PROTEST AGAINST GOD

For Ernest and Evelyn

Psalm 27.10

PROTEST AGAINST GOD
THE ECLIPSE OF A BIBLICAL TRADITION

William S. Morrow

SHEFFIELD PHOENIX PRESS

2007

Copyright © 2006, 2007 Sheffield Phoenix Press

First published in hardback, 2006

First published in paperback, 2007

Published by Sheffield Phoenix Press
Department of Biblical Studies, University of Sheffield
Sheffield S10 2TN

www.sheffieldphoenix.com

A CIP catalogue record for this book
is available from the British Library

Typeset by ISB Typesetting
Printed on acid-free paper by Lightning Source UK Ltd, Milton Keynes

ISBN 978-1-906055-34-9 (paperback)

ISBN 978-1-905048-20-5 (hardback)

ISSN 1747-9614

CONTENTS

Acknowledgements   ix
Abbreviations   xi

Chapter 1
INTRODUCTION   1
  1.1. The History of Biblical Lament in Contemporary
      Scholarship   3
  1.2. Terms of Analysis   8
      1.2.1. Elements of Complaint Prayers   8
      1.2.2. Terms of Dating   11

Chapter 2
INFORMAL LAMENT AGAINST GOD IN BIBLICAL TRADITIONS   13
  2.1. Forms of Complaining Requests in Human Interactions   15
      2.1.1. Complaint with Implied Request for a Group   16
      2.1.2. Complaint with Explicit Request for a Group 16
      2.1.3. Complaint with Implied Request for an Individual 16
      2.1.4. Complaint with Explicit Request for an Individual 17
  2.2. Informal Lament for the Community   17
      2.2.1. Informal Community Laments with Complaint
          against God   19
          2.2.1.1. Implied Petition for a Group. Prayer
               Initiated by a Person   19
          2.2.1.2. Implied Petition for a Group.
               Communication Initiated by God 19
          2.2.1.3. Explicit Petition for a Group.
               Prayer Initiated by a Person 20
          2.2.1.4. Explicit Petition for a Group.
               Communication Initiated by God 20
      2.2.2. Informal Community Laments without
          Complaint against God   21
          2.2.2.1. Implied Petition for a Group.
               Prayer Initiated by a Person 21
          2.2.2.2. Implied Petition for a Group.
               Communication Initiated by God 21
          2.2.2.3. Explicit Petition for a Group.
               Prayer Initiated by a Person 22

2.2.2.4. Explicit Petition for a Group.
          Communication Initiated by God   22
2.3. Informal Laments for Individuals   29
    2.3.1. Informal Individual Laments with
            Complaint against God   30
        2.3.1.1. Implied Petition for an Individual.
                  Prayer Initiated by a Person   30
        2.3.1.2. Implied Petition for an Individual.
                  Communication Initiated by God   30
        2.3.1.3. Explicit Petition for an Individual.
                  Prayer Initiated by a Person   31
    2.3.2. Informal Individual Lament without
            Complaint against God   31
        2.3.2.1. Implied Petition for an Individual.
                  Prayer initiated by a Person   31
        2.3.2.2. Implied Petition for an Individual.
                  Communication Initiated by God   31
        2.3.2.3. Explicit Petition for an Individual.
                  Prayer Initiated by a Person   31
        2.3.2.4. Explicit Request for an Individual.
                  Communication Initiated by God   32
2.4. Origins and Developments of Informal Lament 35

Chapter 3
PSALMS OF INDIVIDUAL LAMENT: CLASSIFICATION AND
LITURGICAL CONTEXTS   42
3.1. Identifying Individual Complaint Psalms   43
3.2. Unity and Diversity in the Psalms of LI   45
    3.2.1. The Unity of the Psalms of LI   45
    3.2.2. Psalms of Plea and Psalms of Protest   48
3.3. Theology, Suffering and Protest in the Psalms of LI   51
    3.3.1. Psalms of Plea   53
    3.3.2. Psalms of Indirect Protest   54
        3.3.2.1. Indirect Protest with Petitions for
                  Forgiveness   55
        3.3.2.2. Indirect Protest with Confession of Sin   55
        3.3.2.3. Indirect Protest in Preventative Prayers 56
    3.3.3. Psalms of Direct Protest   57
        3.3.3.1. Direct Protest of Divine Absence 57
        3.3.3.2. Direct Protest of Divine Affliction   59
3.4. Origins and Liturgical Contexts of the Psalms of LI   60
    3.4.1. The Informal Lament as Precursor to the Psalms   61
    3.4.2. Performers of LI in Ancient Israel   65
    3.4.3. Centralization of the Psalms of LI   69
3.5. Use of the Psalms of LI: Summary and Conclusions 72

Chapter 4
THE PROTEST AGAINST GOD IN COMMUNITY COMPLAINTS 76
  4.1. Psalms of Collective Protest in Biblical Literature 76
  4.2. Biblical Communal Lament and Mesopotamian
      Lamentations 81
      4.2.1. Temporal Relationships between Mesopotamian
           Laments and Israel's Complaints 82
      4.2.2. A Pre-exilic Genre of City-Lament in Ancient
           Judaism? 85
           4.2.2.1. Fragmentary Citations of Corporate
                   Complaint in Prophetic Sources 86
  4.3. Dating the Protests of National Defeat 93
  4.4. Origins of the Protests of National Defeat 96
  4.5. The Development of the Protests of Community Distress 101

Chapter 5
EXILIC CRITIQUE OF THE PROTEST AGAINST GOD 106
  5.1. Lamentations and the Logic of Complaint 107
  5.2. The Second Isaiah and the Transformation of Complaint 120
  5.3. Complaint against God in the Deuteronomistic History 125
  5.4. Protest against God in the Exile 127

Chapter 6
PROTEST AGAINST GOD IN THE AXIAL AGE 129
  6.1. Dialogue and Complaint in Job 3–27; 29–31 131
  6.2. Job and the Emergence of Israel's Axial Age 134
  6.3. Responses to Job's Dilemma 139
      6.3.1. The Wisdom Poem in Job 28 139
      6.3.2. The Elihu Speeches 140
      6.3.3. The YHWH Speeches 142

Chapter 7
COMMUNITY COMPLAINT IN SECOND TEMPLE LITERATURE 147
  7.1. Extra-biblical Second Temple Community Pleas and
      Laments 149
      7.1.1. Laments like those in the Psalter 150
           7.1.1.1. Laments with Petitions for the Community 150
           7.1.1.2. Laments mixing Collective and Individual
                   Petitions 151
      7.1.2. Communal Prayers for Help 152
      7.1.3. Penitential Prayers 152
      7.1.4. Imitations of Lamentations 153
      7.1.5. Informal Laments 154
      7.1.6. Paraphrases of the Biblical Tradition 157
  7.2. Complaints against God in Second Temple Literature 158
      7.2.1. Petitions of Indirect Protest 158

7.2.2. Justification of Divine Righteousness   159
7.2.3. Direct Complaint against God   160
7.3. The Eclipse of Collective Protest by Penitential Prayer   161
7.3.1. Reversal of the Rhetoric of the God-Israel
        Relationship   163
7.3.2. Scriptural Allusions in Penitential Prayers   164
7.3.3. Priestly Influences in the Emergence of Penitential
        Prayer   166
7.4. Protest Prayer in Second Temple Sources   168
7.5. Collective Protest in the New Testament   173
7.6. Summary and Conclusions   176

Chapter 8
PRAYERS FOR INDIVIDUALS IN EXTRA-BIBLICAL SECOND TEMPLE
LITERATURE   178
8.1. Parallels to LI in Extra-Biblical Second Temple Literature 178
8.1.1. Laments like those in the Psalter   178
8.1.2. Informal Lament   181
8.2. Complaints against God in Second Temple LI   181
8.2.1. Petitions of Indirect Protest   181
8.2.2. Justification of Divine Righteousness   182
8.2.3. Direct Complaint against God   182
8.3. Functional Shifts in Second Temple LI   182
8.3.1. Absence of Cultic References in Second Temple LI   183
8.3.2. Scripturalization of Second Temple LI   187
8.3.3. Disputation and Exegesis   188
8.4. Prayers against Demonic Attack in Second Temple Sources   190
8.5. Prayers of the Righteous Sufferer in the New Testament   195
8.6. The Loss of LI as Healing Liturgy   197

Chapter 9
ECLIPSE AND RECOVERY OF PROTEST PRAYER   201
9.1. The Eclipse of Protest Prayer in Biblical Tradition   201
9.2. The Continuity of the Complaint Tradition in Judaism   206
9.3. The Recovery of Lament in Christianity   210

Tables
1   Classification of Informal Community Laments by
      Textual Source and Type   23
2.   Classification of Informal Individual Laments by
      Textual Source and Type   33
3.   Collective Complaint against God in Biblical Poems   79

Bibliography   219
Index of Scripture and Ancient Literature   232
Index of Authors   247

ACKNOWLEDGEMENTS

This book would not have been possible without the generous support of Queen's Theological College, which provided me with leaves in 2001–2002 and 2005–2006. I am also grateful to the Association of Theological Schools in the United States and Canada, which awarded me a Lilly Faculty Fellowship that facilitated my sabbatical in 2001–2002 and provided funding to present research connected with this project in various conferences. In addition, I wish to thank the Catholic Biblical Association of America, under whose auspices I enjoyed a visiting professorship at the École Biblique et Archéologique Française in Jerusalem during the Winter and Spring of 2006. There, I attended to some of the final stages in preparing this volume.

I have appreciated opportunities to refine my ideas in response to questions and comments from many persons. Papers related to this study have been read and discussed at meetings of the Canadian Society of Biblical Studies, the Catholic Biblical Association, the Colloquium on Religion and Violence, the International Organization for the Study of the Old Testament and the Society of Biblical Literature. I have also benefited from dialogue with students and members of the public, who encountered some of this material in various courses and popular lectures. Of course, responsibility for the opinions expressed herein remains solely mine.

Special thanks go to Dawn Clarke for her editorial assistance. Karen Farrar and Ernest Morrow also read drafts of chapters in this book and gave helpful advice for improving them.

I owe the greatest debt of gratitude to my wife, Ruth, who has patiently encouraged this project during its years of gestation and development. This book is dedicated to our children.

Unless otherwise noted translations of biblical texts are taken or adapted from Revised Standard Version of the Bible copyrighted 1971 and 1952 by the Division on Christian Education of the National Council of the Churches of Christ in the USA.

July 31, 2006

ABBREVIATIONS

AB	Anchor Bible
ABD	David Noel Freedman (ed.), *The Anchor Bible Dictionary* (New York: Doubleday, 1992).
AnBi	Analecta biblica
BETL	Bibliotheca ephemeridum theologicarum lovaniensium
Bib	*Biblica*
BibInt	*Biblical Interpretation: A Journal of Contemporary Approaches*
BibOr	Biblica et orientalia
BO	*Bibliotheca orientalis*
BTB	Biblical Theology Bulletin
BZAW	Beihefte zur *ZAW*
CANE	Jack M. Sasson (ed.), *Civilizations of the Ancient Near East* (4 vols.; New York: Charles Scribner's Sons, 1995).
CBQ	*Catholic Biblical Quarterly*
CBQMS	*Catholic Biblical Quarterly*, Monograph Series
ConBOT	Coniectanea biblica, Old Testament
CRINT	Compendia rerum iudaicarum ad Novum Testamentum
DtrH	The Deuteronomistic History
E	Pentateuchal literature considered to belong to the Elohistic source
EvQ	*Evangelical Quarterly*
FOTL	The Forms of the Old Testament Literature
HUCA	*Hebrew Union College Annual*
HSM	Harvard Semitic Monographs
HTR	*Harvard Theological Review*
IEJ	*Israel Exploration Journal*
Int	*Interpretation*
J	Pentateuchal literature considered to belong to the Yahwistic source
JAOS	*Journal of the American Oriental Society*
JBL	*Journal of Biblical Literature*
JCS	*Journal of Cuneiform Studies*
J-E	Pentateuchal literature in the style used by J and E materials
JSOT	*Journal for the Study of the Old Testament*
JSOTSup	*Journal for the Study of the Old Testament*, Supplement Series
JSS	*Journal of Semitic Studies*
KAI	H. Donner and W. Röllig, *Kanaanäische und aramäische Inschriften* (3 vols.; Wiesbaden: Otto Harrassowitz, 3rd edition, 1973).
LI	Psalms and prayers in the form of the individual lament
NCB	New Century Bible

NIGTC	The New International Greek Testament Commentary
NICNT	New International Commentary on the New Testament
NovT	*Novum Testamentum*
OTG	Old Testament Guides
OTS	Oudtestamentische Studiën
OTL	Old Testament Library
P	Pentateuchal literature considered to belong to the Priestly source
SBLDS	SBL Dissertation Series
SBLMS	SBL Monograph Series
SBLSP	SBL Seminar Papers
SJ	Studia judaica
SR	*Studies in Religion/Sciences religieuses*
STDJ	Studies on the Texts of the Desert of Judah
SUNY	State University of New York
TLZ	*Theologische Literaturzeitung*
TQ	*Theologische Quartalschrift*
TRu	*Theologische Rundschau*
TTod	*Theology Today*
VT	*Vetus Testamentum*
VTSup	*Vetus Testamentum*, Supplements
WBC	Word Biblical Commentary
WMANT	Wissenschaftliche Monographien zum Alten und Neuen Testament
ZAW	*Zeitschrift für die alttestamentliche Wissenschaft*
ZTK	*Zeitschrift für Theologie und Kirche*

Chapter 1

INTRODUCTION

Lament psalms constitute the most prominent genre of poetry in the Hebrew Psalter. Yet, it is generally acknowledged that during the Second Temple period this vigorous tradition of biblical poetry became over-shadowed by other forms of prayer.[1] The goal of this book is to account for the eclipse of argumentative prayer in the development of biblical religion. Various groups of intellectuals are implicated in the changing fortunes of the lament tradition, including prophets, priests and sages. Their influence placed various limits on the most salient form of complaint in biblical and extra-biblical Second Temple literature: the protest against God.

This chapter contains a brief survey of past attempts at writing a history of biblical lament (§1.1) and a discussion of methodology and terminology used in the book (§1.2). One use of terminology, however, should be highlighted at the outset. The biblical lament genre has various designations. Along with the term, lament, these texts have also been called prayers of complaint,[2] forms of the arguing with God tradition,[3] and protest prayer.[4] This book uses the terms lament, complaint prayer and argumentative prayer with some flexibility. While it is true that the English word lament is ambiguous (it can mean either a dirge for the dead or an expression of

---

1. See, e.g. Hermann Gunkel and Joachim Begrich, *Introduction to the Psalms: The Genres of the Religious Lyric of Israel* (Mercer Library of Biblical Studies: Macon, GA: Mercer University Press, 1998; 4th German edn, 1985), pp. 197-98; Ottmar Fuchs, *Die Klage als Gebet: Eine theologische Besinnung am Beispiel des Psalms 22* (Munich: Kösel, 1982), pp. 441-45; Karl-Joseph Kuschel 'Ist Gott verantwortlich für das Übel: Überlegungen zu einer Theologie der Anklagen', in G. Fuchs (ed.), *Angesichts des Leids an Gott glauben? Zur Theologie der Klage* (Frankfurt a. M.: Joseph Knecht, 1996), pp. 228-31; Meinard Limbeck, 'Die Klage—Eine verschwundene Gebetsgattung', *TQ* 157 (1977), pp. 13-16.

2. John Day, *Psalms* (OTG; Sheffield: JSOT Press, 1992), p. 20.

3. Anson Laytner, *Arguing with God: A Jewish Tradition* (Northvale, NJ: Jason Aronson, 1990), pp. xvii-xviii.

4. Craig C. Broyles, *The Conflict of Faith and Experience in the Psalms: A Form-Critical and Theological Study* (JSOTSup, 52; Sheffield: JSOT Press, 1989), p. 52; David R. Blumenthal, *Facing the Abusing God: A Theology of Protest* (Louisville, KY: Westminster John Knox, 1993), pp. 249-52.

sorrow), expressions of distress and grief remain tied to the tradition of prayer that is being analyzed here. Moreover, the vocabulary of lament remains common in biblical scholarship which studies the form and content of psalms written for persons and communities in distress. At the same time, the tradition that generated the lament psalms authorizes complaint, often with tones of anger that connote protest against God. These psalms also employ an argumentative form of rhetoric meant to win a decision or seek a change in divine actions.

The phrase 'argumentative prayer' is more or less synonymous with the terminology of 'arguing with God' used by Anson Laytner. But I prefer to use the term argumentative prayer for two reasons. First, arguing with God might imply that the deity's connection to the distress which is the cause of the complaint is always the same. In fact, this is not true. There are distinctions to be made between argumentative prayers that complain against God and those that lament other causes of distress. Secondly, Laytner uses the terminology of arguing with God as a way of characterizing the entire tradition of argumentative prayer in Judaism from the Bible to modern times. While I do not question such a programmatic use of the term, there are distinctions between the use and status of complaining prayer in biblical tradition and later Judaism that this book seeks to highlight. By the same token, I have not used the terminology of the 'law court pattern' of prayer to identify texts of biblical complaint prayer. There can be no question that the rhetoric of lament relies on legal metaphor, but the concept of the law court pattern is used by Joseph Heinemann to describe a certain form of prayer in Talmudic times.[5] I am reluctant to dilute the usefulness of Heinemann's designation by broadening its application.

The preference for the term 'protest' in the title of this book bears on a key assumption of its method. I follow Claus Westermann in his assertion that developments in the complaint against God are indicative for the history of lament.[6] The terms 'protest' and 'protest prayer' refer to expressions of prayer that include direct complaint against God.[7] This book attempts to control a rather large subject, the history of lament, by paying particular attention to complaint against God in prayers from biblical and extra-biblical sources belonging to the Second Temple period of Judaism.

---

5.   Joseph Heinemann, *Prayer in the Talmud: Forms and Patterns* (SJ, 9; Berlin: W. de Gruyter, 1977), pp. 192-93.

6.   Claus Westermann, 'The Complaint against God', in Tod Linafelt and T. K. Beal (eds.), *God in the Fray: A Tribute to Walter Brueggemann* (Minneapolis: Fortress Press, 1998), p. 233.

7.   See Walter Brueggemann, *Old Testament Theology: Essays on Structure, Theme, and Text* (Minneapolis: Fortress Press, 1992), p. 29.

It will show that, when protest against God was permitted as a part of the worshipping experience of Israel, the lament tradition was strong. But as theological constructs shifted and became increasingly uncomfortable with protest against God, the argumentative prayer tradition was eclipsed by other forms of supplication.

1.1. *The History of Biblical Lament in Contemporary Scholarship*

Though they were by no means the first studies on the theology of biblical lament psalms in critical scholarship, the works of Walter Brueggemann and Claus Westermann signal the practical beginning of what has become a growing movement for the recovery of lament in the Church on both sides of the Atlantic.[8] An inspection of the database of the American Theological Library Association shows that the bulk of articles and books devoted to the subject of complaint prayer date from the 1970s. Prior to this time, the material available on lament is mainly of a technical nature. But the past three decades have seen a burgeoning number of studies on both sides of the Atlantic devoted not simply to scholarly questions but also urging the relevance of lament rhetoric for broader theological and pastoral agenda. In English-speaking scholarship, there is a case for dating the resurgence of awareness of complaint prayer to the 1974 issue of *Interpretation*, which contained the first of Brueggemann's provocative essays on the recovery of lament in the Church and a translation of Westermann's, 'The Role of the Lament in the Theology of the Old Testament'.[9] However, the movement to recover lament began earlier in Germany under the influence of Westermann's scholarship on the psalms.[10]

The fascination with lament has also registered in Jewish circles. In recent times it has been marked by Laynter's comprehensive survey of the arguing with God tradition in Judaism. Though restricted by the end of Second Temple times,[11] the arguing with God tradition has a rich history

8. Sally A. Brown and Patrick D. Miller (eds.), *Lament: Reclaiming Practices in Pulpit, Pew, and Public Square* (Louisville, KY: Westminster John Knox, 2005), p. xiv.

9. Walter Brueggemann, 'From Hurt to Joy, from Death to Life', *Int* 28 (1974), pp. 3-19; Claus Westermann, 'The Role of the Lament in the Theology of the Old Testament', *Int* 28 (1974), pp. 20-38.

10. See Claus Westermann, 'Struktur und Geschichte der Klage im Alten Testament', *ZAW* 66.1-2 (1954), pp. 44-80. Westermann began his highly influential *Das Loben Gottes in den Psalmen* (the second edition of 1961 was translated into English in 1965) in a prison camp during World War II; see Samuel E. Balentine, *Prayer in the Hebrew Bible: The Drama of Divine–Human Dialogue* (Overtures to Biblical Theology; Minneapolis: Fortress Press, 1993), p. 258.

11. Laytner, *Arguing with God*, pp. 103-11; see also David Kraemer, *Responses to Suffering in Classical Rabbinic Literature* (New York: Oxford University, 1995), pp. 211-18.

in rabbinic Judaism and its tradents. Laytner joins other Jewish voices in advocating the recovery of the rhetoric of complaint in the post-Holocaust era.[12]

A survey of scholarly literature on the lament would require considerable space. But an overview of attempts to sketch the history of the lament form in biblical and Second Temple extra-biblical literature may be undertaken more economically. For there is no book-length study of the history of biblical lament prayer in contemporary scholarship.

Before the Second World War, as part of his magisterial study of the psalms (completed by Joachim Begrich), Hermann Gunkel suggested that the history of lament prayer was a story of the gradual dissolution of a form of prayer that originated in the cult. Even in the pre-exilic period, the lament became separated from its cultic context. It developed into a kind of spiritual poetry whose form gradually became compromised by mixtures with other genres. By Maccabean times, the original genre had come to an end.[13]

The most influential history of biblical lament, however, remains that of Westermann.[14] Westermann proposed a three-stage model. Early in Israel's history, lament was mainly protest against God. The evidence is found in brief lay complaint prayers contained in biblical narratives. This tradition was taken up and developed in the cult, where it assumed a tripartite lament pattern containing not only God-complaint, but also descriptions of personal suffering (I/we-complaint) and enemy-complaint. After the exile, the movement between protest and praise, so characteristic of the biblical lament psalm, was truncated by the development of a theology which justified the suffering of the people as God's righteous actions.[15] The final blow, in terms of Christian practice, came either because of theological developments in the New Testament or through the encounter of the early Church with Hellenistic philosophy, especially

---

12. Laytner, *Arguing with God*, pp. 231-46. The list of contemporary Jewish literature influenced by the lament tradition is lengthy. Besides the bibliography provided by Laytner (*Arguing with God*, pp. 196-227) cf. e.g. David G. Roskies (ed.), *The Literature of Destruction: Jewish Responses to Catastrophe* (Philadelphia: Jewish Publication Society, 1989), pp. 565-612; Blumenthal, *Facing the Abusing God*, pp. 252-57.

13. Gunkel and Begrich, *Introduction to the Psalms*, pp. 194-98. According to Gunkel, the *Psalms of Solomon* are particularly significant for showing the attenuation of the form of lament and its devolution into 'reflection'.

14. First published in 1954, Claus Westermann's essay 'Struktur und Geschichte der Klage im Alten Testament' was reprinted in the fifth edition of *Das Loben Gottes in den Psalmen*, when the book was given the new title *Lob und Klage in den Psalmen* (1977). The book was translated as *Praise and Lament in the Psalms* (Atlanta: John Knox Press, 1981); for further information see the remarks of the translator on p. 3.

15. Westermann, *Praise and Lament in the Psalms*, pp. 195-213.

Stoicism.[16] Westermann's general thesis has found support in more recent treatments of the history of lament.[17]

Westermann is not alone in attempting to sketch the early history of lament. Important contributions have been made by Anneli Aejmelaeus, Rainer Albertz and Erhard Gerstenberger. Gerstenberger is prominent for his comparison of the biblical psalms of individual lament with prayers and ceremonies for suffering persons found in cuneiform collections from Mesopotamia. He has suggested that the laments were administered by ritual experts, who like those in Mesopotamia were affiliated with cultic institutions. But he has also introduced a sociological distinction between the religious practices of the 'large group' and the 'small group' in biblical culture. As an expression of small group piety, the lament was not necessarily performed in sacred space, but also in homes as was true for the cuneiform incantations.[18] The reconstruction of the original setting of individual lament by Albertz is similar to Gerstenberger's, but Albertz has attempted to describe in more detail the distinctions between small and large group in ancient Israel.[19] Building on the work of Gerstenberger, Aejmelaeus has studied the origins of what she discerns as the basic rhetorical form of lament (address, petition, motivation clause). In her opinion this is a natural form of human speech that points to a non-cultic origin for the lament form. She posits the existence of an oral tradition behind the laments in the Psalter, suggesting that they were not fixed into written forms until later in the history of the genre.[20]

Such constructions have not gone without criticism, however. Henning Reventlow's discussion of prayer reacts to the work of Albertz, Gerstenberger and Westermann. His investigations cast doubt on assertions that

16. Westermann, 'The Role of the Lament in the Theology of the Old Testament', p. 25.

17. For the seminal importance of Westermann in lament studies, see Walter Brueggemann, 'The Costly Loss of Lament', *JSOT* 36 (1986), pp. 57-71 (57). Other scholars who follow Westermann's account of the history of lament include Balentine, *Prayer in the Hebrew Bible*, p. 28; Fuchs, *Die Klage als Gebet*, pp. 304-306 and Patrick D. Miller, *They Cried to the Lord: The Form and Theology of Biblical Prayer* (Minneapolis: Fortress Press, 1994), p. 86.

18. Erhard S. Gerstenberger, *Der bittende Mensch: Bittritual und Klagelied des Einzelnen im Alten Testament* (WMANT, 51; Neukirchen–Vluyn: Neukirchener Verlag, 1980), pp. 167-69; summarized in Patrick D. Miller, *Interpreting the Psalms* (Philadelphia: Fortress Press, 1986), pp. 6-7.

19. For example, Rainer Albertz, *A History of Israelite Religion in the Old Testament Period* (OTL; 2 vols.; Louisville, KY: Westminster John Knox, 1994), I, p. 100, summarized in Balentine, *Prayer in the Hebrew Bible*, pp. 211-12.

20. Anneli Aejmelaeus, *The Traditional Prayer in the Psalms* (BZAW, 167; Berlin: W. de Gruyter, 1986), pp. 99-103; summarized in Balentine, *Prayer in the Hebrew Bible*, pp. 209-10.

early biblical laments were characteristically short or that a 'lay piety' can be discerned in the narratives of the Hebrew Bible. Even if the narrative traditions that Westermann appeals to for his typology of early lay lament contain only short prayers, this may be a function of the needs of narrative rather than a reflection of early practice. Reventlow points out that there are short prayers in narrative that show the elements typical of lament psalms. Moreover, the sociological conditions of the text defy attempts to discover a form of lay piety. As a rule, petitioners in biblical narrative are not private individuals in the modern sense but leaders and representatives of the nation.[21] Reventlow also acknowledges Albertz's distinction between a personal and national deity only to conclude that while the destination offers wide ranging implications for understanding prayer in the Hebrew Bible, it is by no means considered proven. There are other conceptions of the relationship between individual and nation in the YHWH-faith.[22]

Mention should also be made of the description of biblical prose prayer by Moshe Greenberg who has challenged the idea that an evolutionary perspective on biblical prayer can be derived from considering the form of lament in prose sources. He suggests that a distinction should be made among three levels of prayer with varying degrees of formality. Alongside the psalms (the most formal kind of prayer), which Greenberg associates with temple worship, individuals could have prayed extemporaneously based on formal models, or composed free prayers spontaneously. For example, Samson can be depicted in narrative using a spontaneous free form on one occasion (Judg. 15.18) and a more carefully patterned complaint on another (Judg. 16.28).[23]

The history of lament prayer in post-biblical times has also been the subject of new studies.[24] These have been particularly focused on the replacement of communal lament by penitential prayer, a development

21. Henning G. Reventlow, *Gebet im Alten Testament* (Stuttgart: Kohlhammer, 1986), pp. 98-100.

22. Reventlow, *Gebet im Alten Testament*, p. 87. See also his discussion of the address to YHWH in Psalm 3 (p. 181).

23. Moshe Greenberg, *Biblical Prose Prayer as a Window to the Popular Religion of Ancient Israel* (The Taubman Lectures in Jewish Studies, Sixth Series; Berkeley: University of California Press, 1983), p. 46.

24. See, e.g. Richard J. Bautch, *Developments in Genre between Post-Exilic Penitential Prayers and the Psalms of Communal Lament* (Academia biblica, 7; Atlanta: Society of Biblical Literature, 2003); Mark J. Boda, *Praying the Tradition: The Origin and Use of Tradition in Nehemiah 9* (BZAW, 277; Berlin: W. de Gruyter, 1999); Rodney A. Werline, *Penitential Prayer in Second Temple Judaism: The Development of a Religious Institution* (Early Judaism and its Literature, 13; Atlanta: Scholars Press, 1998).

noted by Westermann.[25] There has been little attention to the fate of individual lament prayer in post-biblical Second Temple literature, however. This lack seems to be based on an assumption that the fate of communal and individual complaint prayer was the same.

The views surveyed above raise several questions that deserve further reflection. First, is it possible to place the psalms at a mid-point in the development of lamenting prayer, contrasting with an earlier period and a later one? What can be said about the development of the psalms of lament in relationship to other forms of complaining discourse (including Lamentations)? What was the function of the cultic context which was alluded to in complaint psalms and which was responsible for the collection of the complaint psalms now extant in the Bible? Is it true that individual and communal lament suffered the same fate in the Second Temple period. If so, how does one account for the continuity of the arguing with God tradition in later Judaism as demonstrated by Laytner?

It is also necessary to address the idea that the complaint psalm genre fell by the wayside because of Judaism's profound encounter with Hellenistic civilization.[26] This explanation is important because it seems to provide a bridge of understanding to the modern situation. But there are also inner biblical developments that condition the eclipse of the complaint tradition and allow it to happen in Hellenistic times. These need to be accounted for.

The relationship between forms of argumentative prayer and social organization in ancient Israel is complex. Brueggemann has underscored connections between argumentative prayer and the stance of theological advocacy for the marginalized that he refers to as 'pain embrace'. In this construction, lament is a way of protesting against the common theology of 'structure legitimation'.[27] As valid as these observations are, it would be incorrect to propose a simple opposition between the constructs of structure legitimation and pain embrace in ancient Israel. The mystery of the disappearance of lament is connected to the fact that protest against God was expressed in traditions of prayer legitimated by social institutions. Hence the eclipse of the complaint against God is associated with large-scale social transitions which affected the nature of biblical institutions and their theological assumptions.

Westermann's fertile ideas and influential model of the history of lament will provide a constant point of reference as well as a foil for the study that follows. Chapters Two–Four survey biblical evidence for the use of

25. Westermann, *Praise and Lament*, p. 206.

26. Sheila Carney, 'God Damn God: A Reflection on Expressing Anger in Prayer', *BTB* 13 (1983), p. 117.

27. Brueggemann, *Old Testament Theology*, p. 27.

protest prayer in pre-exilic prose and prophetic contexts as well as in the psalms. Chapters Five and Six review biblical literature from the exilic period and postexilic period that signal shifts in the theological underpinnings of the lament tradition. Chapters Seven and Eight discuss the fate of communal and individual lament respectively as the biblical tradition developed into its canonical forms and was appropriated by extra-biblical Second Temple texts. Chapter Nine summarizes the conclusions of this study and offers an explanation for the contemporary interest in recovering the complaint tradition in the light of its findings.

1.2. *Terms of Analysis*

The following discussion touches on issues of terminology. Form criticism has discovered that lament psalms use stereotypical contents, which may referred to as 'elements' of the form.[28] It is important to clarify how the elements of complaint prayers are described in the chapters that follow (§1.2.1). Dating of texts is significant for the present study, so there is also an indication of how various eras in biblical and post-biblical history are designated (§1.2.2).

1.2.1. *Elements of Complaint Prayers*
Identification of argumentative prayers assumes that they have a family resemblance that allows a reader to discern them in a number of different settings. The fullest description of the markers of the lament genre comes from work on the psalms. There are a number of excellent descriptions of the stereotypical elements of complaint psalms.[29] An important assumption of this book is that complaint prayers outside the biblical psalms can be identified because they possess similar elements to those ascribed to the form of lament psalms. Particular attention is paid to the definition of protest against God, as this motif is of central concern to my study of the biblical tradition of argumentative prayer.

Address
The element of address consists of vocatives (i.e. direct address) that name the deity. Often the vocative is accompanied by epithets that further identify the one who is being addressed. There is a tendency for the epithets to be expanded into confessions of trust, which describe the relationship of

---

28. Gestenberger, *Der bittende Mensch,* p. 63.

29. See, e.g. Walter Baumgartner, *Jeremiah's Poems of Lament* (Sheffield: Almond Press, 1988), pp. 19-40; Erhard S. Gerstenberger, *Psalms: Part 1 with an Introduction to Cultic Poetry* (FOTL, 14; Grand Rapids: Eerdmans, 1988), pp. 11-14; Miller, *They Cried to the Lord,* pp. 58-133; Westermann, *Praise and Lament,* pp. 52-78.

the petitioner to YHWH or expressconfidence in the nature of the deity. Frequently, the address is reinforced by petitions calling on God to 'listen', 'see', or 'pay attention'. But there is an obvious overlap between the petitions that accompany the address and those that stand as calls for help and salvation.[30] For that reason, I restrict the identification of address to naming of the deity.[31]

Complaint

A key question is whether descriptions of sources of suffering are best identified as elements of lament or complaint.[32] Here I give precedence to the terminology of 'complaint'. There is an analogy between human interactions seeking remedy for grievances and the argumentative prayer tradition. One seeks not only to identify the cause of one's distress by complaining of it, but also to find a remedy.[33] The reasons for naming one's source of distress in protest prayer suggest the terminology of complaint is more apt than lament.[34] There are three categories of the element of complaint:

a) *I-Complaint/We-complaint.* These are descriptions of the physical and emotional suffering of the poet or the community. Though often in the first person singular or plural, complaints of personal or community suffering can also appear in third person accounts (e.g. Isa. 33.7-9; Joel 1.16-18).

b) *Enemy-Complaint.* This category describes the actions and words of persons hostile to the petitioner(s) and inimical to God's own interests.

c) *God-complaint.* It is typical to find God-complaint in both statements (e.g. Pss. 44.10-15; 102.11, 24b; Lam. 3.43-44) and questions predicated of God (e.g. Pss. 13.2; 74.11).[35] Following Claus Westermann, questions using the words 'How long?' and 'Why?' (or complaints that imply a why-question) are analysed as God-complaints.[36] There are also indications that the question 'Where?' can imply God-complaint (e.g. 1 Sam. 4.21; Isa. 63.15).[37]

---

30. Baumgartner, *Laments of Jeremiah*, p. 29.

31. See Miller, *They Cried to the Lord*, pp. 58-63.

32. See the discussion in Miller, *They Cried to the Lord*, pp. 68-69.

33. Gerstenberger, *Der bittende Mensch,* pp. 49-51.

34. Erhard S. Gerstenberger, 'Jeremiah's Complaints: Observations on Jer 15.10-21', *JBL* 82 (1963), pp. 393-408 (405).

35. Broyles, *Conflict of Faith and Experience,* pp. 37-39; Walter Gross, 'Trifft ein Unglück die Stadt, und der Herr war nicht am Werk? Amos 3,6', in Fuchs, *Angesichts des Leids*, pp. 97-98.

36. Westermann, *Praise and Lament,* pp. 176-78, 183-84; see also Broyles, *Conflict of Faith and Experience,* pp. 37-39; Gross, 'Trifft ein Unglück die Stadt', pp. 97-98.

37. See Joel S. Burnett, 'The Question of Divine Absence in Israelite and West Semitic Religion', *CBQ* 67 (2005), pp. 221-23.

Not all statements about God can be considered complaint, however. Craig Broyles would rule out statements such as 'let the bones which you have broken rejoice' (Ps. 51.10) and 'for they have persecuted him whom you have smitten' (Ps. 69.27) as God-complaint.[38] Common to both is the fact that the statement about a divine action directed against the petitioner is in a relative clause that is subordinate to another element in the lament. In these cases, God's actions are only incidental to the complaint or petition.

Patrick Miller has argued that expressions of shame, the humiliation of taunts and mockery, are another facet of the complaint against God. Texts such as Jer. 20.18; Pss. 39.8-10; 69.9-10 indicate that because of what God has done the psalmist fears the scorn of his foes. The shame of the faithful sufferer suggests God's indifference or powerlessness in the situation.[39] However, the shame that Miller describes is experienced through encounters with the poet's enemies and erstwhile friends. One can argue that the attacks of the psalmist's enemies generally imply divine indifference or inactivity, a situation which the lament psalms are attempting to remedy.

Therefore, I have taken a fairly conservative approach to the identification of protest against God. For the sake of clear categories, I do not use Miller's expanded definition of God-complaint. God-complaint is restricted to accusatory statements and questions about divine actions. But the accusatory statement must not be subordinated to another element of the lament genre in a relative clause. Why-, how long- and where-questions in prayers are regarded as complaints against God regardless of the subject of the verb. Other questions may be considered complaints against God only if God is the subject of the verb; but such usage must be distinguished from cases in which rhetorical questions are being used as affirmations of divine character.[40]

Confession of Trust/Retrospect

Confessions of trust include claims about the trustworthiness of the petitioner. They may also contain accounts of past good relations between God and the petitioner and statements of confidence in God's justice and integrity. In community complaint psalms, the account of past good relations amounts to a retrospective review of salvation history.[41] Statements about the petitioner may consist of affirmations of loyalty and

---

38. Broyles, *Conflict of Faith and Experience*, pp. 39-40.
39. Miller, *They Cried to the Lord*, pp. 77-78.
40. E.g. the rhetorical questions in Jehoshaphat's prayer in 2 Chron. 20.6-12 are not God-complaint but are tantamount to a form of praise, see Balentine, *Prayer in the Hebrew Bible*, pp. 99-100.
41. Westermann, *Praise and Lament*, pp. 55-57.

faithfulness to God and God's people and assertions of innocence and righteousness. Gerstenberger regards the assertion of innocence as an element separate from the confession of trust.[42] But just as the complaint element can be classified by several categories including descriptions of God and the petitioner, so also can the confession of trust.[43]

Confession of Sin

Gerstenberger notes that the confession of sin represents the polar opposite of the declaration of innocence.[44] I have already indicated my reluctance to accord the declaration of innocence the status of a separate element in the complaint prayer paradigm. But it is worth highlighting instances of the confession of sin, because confessions of sin are unusual in some forms of biblical lament, e.g. psalms of communal complaint.

Petitions

Petitions and wishes are attested in all three persons, although first person expressions are not common (e.g. Ps. 25.20b). Usually petitions are found in the form of second person commands (mainly positive and negative Imperatives) to YHWH and third person wishes. Third person wishes or curses against the enemy are designated as 'imprecations'. Petitions may be accompanied by motifs of complaint and trust.[45]

Vow of Praise/Assurance of Being Heard/Praise

A number of lament prayers end with a shift in tone containing an expression of thanksgiving, praise or vowing the same in return for a positive answer to the complaint prayer. Though it is possible to distinguish the vow of praise from the assurance of being heard, and both from expressions of praise,[46] this category is not of principle concern in the following study. Most significant is to observe what structures of lament contain this concluding element, as it is often missing in biblical texts belonging to the tradition of argumentative prayer.

1.2.2. Terms of Dating

The Bronze Age of ancient Near Eastern history is considered to have ended c. 1200 BCE. Where the Iron Age is referred to, it designates a period running from c. 1200 to the beginning of the Persian era in biblical history

---

42. Gerstenberger, *Psalms*, I, p. 13.

43. Miller, *They Cried to the Lord*, pp. 127-28

44. Gerstenberger, *Psalms*, I, p. 13.

45. Aejmelaeus, *Traditional Prayer in the Psalms*, pp. 59-83; Miller, *They Cried to the Lord*, pp. 114-26

46. See, e.g. Baumgartner, *Jeremiah's Poems of Lament*, pp. 35-38; Westermann, *Praise and Lament*, pp. 75-81.

(c. 539). Typical divisions in biblical history between the pre-exilic, exilic and postexilic eras are observed in this book. The pre-exilic period can be divided into a monarchical era (c. 1000–587; its end overlaps slightly with the exilic era) and a pre-monarchical era.

The religion of the pre-exilic era is referred to as 'ancient Israelite' religion. For the sake of variety, the same institutions are comprehended by the expression, 'ancient Judaism'. I recognize that it is a matter of controversy at what point a distinctly Jewish religion developed in the biblical era. Some would not want to identify the emergence of an identifiable Judaism before the exile. However, I assume that the earliest identifiable forms of Judaism have roots in the pre-exilic period and for that reason, the pre-exilic period is sometimes glossed here as ancient Judaism.

Although sometimes dated from the promulgation of the Cyrus decree (c. 538), the start of the postexilic era may be regarded as coeval with the beginning of the 'Second Temple' period in Jewish history. The foundations for the Second Temple were laid under the aegis of exiles returning from Babylon in 520 BCE. The exilic period is dated, therefore from the first exile of Jerusalem to the founding of the Second Temple (597–520 BCE).[47]

Though it had suffered previous assaults, the Second Temple was finally destroyed in 70 CE when the Romans captured Jerusalem. Nevertheless, in many ways the Second Temple era only ended in 135 CE when all hopes for rebuilding and reconsecrating the Second Jerusalem Temple were dashed by the Roman suppression of the Jewish rebellion led by Bar Kochba. Therefore, the Second Temple period can be dated from 520 BCE to 135 CE. There were various expressions of Judaism during this era, but their common characteristics may be comprehended by the term, 'Second Temple Judaism'. The first half of the Second Temple period is coeval with the postexilic period of biblical history. For practical purposes, the postexilic era runs to the composition of the book of Daniel (c. 168 BCE), the latest substantial literary work to enter the canon of the Hebrew Bible. Taken together, the biblical and later Second Temple periods are referred to as 'early Judaism'. This epithet distinguishes the literature and institutions of these eras from the developments of rabbinic Judaism, which emerged as normative after Second Temple times.

47. Rainer Albertz, *Israel in Exile: The History and Literature of the Sixth Century B.C.E.* (Studies in Biblical Literature, 3; Atlanta: Society of Biblical Literature, 2003), p. 2.

Chapter 2

INFORMAL LAMENT AGAINST GOD IN BIBLICAL TRADITIONS

A significant feature of biblical prose and prophetic texts is the presence of forms of argumentative prayer that are less complete in their structures than the psalms of lament. This type of prayer can be called 'informal lament'. Such prayers point to a tradition of informal complaint that was used by individuals in distress early in the monarchical era. The rhetoric of informal complaint was subsequently appropriated by prophets in order to intercede for the nation. The prestige of the prophets also appears to have affected the depiction of informal protest prayer in the Hebrew Bible. The scriptural tradition confined individual protest prayers by non-prophetic types to the pre-monarchical period.

The agenda for this chapter has been set by the influential views of Claus Westermann. He observed that many complaint prayers in prose sources differ from the laments found in the psalms: prose complaint prayers often consist of a strong element of God-complaint and no explicit petition. Westermann held that such informal laments represented an expression of lay piety in Israelite religion that predated the complaint psalms.[1]

Westermann's ideas about the priority of informal lament to the composition of the psalms have significant resonances in contemporary scholarship. Four interconnected assumptions can be highlighted:

- formal patterns of prayer in individual lament psalms are derived from conventions of human speech;[2]
- informal complaint prayers preceded the composition of the psalms;[3]

---

1. Claus Westermann, *Praise and Lament in the Psalms* (Atlanta: John Knox Press, 1981), pp. 195-201; restated in Claus Westermann, 'The Complaint against God', in Tod Linafelt and T.K. Beal (eds.), *God in the Fray: A Tribute to Walter Brueggemann* (Minneapolis: Fortress Press, 1998), pp. 233-35.

2. E.g. Anneli Aejmelaeus, *The Traditional Prayer in the Psalms* (BZAW, 167: Berlin: W. de Gruyter, 1986), pp. 89-91.

3. E.g. Ottmar Fuchs, *Die Klage als Gebet: Eine theologische Besinnung am Beispiel des*

- the practice of individual lament preceded communal lament;[4]
- Israel's social structure originally located the lament in the family or clan before the practice moved to the temple.[5]

These four assumptions will be addressed in this chapter and also Chapters Three and Four. This chapter investigates the origin and history of informal laments. The next chapter will discuss the relationship between informal laments and the individual complaint psalms. Chapter Four will discuss historical connections between individual and community lament psalms.

There are a number of reasons for revisiting Westermann's study. First, it was focused on a few examples of complaint prayer from supposedly early texts. Westermann based himself on the work of Adolf Wendel, who held that a small group of prayers could be isolated from the period of the judges in Israel's early history to present a picture of complaint practice prior to the composition of the biblical psalms. All pertained to the distress of the people, even though some were personal laments of a covenant mediator: Josh. 7.7-9; Judg. 6.22; 15.18; 21.3 and Hos. 8.2. Westermann questioned the inclusion of Hos. 8.2 but added Gen. 25.22 and 27.46 as examples of individual lament.[6] The dating of many of these texts is now disputed.

Second, Westermann did not test his thesis against a complete catalogue of informal laments in prose sources. This fuller narrative and prophetic context must be reconstructed in order to describe the function and origin of the informal lament against God. A significant feature of this chapter is that it surveys a larger number of texts than Westermann used. This provides a surer base for establishing the function and distribution of the informal lament.

Finally, Westermann himself noted, but did not develop, the observation that complaints implying requests for help often appear in biblical discourses between human beings.[7] Many of the relevant examples have not been investigated. One of the goals of this chapter is to examine the

---

Psalms 22 (Munich: Kösel, 1982), pp. 304-312; Patrick D. Miller, *They Cried to the Lord: The Form and Theology of Biblical Prayer* (Minneapolis: Fortress Press, 1994), p. 86.

4. E.g. Erhard S. Gerstenberger, *Psalms: Part 2 and Lamentations* (FOTL, 15; Grand Rapids: Eerdmans, 2001), p. 214.

5. See the discussion and review of literature in Samuel E. Balentine, *Prayer in the Hebrew Bible: The Drama of Divine–Human Dialogue* (Overtures to Biblical Theology; Minneapolis: Fortress Press, 1993), pp. 208-210.

6. Westermann, *Praise and Lament*, p. 195; cf. Adolf Wendel, *Das freie Laiengebet im vorexilischen Israel* (Leipzig: Pfeiffer, 1931), pp. 123-43.

7. Westermann, *Praise and Lament*, pp. 195-96.

relationship between complaint in human speech and informal lament systematically.

The discussion below is divided into four sections. The first will identify forms of complaining speech in human interactions (§2.1). This review is important because of the rhetorical structure (form) of complaining requests outside of the psalms. The same forms are used both to make requests of other human beings and to present complaining petitions to God in prayer. The fact that similar rhetorical structures can be used in both circumstances is important because it sharpens questions about cultural origins and functions of informal lament. When could human beings make demands of the biblical God in the same argumentative way they made demands of one another?

The survey of informal complaint prayers in narrative prose and prophetic texts is divided into two sections: one each for laments of the community (§2.2) and the individual (§2.3). Their description does not begin by making distinctions on the basis of source or chronology. Obviously, these texts were written in different times and transmitted in various ways. But source criticism of the biblical books remains controversial and it is worth describing the overall picture before sifting the results for any historical developments. The descriptions in §§2.2–3 survey prayers for the group before prayers for individuals because some features of informal lament for individuals are best discussed in comparison to traits adduced for communal prayers.

The fourth section will synthesize the results of the first three sections (§2.4). I will agree with Westermann that the biblical record contains evidence of a tradition of lay lament that has an ancient pedigree: it actually reaches back into the Bronze Age. I also conclude that informal lay lament with complaint against God shows historical development in terms of its preferred practitioners. At some point in the monarchical period, the practice seems to fall under the aegis of prophetic functionaries.

2.1. *Forms of Complaining Requests in Human Interactions*

My study of complaining speech in human interactions follows the earlier work of Erhard Gerstenberger; the examples cited in this section are taken from his study on biblical petitions.[8] The condition for inclusion in my study was the communication of a request in which an element of complaint was explicit. The following criteria are used to classify complaints in human interactions:

---

8.   Erhard S. Gerstenberger, *Der bittende Mensch: Bittritual und Klagelied des Einzelnen im Alten Testament* (WMANT, 51; Neukirchen–Vluyn: Neukirchener Verlag, 1980), pp. 47-50.

- distinction between requests made on behalf of a group or an individual
- distinction between texts with explicit and implicit requests/ demands

The distinction between petitions made on behalf of the community and those made for an individual is important in the study of lament psalms. For that reason, the distinction is also made here. In addition, it is worth distinguishing speeches with explicit as opposed to implicit requests because of Westermann's thesis about the significance of the form of informal lament in which only the element of complaint is explicit. Ordinarily requests use the Imperative or a wish-form. However, an implicit request contains no Imperative or analogous form. So, e.g. the speeches with why-questions in 1 Sam. 28.15 and 2 Sam. 20.18-19 are treated as connoting implicit requests because there is no explicit demand to answer the question (cf. 2 Kings 5.8).

These criteria generate the following four classes of complaining speeches in human conversations:

2.1.1. *Complaint with Implied Request for a Group*
The Israelite supervisors complain to Pharaoh with an implied request to restore their former supplies of straw,

> Why do you deal thus with your servants? No straw is given to your servants, yet they say to us, 'Make bricks!' And behold, your servants are beaten; but the fault is in your own people. (Exod. 5.15-16)

Other examples include Josh. 17.14; 2 Sam. 20.18-19; 1 Kgs 1.24-27; 2 Kgs 2.19; 4.40; 6.15.

2.1.2. *Complaint with Explicit Request for a Group*
The starving Egyptians cry out to Joseph,

> Give us food; why should we die before your eyes? For our money is gone. (Gen. 47.15)

Other examples include Gen. 47.18-19; Exod. 10.7; Num. 27.3-4; Deut. 5.21-24 (24-27).

2.1.3. *Complaint with Implied Request for an Individual*
Jephthah's lament on seeing his daughter carries with it an implied request for her forgiveness,[9]

---

9.   Gerstenberger, *Der bittende Mensch*, p. 48

> Alas, my daughter! you have brought me very low, and you have become the cause of great trouble to me; for I have opened my mouth to YHWH, and I cannot take back my vow. (Judg. 11.35)

Other examples include: Gen. 42.36; Num. 22.28; 1 Sam. 28.15 (Samuel); 1 Kgs 17.18; 2 Kgs 4.1, 28; 6.5.

2.1.4. *Complaint with Explicit Request for an Individual*
Elisha sends a message to the king of Israel, who is in distress on account of the letter from the king of Aram seeking healing for Naaman, his commander-in-chief,

> Why have you rent your clothes? Let him come now to me, that he may know that there is a prophet in Israel. (2 Kgs 5.8)

Other examples include Exod. 2.20;[10] 1 Sam. 24.10-16; 26.18-20; 2 Sam. 14.32aβ.b; 2 Kgs 2.16.

The cases above show that biblical writers considered the communication of a request, motivated by complaint, to be a common form of speech and suitable for various kinds of social interchanges. A number of examples involve requests by social inferiors to their superiors in rank or class. In human interactions, complaint is used especially in petitions or requests when the person addressed is connected to the cause of the petitioner's distress.[11] There is a tendency for a request to remain unstated when the solution to the dilemma is implied in the complaint. Where the relationship between the complaint and the request is unclear, or in lengthy or elaborate speeches such as those made by David to the pursuing Saul (1 Sam. 24.10-16; 26.18-20), the request is explicit.

2.2. *Informal Lament for the Community*

Resources for identifying biblical prayers outside the Psalms include the lists of Moshe Greenberg, Hermann Gunkel and Patrick Miller.[12] A prayer is defined as a speech in which a person or community brings a concern

---

10. Jethro's commands to his daughters might suggest a classification as group request, but the final clause indicates the focus is on the care of Moses.

11. Gerstenberger, *Der bittende Mensch*, pp. 47-48.

12. Moshe Greenberg, *Biblical Prose Prayer as a Window to the Popular Religion of Ancient Israel* (The Taubman Lectures in Jewish Studies, Sixth Series; Berkeley: University of California Press, 1983), pp. 59-60; Hermann Gunkel and Joachim Begrich, *Introduction to the Psalms: The Genres of the Religious Lyric of Israel* (Mercer Library of Biblical Studies; Macon: Mercer University, 1998; 4th German edn, 1985), pp. 82, 121; Miller, *They Cried to the Lord*, pp. 337-57.

before God.[13] All prayers analysed below contain a formal element of complaint. This was *the* criterion used to identify examples for discussion. While address or petition might be implied by the context, a complaint prayer is only included if it actually contains a reference to distress. Requests for help that are not accompanied by complaint are excluded,[14] as are curses and wishes not clearly in a context of prayer.[15]

For the purpose of analysis a number of conditions are distinguished:

- prayers on behalf of a group as opposed to an individual
- prayers containing explicit as opposed to implicit requests.
- prayers containing God-complaint as opposed to those that do not
- prayers uttered in a vision as opposed to those that are not

The first two criteria are similar to those used in analysing complaint in human interactions. The third consideration appears because distinguishing between prayers with and without complaint against God ought to help in determining whether there is an informal lament-form where the complaint against God is prominent. Finally, Samuel Balentine has suggested that a prayerful speech in the midst of a communication initiated by God (e.g. in a vision) is different from the situation in which a person has initiated the prayer.[16] Consequently, I distinguish contexts in which a prayer appears in visionary circumstances from those initiated by human beings.

There are two possible categories of informal community complaint prayers. First, there are citations of community laments where the performer(s) is not identified (anonymous). These occur mainly in prophetic texts and will be considered along with other community complaints in Chapter Four. Second, there are a number of prayers that the scriptural tradition attributes to a specific person. It is this second category that is relevant here because Westermann's discussion has focused on the prayers of named individuals as a clue to the history of complaint prayer. Identification of named community mediators is usually straightforward in

---

13. Henning G. Reventlow, *Gebet im Alten Testament* (Stuttgart: Kohlhammer, 1986), p. 89. Reventlow would define an isolated cry such as 'violence!' as a short form of lament (cf. Jer. 20.8; Hab. 1.2; Job 19.7). But each of these statements occurs in a larger unit of discourse, so I have not treated these one word complaints as discrete prayers.

14. Examples of corporate requests for help without an element of complaint include: 2 Sam. 7.18-29; 1 Kgs 8.23-53; 18.36-37 and 1 Chron. 29.10-19. Examples of individual requests for help without an element of complaint include: Gen. 24.12-14; 30.24; Exod. 4.13; Deut. 3.24-25; Judg. 13.8; Neh. 13.14, 22, 31.

15. E.g. Gen. 43.14 and 2 Sam. 3.39.

16. Balentine, *Prayer in the Hebrew Bible*, p. 54.

prose sources. I have also included prayers of named functionaries in narratives of visionary experiences found in prophetic texts and in other contexts where a reference to the prophet after whom a book is named seems evident (e.g. Joel 1.19-20).

Even in cases in which the petitioner is named, a number of community prayers are not analysed since, though they imply scenarios of lament, they do not contain a formal element of complaint.[17] Also left aside are penitential prayers, such as those found in Dan. 9.4-19; Ezra 9.6-15; Neh. 1.5-11; 9.5-37. The relationship of penitential prayers to the lament genre will be explored in Chapter Seven.

2.2.1. *Informal Community Laments with Complaint against God*
2.2.1.1. *Implied Petition for a Group. Prayer Initiated by a Person.* Moses initiates a complaint to God on behalf of the people,

> YHWH, why have you done evil to this people? Why did you ever send me? For since I came to Pharaoh to speak in your name, he has done evil to this people, and you have not delivered your people at all. (Exod. 5.22-23)

Other cases include Josh. 7.7-9; 1 Sam. 4.21; Hab. 1.2-4.

2.2.1.2. *Implied Petition for a Group. Communication Initiated by God.* Ezekiel breaks out into a cry of intercession to YHWH in the middle of a vision of the terrible judgment coming upon Jerusalem. Both 9.8 and the near parallel in 11.13 are composed of complaints directed at YHWH's actions, accusations which carry an implied plea for mercy. The intercession is refused in Ezek. 9.9-10. It is answered somewhat elliptically in 11.14-21 as a promise of redemption for those in exile, but not for those left in Jerusalem.[18]

> Ah, Lord YHWH! will you destroy all that remains of Israel in the outpouring of your wrath upon Jerusalem? (Ezek. 9.8)

Other cases occur in Judg. 6.13; Isa 6.11a;[19] Jer 4.10; Ezek 11.13; Hab. 1.12-17;[20] Zech. 1.12; Dan. 8.13; 12.6.

---

17. Exod. 32.31-32; Judg. 10.10, 15; 2 Sam. 15.31; 2 Chron. 14.10.

18. For the structure of this complaint, see Miller, *They Cried to the Lord*, p. 356.

19. The cry, 'How long, YHWH?' can be construed as a short prayer of prophetic intercession. There is a connection between the prophetic vocation (Isa. 6.8) and the call to preach until the people are insensible to the prophet's message (v. 9). In Isa. 6.11 the prophetic mediator intercedes for the community under judgment; see Reventlow, *Gebet im Alten Testament*, pp. 249-50.

20. Hab. 1.2–2.4 is an extended dialogue between the prophet, Habakkuk, and God. It consists of two complaint prayers (1.2-4 and 12-17) each accompanied by a divine response in 1.5-11 and 2.2-4 (Balentine, *Prayer in the Hebrew Bible*, p. 183). I assume that

2.2.1.3. *Explicit Petition for a Group. Prayer Initiated by a Person.* One case of this category occurs in Jer. 8.18-19aα, 21-23. The personified community or city speaks in vv. 19aβ, 20. An explanatory gloss has been added in v. 19b to explain the reason for the destruction (the people's idolatry). The voice of the community is cited by another complaining voice that consistently uses the first person singular in vv. 18, 21-23. This first person singular text can be considered the words of Jeremiah's own agonized lament for his shattered people.[21] Complaint against God is indicated by the why-question in v. 22. This passage ends with an unusual wish-form as its petition.

William Holladay proposes a rather complex division of voices in which Jeremiah speaks in vv.18-19aα, 21, 22b-23, the people complain in vv.19aβ, 20 and YHWH speaks in vv. 19b and 22a.[22] Apart from the secondary presence of v.19b, Robert Carroll holds the opinion that there is really only one voice throughout Jer 8.18-19a, 20-23. Since the covenant mediator speaks for the people, the composition remains the people's prayer throughout.[23] As my study is interested in distinguishing the protests of the prophetic mediator from those of the people, identifying separate voices is important. Jer 8.18-19aα, 21-23 can be considered the words of the prophet himself. I do not follow Holladay in assigning v. 22a to the voice of YHWH. Where YHWH does speak in this text, there is an obvious gloss. Moreover, the phrase 'my people' links v. 22a with v. 23. Since Holladay thinks the latter is spoken by Jeremiah, the parallelism would suggest that the former is the prophet's speech as well.

2.2.1.4. *Explicit Petition for a Group. Communication Initiated by God.* Gen. 18.23-32 belongs to a lengthy section of discourse initiated by YHWH's arrival at the tent of Abraham and the decision not to hide from him the impending divine judgment on Sodom (18.17). The text contains both explicit and implied petitions. The initial prayer in vv. 23-25 begins with a question that implies petition, 'Will you indeed destroy the righteous with the wicked?' which is repeated in v. 24.[24] This speech ends with a strong negative wish in v. 25, 'Far be it for you to do such a thing, to slay the righteous with the wicked'.[25] This wish is the controlling petition of

vv. 12-17 follow the first divine response, so these verses have as their context divinely initiated discourse.

   21. John Bright, *Jeremiah* (AB, 21; Garden City, NY: Doubleday, 1965), p. 65.

   22. William L. Holladay, *Jeremiah* (Hermeneia; 2 vols.; Philadelphia: Fortress Press, 1986, 1989), I, pp. 290-91.

   23. Robert P. Carroll, *Jeremiah* (OTL; London: SCM Press, 1986), pp. 235-36.

   24. See Miller, *They Cried to the Lord*, p. 337.

   25. Gen. 18.25 is marked by a particle that signals a negative oath. Oaths and wishes

the passage, and it is presupposed by the bargaining queries in vv. 27-32. Abraham's questions are a form of complaint; their repetition and his persistence model the tradition of argumentative prayer.[26]

Exod. 32.11-13 contains another case of protest prayer in an extended discourse initiated by YHWH (note the why-question in v. 11).

2.2.2. *Informal Community Laments without Complaint against God*
2.2.2.1. *Implied Petition for a Group. Prayer Initiated by a Person.* Moses cries out to YHWH in exasperation over the complaints of the people in the wilderness,

> What shall I do with this people? They are almost ready to stone me. (Exod. 17.4)

As the interrogative form does not seem to imply the question 'why?', Moses' question is treated as an implied request for help. Other cases of implied petition occur in Joel 1.19-20;[27] 2 Chron. 20.6-12.[28]

2.2.2.2. *Implied Petition for a Group. Communication Initiated by God.* Jer. 14.1–15.4 is a complex text subject to different analyses. Commentators are divided as to whether the text can be read as a unit (and what the unit is) and where elements of lament may be found. For example, Jenö Kiss believes that Jer. 14.13-16 is an exilic or early postexilic addition to a text that originally contained a we-complaint in vv. 2-7 and a divine answer in vv. 10-12.[29] By contrast Mark Boda contends that, even if one regards Jer. 14.1–15.4 as an exilic product, the laments and descriptions of divine interaction in this unit cannot be derived from Deuteronomistic activity.

---

have similar syntax on Biblical Hebrew; see Bruce K. Waltke and Michael P. O'Connor, *An Introduction to Biblical Hebrew Syntax* (Winona Lake, IN: Eisenbrauns, 1990), §40.2.2.

26. Anson Laytner, *Arguing with God: A Jewish Tradition* (Northvale, NJ: Jason Aronson, 1990), pp. 3-8.

27. While vv. 16-18 appear to be a citation of collective lament by the people, the self-reference in v.19b suggests that it is the prophet who is speaking; see James L. Crenshaw, *Joel* (AB, 24C; New York: Doubleday, 1995), p. 111

28. The prayer in 2 Chron. 20.6-12 begins with rhetorical questions in vv. 6-7. It ends with a question in similar form in v. 12, which I analyse as an implied petition because of its placement at the end of the speech, where petitions often occur in prayers. The syntax of *hălō'* in 2 Chron. 20.6-12 is discussed by Balentine (*Prayer in the Hebrew Bible*, pp. 99-100), who regards the use of this interrogative particle not as an expression of complaint, but as a positive assertion bordering on doxology.

29. Jenö Kiss, *Die Klage Gottes und des Propheten: Ihre Rolle in der Komposition und Redaktion von Jer 11–12, 14–15 und 18* (WMANT, 99; Neukirchen–Vluyn: Neukirchener Verlag, 2003), p. 210.

Hence, Boda would trace the dialogue represented in vv. 10-16 back to Jeremiah himself.[30]

The fact that Jeremiah may be both a historical figure and a literary creation does not appreciably affect the analysis here. The book records the experiences of a prophet named Jeremiah who attempts to intercede with YHWH for the people. A divine prohibition against interceding for the people appears in Jer. 7.16 and 11.14. But Jeremiah responds to the same divine prohibition in 14.11-12 by complaining on behalf of the people that they are being deceived by their prophets.

> Ah, Lord YHWH, behold, the prophets say to them, 'You shall not see the sword, nor shall you have famine, but I will give you assured peace in this place'. (Jer. 14.13)

2.2.2.3. *Explicit Petition for a Group. Prayer Initiated by a Person*. The book of Nehemiah intersperses its narrative with short prayers. After recounting the insults of their enemies, who wish to prevent the Jews from rebuilding the walls of Jerusalem, Nehemiah breaks out in imprecation:

> Hear, O our God, for we are despised; turn back their taunt upon their own heads and give them up to be plundered in a land where they are captives. Do not cover their guilt, and do not let their sin be blotted out from your sight; for they have provoked you to anger before the builders. (Neh. 3.36-37)

Other cases occur in 2 Sam. 24.17; 2 Kgs 19.15-19 (= Isa. 37.16-20); Neh. 13.29.

2.2.2.4. *Explicit Petition for a Group. Communication Initiated by God*. There are four related visions in Amos 7.1-3, 4-6, 7-9 and 8.1-3. Their cumulative effect is to demonstrate that prophetic intercession will not lead to atonement with YHWH.[31] The first two, however, contain prayers that seek to turn aside divine judgment. The structure of Amos 7.2 ends with a complaining question that reinforces the Petition. As the question is neither prefaced by 'how long' nor implies 'why', I do not analyse it as complaint against God.

> O Lord YHWH, forgive, I beseech you! How can Jacob stand? He is so small. (Amos 7.2)

Another case occurs in Amos 7.5.

---

30. Mark J. Boda, 'From Complaint to Contrition: Peering through the Liturgical Window of Jer 14,1–15,4', *ZAW* 113 (2001), pp. 190-93.

31. Reventlow, *Gebet im Alten Testament*, pp. 247-48.

Table 1. *Classification of Informal Community Laments by Textual Source and Type*

Source	Laments with God-Complaint		Laments without God-Complaint	
	Not-	In a Vision	Not-	In a Vision
Pentateuch				
J	Exod. 5.22-23	Gen. 18-23-32		
J or E		Exod. 32.11-13	Exod. 17.4	
DtrH	Josh. 7.7-9	Judg. 6.13	2 Sam. 24.17	
	1 Sam. 4.21		2 Kgs 19.15-19	
Prophets	Jer. 8.18-23	Isa. 6.11	Joel 1.19-20	Jer. 14.13
	Hab. 1.2-4	Jer 4.10		Amos 7.2
		Ezek. 9.8		Amos 7.5
		Ezek. 11.13		
		Hab. 1.12-17		
		Zech. 1.12		
		Dan. 8.13		
		Dan. 12.6		
Chronicler			Neh. 3.36-37	
			Neh. 13.29	
			2 Chron. 20.6-12	

As a general rule, I assume that a narrative source reflects beliefs and ideas current in the times in which it was written down. True, there may be anachronisms and memories of a past at variance with present practices, but on the ideological level I suppose that stories are told and transmitted because they speak to the persons who preserve them and want to hear them. Therefore, when it comes to dating sources I assume that the stories they contain give information about beliefs and practices at the time of writing or in the centuries immediately before, when the oral or textual material at the basis of these writings may have circulated. A consequence of this approach is that I do not think that most of the texts surveyed in §2.2 can really cast light on ancient Jewish practice before the middle of the monarchical period. The one exception is 1 Sam. 4.21.

Sources for texts from the Pentateuch were determined with reference to standard syntheses of the critical consensus.[32] Dating of the sources J and E as well as their existence is hotly contested. While the nature of E has been debated for some time, in recent decades scholars have also cast considerable doubt on the nature of J. In fact, the unity of J has been a

---

32. See Samuel R. Driver, *An Introduction to the Literature of the Old Testament* (Cleveland: Meridian Books, 1967) and Norman K. Gottwald, *The Hebrew Bible: A Socio-Literary Introduction* (Philadelphia: Fortress Press, 1985).

perennial problem in critical scholarship.[33] My approach to this problem
is to recognize that the unity of J (and of J-E) is, first of all, a matter of
style, not date or source. Computer analysis of Genesis shows an inability
to distinguish J from E, but the combination of J and E texts is distin-
guishable from the texts assigned to P.[34] My work here, therefore, accepts
a basic distinction between P and non-P strands in Pentateuchal narrative.

Critical consensus assumes that the Pentateuch received its present
form (more or less) around the end of the 5th century BCE.[35] A significant
body of scholarship still dates J to the 10th century BCE, assuming that it
may contain even older materials. Such assumptions about the date of J
underlie the work of Westermann.[36] But a newer school of Pentateuchal
criticism dates the narrative source J to the exilic period.[37] I take the
position, that the combined material of J and E reflects tales told in a style
which had considerable stability during the Iron Age. While there are
undoubtedly materials in the J-E style from the monarchical period, it is
also apparent that some strands must stem from the exilic era.[38]

Theoretically, therefore, J-E materials could reflect conditions of the
monarchical period through to the exilic period (i.e. most of the Iron
Age). In fact, the window for dating the materials in §2.2 is narrower than
this, because the Pentateuchal references mainly concern Moses. Many of
the prayers and complaints associated with the Mosaic tradition echo
typologies of prophetic practice during the later monarchy, perhaps especially with Jeremiah.[39] There are analogues between the lament reports

33. Albert de Pury, 'Yahwist ('J') Source', *ABD*, VI, p. 1013.

34. Y.T. Radday and Haim Shore, *Genesis: An Authorship Study* (AnBib, 103; Rome:
Biblical Institute Press, 1985), p. 189.

35. Gottwald, *The Hebrew Bible*, pp. 102-103. See also the conclusions of John Van
Seters, *The Pentateuch: A Social-Science Commentary*, (Trajectories, 1; Sheffield: Sheffield
Academic Press, 1999) pp. 188-89, 213.

36. Westermann, *Praise and Lament*, p. 195. For the continuing importance of the
traditional dating of J, see, Harold Bloom and David Rosenberg, *The Book of J* (New
York: Vintage, 1991), p. 9 and many modern textbooks, e.g. Gottwald, *The Hebrew Bible*,
p. 137.

37. E.g. Van Seters, *The Pentateuch*, p. 122; E. Theodore Mullen, *Ethnic Myths and
Pentateuchal Foundations: A New Approach to the Formation of the Pentateuch* (Atlanta:
Scholars Press, 1997), pp. 10-12

38. Work on J has underscored parallels with Akkadian mythology, including
Gilgamesh (Van Seters, *The Pentateuch*, p. 119) and Atrahasis (Bernard F. Batto, *Slaying
the Dragon: Mythmaking in the Biblical Tradition* [Louisville, KY: Westminster John Knox
Press, 1992], pp. 44-46). My opinion is that a writer of Hebrew literature could not
have encountered such material before the exile to Mesopotamia as there was only
limited familiarity with Akkadian texts in the pre-exilic era, see William S. Morrow,
'Cuneiform Literacy and Deuteronomic Composition', *BiOr* 62 (2005), pp. 204-13.

39. Brevard S. Childs, *The Book of Exodus* (OTL; Philadelphia, Westminster Press.

found in prophetic sources and those attributed to Moses. A similar structure of complaint and divine response is visible.

The books of Joshua–2 Kings belong to the Deuteronomistic History (DtrH). The composition history of the DtrH is disputed. Following the work of Frank Moore Cross, many scholars believe that a first edition (or block) was composed in the late pre-exilic period with a second completed during the exile. Another influential view, associated with Rudolf Smend, thinks that redaction criticism can expose three different versions (or strata) of the DtrH: two composed during the exile and a third in the postexilic period. In fact, both the beginning and the end of the period in which the DtrH was composed are debatable.[40] But the weight of these two theories suggests that the DtrH was substantially composed by the end of the exilic period. Nevertheless, it would not be amiss to assume that some of the traditions contained in the DtrH were circulating in the late monarchical period. There are grounds for assuming use of earlier material such as some of the Samson narratives in Judges or the ark narrative in Samuel. But in the absence of indications that the writers of the DtrH are drawing on material inimical to their own worldview, I assume that the texts from the DtrH basically indicate what thinkers from the late monarchical and exilic period thought of as acceptable lament practice.

The material connected to the source called 'Chronicler' is derived from more than one postexilic writer. While they show similarities in style, it is now generally accepted that the writer of Chronicles is not identical with the authors of Ezra and Nehemiah, each of which has its own history of transmission. My use of the label of Chronicler, therefore, is stylistic in intent. The material in Chronicler style probably stems from the 4th century BCE.[41]

The prophetic books have been subject to editing, some of them quite heavily. The texts I have surveyed stem from constellations of speech and story centered on the eighth century prophets Amos and the Isaiah of Jerusalem, the seventh–sixth century prophet Jeremiah, and the exilic prophets Ezekiel and Habakkuk. For the most part, I have not made rigid

1974), pp.144-49; John Van Seters, *The Life of Moses: The Yahwish as Historian in Exodus–Numbers* (Louisville, KY: Westminster John Knox, 1994), pp. 171-75; Timo Veijola, 'Das Klagegebet in Literatur und Leben der Exilsgeneration am Beispiel eigenen Prosa-texte', in J.A. Emerton (ed.), *Congress Volume: Salamanca 1983* (VTSup, 36; Leiden: Brill, 1985), p. 306.

40. See the review of current literature on the composition of the DtrH in Timo Veijola, 'Deuteronomismusforschung zwischen Tradition und Innovation (III)', *TRu* 68 (2003), pp. 41-44.

41. Ralph W. Klein, 'Chronicles, Book of 1-2', *ABD,* I, pp. 994-95.

distinctions between a prophet and his editors. While dating individual texts is difficult, one will not go far wrong to assume that the complaints extracted from the prophetic books reflect beliefs and rhetoric current from the mid-monarchical period thought to the exile, depending on the source.

The evidence in Table 1 militates against the assumption that informal community laments with God-complaint were a typical expression of lay piety. The passages in the Chronicler style do not help, because they contain no cases of God-complaint. Therefore, the evidence comes from Pentateuchal sources, the Deuteronomistic History and Iron Age prophecy. These three sources speak with a similar voice.

Accounts of community intercession using complaint against God are mainly put into the mouths of persons whom the tradition identifies as prophets. The list includes Isaiah, Jeremiah, Ezekiel, and Habakkuk. Two cases are attributed to Moses; but Moses can also be considered as a prophetic type, because there is a connection between the figure of Moses as a community intercessor and the prophetic office.[42]

The same connection can be made with Joshua. Moses lays hands on him in Deut. 34.9 and Joshua is told he will be addressed by YHWH in ways similar to Moses (Josh. 1.5). While Westermann wished to date the narrative in Josh. 7.7-9 to the early monarchical period, the story seems to reflect exilic concerns.[43] Joshua's intercession on behalf of the people in Josh. 7.7-9, therefore, appears to be an extension of the type of intervention common to Moses and other prophetic types.

Judg. 6.13 falls under suspicion because the text is connected to the genre of prophetic narrative called the 'call narrative'. In other words, the complaint prayer occurs in the context where Gideon receives his commission to be a kind of covenant mediator. His intercession for the people under ecstatic circumstances, therefore, is connected to prophetic motifs.[44]

---

42. Robert R. Wilson, *Prophecy and Society in Ancient Israel* (Philadelphia: Fortress Press, 1984), pp. 151-56.

43. Veijola, 'Das Klagegebet', p. 304. Veijola assumes that the Achan narrative reflects Deuteronomisitic ideology; it is possible, however, that it also contains motifs of a priestly provenance, see Mark J. Boda, *Praying the Tradition: The Origin and Use of Tradition in Nehemiah 9* (BZAW, 277; Berlin: W. de Gruyter, 1999), pp. 59-61. In either case, Josh. 7.7-9 appears to be a text stemming from much later times than Westermann thought.

44. Norman C. Habel ('The Form and Significance of the Call Narratives', *ZAW* 77 [1965], pp. 316-17) argues that the calls of Moses in Exodus 3–4 and Gideon influenced the call narratives of the prophets (cf. Isaiah 6; Jeremiah 1 and Ezekiel 1–3). But the influence probably runs in the other direction, because the figure of Moses cannot be easily separated from prophetic typology.

Before turning to the cases of Gen. 18.23-32 and 1 Sam. 4.21, it is worth drawing out some implications of the discussion above. It begs the question of the identity of the prophets. In fact, the designation 'prophet' covers a wide variety of types of divinely inspired persons in biblical culture.[45] But I use the term to mean the type of visionary to which the canonical prophets and Moses were considered to belong. That is, the so-called 'classical prophets' who professed to be privy to YHWH's counsel and possessed by the revelation of the effective word of Israel's deity. These functionaries also claimed to be subject to both visions and auditions of a supernatural kind.[46]

Additional evidence for the dominance of prophetic functionaries may be derived from cases of community complaints in the Exodus traditions that occur outside the context of prayer. These include Exod. 16.3; 17.2-3 (read as a single speech, though separated by a short narrative); Num. 11.20; 14.2-3; 21.5 and Deut. 1.27-28. These are not texts of prayer, yet the narrative indicates that God is the object of the people's complaints, though the speeches are directed at Moses. These wilderness traditions clarify who customarily voiced such protests in prayer. Evidently, group leaders could bring the community's distress to a prophet's attention using complaint forms common in human interactions, but the community's leaders did not complain against God in prayer. That was left to a prophetic intermediary like Moses.

This claim can be tested by considering community laments without complaint against God. Those unconditioned by visionary experience involve the non-prophetic figures, Hezekiah (2 Kgs 19.15-19), Jehoshaphat (2 Chron. 20.6-12) and Nehemiah (Neh. 3.36-37; 13.29). One need not question the idea that non-prophetic mediators such as kings had liturgical responsibilities (cf. Solomon's intercessory prayer in 1 Kings 8), but it is noteworthy that these community leaders do not complain against God in their prayers.

The prayer of Abraham in Gen. 18.23-32 needs to be considered against the background of all of the prayers for groups in a visionary context. Altogether there are 14 cases of informal laments for the community uttered under ecstatic conditions. These are listed in Table 1. Twelve are associated with prophetic experience (including Dan. 8.13 and 12.6). The two remaining are Gen. 18.23-32 and Judg. 6.13. The fact that Abraham and Gideon belong to the pre-monarchical period should not be ignored. These data are commensurate with the suggestion that Israel's storytellers gradually constricted the record of divine encounter from a broad

45. J.J. Schmitt, 'Prophecy (Preexilic Hebrew)', *ABD*, V, pp. 482-89 (482).
46. See the description in J. Lindblom, *Prophecy in Ancient Israel* (Oxford: Basil Blackwell, 1962), pp. 105-37.

popular base to include only prophets in monarchical times.[47] In other words, key figures in Israel's early history were thought to have had an intimacy with divine reality considered characteristic of prophetic mediators.

The best case for discovering a lay community lament, therefore, occurs in 1 Sam. 4.21. The name given by the wife of Phineas to her new-born son as she was dying in child-birth was Ichabod, literally, 'Where is the glory?' This prayer of complaint reflects a typical Semitic naming pattern associated with problematic births.[48] Ichabod is related to a type of personal name well-attested in various sources from the Second Millennium that has the form 'Where is (divine name or epithet)?' West Semitic examples include, *'Ayya-'abi-'ilu* ('Where is my Father, the God?') and *'Ayya-ma-'ilu* ('Where is God?').[49] The use of the form of the personal name 'Where is (divine epithet)?' is found in both Bronze and Iron Age contexts. There are several biblical examples, including Ayyah (Gen. 36.24; 2 Sam. 3.7), Ithamar (Exod. 6.23), Iezer (Num. 26.30), Ehud (Judg. 3.15) and Jezebel (a Phoenician name alluding to the storm-god, Baal-Hadad). These names belong to the religious experience of the family. Typically, such names recall a lament that is considered answered by a child's birth and serves as a reminder of the divine response to a human predicament. In these personal names, a question of divine absence (voiced as a complaint predicated by the question 'Where?') has been turned an affirmation of divine presence by the person living with this type of name.[50]

Unlike other examples, the complaining question in the name Ichabod appears to publicize and perpetuate a lament rather than signal its answer. The family distress in the birth narrative of Ichabod involves the deaths of the nameless woman's husband and father-in-law, but this is not the main reference of the name. Twice the text underscores the connection between the lament 'Where is the glory' and the loss of the divine ark housed in the Shiloh shrine (1 Sam. 4.21-22).

The case of 1 Sam. 4.21 is an exception to the pattern of prophetic intermediaries bringing complaint against God to expression in informal laments by virtue of their intimate association with YHWH. But YHWH was thought to have special care over two significant transitions in the lives of

---

47. See Balentine, *Prayer in the Hebrew Bible*, 20.

48. Karl van der Toorn, *Sin and Sanction in Israel and Mesopotamia: A Comparative Study* (Studia semitica neerlandica; Assen: Van Gorcum, 1985), p. 57.

49. Joel S. Burnett, 'The Question of Divine Absence in Israelite and West Semitic Religion', *CBQ* 67 (2005), pp. 221-22.

50. Burnett, 'The Question of Divine Absence', pp. 223-26.

individuals: birth and death.[51] Below, I will adduce further evidence to show the importance of these two events for informal individual lament. Birth and death come together in the narrative of 1 Sam. 4.21. While the unnamed mother of Ichabod is not a prophet, as she experiences her own premature death at the moment of the birth of her son she is arguably in a transitional state in which YHWH is thought to have a particular interest. Hence, she takes the opportunity to lament not only her own misfortunes but also those of her people with her dying breath.

2.3. *Informal Laments for Individuals*

Distressed individuals also pray on their own behalf, not simply as community representatives. This is a sticky point, because it can be argued that the biblical individuals depicted in acts of protest prayer are all larger-than-life, national heroes.[52] The list of individual examples includes prayers by covenant mediators that register personal distress, e.g. Gideon in Judg. 6.22 and Jacob in Gen. 32.10-13.[53]

Criteria for classification are similar to those used for informal community laments (§2.2). Only individual prayers containing a formal element of complaint are analysed. Some texts are missing that imply individual lament: e.g. David's confession of sin in 2 Sam. 12.13, in which Nathan's reply recognizes a plea not to die, and Hezekiah's prayer for healing in 2 Kgs 20.3 (= Isa 38.3). These texts lack an explicit complaint element. Another set of texts left out of consideration are the so-called 'Confessions' of Jeremiah (Jer. 11.18-20; 12.1-4; 15.15-18; 17.14-18; 18.19-23; 20.7-13, 14-18). Their similarities to the rhetoric of the psalms put them in a different category than the prayers surveyed here.[54] The significance of

---

51. Hans W. Wolff, *Anthropology of the Old Testament* (Philadelphia: Fortress Press, 1974), pp. 96-98, 107-108.

52. Reventlow, *Gebet im Alten Testament*, p. 99.

53. I agree with Reventlow (*Gebet im Alten Testament*, p. 98) that Gen. 32.10-13 contains the prayer of a clan chief responsible for a large number of people. But the narrative leads us to understand that Jacob is deeply anxious for his personal survival.

54. See Robert P. Carroll, *From Chaos to Covenant: Prophecy in the Book of Jeremiah* (New York: Crossroad, 1981), p. 108; Klaus Koch, *The Prophets* (2 vols.; Philadelphia: Fortress Press, 1983, 1984), II, p. 38. Some scholars have referred to these poems as the 'confessions of Jeremiah' on analogy with the famous confessions of St Augustine, because they seemed to be first person accounts of the spiritual life. A less contentious term would be the 'psalms of the book of Jeremiah', see J. Vermeylen, 'Essai de Redaktionsgeschichte des «Confessions de Jérémie»', in P.M. Bogaert (ed.), *Le livre de Jérémie: Le prophète et son milieu, les oracles et leur transmission* (BETL, 54; Leuven: Peeters, 1981), p. 268

these poems in Jeremiah for a history of the complaint against God will
be addressed in the next chapter.

2.3.1. *Informal Individual Laments with Complaint against God*
2.3.1.1. *Implied Petition for an Individual. Prayer Initiated by a Person.*
Samson's lament is personal, though he is a type of covenant mediator.
His complaint reproaches YHWH with a contrast between what God had
done earlier and what he is presently doing. The contrast implies the
question 'Why?'[55]

> You have granted this great deliverance by the hand of your servant; and
> shall I now die of thirst and fall into the hands of the uncircumcised? (Judg.
> 15.18)

Similar cases include Gen. 25.22 (but not 27.46b);[56] 2 Kgs 2.14;[57] Jer
32.17-25;[58] 45.3.[59]

2.3.1.2. *Implied Petition for an Individual. Communication Initiated by God.*
Cain complains to God when he hears of his banishment from the ground,

> My punishment is greater than I can bear. Behold, you have driven me this
> day away from the ground; and from your face I shall be hidden; and I
> shall be a fugitive and a wanderer on the earth, and whoever finds me will
> slay me. (Gen. 4.13-14)

Another case occurs in Gen. 15.2-3.

---

55. Westermann, *Praise and Lament*, p. 198.

56. Westermann (*Praise and Lament*, p. 195) considered both Gen. 25.22 and 27.46b as
examples of early complaint. His opinion is followed by Reventlow (*Gebet im Alten
Testament*, p. 95). But Gen. 27.46 is better analysed as inter-human communication. The
person to whom Rebecca directs her question, in the first place, is Isaac. Her complaint
contains an implied request that Jacob marry a relative. Isaac responds in the next
verse, where he calls Jacob in, blesses him and sends him to his uncle's people (28.1).

57. 2 Kgs 2.14 is not usually considered as a complaint prayer. But 'Where is
YHWH...?' can be considered a form of lament (cf. 1 Sam. 4.21; Isa. 63.11-12, 15).

58. For the structure of this complaint, see Miller, *They Cried to the Lord*, pp. 355-56.
The more original form of this text probably comprised vv. 17, 21-25. Jeremiah's dismay
at YHWH's instructions to redeem his family patrimony is conveyed in the phrase 'Ah,
Lord YHWH' in v. 17. Verses 24-25 give the details of the prophet's bafflement, in effect,
complaining that the city is under siege (Holladay, *Jeremiah*, II, pp. 208-209). Despite
the personal note, the language of the prayer is Deuteronomistic and akin to group
prayers found in the Persian period and later (cf. Dan. 9.4-19). As the leader of the
prayer, Jeremiah is presented as a major liturgical figure (Carroll, *Jeremiah*, p. 625). In
other words, Jer. 32.17-25 is a prayer of a covenant mediator which also contains a note
of personal distress.

59. For the structure of this complaint, see Miller, *They Cried to the Lord*, p. 357.

2.3.1.3. *Explicit Petition for an Individual. Prayer Initiated by a Person*. Elijah's prayer for the widow's son is not usually considered when the complaint genre is discussed. Nevertheless, it bears sufficient formal similarity for consideration here, because it contains an implied question 'why?' The analysis treats the words of Elijah as one prayer, though there are two separate speeches,

> YHWH, my God, have you brought calamity even upon the widow with whom I sojourn, by slaying her son? ... YHWH, my God, let this child's life come into him again. (1 Kgs 17.20-21)

Other cases are found in Num. 11.11-15 and Jon. 4.2-3.[60]

2.3.2. *Informal Individual Lament without Complaint against God*
2.3.2.1. *Implied Petition for an Individual. Prayer initiated by a Person*. Desperate for a child, Hannah makes a vow to YHWH. There is no Imperative or explicit wish formula; the request is implied by the conditional form of the vow. The complaint is indicated by the phrase 'the affliction of your maidservant',

> O YHWH of hosts, if you will indeed look on the affliction of your maidservant, and remember me, and not forget your maidservant, but will give to your maidservant a manchild, then I will give him to YHWH all the days of his life and no razor shall touch his head. (1 Sam. 1.11)

2.3.2.2. *Implied Petition for an Individual. Communication Initiated by God*. The prophet Jeremiah attempts to avoid the divine commission by complaining about his youth:

> Ah, Lord YHWH! Behold, I do not know how to speak, for I am only a youth. (Jer. 1.6)

Other cases occur in Exod. 4.10; Judg. 6.22; 1 Kgs 19.10(= v. 14); Ezek. 21.5.[61]

2.3.2.3. *Explicit Petition for an Individual. Prayer Initiated by a Person*. Samson calls on YHWH so he can take personal revenge on the Philistines who have captured and blinded him,

---

60. For the structure of this complaint, see Miller, *They Cried to the Lord*, p. 357. Jonah's complaint against God is ironic, the traditional doxology of divine graciousness has become the source of the prophet's disappointment.

61. Ezekiel complains that the people he addresses accuse him of being a maker of allegories. The lament is an elliptical request for an interpretation of the allegory that he has been told to proclaim in Ezek. 21.1-4. The divine response in 21.6-10 makes explicit the meaning of the allegory, see John W. Wevers, *Ezekiel* (NCB; London: Nelson, 1969), p. 163.

> O Lord YHWH, remember me, I pray you, and strengthen me, I pray you,
> only this once, O God, that I may be avenged upon the Philistines for one
> of my two eyes. (Judg. 16.28)

Other cases include Gen. 21.16;[62] 32.10-13; 1 Sam. 23.10-11;[63] 1 Kgs 19.4;
Neh. 6.14.[64]

2.3.2.4. *Explicit Request for an Individual. Communication Initiated by God.*
Lot implores the angels who want his family to flee into the hills away
from the impending doom on Sodom,

> Oh, no, my lords; behold, your servant has found favour in your sight, and
> you have shown me great kindness in saving my life; but I cannot flee to
> the hills, lest the disaster overtake me and I die. Behold, yonder city is near
> enough to flee to, and it is a little one. Let me escape there — is it not a little
> one? — and my life will be saved! (Gen. 19.18-20)

Another case occurs in 1 Kgs 3.6-9.[65]

Literary-critical assumptions are similar to those set out in §2.2. But some
cases require comment. Even scholars who wish to place the composition
of the patriarchal narratives in the exile acknowledge that some of these
narratives are based on pre-existing traditions.[66] The complaints of Hagar
(Gen. 21.16) and Rachel (25.22) almost certainly belong to these early traditions. There are also grounds for discerning an older form of Gen. 32.10-13

---

62. Analysed as a prayer by Miller, *They Cried to the Lord,* p. 338. The element of
complaint is the object of the negative wish.

63. Veijola ('Klagegebet', p. 290) analyses 1 Sam. 23.10-11 as a narrative in which a
Deuteronomistic author has revised an earlier request for an oracle into an individual
complaint. Elements of lament include Address, Enemy-complaint (v.10) and Petitions
(v. 11).

64. As in Judg. 16.28, Nehemiah is praying for revenge on those who have hurt him.
This is a prayer for individual distress on analogy with imprecatory prayers against
the enemies in the complaint psalms (e.g. Pss. 140.10-12; 141.6).

65. Although Solomon is conscious of the impact of his actions on the nation as a
whole, his prayer indicates personal concerns. Balentine (*Prayer in the Hebrew Bible,* p.
57) describes 1 Kgs 3.6-9 as a report of a dream epiphany that has the 'look of prayer'
but functions differently because it is in a vision initiated by God. But 1 Kgs 3.6-9 does
represent a human communication to a divine figure in which a request for help is
made using a pattern of speech common to the complaint form. Solomon complains in
v. 7 that 'I am but a little child; I do not know how to go out or come in'. Even if this
protest is more a matter of convention than sincerity, it has an analogy to Jeremiah's
protest in Jer. 1.6.

66. See, e.g. Van Seters, *The Pentateuch,* pp. 127-28; 130-31; Rainer Albertz, *Israel in
Exile: The History and Literature of the Sixth Century B.C.E.* (Studies in Biblical Literature,
3; Atlanta: Society of Biblical Literature, 2003), pp. 255-56.

Table 2. *Classification of Informal Individual Laments by Textual Source and Type.*

Source	Laments with God-Complaint		Laments without God-Complaint	
	Not-	In a Vision	Not-	In a Vision
Pentateuch				
J		Gen. 4.13-14		
J/E		Gen. 15.2-3		
J				Gen. 19.18-20
E			Gen. 21.16	
J	Gen. 25.22			
J/E			Gen. 32.10-13	
J				Exod. 4.10
J/E	Num. 11.11-15			
DtrH	Judg. 15.18		Judg. 16.28	Judg. 6.22
	1 Kgs 17.20-21		1 Sam. 1.11	1 Kgs 3.6-9
	2 Kgs 2.14		1 Sam. 23.10-11	1 Kgs 19.10
			1 Kgs 19.4	
Prophetic	Jer. 32.17-25			Jer. 1.6
	Jer. 45.3			Ezek. 21.5
	Jon. 4.2-3			
Chronicler			Neh. 6.14	

from the present narrative (probably vv. 10a.12).[67] Some of the references to lament in the DtrH may also reflect pre-existing sources, e.g. traditions surrounding Samson (Judg. 15.18),[68] Samuel (1 Sam. 1.11) and Elijah (1 Kings 17.20-21).

I also assume that prophetic intermediaries are not lay persons in the ordinary sense of the word. Therefore, an investigation of lay complaints in biblical culture ought to distinguish prayers uttered by prophetic functionaries from other cases. Another potentially important methodological question arises from the distinction between prayers initiated by human beings and laments that occur within responses to communication initiated by the deity.

In the case of informal individual laments in non-visionary conditions, 6/15 cases involve prophets, including Moses (Num. 11.11-15), Elijah

67. Reventlow, *Gebet im Alten Testament*, pp. 97-98. See also the study of the current form of Gen. 32.10-12 in Judith H. Newman, *Praying by the Book: The Scripturalization of Prayer in Second Temple Judaism* (Early Judaism and its Literature, 14; Atlanta: Scholars Press, 1999), pp. 29-33. Newman's discussion supports the idea of Reventlow that an early version of Jacob's prayer has been expanded by appeal to written traditions.

68. Reventlow (*Gebet im Alten Testament*, p. 92) identifies Judg. 15.18 as part of an aetiological narrative that was incorporated into the Samson cycle.

(1 Kgs 17.20-21; 19.4), Elisha (2 Kgs 2.14), Jeremiah (Jer. 32.17-25) and
Jonah (Jon. 4.2-3). Of the nine texts not uttered by prophetic functionaries,
evidence for lay lament with complaint against God depends on the
prayers of Baruch, Rebecca and Samson.

Jer. 45.3 has associations with prophetic practice. Jer 45.3-5 contains
both Baruch's lament (v. 3) and an oracular reply by Jeremiah (vv. 4-5).
The divine response indicates that the social upheaval caused by YHWH
will affect everyone in Jerusalem, but Baruch's life will be preserved. The
exact context in which Baruch's complaint was uttered is unclear. But it
looks as if Baruch's lament was originally addressed not to YHWH, but to
Jeremiah.[69] In other words, Baruch did not put his complaint to YHWH
directly but through a recognized intermediary.

Rebecca's pregnancy causes her to cry out, 'If it is thus, why do I live?'
The context indicates the speech was directed to God, because Rebecca
seeks the answer to her query in sacred space, 'So she went to inquire of
YHWH' (Gen. 25.22b). Does this mean that Rebecca's complaint led to
mediation by a ritual expert as in the case of Jer 45.3? The fact that Rebecca
seeks an answer to her query does not invalidate the picture presented in
the text: a pregnant lay-woman complains to God, using the self-contained
lament form, in her own home. Rebecca's prayer accords with other evidence that birthing was a typical context for lay complaint. References
were cited above in connection with 1 Sam. 4.21.

Samson was not an ordinary layperson. According to the biblical record,
he was invested with the spirit of God on a regular basis (e.g. Judg. 13.25;
14.19). He was also peculiar among his fellow Israelites because he was to
be a Nazarite (a person dedicated to God who neither drank wine nor cut
his hair) from the day of his birth (Judg. 13.5). Nevertheless, there seems
to be no particular relationship between his religious status and his forms
of prayer. Westermann distinguishes Samson's prayer for help from that
of ordinary lay-people by describing 15.18 as a lament of the mediator.[70]
But, in contrast to Westermann's other examples (Judg. 6.13 and 21.3),
Samson is clearly complaining on his own behalf—not the nation's. Despite
the unusual status of Samson, I take Judg. 15.18 as an example of lay piety
using the self-contained lament.

There is also indirect biblical testimony to the practice of lay complaint
against God. This includes Naomi's bitter complaint in Ruth 1.20-21 and
the speeches of the suffering Job (e.g. Job 6–7; 9–10; 12–14). Given the
proximity between conventions of social discourse and informal complaining prayers, it would be surprising if such complaints did not spill

---

69. Holladay, *Jeremiah*, II, p. 309.
70. Westermann, 'Complaint against God', p. 234.

over into unmediated laments against God on certain occasions, as represented in the book of Job.

Evidence for lay practice includes examples of informal lament without God-complaint. There are two categories. First, there are prayers of (would-be) mothers in extreme circumstances including Hagar (Gen. 21.16) and Hannah (1 Sam. 1.11). These prayers have connections with women's laments in Gen. 25.22 (Rebecca) and 1 Sam. 4.21 (the mother of Ichabod). Second, there are prayers for those facing imminent death at the hands of enemies, asking for either revenge (Judg. 16.28; Neh. 6.14) or protection (Gen. 32.10-13; 1 Sam. 23.10-11; 1 Kgs 19.10).

Now that the probability of informal lay complaint by individuals has been established, the cases of Cain and Abram may be considered. Gen. 4.13-14 and 15.2-3 occur in visionary situations. The circumstances of Cain and Abram's complaints to God, therefore, resemble cases in which the intimacy of prophetic experience has been projected onto significant persons in the pre-monarchic period. But apart from this observation, it would appear that both texts provide evidence for the practice of protest prayer in lay circles. In the case of Cain, his sentence of banishment is perceived as a death-sentence, since anyone who encounters him will feel free to slay him. Informal laments of persons facing imminent death are also attested in Gen. 32.10-13; Judg. 6.22; 15.18; 1 Kgs 19.10 and Neh. 6.14. Abram protests the fact that God has left him without an heir — a situation which has dire consequences for his welfare after death as well as for the transfer of his property.[71] There are other laments by persons struggling with birth difficulties in Gen. 25.22 and 1 Sam. 1.11. There is reason to assume, therefore, that Gen. 4.13-14 and 15.2-3 reflect circumstances in which informal lament with God-complaint was typically expressed.

2.4. *Origins and Developments of Informal Lament*

The chapter opened by listing four concerns that are connected with the study of the informal lament. The evidence surveyed in §§2.2-3 allows commentary on two:

- formal patterns of prayer in individual lament psalms are derived from conventions of human speech;
- the practice of individual lament preceded communal lament.

Can one can assign a formal significance to the informal laments with God-complaint that only imply petition? A total of 16/26 informal community laments contain God-complaint. A total of 10/24 informal individual

71. See H.C. Brichto, 'Kin, Cult, Land and Afterlife — a Biblical Complex', *HUCA* 44 (1973), pp. 27-28.

laments contain God-complaint. So 52% of the total number of prayers surveyed involve an element of protest. Of the protest prayers, 20/26 (roughly 75%) do not possess an explicit petition. The percentage is not as significant when prayers without God-complaint are counted, as 10/24 (roughly 40%) have no explicit petition.

Superficially, these results appear to support Westermann's thesis, that there was a form of informal lament characterized by the element of God-complaint without explicit petitions. But another explanation is possible in view of the survey of inter-human requests in §2.1 above. Why choose the self-contained lament pattern instead of a petitionary form when the complaint is against God? Most obviously, because the complaint and the request are not divided. In the case of the complaint against God, they are two sides of same coin. To have complained about divine action is already to have indicated the solution that is sought for. This abbreviated tactic of communication shows similarities to cases of biblical conversations between persons. Complaint in conversation between persons often implies rather than expresses request when the person addressed is held directly responsible for the petitioner's distress. If petition is more common in cases of informal laments not motivated by God-complaint, it is because God was not necessarily held to have the same degree of responsibility for the predicament. One cannot conclude with Westermann, therefore, that there was a stereotypical speech-form reserved for complaint against God in ancient Israel. The rhetoric of informal lament is actually a common conversational strategy. Its use was dependent on the perceived relationship of God to the cause of the complaint.

What about the priority of individual to community complaint? Before proceeding to discuss this question, one caveat is in order. Biblical form criticism assumes that stereotypical speech forms (or formulas) were typically used in particular cultural contexts. A problem involved in discussing the cultural context of a particular speech form in the Bible arises from making the leap from observations about biblical context to the practices of ancient Israel. The question of biblical witness to ancient religious practice touches on a concern that has wider ramifications than the history of argumentative prayer. Scholars researching other types of texts have also had to ask about the extent to which ancient Jewish society can actually be constructed from the biblical evidence. There is reason to believe that the picture presented by the normative scriptural documents is removed, to some degree, from the social reality of the times.[72]

---

72. See, e.g. Cheryl B. Anderson, *Women, Ideology, and Violence: Critical Theory and the Construction of Gender in the Book of the Covenant and the Deuteronomic Law* (JSOTSup, 394; London: Continuum, 2004), pp. 14-17.

Making determinations about the history of informal lament is difficult because the records deal with different periods of history and different themes. One expects, e.g. the DtrH to concentrate on prophetic functionaries, as is also the case for the traditions from the writing prophets. There are a few clues to suggest, however, that there may have been some development in the use of informal laments with complaint against God.

Half of the texts containing complaint against God occur during visionary experiences (13/26); of those not involving ecstatic conditions, only 3/13 avoid the typology of prophetic experience or practice (Gen. 25.22; Judg. 15.18; 1 Sam. 4.21). These three texts seem to reflect fairly early traditions. References are not specific enough to identify either of the Genesis traditions with Bronze Age culture.[73] So I assume these narratives all represent lament practice of the earlier monarchical period.

Westermann assumed that early in Israelite history lay people had the right to complain against God in prayer outside sacred space, unmediated by any liturgical expert. Other thinkers about the nature of biblical prayer also imply such a possibility.[74] There can be little doubt, that the biblical tradition knows of a practice of informal lay prayer for individuals. The evidence of Gen. 25.22; Judg. 15.18 and 1 Sam. 4.21 can be supplemented by five other cases of informal individual lament in non-visionary circumstances: Gen. 21.16; 32.10-13; Judg. 16.28; 1 Sam. 1.11; Neh. 6.14. The fact that these latter five do not show God-complaint and contain requests cannot be pushed too far. The cause of the distress dictates the form of the prayer. We may conclude, therefore, that individuals living in Iron Age Israel or Judah would have occasionally felt themselves in such extreme life and death situations that informal protest prayer was justified.

One can suggest that individual practice preceded appropriation of the informal lament tradition for community distress, because of the connection between protests against God in community intercession and prophetic discourse. Attributions of prophetic typology to Abraham, Moses, Joshua and Gideon must have taken place in the later monarchic period. The visionary circumstances they often assume have their best parallels in prophetic experiences reported no earlier than the eighth century. It would require some time for this type of ecstatic experience to be predicated of pre-monarchical figures. Therefore, traditions putting informal lament on behalf of the community in the mouths of pre-monarchical characters are probably from the later monarchic period. The same conclusion is not

---

73. See John Van Seters, *Abraham in History and Tradition* (New Haven, CT: Yale University, 1975), pp. 120-21; Moshe Anbar, 'Mari and the Bible [Modern Hebrew]', *Bet Miqra* 170 (2002), p. 197.

74. See Greenberg, *Biblical Prose Prayer*, p. 46 and Miller, *They Cried to the Lord*, p. 86.

required, however, for traditions of individual informal lament in cases such as Rachel (Gen. 25.22) and Samson (Judg. 15.18).

It looks as if Iron Age prophets took over a tactic of prayer employed by individuals to intercede for the nation in distress. The prominence of the complaint against God in visions is instructive. It points to a convergence of personal encounter with community need. The prophets' personal encounters with divine reality and their presumed intimacy with the supernal realm are the conditions under which informal complaint for the community most often takes place when the complaint against God is employed.

Israel's tradents and storytellers assumed that a close encounter with the divine reality was an appropriate condition for protest prayer. In the case of individuals, most informal laments against God occur at moments of birth and imminent death, situations in which YHWH was thought to be intimately connected with individual lives. The perception of intimacy with the divine links prophetic practice and individual practice in expressing informal laments with God-complaint. Prophetic representatives were thought to possess both the office and the intimate access to YHWH's counsel necessary to confront the divine king with inconsistencies in the sphere of divine sovereignty. It follows that those thought to be most familiar with God were most entitled — and most likely — to confront God with protest on behalf of the community/state.

The prominence of the prophetic office is associated with the fortunes of the state in ancient Israel and Judah.[75] It is likely that prophets took over a practice of informal individual lament in order to make intercession for the state when its very life became threatened. It is no accident, therefore, that the earliest datable prophetic intercessions using the informal lament form stem from eighth century traditions (Amos and the Isaiah of Jerusalem). This was the era which witnessed Assyrian domination of the Levant.

A good illustration of the prophetic mediation of both community and individual concerns occurs in the developed narratives about Elijah and Elisha. These stories probably reached something like their present form in the late monarchy.[76] They emphasize the competence of YHWH over all

75. Don C. Benjamin, 'An Anthropology of Prophecy', *BTB* 21 (1991), p. 136.

76. Many of the stories about Elijah and Elisha were in their present form prior to inclusion in the DtrH; see Keith W. Whitelam, 'Elisha', *ABD*, II, p. 472. According to Alexander Rofé (*The Prophetical Stories: The Narratives about the Prophets in the Hebrew Bible, their Literary Types and History* [Publications of the Perry Foundation for Biblical Research in the Hebrew University of Jerusalem; Jerusalem: Magnes Press, 1988], pp. 189-90), the stories about Elijah's struggle with Baal in 1 Kings 16.29–19.18 may be dated to the time of Manasseh.

spheres of life: both national and personal concerns are registered. On the national level, YHWH brings and relieves drought (1 Kgs 17.1; 18.41-46), makes and deposes rulers (1 Kgs 19.15-17; 2 Kgs 8.7-15; 9.1-10) and gives military victory through his prophets (2 Kgs 6.24–7.20; 13.14-19). But the messengers of YHWH are also involved in the lives of individuals. Along with healing (e.g. 2 Kgs 5.1-27), YHWH's prophets solve difficulties in conception (2 Kgs 4.14-17) and save persons from premature death (1 Kgs 17.17-24; 2 Kgs 4.17-37, 38-41; 13.20-21). These are typical concerns of the informal individual lament tradition.

Despite evidence for the persistence of the practice of informal complaint by lay persons during the Iron Age, there are some indications that prophets became the preferred mediators of individual complaints against God in the later monarchical period. The testimony of Jer 45.3 can be augmented by considering the complaining questions that arise in the stories of Elijah (1 Kgs 17.18) and Elisha (2 Kgs 4.28) from mothers of suddenly-dead children. In both cases, the complaints act as implied requests for the restoration of the children's lives. It is significant that the mothers complain to the prophet, but the prophet complains to God (1 Kgs 17.20-21). This portrayal accords with the suggestion that a prophetic intermediary was the preferred resource for healing in the monarchical period, when available.[77]

So far, the exceptional case of 1 Sam. 4.21 has not been addressed. The name Ichabod is unusual as a form of informal community lament in biblical narrative. There is reason to think that names of the type 'Where is (divine epithet)' became less common after the Bronze Age. A number of prominent biblical examples involve individuals of priestly lineage. Names of this kind may have had special associations with the priesthood or other families involved in religious leadership in Iron Age Israel.[78] These observations suggest that customs involving informal complaint may have been changing by the early monarchical period.

The biblical narrative traditions themselves imply that informal lay complaint involving complaint against God was restricted to earlier times. Prophetic functionaries are represented as the legitimate tradents of this rhetoric in the monarchical period and later. By limiting instances of informal God-complaint among the laity to the pre-monarchical period, the elite writers of the biblical record may have intended to produce an institutional brake on the practice for the period (later Iron Age) in which they were writing.

---

77. See Hector Avalos, *Illness and Health Care in the Ancient Near East: The Role of the Temple in Greece, Mesopotamia, and Israel* (HSM, 54; Atlanta: Scholars Press, 1995), pp. 263-70.

78. Burnett, 'Question of Divine Absence', pp. 226-27.

In other words, the biblical witness to the religious reality of ancient Israel has both an idealistic bias and useable data. The assignment of the weight of informal protest against God in favour of the prophets reflects a development in biblical religion. It is also, however, an idealized picture. Clearly, lay people are depicted as uttering laments in informal situations during the monarchy and after, as in the case of Nehemiah. The fact that these non-prophetic individuals do not use God-complaint should not be over emphasized. The use of laments with implied petitions is a feature of the conversational context, rather than formally significant. If complaint prayer remained a viable option for non-prophetic types, the use of God-complaint should be expected, even if not approved. It would appear that by placing informal prayers with God-complaint under prophetic aegis, one encounters an attempt by biblical thinkers to control the complaint against God.

Why does the right to protest divine actions appear to devolve onto prophets during the monarchical period and later? One explanation arises from the observation that the ancient world was alive to the power of words.[79] Confronting a divine being with negative speech (e.g. complaint) would have been considered a dangerous enterprise, only to be attempted under special conditions. It would be attractive to employ specialists when they became available and as their prestige grew. The reputation of the prophets as intimates of the divine would recommend their resources when complaint against God was called for. A complementary explanation has to do with the prestige of the prophets as community mediators. This prestige would enhance their usefulness for prayers of individual healing. So, e.g. the scriptural record shows the wife of Jeroboam seeking prophetic healing for her ill son in 1 Kgs 14.1-5 and the foreign dignitary Naaman seeking out Elisha in 2 Kings 5.

Two results of this study are significant as it unfolds in the following chapters. First, closeness with YHWH was a condition for informal protest prayer in ancient Israelite religion. This proximity was presumed by individuals in time of difficult life passages in which the deity was thought to be especially involved: birth and premature deaths. Second, during the monarchical period, prophetic functionaries of the classical type claimed a quality of intimacy with the divine that allowed them to bring complaint against God about national or state problems. Their prestige as intercessors probably induced individuals to seek out prophetic mediation when complaint against God seemed called for. As a result, one can propose a certain institutionalization of the informal complaint against

79. See John W. Wevers, 'A Study in the Form Criticism of Individual Complaint Psalms', *VT* 6 (1956), pp. 82-83.

God in prophetic circles by the late monarchical period. It follows that changes in the perception of divine proximity and prophetic self-understanding would affect the tradition of argumentative prayer as biblical religion developed.

Chapter 3

Psalms of Individual Lament: Classification and Liturgical Contexts

According to Walter Brueggemann, pain embrace finds a classical expression in individual lament psalms.[1] This chapter concludes that the categories of pain embrace and structure legitimation are not necessarily at odds in the generation and use of complaint psalms. By the end of the monarchical period, the individual lament psalms found in the Psalter had come under the aegis of the major cultic institution that legitimated political and religious structures in ancient Israel: the Jerusalem temple. Protest prayer was permitted to users of the psalms only under controlled circumstances.

The chapter proceeds in five sections. First, the corpus of individual lament psalms is identified (§3.1). A discussion of models for describing the unity of this group of poems follows (§3.2). The corpus of individual lament psalms shows both unity and diversity. There is reason to distinguish the psalms that contain indirect and direct protest against God from another group of complaint prayers designated as 'psalms of Plea'. The third section discusses the theology of the lament psalms according to these three categories: psalms of Plea, psalms of Indirect Protest and psalms of Direct Protest (§3.3). The fourth section deals with questions of origin and use of the individual laments in the Psalter (§3.4). This discussion will address questions raised at the beginning of the last chapter, including the relationship between prayers of informal and formal lament, and the postulated movement of lament from the home to the temple. The last section will point out some consequences of the institutionalization of individual lament (§3.5).

---

1.   Walter Brueggemann, *Old Testament Theology: Essays on Structure, Theme, and Text* (Minneapolis: Fortress Press, 1992), p. 29.

3.1. *Identifying Individual Complaint Psalms*

The number of poems classified as laments of the individual varies.[2] Many questions about classification have to do with problems in form or content. For instance, a question of form arises with Psalms 4 and 11. Though they have certain elements in common with other complaint psalms, they seem to lack petitions for help from God. Content problems also arise; e.g. Fredrik Lindström would not classify Psalms 25; 39; 51 and 130 with other laments because they do not appear to deal with life-threatening situations.[3]

Another problem concerns mixed forms. For example, the distinction between individual and community complaint is not as neat as introductory discussions may suggest. There are a number of psalms of lament that move between imagery describing the distress of individuals and an afflicted community (e.g. Psalms 9–10; 77; 94). Mixed forms also raise the possibility of a history of composition. In a number of cases, scholars suggest that a psalm has its present form because it was supplemented with newer material after it had been first composed. Prominent examples include Psalms 27; 40 and 41, where there are lengthy introductory sections of trust or praise.

A third problem concerns the identity of the 'I' of the complaint psalms. I follow those commentators who set themselves against an interpretation of the majority of 'I' laments as 'royal compositions' or as the utterances of community representatives.[4] Obviously, these categories are not mutually exclusive. Kings did act as covenant mediators and community intercessors (e.g. 1 Kgs 8.22-53; 2 Kgs 19.15-19). Moreover, there are cases in

---

2.   The following studies were consulted: Rainer Albertz, *Persönliche Frömmigkeit und offizielle Religion: Religionsinterner Pluralismus in Israel und Babylon* (Calwer Theologische Monographien Reihe A, Bibelwissenschaft 9; Stuttgart: Calwer Verlag, 1978), p. 41; Bernhard W. Anderson, *Out of the Depths: The Psalms Speak for Us Today* (Philadelphia: Westminster Press, rev. edn, 1983), pp. 239-42; John Day, *Psalms* (OTG; Sheffield: JSOT Press, 1992), p. 19; Georg Fohrer, *Introduction to the Old Testament* (London: SPCK, 1965), pp. 285-93; Erhard S. Gerstenberger, *Psalms: I–II* (FOTL, 14–15; Grand Rapids: Eerdmans, 1991, 2001); Hermann Gunkel and Joachin Begrich, *Introduction to Psalms: The Genres of the Religious Lyric of Israel* (Mercer Library of Biblical Studies; Macon, GA: Mercer University, 1998; 4th German edn, 1985), p. 121; James Limburg, 'Psalms, Book of', *ABD*, V, p. 532; Fredrik Lindström, *Suffering and Sin: Interpretations of Illness in the Individual Complaint Psalms* (ConBOT, 37; Stockhom: Almqvist & Wiksell, 1994), pp. 43-44.

3.   Lindström, *Suffering and Sin*, p. 44.

4.   See, e.g. Albertz, *Persönliche Frömmigkeit*, pp. 23-24; Gunkel and Begrich, *Introduction to Psalms*, pp. 122-23; Mark Z. Brettler, *God is King: Understanding an Israelite Metaphor* (JSOTSup, 76; Sheffield: JSOT Press, 1989), p. 25.

which the first person singular stands for the community (cf. Josh. 17.14; Lam. 3.1-24). Nevertheless, an individual interpretation is to be preferred for psalms of individual complaint unless there are strong indications in the poem itself to interpret it otherwise.[5]

My classification of individual laments is restricted to those poems in which the complaint-element does not mix individual and community references. Psalms that merge complaint about individual and community suffering (e.g. Psalms 9–10; 77) will be addressed in the next chapter. I have included two poems that do not have a separate element of complaint, but allude to individual distress in their address (cf. Pss. 61.3; 130.1).

The element of petition also requires some attention. Psalms in which expressions of trust or a hymnic element dominates and in which there are no explicit petitions for an individual have been eliminated (e.g. Psalms 11; 52; 63; 139). Arguably, there is a petition in Ps. 4.2, in which the cry for a hearing is combined with a prayer for help.[6] Like Psalms 7; 17; 26 and 27, Psalm 4 seems to be designed for the rehabilitation of socially suspect persons.[7] Psalms 88 and 130 lack explicit petitions. But an explicit petition is not necessary in order to generate a prayer of complaint, as the discussion of the informal lament in the last chapter demonstrated. Of the two, Psalm 88 most clearly belongs to the lament genre because of its extensive complaints and accusatory questions against God.[8] In the case of Psalm 130, there may be an indirect petition in v. 4, but this interpretation can be disputed.[9] Psalm 130 is accepted here because complaint psalms may contain confessions of sin (e.g. Pss. 38.4-5 and 41.5). In fact, penitential psalms such as Psalms 51 and 130 appear to be the exact opposite of another class of lament that emphasizes the innocence of the psalmist (e.g. Psalms 7; 17 and 26).[10]

Reuse of older materials is a well-known technique in the production of ancient liturgies. Yet a work that combines older materials still stands

---

5.   Day, *Psalms*, pp. 21-25. Psalm 144, e.g. seems to be a prayer for a king, who is by definition a representative of the community.

6.   Erhard S. Gerstenberger, *Der bittende Mensch: Bittritual und Klagelied des Einzelnen im Alten Testament* (WMANT, 51; Neukirchen–Vluyn: Neukirchener Verlag, 1981), p. 123.

7.   Gerstenberger, *Psalms*, II, p. 56.

8.   Gerstenberger, *Psalms*, II, p. 145.

9.   A.A. Anderson, *Psalms* (NCB; 2 vols.; Grand Rapids: Eerdmans, 1989, original edn, 1972), II, p. 876; Gerstenberger, *Psalms*, II, pp. 355-57.

10.   John W. Wevers (*The Way of the Righteous* [Philadelphia: Westminster Press, 1961], pp. 24-27) argues for the exclusion of Psalms 51 and 130 from the genre of individual complaint psalms; but see Anderson, *Psalms*, I, p. 38 and Gerstenberger, *Psalms*, I, p. 13.

as a composition that should be analyzed in its own right.[11] For this reason I read Psalms 27; 40 and 41 in their canonical form as examples of the individual complaint genre. This principle will also be extended to the analysis of other poems in which there may be grounds for discerning later additions (e.g. Ps. 51.20-21).

Therefore, the following poems are regarded as individual laments for the purposes of this study: Psalms 3; 4; 5; 6; 7; 13; 17; 22; 25;[12] 26; 27; 28; 31; 35; 38; 39;[13] 40; 41; 42–43; 51; 54; 55; 56; 57; 59; 61; 64; 69; 70–71; 86; 88; 102; 109; 120; 130; 140; 141; 142; 143. This list assumes that in two cases psalms now regarded as separate in the biblical text originally made up one poem (Pss. 42–43 and 70–71). The abbreviation LI (Lament of the Individual) is used to refer to these psalms as a group and the genre they represent.

3.2. *Unity and Diversity in the Psalms of LI*

Is it possible to treat this large group of psalms as a unity? Accounts of the unity of the psalms of LI have focused on the identity of their putative performer, their content and their form. Common form is the best clue to the unity of the psalms of LI.

3.2.1. *The Unity of the Psalms of LI*
Thirty-four poems in the list of LI established above are connected to David (*ldwd*). Two are associated with the sons of Korah (Psalms 42–43 and 88). One is said to be the prayer of an unnamed distressed person (Psalm 102) and two others have no attribution (Psalms 120 and 130). Eight of the David psalms are also supplied with biographical details that relate the psalm to a specific incident in David's life (Psalms 3; 7; 51; 54; 56; 57; 59 and 142).

Although its meaning is ambiguous (it could mean 'for David', or 'belonging to David'), the phrase *ldwd* appears to claim that David composed (or performed) the psalm.[14] The biblical tradition as we now have it,

---

11. Gerstenberger, *Psalms*, II, pp. 253-54.

12. Psalm 25 has an unusual mode of composition: each verse begins with a letter of the Hebrew alphabet (acrostic organization). This feature has caused doubts about its genre membership (Gerstenberger, *Psalms*, I, p. 119-21; Lindström, *Suffering and Sin*, p. 44). But apart from its acrostic form, it generally resembles an individual complaint psalm (Anderson, *Psalms*, I, p. 206).

13. The final petition of Psalm 39 is unusual because it asks God to 'turn your gaze away' (v. 13) while most examples of this genre try to attract God's attention. Nevertheless, Psalm 39 generally conforms to the type of individual lament; see Walter Brueggemann, 'The Costly Loss of Lament', *JSOT* 36 (1986), pp. 65-66.

14. Day, *Psalms*, pp. 114-15.

therefore, supports an interpretative perspective that can be called 'biographical': the psalms of LI are to be understood as utterances of particular individuals in identifiable circumstances. One might claim in support of a biographical perspective the prose prayers studied previously. But to do so would ignore some important distinctions. As Moshe Greenberg explains, the content of a prose prayer is determined by the circumstances in which it arises. Hence, it cannot be reused. But the psalms show careful literary crafting of contents that are generally not determined by specific circumstances.[15] I follow the consensus of critical scholarship in rejecting the biographical perspective. The attribution of authorship to the psalms of LI is important, however, for the history of the interpretation of these poems in later Second Temple Judaism. For that reason, the concept of Davidic performance will be revisited in Chapter Eight.

Another approach to the unity of the psalms of LI is through their contents. For example, by using modern medical insights into the nature of illness (especially how it is felt subjectively) Lindström believes that almost all psalms of LI can be understood as psalms of sickness.[16] But such a unifying vision is too narrow. Though it is typical to identify a number of LI as referring to sickness (e.g. Psalms 6; 38; 41; 69 and 102),[17] in others the major distress appears to come from social conflict. Much of the enemy language in the psalms of LI seems to reflect the bitter social rivalries of village life.[18] Hence, social persecution and disease are both key types of human suffering that the psalms of LI respond to. But many psalms cannot be categorized so easily. Though the affliction described by all of them can be termed 'dis-ease', the distress they imply could arise from a variety of circumstances.[19]

Unity, however, can also be a function of form (rhetorical structure). The formal unity of the poems of complaint has been emphasized by Westermann.[20] While not every poem contains the same organization, every possible stereotypical motif, or gives the same weight to the elements it uses,

---

15. Moshe Greenberg, *Biblical Prose Prayer as a Window to the Popular Religion of Ancient Israel* (The Taubman Lectures in Jewish Studies, Sixth Series; Berkeley: University of California Press, 1983), p. 17.

16. Lindström, *Suffering and Sin*, pp. 431-32. A similar suggestion is offered for consideration in Albertz, *Persönliche Frömmigkeit*, pp. 46-47.

17. Erhard S. Gerstenberger and Wolfgang Schrage, *Suffering* (Biblical Encounters Series; Nashville: Abingdon Press, 1980), p. 40.

18. Gerstenberger, *Der bittende Mensch*, pp. 144-46; and *Psalms*, I, p. 53.

19. Patrick D. Miller, *They Cried to the Lord: The Form and Theology of Biblical Prayer* (Minneapolis: Fortress Press, 1994), p. 80.

20. Claus Westermann, *Praise and Lament in the Psalms* (Atlanta: John Knox Press, 1981), pp. 64-81.

all can be shown to be working with and reacting to a similar form of argumentation.[21]

The elements of Address, Complaint, Trust, Petition and Praise which the psalms of LI express and play with presuppose a single social metaphor: an audience with a powerful and righteous judge.[22] Babylonian parallels to LI show a similar mode of argumentation, as if the petitioner has approached some oriental magnate for redress of injustice.[23] In a quasi-legal argument, a petitioner calls on the (divine) judge to hear his case (Address), sets out the distress that he experiences (Complaint), expresses his confidence in the power and justice of the judge and also his own loyalty and innocence (Trust), and calls out for help, deliverance and destruction of the evil-doers (Petition). Frequently, the LI end with praise expressing assurance that the judge will respond favorably.

Juridical interpretations of the psalms of LI have been proposed previously.[24] There are a number of problems if the concept is taken literally, and one assumes actual trial conditions.[25] But the juridical metaphor is useful as a way of understanding the rhetorical form of the psalms of LI.[26]

The juridical metaphor has recently been used by Oswald Loretz as a way of approaching the well-known problem of the change of tone at the end of many psalms of LI. It is typical to explain the element of vow of praise/assurance of being heard as a consequence of receiving an oracle of salvation after the petition.[27] But the form of the psalms themselves does not give this theory the support it requires.[28] There are isolated cases in which an oracle is incorporated into a psalm (e.g. Pss. 12.6; 60.8-10) but

21. See, e.g. Craig C. Broyles, *The Conflict of Faith and Experience in the Psalms: A Form-Critical and Theological Study* (JSOTSup, 52; Sheffield: JSOT Press, 1989), p. 16; Gerstenberger, *Psalms*, I, pp. 11-14; Miller, *They Cried to the Lord*, pp. 125-26.

22. Miller, *They Cried to the Lord*, p. 47.

23. Werner Mayer, *Untersuchungen zur Formensprache der babylonischen 'Gebetsbeschwörungen'* (Studia Pohl Series Maior, 5; Rome: Pontifical Biblical Institute, 1976), p. 119.

24. For previous bibliography see Brueggemann, 'The Costly Loss of Lament', p. 58; Patrick D. Miller, *Interpreting the Psalms* (Philadelphia: Fortress Press, 1986), pp. 4-5.

25. Day, *Psalms*, pp. 27-29.

26. Walter Baumgartner, *Jeremiah's Poems of Lament* (Sheffield: Almond Press, 1988), p. 30; Gerstenberger, *Der bittende Mensch*, pp. 155-56.

27. See the literature review in Oswald Loretz, 'Der altorientalische rechtliche Hintergrund der biblischen 'Klage Des Einzelnen'', in Klaus Kiesow and Thomas Meurer (eds.), *Textarbeit: Studien zu Texten und ihrer Rezeption aus den Alten Testament und der Umwelt Israels: Festschrift Peter Weimar* (Münster: Ugarit-Verlag, 2003), pp. 287-99.

28. See, e.g. the discussions of John W. Wevers, 'A Study in the Form Criticism of Individual Complaint Psalms', *VT* 6 (1956), pp. 81-82; and Ottmar Fuchs, *Die Klage als Gebet: Eine theologische Besinnung am Beispiel des Psalms 22* (Munich: Kösel, 1982), pp. 314-20.

these psalms do not record a change in tone as a result. While there are grounds for thinking that a lamenting petitioner could receive an oracle of assurance (e.g. Ps. 5.4),[29] this practice cannot explain the change in tone at the end of so many LI. Loretz proposes that the theology behind the ceremony in which the LI was used provides a better explanation for the change of tone. The practice of LI is connected (metaphorically) to legal process. The change of tone is a further expression of the confidence that caused the individual petitioner to seek divine help in the first place. The lamenter expects from God a just trial with a judgment that will resolve the distress.[30]

An analogy to the legal fiction of the lament psalms can be found in the story of the widow from Tekoa in 2 Samuel 14. The widow seeks an audience with the king to complain of a tribal vendetta that threatens to wipe out her dead husband's family name and surviving posterity. As judge, the king must decide whether to intervene or let local justice take its course. The legal fiction assumed by the argument of the complaint psalms is not much different. In biblical Israel, it was primarily the responsibility of the injured party to seek juridical recompense.[31] The God addressed by complaint prayer was neither 'impassable' nor 'immutable'.[32] YHWH as monarch and judge had the right to intervene. But he might not. The psalmists assumed they had to present themselves as victims of injustice and plead for the righteous judge to act on their behalf.

3.2.2. *Psalms of Plea and Psalms of Protest*
Craig Broyles has argued for a distinction between laments that contain complaint against God (protest) and those that do not. In his opinion, psalms containing complaint against God are a subset of a larger group of laments. My analysis has points of convergence with, and divergence from, Broyles's position. It is valid to distinguish psalms of lament that do not contain protest against God from those that do. But this division should not ignore the fact that there is formal continuity between the two

---

29.   Loretz, 'Klage des Einzlenen', p. 298; see also Rainer Albertz, *Israel in Exile: The History and Literature of the Sixth Century B.C.E* (Studies in Biblical Literature, 3; Atlanta: Society of Biblical Literature, 2003), pp. 170-71; Gerstenberger, *Der bittende Mensch*, p. 151.

30.   Loretz, 'Klage des Einzlenen', pp. 299-301. Loretz's thesis of a motivating confidence in the form of LI has resonances with the explanation of the change of tone by Wevers ('Form Criticism', pp. 82-87), who proposes that it is confidence in the power of the name of YHWH that motivates the shift to praise at the end of the psalms of LI.

31.   Ze'ev W. Falk, *Hebrew Law in Biblical Times* (Provo, UT/Winona Lake, IN: Brigham Young University/Eisenbrauns, 2nd edn, 2001), p. 56.

32.   Miller, *They Cried to the Lord*, p. 126.

groups in terms of their basic structure. This continuity is underscored by the fact that a third group of psalms can be distinguished that holds an intermediate position between the laments of complaint against God and those better described as psalms of plea. This intermediate group is distinguished by a rhetoric of indirect complaint against God.

Broyles isolated Pss. 6; 9–10; 13; 22; 35; 39; 42–43; 44; 60; 74; 77; 79; 80; 85; 88; 89; 90; 102 and 108 as psalms containing God-complaint. According to Broyles, a psalm of plea focuses on a situation, whereas a complaint contains a note of blame or rebuke. The psalms Broyles lists as complaints differ in how they describe the situation of distress, how they interpret it, and how they appeal to God.[33] In the discussion that follows, I will designate the poems Broyles calls complaints as 'psalms of Protest'. I reject the restriction of the term 'complaint' to protest against God. In the introductory chapter, I argued for the use of 'complaint' as a meaningful description for all the motifs of distress in the psalms. Moreover, Broyles uses his insights to suggest that the primary polarity that the psalms depend upon is between praise and protest.[34] For these reasons, psalms containing complaint directed against God will be designated as psalms of Protest.

Broyles's discussion of the form and content of what he calls psalms of complaint mixes examples of LI with prayers for the community. In keeping with most scholarship, I prefer to discuss individual laments apart from those for the community. Therefore, the psalms of Protest relevant to this chapter are Psalms 6; 13; 22; 35; 39; 42–43; 88 and 102, a subset of Broyles's list. I used simpler criteria than Broyles to reach this result. Out of the 39 psalms of LI, I isolated those that contained either direct questions to God of the kind 'Why?' (Pss. 22.2; 42.10; 43.2; 88.15) and 'How long?' (Pss. 6.4; 13.2-3; 35.17) or direct statements complaining of God's actions (Pss. 39.11-12; 88.7-9, 16-17, 19; 102.11, 24).

The fact that my results (though reached somewhat differently) accord with those of Broyles raises a question of mixed membership his own work does not address. Broyles notes that there is an overlap between the psalms of plea and protest in the use of petitions with the negative Imperative directed at God. Broyles claims that negative petitions of the kind 'do not...' occur relatively more frequently in the psalms of Protest than in the psalms of Plea.[35] But he ignores the possibility that this speech form implies some criticism of YHWH in both groups. Implied protest seems particularly strong in psalms of lament where negative Imperatives are repeated. In Psalm 70–71, e.g. God is implored not to delay (70.6), not to let the petitioner be put to shame (71.1), not to cast him off

---

33. Broyles, *Conflict of Faith*, pp. 40-41.
34. Broyles, *Conflict of Faith*, p. 52.
35. Broyles, *Conflict of Faith*, p. 46.

(71.9), be far off (71.12), nor forsake him (71.9, 18). Another example of multiple negative Imperatives appears in Ps. 27.9,

> Hide not your face from me. Turn not your servant away in anger, you who have been my help. Cast me not off, forsake me not, O God of my salvation!

Walter Brueggemann refers to such argumentation as 'countertestimony'. Not only is there a legal argument for the divine judge to act, there is also an indictment of the judge's present inactivity.[36] Other scholars have also recognized the negative Imperatives in the psalms of LI as a form of protest against God.[37]

Another consideration that supports the idea that the negative Imperatives directed towards God have a formal significance comes from surveying their distribution in the Psalter. There are only three psalms, outside those that can be considered laments of the community or individual, in which a negative Imperative is directed at God. These cases include Pss. 119.8, 10, 19, 31, 43, 116, 133; 132.10 and 138.8. These exceptions are less telling than they may appear. Psalm 119 has been written under the influence of the LI genre.[38] Psalm 138 is a thanksgiving psalm for an individual;[39] therefore, it has a thematic connection with the rhetoric of LI by virtue of its membership in the lament-thanksgiving cycle of liturgical poetry. This leaves only Psalm 132 outside the ambit of the rhetoric of LI. I have no explanation for such an exception save to note that the lament genre has proven capable of influencing the composition of various sorts of mixed forms.[40] By far the majority of negative Imperatives belongs to the genre of LI or can be associated with the influence of its rhetoric. I regard the negative Imperative directed at God as a characteristic expression of argumentative prayer.

---

36. Walter Brueggemann, *Theology of the Old Testament: Testimony, Dispute, Advocacy* (Minneapolis: Fortress Press, 1997), pp. 375-76.

37. Anneli Aejmelaeus, *The Traditional Prayer in the Psalms* (BZAW, 167; Berlin: W. de Gruyter, 1986), pp. 45-47; Walter Gross, 'Trifft ein Unglück die Stadt, und der Herr war nicht am Werk? Amos 3,6', in G. Fuchs (ed.), *Angesichts des Leids an Gott glauben? Zur Theologie der Klage* (Frankfurt a. M.: Joseph Knecht, 1996), p. 99; Miller, *They Cried to the Lord*, pp. 76-77.

38. See Will Soll, *Psalm 119: Matrix, Form, and Setting* (CBQMS, 23; Washington: Catholic Biblical Association, 1991), pp. 66-69, 110. Though often labeled a composition of mixed genre, Soll's study suggests that the logic of Psalm 119 can be explained as a movement from individual lament to assurance that occurs several times in the poem. The length and contrived artistry of Psalm 119 distinguish the poem from cases of LI, but its use of negative Imperatives is derived from lament rhetoric.

39. Gerstenberger, *Psalms*, II, pp. 399-400.

40. Gunkel and Begrich, *Introduction to the Psalms*, p. 121.

It is possible, therefore, to divide the poems of LI into three groups on the basis of their complaining rhetoric:

- Psalms of Plea: 3; 4; 5; 7; 17; 31;[41] 54; 56; 57; 61; 64; 86; 120; 130; 142
- Psalms of Indirect Protest: 25; 26; 27; 28; 38; 40; 41; 51; 55; 59; 69; 70–71; 109; 140; 141; 143
- Psalms of Direct Protest: 6; 13; 22; 35; 39; 42–43; 88; 102

The distinction of these three groups has more than a formal significance. The isolation of the group of psalms containing Indirect Protest implies that complaint rhetoric in the psalms of LI has degrees of severity. While many psalms of LI allow for none; almost the same number allow for implicit criticism of God. A small number of compositions are permitted to go farther in their accusations against God. But the fact that psalms of Direct Protest also share the same formal fiction (legal appeal to a sovereign power) as the psalms of Plea needs to be considered before the uniqueness of the psalms of Direct Protest is addressed. Some features of the psalms with complaints against God are best explained within the context of the larger group of LI. This includes their theological premises.

3.3. *Theology, Suffering and Protest in the Psalms of LI*

At the heart of the psalms of LI is a kind of dualism that Martin Buber identified with the basic myth of Judaism: the ontological distinction between God (the Creator) and the (human) world.[42] This distinction creates the possibility of dialogue,[43] an aspect of the theology of lament.[44] But dialogue is often only potential in the world of the Hebrew Bible; it can also be refused and frustrated. Therefore, it is necessary to assume another dimension of biblical mythology, namely YHWH's struggle against chaos.[45] The created world exists as a result of an action in which God has 'liminated' rather than eliminated the forces of chaos that resisted creation.

41. Psalm 31 belongs to this list though the Masoretic text reads in v.11 'my strength fails because of my iniquity'. Critical scholarship regards the original reading to be 'because of my misery' following the Septuagint and the Syriac. It appears that the Hebrew vocalization of the word marks the intrusion of a penitential theology from postexilic times; see Gerstenberger, *Psalms*, I, p. 130.

42. Martin Buber, 'Myth in Judaism', *Commentary* 9 (1950), p. 566.

43. Joshua Amir, 'Monotheistic Myth in the Bible [Modern Hebrew]', *Bet Miqra* 146 (1996), p. 208.

44. See, e.g. Walter Brueggemann, 'From Hurt to Joy, From Death to Life', *Int* 28 (1974), p. 4; Miller, *They Cried to the Lord*, p. 133

45. Dharmakkan Dhanaraj, *Theological Significance of the Motif of Enemies in Selected Psalms of Individual Lament* (Orientalia biblica et Christiana, 4; Glückstadt: J.J. Augustin, 1992), pp. 277-83.

Despite the fact that these forces have been pushed to the margins of the known world, they are believed to still be able to assert themselves in actions of aggression against the divine order (just as the ocean retains its capacity to devastate dry land through wave and storm, and marauders and bandits are able to breach the borders of a civilized state). Due to this possibility, divine mastery over creation is often in need of reactivation and reassertion. Complaint prayer often records the perception that divine control over the world is painfully distant from ordinary experience, a memory and a hope rather than a current reality.[46]

What does such a worldview say about divine 'omnipotence?' The world-view of the psalmists is not one in which God is in charge of everything all the time. It is true to say, however, that God is always regarded as having the power to defeat the forces of chaos and reassert the good order of creation. In other words, divine omnipotence is always potential in the world of the psalmists, but not always actual.

There are human and non-human forces that refuse to dialogue with God and desire a return to chaos. These are the enemies of God. Enemies of God and agents of chaos are sinners. Throughout the psalms, God is expected to behave towards sinners in a consistent fashion: they are to be punished and destroyed. For such divine action to take place, however, the powerful and righteous judge must be convinced that right is on the side of the complainant—hence the need for quasi-legal argument. The judge must be satisfied that the sufferings of the victim are undeserved. The laments must satisfy the divine judge of the injustice of the suffering and the innocence and probity of the victim if the appeal of help is to be successful.

What are the causes of suffering that the petitioner brings to the divine judge? There are two: divine action and enemy action. Such an opinion stands against assertions that God is always regarded as the cause of suffering in psalms of LI.[47] Equally untenable, however, is the proposal that YHWH originally was never blamed for suffering in the psalms of LI.[48] A dualistic perspective on the causes of suffering can be defended in a number of ways. First, there are a number of psalms in which there is no suggestion of another cause for suffering than the attack of enemies.[49] Second, Babylonian parallels also allow for the possibility that distress

---

46. Jon D. Levenson, *Creation and the Persistence of Evil: The Jewish Drama of Divine Omnipotence* (San Francisco: Harper & Row, 1988), p. 47.

47. See, e.g. K. Seybold and U.B. Mueller, *Sickness and Healing* (Biblical Encounters Series; Nashville: Abingdon Press, 1978), p. 96.

48. Lindström, *Suffering and Sin*, pp. 429-31.

49. Pss. 3; 5; 7; 17; 31; 54; 55; 56; 57; 59; 61; 64; 86; 109; 120; 140 and 142.

and sickness can be diagnosed as the result of random inflictions or due to divine punishment.[50] Third, the response of David to Saul's continuing persecution is telling:

> If it is YHWH who has stirred you up against me, may he accept an offering; but if it is men, may they be cursed before YHWH...(1 Sam. 26.19)

Here David acknowledges the possibility of two potential causes for Saul's hostility.[51]

3.3.1. *Psalms of Plea*

The psalms of Plea include 3; 4; 5; 7; 17; 31; 54; 56; 57; 61; 64; 86; 120; 130 and 142. Enemy action is the main cause of lament;[52] I-complaint appears less frequently.[53] The enemies belong to one of two categories. Some are described as members of the psalmist's social group (e.g. Ps. 31.12). But a large number are less identifiable malevolent beings. There can be many, even thousands of them (Ps. 3.2, 7). They can be characterized not only as human beings but as wild animals (e.g. Pss. 7.3; 17.12; 57.5).

What is the significance of these two categories? The first describes social enmity on the part of the village or community to whom the psalmist belongs. Similar motifs appear in Mesopotamian literature. Akkadian compositions such as 'I Will Praise the Lord of Wisdom', the 'Babylonian Theodicy' and the Sumerian 'Man before his God' describe the sufferings of high-ranking persons who are thrust down into the lowest levels of social status as a result of misfortune and disease. Sickness, however, is not what they primarily lament. Motifs of social ostracism and persecution by former friends, colleagues and companions dominate these works. Similar imagery is found in the individual complaint psalms.[54] The victim's loss of status, for whatever reason, was explained by his peers as divine judgment and afforded a pretext for violence and ostracism by members of the larger group. A primary goal of the complaint psalms was to rehabilitate the individual to the larger group (who also worship YHWH) by affirming the undeserved suffering of the petitioner, an affirmation that is

---

50. Graham Cunningham, *'Deliver Me From Evil': Mesopotamian Incantations 2500–1500 B.C.* (Studia Pohl Series Maior, 17; Rome: Pontifical Biblical Institute, 1997), pp. 129, 179; Karl van der Toorn, *Sin and Sanction in Israel and Mesopotamia: A Comparative Study* (Studia semitica neerlandica; Assen: Van Gorcum, 1985), p. 72.

51. Gerstenberger, *Der bittende Mensch*, p. 49.

52. Pss. 3.2; 5.9; 7.2; 17.10-12; 31.12-14; 54.5; 56.2-3, 6-7; 57.4, 7; 64.3-6; 86.14; 120.7; 142.7.

53. Pss. 4.3; 31.10-11; 57.5; 61.3; 86.1; 120.5-6; 130.1; 142.4.

54. Lea Jakobzen, 'The Individual's Sufferings in Psalms and in Mesopotamian Narratives [Modern Hebrew]', *Bet Miqra* 168 (2001), pp. 33, 39-55.

intended to arrest both his social exclusion and also the justification of group violence against him.[55]

A second group of enemy images is characterized by such wildness and complete hostility that one wonders if these enemies represent interpersonal actors at all. Their status seems to be that of rather undefined demonic powers.[56] This is commensurate with a world-view that did not possess a well-developed concept of impersonal causation for suffering. Beside the life-giving realm of God and temple there was also a belief in the presence of deadly, rather undefined, life-threatening powers that had the capacity to harm human beings. The imagery of the psalms can pass easily from human to inhuman characteristics (e.g. Ps. 17.10-12). Therefore, though one may distinguish social and demonic imagery in theory, in the imagination of the psalmists the agents of social conflict and chaos often combine.[57]

The attitude towards the suffering represented by the psalms of Plea has motifs of structure legitimation. As creator, God is expected to reassert the divine order in the face of rising chaos. Not only is the psalmist to be saved and rescued (e.g. Pss. 3.8; 5.9; 17.13; 31.16-17; 142.7-8), but the agents of chaos are to be punished and destroyed (e.g. Pss. 5.11; 7.1; 17.13-14; 31.18-19).

3.3.2. *Psalms of Indirect Protest*
The psalms of Indirect Protest include 25; 26; 27; 28; 38; 40; 41; 51; 55; 59; 69; 70-71; 109; 140; 141; 143. The psalms of Indirect Protest are a transitional group that has affinities with both of the other groups. As with the psalms of Direct Protest, pain embrace is suggested by prayers addressed to the deity in the negated Imperative.[58] There is also overlap with the psalms of Plea, because a number of psalms of Indirect Protest describe attacks of the enemy as a major cause of distress: 27; 55; 59; 70-71; 109; 140.

Two traits distinguish the psalms of Indirect Protest from the psalms of Plea, however. Formally, the psalms of Indirect Protest contain negative

---

55. Albertz, *Persönliche Frömmigkeit*, p. 44; Gerstenberger, *Der bittende Mensch*, pp. 156-60.

56. Albertz, *Persönliche Frömmigkeit*, pp. 44-46.

57. Gerstenberger and Schrage, *Suffering*, pp. 62-65; Hans-Peter Müller, 'Feinde, Tiere und Dämonen: Ein kleiner Beitrag zu den Klage- und Bittpsalmen des Einzelnen', in Kiesow and Meurer (eds.), *Textarbeit*, pp. 329-30.

58. Negative Imperatives addressed to God using the particle *'al* and a form of the second person Imperfect are distributed as follows, Psalms of Indirect Protest: 25.7; 26.9; 27.9[tris], 12; 28.1, 3; 38.2, 22[bis]; 40.18; 41.3; 51.13[bis]; 55.2; 59.6, 12; 69.18; 70.6; 71.1, 9[bis]; 12, 18; 109.1; 140.9[bis]; 141.4, 8; 143.2, 7; Psalms of Direct Protest: 6.2[bis]; 22.12, 20; 35.22[bis]; 39.9, 13; 102.3, 25.

Imperatives directed at God. On the level of content, the psalms of Indirect Protest have a significant number of references to human sin. In fact, this trait helps to set the psalms of Indirect Protest apart from either the psalms of Plea or Direct Protest. Only 1/15 psalms of Plea (130) alludes to the sin of the petitioner. Only 2/8 psalms of direct Protest (6 and 39) allude to sin on the part of the petitioner. But 7/16 psalms of Indirect Protest make mention of the poet's guilt (25; 38; 40; 41; 51; 69) and four others seem to have a prophylactic rhetoric meant to ward off the possibility of being classed among sinners by God (26; 28; 141 and 143).

Suffering can come from God as a consequence of sin in two different ways. An instructive passage concerns the punishment for David's census of the people in 2 Sam. 24.12-14. David must choose either three years of famine, three months of persecution by his foes or three days of plague. His reply is telling: 'let us fall into the hand of YHWH, for his mercy is great; but let me not fall into the hand of man' (2 Sam. 24.14). As a result a plague ravages the nation for three days. The choice, apparently, is between being abandoned by God to Israel's social enemies or receiving direct affliction from God in the form of sickness or drought.

A number of psalms of Indirect Protest allude to divine judgment for sin (25; 26; 28; 38; 40; 41; 51; 69; 141; 143). The description of the rhetoric of sin in the Psalms of Indirect Protest is broken into three sections. First, psalms with petitions for forgiveness are discussed (§3.3.2.1). Next are psalms that contain confessions of sin but have no explicit petitions for forgiveness (§3.3.2.2). Finally, there is a group of poems with allusions to sin but without a confession of sin (§3.3.2.3).

3.3.2.1. *Indirect Protest with Petitions for Forgiveness.* Two poems contain explicit prayers for forgiveness: Pss. 25.7, 11, 18 and 51.3, 4, 11. The exact nature of the affliction that besets the poet in Psalm 51 is difficult to determine.[59] In Psalm 25 the major distress faced by the poet comes from the enemy. Several petitions ask for actions against the enemy (Ps. 25.2, 3, 19). Evidently in Israel, as in Babylonia, the personal God could abandon his worshipper out of displeasure and leave him open to (demonic) attack.[60]

3.3.2.2. *Indirect Protest with Confession of Sin.* The psalms that contain a confession of sin (Pss. 38; 40; 41 and 69) but do not have a prayer for

---

59. Although Ps. 51.10 prays 'let the bones that you have broken rejoice', it is not clear if this is a reference to physical or psychological anguish. It is also unclear in Ps. 51.16 whether the bloodshed that the poet needs to be delivered from is caused by his deeds or is an external threat; see Anderson, *Psalms,* I, pp. 397, 400.

60. Jakobzen, 'The Individual's Suffering in Psalms and in Mesopotamian Narratives', pp. 38-39.

forgiveness confirm the possibility that God may leave the psalmist open to enemy attacks, or bring about physical affliction. Psalm 38 is the best representative of this group. Description of personal suffering (vv. 3-11, 14-15, 18b) is a major feature, but there are also references to the deeds of the enemies (vv. 12-13, 20-21). It is important to notice, however, that all mention of sin occurs within descriptions of the physical distress of the poet (vv. 4-6, 19). This implies that sickness has been visited on the poet by God (v. 3). But the situation also promotes the machinations of the enemy (vv. 20-21).

Both the imagery of divinely caused sickness and of enemy attack occur in Psalm 41. Psalm 41.5 connects the prayer for healing with an explicit confession of sin. The poem then goes on to describe the behavior of the enemy in vv. 6-10. Apparently, the foes are taking advantage of a deadly illness and waiting for the psalmist's demise. The prayer in v. 11 also alludes to the divine cause of the calamity. God is called upon to raise the poet up, so the psalmist can take revenge on the enemies. Such a petition stands in contrast to other cases in which God is called upon to destroy or punish the enemies directly.

As in Psalm 41, there is a contrast between what God has done and what the enemy is doing in Psalm 69. Judging from the statement in 69.6, the psalmist has committed some wrong in the past. But the enemy is not content to let divine punishment take its course. According to 69.27, 'they persecute him whom you have smitten, and him whom you have wounded they afflict still more'.[61] As a result, the psalm ends in a series of curses against the poet's opponents (vv. 23-29) and prayer for divine protection (v. 30).

The statement in Ps. 40.13 that iniquities have overtaken the psalmist is not attached to a clear description of physical suffering. The psalm seems to have a certain community of thought with Psalm 25 (cf. §3.3.2.1). Psalm 40 registers a fear that God might hand the petitioner over to the predations of the enemy due to transgressions. Past sins may be a precondition for suffering, but Psalm 40 pleads with God not to abandon the poet to anti-social forces that threaten to destroy him (vv. 14-16). As far as divine action is concerned, there are no expressed prayers for healing. God is called on not to withhold mercy (v. 12), for help and deliverance (v. 14) and not to delay (v. 18).

3.3.2.3. Indirect Protest in Preventative Prayers. A third class of psalm of Indirect Protest seems to be prophylactic in character (26; 28; 141; 143).

---

61. Following the text of the RSV emended on the basis of the Septuagint and Syriac.

While no cause of suffering is detectable in Psalm 26, the poet prays not to be swept away with the wicked (v. 9). Dissociation from malefactors is a prominent goal of LI in order to avoid their fate (cf. 28.3).[62] A similar logic drives the prayers for right speech in Psalm 141.3-4, otherwise the poet might be left without divine defense (v. 8). So too, in Psalm 143 the poet fears entering into a condition of divine judgment for sin (v. 2). Since the psalmist is under enemy attack (v. 3), it is imperative not to be abandoned (v. 7) as would be the case for a wicked person. Psalm 130 (a psalm of Plea) may also be connected to the psalms concerned with preventing divine punishment.

Prayers that anticipate or analyze suffering as a result of sin assume that God can act as a structure legitimator. YHWH does so either by afflicting the poet with sickness or by withdrawing divine protection and leaving the psalmist exposed to attacks by enemies. The poets, for their part, fear God's power to punish. But, on the other hand, they are also prepared to protest when the punishment does not seem to fit the crime.[63] This note of pain embrace occurs frequently in psalms that allude to the poet's sins as a cause of suffering. There are petitions not to be deprived of the divine presence (Pss. 38.22; 40.12; 69.18; 141.8; 143.7) nor to be arbitrarily lumped in with sinners (Pss. 26.9 and 28.3). For the most part, these negative Imperatives present indirect complaint of divine absence. Despite the obvious injustice of their situations, God has not exerted his sovereignty against the psalmists' godless enemies. There is also a risk that the psalmists may be abandoned to a fate they do not desire (e.g. Pss. 27; 70–71).

3.3.3. *Psalms of Direct Protest*
A small group of psalms appears to be especially devoted to protesting divine actions: Psalms 6; 13; 22; 35; 39; 42–43; 88; 102. God may withdraw protection and abandon the poet to enemy attacks, or God may actively bring about affliction through sickness.[64] Therefore, two classes of objections can be distinguished: One group complains about divine absence (Psalms 13; 22; 35; 42–43), the other remonstrates against divinely directed affliction (Psalms 6; 39; 88; 102).

3.3.3.1. *Direct Protest of Divine Absence.* There are numerous psalms wherein the psalmists portray themselves as disheartened while enemies prevail. But, unlike Psalm 13, they do not charge God with neglect or betrayal. The motivation for the accusatory questions in Ps. 13.2-3 seems to arise

62. See Gerstenberger, *Psalms*, 1, p. 128.
63. Brueggemann, *Theology of the Old Testament*, p. 373.
64. Brueggemann, *Theology of the Old Testament*, pp. 375-78.

from a correlation between a perceived lack of divine response and nearness to death (v. 4). In other words, grounds for protest arise from the extreme nature of the distress and undue delay in deliverance.[65]

Psalm 22 contains ambiguous images that suggest divine abandonment (vv. 2-3) and perhaps direct affliction: 'you lay me in the dust of death' (v. 16b). Broyles counsels the reader not to press the poetic language of v. 16 too far; he hesitates to conclude either that the psalmist envisages YHWH as the agent causing death, or that YHWH has simply left the poet at death's door.[66] But there are several clues that point to divine absence as the overwhelming problem. First, apart from v. 16b physical suffering is related to enemy attacks. Second, when the poet calls for divine intervention, the pleas are that God not be far off (vv. 12 and 20) and for deliverance from enemy actions (vv. 21-22). Finally, there is a grammatical clue at the beginning of v. 17. If the *kî* clause opening v. 17 is explanatory to v. 16b, then the divine action is to be understood as abandonment to the predations of the poet's foes.[67] For these reasons, it is most likely that the protest of Psalm 22 arises from a perception of divine abandonment. Left near to death (v. 16b),[68] the poet is at a loss as to why God has failed to answer earlier prayers (vv. 2-3).

Divine abandonment is also the subject of complaint in Psalms 35 and 42–43. The accusatory question of Ps. 35.17, 'Lord, how long will you look on?' is only delivered after a lengthy description of enemy actions (vv. 11-16). YHWH has no active involvement in the poet's distress. But his delay in delivering the psalmist makes the deity in some measure responsible for it.[69]

In Psalm 42–43, the psalmist is alienated from the temple. Mention is made of an enemy oppressing the psalmist, but the primary source of distress appears to be God. The psalmist not only expresses apprehension about God's disposition (42.10; 43.2), but also an assertion that God has actually brought this affliction upon the poet (42.8).[70] Nevertheless, the statement in 42.8 seems to possess the same inference as 22.16b. The petitions of 43.3-4 underscore the perception that it is a prolonged divine refusal to intervene and provide the psalmist access to the temple that is the principal problem.

---

65. Broyles, *Conflict of Faith and Experience*, pp. 184-85.
66. Broyles, *Conflict of Faith and Experience*, p. 190.
67. Broyles, *Conflict of Faith and Experience*, p. 254.
68. Gerstenberger, *Psalms*, I, p. 112.
69. Broyles, *Conflict of Faith and Experience*, p. 194.
70. Broyles, *Conflict of Faith and Experience*, p. 102.

3.3.3.2. *Direct Protest of Divine Affliction.*

These psalms can be subdivided between those that contain no allusion to sin (88 and 102) and those that do (6 and 39).

Death is the subject of Psalm 88; but a specific sickness cannot be identified. There are no hostile enemies in the psalm. Even though the psalmist describes social estrangement (v. 19), this is also regarded as YHWH's doing. Broyles holds that the principle reason the psalmist believes that YHWH is the cause of his affliction arises from a lack of response to his prayers (vv. 14-15). Since no divine help is evidently forthcoming, the poet concludes that YHWH has rejected him. In that sense, the terrors of suffering and death are from YHWH (vv. 16-17).[71] But such a viewpoint does not adequately take into account the assertions that God has brought the poet to the brink of Sheol. There is not simply abandonment; YHWH is attacking the poet as an enemy (vv. 7-8, 17-18). Though God is characterized by 'steadfast love' (v. 12), there is none for the poet.[72] Curiously, there are no petitions for healing or salvation. The psalmist is content to let descriptions of his extreme misery and cruel actions speak for themselves. Petition is only implied. There is an analogy, therefore, between the form of Psalm 88 and protest prayers in prose and prophetic texts outside the Psalms with no explicit petitions (§2.3.1.1).

The motif of YHWH's rebuilding Zion in Ps. 102.13-18 suggests that the poet is alienated from the temple and probably in exile. Discerning the cause of the poet's distress is difficult; yet the poet represents God not simply as indifferent to his plight, but actively hostile (vv. 11, 24).[73] We saw in the previous chapter that one of the typical circumstances in which individuals appealed to YHWH's help was when they faced premature death. This observation is applicable to Psalm 102, which holds up to God the unfairness of being cut off in the midst of life (vv. 4, 25).

Psalm 102 suggests three arguments for being saved from death. First, there is an *a fortiori* argument. If God can restore Zion (vv. 13-17), which was also cut-off in mid-life by the Babylonian exile, he must be able to restore the psalmist at mid-life also. Moreover, Zion exists for the prayers of the destitute (vv. 18-22); therefore it would be a contradiction in terms if the God of Zion did not to respond to the poet's plea. Finally, eternal life is characteristic of God (vv. 27-28). By implication, it is a contradiction in the divine character not to bestow long life on the psalmist.

---

71. Broyles, *Conflict of Faith and Experience*, pp. 206-207.
72. Ingvar Fløysvik, *When God Becomes My Enemy: The Theology of the Complaint Psalms* (St Louis: Concordia Press, 1997), pp. 111-12.
73. Broyles, *Conflict of Faith and Experience*, p. 210; Fløysvik, *When God Becomes My Enemy*, p. 150.

God is also capable of causing suffering through illness. Sickness can be experienced as a result of sin. But there are situations when such suffering seems unjustified, because it more than fits the crime.

Psalm 6 opens with words that suggest a penitential context: 'YHWH, rebuke me not in your anger, nor chasten me in your wrath (v. 2)'. Though awareness of sin seems presupposed by terms such as 'rebuke' and 'chasten', the chief concern of the psalm is not with the exercise of divine punishment, but with its severity (v. 3) and its persistence (v. 4).[74] Psalm 6 is usually regarded as a psalm for the relief of a sick person, though its generalized language probably allowed its imagery to be extended to other kinds of extreme distress.[75] Though enemies are mentioned (vv. 8, 11), there is no petition directed against them. Consequently, it appears that their harassments are not the cause of the poet's afflictions. As Ingvar Fløysvik notes, 'God is the problem and God the solution'.[76]

It appears that Psalm 6 protests a situation in which punishment for sin in the form of suffering has reached the point of diminishing returns not only for the psalmist but also for God. YHWH is about to lose one dedicated to his praise to the grave (v. 6). Psalm 6, therefore, seems to presuppose a situation in which a psalm like Psalm 38 has been used, but to no avail. Sin may have been the problem once, but it is no longer. YHWH's punitive wrath has created a situation with no further benefit for either party.

A similar situation appears in Psalm 39. Though the wicked are mentioned, they are not considered the immediate cause of the psalmist's distress. The problem appears to be the prospect of imminent death (v. 14) as a result of divine action (v. 10). The poet protests that life is already too short and that his premature death is an excessive exercise of divine reproof.[77] Unlike Psalm 102, however, Psalm 39 alludes to punishment for sin as an explanation for the poet's suffering (vv. 9, 12). In this motif, Psalm 39 shows a thematic overlap with a number of the psalms of Indirect Protest.

3.4. *Origins and Liturgical Contexts of the Psalms of LI*

The discussion in Chapter Two noted two related claims in defining connections between informal lament and the psalms of LI:

---

74. Broyles, *Conflict of Faith and Experience*, p. 181.
75. Fløysvik, *When God Becomes My Enemy*, p. 45; Gerstenberger, *Psalms*, I, 62.
76. Fløysvik, *When God Becomes My Enemy*, p. 45; see also Broyles, *Conflict of Faith and Experience*, p. 180.
77. Broyles, *Conflict between Faith and Experience*, pp. 198-99.

- informal complaint prayers preceded the composition of the psalms
- Israel's social structure originally located the lament in the family or clan before the practice moved to the temple

The following discussion is devoted to commenting on these two claims. The first point must be qualified because the biblical evidence is too limited to determine when forms of complaint prayer were first derived from patterns of complaining speech (§3.4.1). The history of individual lament also requires conjecture about who performed the psalms of LI. Evidence points to a circle of expert oral poets who could perform in a variety of venues including home and temple (§3.4.2). It is probable, however, that the extant psalms of LI reflect some process of centralization in which the prayers of complaint came under the aegis of the Jerusalem temple by the late pre-exilic era (§3.4.3).

3.4.1. *The Informal Lament as Precursor to the Psalms*

It is plausible that the rhetoric of lament prayer is not simply related to, but ultimately derived from, conventions of human speech.[78] The question is whether this process can actually be observed in the Bible. The previous chapter identified Gen. 21.16; 25.22; 32.10-13; Judg. 15.18; 1 Sam. 1.11; 4.21 as texts that reflected lay practice during early monarchical times. A scrutiny of the literary contexts of these complaint prayers indicates that they portray lay lament functioning in connection with cultic institutions besides those of the family. This is evident in the cases of Gen. 25.22 and 1 Sam. 1.11; 4.21.

In the throes of a difficult pregnancy, Rachel complains with a why-question in her home. Then she goes to consult YHWH. The text does not tell the reader where she goes or whom she consults, but the vocabulary used (root *drš*) is consistent with seeking an oracle from a prophet (cf. 1 Sam. 9.9; 2 Kgs 22.18; Ezek. 20.1). In other words, individual lament and consultation with a religious institution outside the family are already combined in this biblical narrative. It might be argued that the Genesis tradition illustrates by piety in the pre-monarchical period. But this does not appreciably change the testimony of Rachel's story with respect to the history of lament. Whatever the truth of the patriarchal traditions or the settlement of Canaan by a group called 'Israel', Bronze Age Canaan and Syria were well endowed with temples and we should imagine a complex relationship between family religion and large group institutions as far back in time as one may wish to locate the origins of the Israelite experience.

---

78. Aejmelaeus, *Traditional Prayer*, pp. 88-90.

The conclusion of the last paragraph can be illustrated by the two informal laments associated with the pre-monarchical cult-place at Shiloh. Hannah utters a silent vow at the threshold of the temple there (1 Sam. 1.11). It is significant that she chooses to complain to YHWH at his cult-place, although her difficulty is connected to her status in the family (small group). The unnamed mother of Ichabod is a member of the priestly family in charge of Shiloh. Her informal lament is embodied in the name of her child and recalls the disaster that came over the large group at the capture of the ark of the covenant (1 Sam. 4.21-22).

Chapter One noted Moshe Greenberg's opposition to the idea that an evolutionary perspective on biblical complaint prayer can be derived from texts of informal lament. He suggests that a distinction should be made between three levels of prayer with varying degrees of formality. Alongside the psalms (the most formal kind of prayer), which Greenberg associates with temple worship, individuals could have prayed extemporaneously based on formal models or composed free prayers spontaneously.[79] Although I hesitate to link formal psalms of complaint as closely to temple worship as Greenberg has, I generally concur with his thesis. It is important, however, not to put too much distance between the three practices of prayer that Greenberg distinguishes. By way of illustration, one may consider the composition of Psalm 88 and the informal psalm-like prayers of Jeremiah.

Psalm 88 provides a good example of how closely informal and formal lament may be related. It stands out from other psalms of LI by the fact that it consists of a long list of lamenting statements in which God-complaint dominates. Moreover, it contains no explicit petition. Therefore, although more elaborate, its structure is similar to the structure of informal laments. In contrast to informal laments, however, Psalm 88 is deeply invested in formulaic and mythical language.[80] Here the conversational strategy of informal lament has been taken up and worked into a poem. But this form of poetic elaboration does not disguise a rather simple construction which maintains a similarity to the conventions of protest prayers preserved in prose.[81]

The lament-like prayers of Jeremiah provide a good illustration of extemporaneous prayer holding an intermediate position between informal lament and the psalms of lament. In their present form, the complaints of Jeremiah span eight poems: Jer. 11.18-23; 12.1-6; 15.10-14, 15-21; 17.14-18;

79. Greenberg, *Biblical Prose Prayer*, p. 46.

80. For details, see Gerstenberger, *Psalms*, II, pp. 142-44.

81. Aejemaleaus (*Traditional Prayer*, p. 91) describes the structure of Psalm 88 as 'archaic'.

18.19-23; 20.7-13, 14-18.[82] These can be classified into two groups. Six poems show affinity through their common use of five elements: invocation of God, speeches of the enemy, declarations of innocence, prayers for vengeance and occasionally words of divine response. However, the divine responses seem to be secondary to the composition of most these poems.[83] Therefore, the first group comprises Jer. 11.18-20; 12.1-4; 15.15-18; 17.14-18; 18.19-23 and 20.7-13. The second group of poems is characterized by self-curses. These occur in Jer. 15.10 and 20.14-18.[84]

Scholarly discussion of the complaint poems of Jeremiah is extensive and complex. There are disagreements about what to call these poems ('confessions' or 'laments'), how many of them there are, what their textual limits might be, their relationship to the historical Jeremiah, and their function in the book. Associations between the complaints of Jeremiah and experiences of individual suffering have not gone unchallenged. Sometimes these poems have been seen to voice the anxiety of the Judean community in exile.[85] But the attitude taken by the editors of the book of Jeremiah towards these poems as well as their resemblance to psalms of LI suggest an individual subject. The canonical placement of these poems is due to extensive activity on the part of (Deuteronomistic) editors.[86] In their present form, these complaint poems serve an apologetic function that helps to justify YHWH's judgment on Judah. Jeremiah is presented as a model of righteousness in contrast with the nation's corrupt leadership. The desperate wickedness of the people is highlighted through their unjustified persecution of the exemplary prophet.[87]

There are several reasons for believing that the complaints of Jeremiah are not simply an editorial fiction. First of all, the poems are not well

---

82. Following the divisions of A.R. Diamond, *The Confessions of Jeremiah in Context: Scenes of a Prophetic Drama* (JSOTSup, 45; Sheffield: JSOT Press, 1987), pp. 21-121 and Mark S. Smith, *The Laments of Jeremiah and their Contexts: A Literary and Redactional Study of Jeremiah 11–20* (SBLMS, 42; Atlanta: Scholars Press, 1990), p. 2.

83. The elements of the first group are presented in chart form in Smith, *Laments of Jeremiah*, p. 2. Jenö Kiss (*Die Klage Gottes und des Propheten: Ihre Rolle in der Komposition und Redaktion von Jer 11–12, 14–15 und 18* [WMANT, 99; Neukirchen-Vluyn: Neukirchener Verlag, 2003], p. 206) would include the divine response of v. 19 in the original form of Jer. 15.10-20, which he reconstructs as 15.10, 15aα, 16-19.

84. Smith, *Laments of Jeremiah*, p. 2. The divine response in Jer. 15.11-14 has a redactional history; but it is more difficult to defend the thesis of editorial intervention in the case of Jer. 20.14-18; see, Diamond, *Confessions of Jeremiah*, pp. 55-58, 116-18.

85. E.g. Robert P. Carroll (*From Chaos to Covenant: Prophecy in the Book of Jeremiah* [New York: Crossroad, 1981], p. 123) believes that the poems originated as community complaints that were later read back into the life of the prophet.

86. Smith, *Laments of Jeremiah*, pp. xv-xvi.

87. Diamond, *Confessions of Jeremiah*, p. 187.

marked by the style of the Deuteronomistic editors.[88] The redactors and authors implicated in the book of Jeremiah thought that they were providing a picture of a particular practice of prayer which can be associated with a figure of the late monarchical period. I see no reason to dispute the idea that this picture may be reasonably accurate. Secondly, the poems contain elements that are atypical of psalms of complaint. These include the direct accusation against God for deceiving the poet,[89] and the complaint of being overwhelmed by the prophetic office.[90] Such features support the traditional ascription of the core of the poems to Jeremiah himself.[91]

Jeremiah's prayers show a theology of suffering that is identical with that of the psalms of LI: suffering can be ascribed to either agents of sin and chaos (the enemy) or to God.[92] Evidence of the extemporaneous nature of Jeremiah's prayers can be taken from the laments containing self-curses. Recognizable elements of LI in 15.10 include a declaration of innocence, 'I have not lent nor have I borrowed', followed by a description of enemy actions, 'yet all of them curse me' (cf. the description of the enemies as cursers in Ps 109.28).[93] A complaining question against God can be found in 20.18, 'Why did I come forth from the womb to see toil and sorrow, and spend my days in shame?' In both cases, however, the reader familiar with the LI genre is unprepared for complaint that rues the day the poet was born. In 15.10, the complaint begins with the language of a funeral dirge: 'woe is me'.[94] In other words, the human conflict the prophet experiences leads him to assume that he is effectively dead as far as his social isolation is concerned.[95] The wording of 20.14-18 is even stronger. Though cursing enemies is well attested in the psalms of LI (e.g. Pss. 17.14; 69.23-26; 109.6-19), self-cursing is unprecedented. The prophet's very life has become such a source of suffering that he prefers death. This motif, though extreme, has parallels in the informal complaint prayers of 1 Kgs 19.4 and Jon 4.2-3.

What is striking about the psalms of Jeremiah, from the point of view of performance, is that Jeremiah is able to lament using formulas like those found in the psalms apparently without reference to either a human

---

88.   Smith, *Laments of Jeremiah*, p. xviii.

89.   Smith, *Laments of Jeremiah*, p. 1.

90.   Klaus Koch, *The Prophets* (2 vols.; Philadelphia: Fortress Press, 1983, 1984), II, p. 44.

91.   See also Diamond, *Confessions of Jeremiah*, pp. 189-90.

92.   Samuel E. Balentine, *Prayer in the Hebrew Bible: The Drama of Divine–Human Dialogue* (Overtures to Biblical Theology. Minneapolis: Fortress Press, 1993), p. 161.

93.   Diamond, *Confessions of Jeremiah*, pp. 55-58, 116-18.

94.   Diamond, *Confessions of Jeremiah*, p. 53.

95.   See Koch, *Prophets*, II, p. 40.

intermediary or cultic actions. One might object, perhaps, that Jeremiah's prophetic function gave him a privilege when it came to lament that others would not possess. But Jeremiah protests in spite of his prophetic office, which he regards as a burden (20.7-9).

The proximity of Psalm 88 to informal lament and the ability of Jeremiah to compose extemporaneous prayers using lament-like elements should give commentators pause about proposing neat lines of historical development between informal and formal compositions of individual lament. In the last chapter, I proposed that the *context* of complaint was a better guide to the use of the complaint against God than assumptions about historical development. The same conclusion seems warranted for the connection between forms of informal and formal laments for individuals. Rather than deriving one from the other, it appears that biblical tradition recognizes different forms of complaint appropriate for different kinds of circumstances. There was a type of extemporaneous conversational prayer in which the informal lament was common. There was also a more formal type of complaint characteristic of the psalms, probably used when prolonged distress required a more deliberate approach to finding a solution.

3.4.2. *Performers of LI in Ancient Israel*

Scholars have long noted parallels between Babylonian prayers and liturgies for distressed individuals and their biblical counterparts.[96] The structure of the Israelite lament is similar to the Babylonian incantations called *šu'illa*. Both contain address to the god (often expanded by clauses expressing praise), laments and descriptions of distress, pleas for aid, confession of sins, and vows to present a thank-offering. As is the case with LI, in the *šu'illa* some elements may be missing and the order in which they occur is not fixed.[97]

The Babylonian materials were scribal compositions, copied and transmitted by personnel trained and employed in large group institutions, i.e. temple and royal administrations. The *šu'illa* required recitation and liturgical staging by the ritual expert called an *āšipu*. This profession was one of an educated, scribal class, which had affiliations both with the palace and temple. In Neo-Assyrian times, the *āšipu* even attained the status of royal advisors. While they had a number of ritual functions, the *āšipu* had an important role in the health care system, and customarily

---

96. Gerstenberger, *Der bittende Mensch*, pp. 64-112; Miller, *They Cried to the Lord*, pp. 10-25.

97. Helmer Ringgren, *Israelite Religion* (Philadelphia: Fortress Press, 1975), p. 180.

went to the houses of afflicted persons to perform healing rites and incantations.[98]

Despite the suggestive possibilities of Mesopotamian parallels, there are problems in translating the picture of lament practice obtained in cuneiform documents directly to ancient Israel.[99] First, it is not clear that the most likely intermediaries for LI in ancient Israel always shared the same connections with large group institutions. Second, there is evidence for an oral tradition of lament psalms which sets them apart from the Mesopotamian parallels.

The biblical evidence is fairly consistent in identifying the prophet as the legitimate health care consultant who operated outside the temple during the monarchical period.[100] But there is a gap between prophetic practice as described in biblical sources outside the psalms and the liturgical role necessary for mediating LI.[101] Prophets engage in informal and mainly ad hoc intercessions in prose and prophetic texts. Besides cases such as 1 Kgs 17.20-21 and Jer. 45.3, there are also narratives of prophetic healing power in 1 Kgs 14.1-5 and 2 Kgs 5.1-14. Both Naaman and the wife of Jeroboam come to a prophet's house to seek healing. There is no suggestion of liturgical speech or action, however.

Hector Avalos notes that the advice of Isaiah to the ailing Hezekiah in 2 Kgs 20.7-11 has connections with actions that can be connected to two kinds of Mesopotamian healers. Like the *asû*, Isaiah prescribes a medical treatment: the poultice of figs in v. 7. But Isaiah operates like an *āšipu* in that he interprets omens that portend the course of the illness (vv. 8-9). Nevertheless, there is a significant difference between the way Isaiah and the other classical prophets operate and the technical expertise of the Mesopotamian health-care consultant. Expertise in complex healing

---

98.   Robert D. Biggs, 'Medicine, Surgery, and Public Health in Ancient Mesopotamia', *CANE*, III, pp. 1920-21; Walter Faber, 'Witchcraft, Magic, and Divination in Ancient Mesopotamia', *CANE*, III, pp. 1902-1903.

99.   Revenlow, *Gebet im Alten Testament*, p. 228.

100. H. Avalos, *Illness and Health Care in the Ancient Near East: The Role of the Temple in Greece, Mesopotamia, and Israel* (HSM, 54; Atlanta: Scholars Press, 1995), pp. 260-61; Yehezkel Kaufmann, *The Religion of Israel: From the Beginnings to the Babylonian Captivity* (New York: Schocken Books, 1972), pp. 107-108.

101. Hermann Gunkel (Gunkel and Begrich, *Introduction to the Psalms*, pp. 129-30) hesitated to conclude that the psalms of LI were composed solely for liturgical purposes. But this opinion was based upon the assumption that many of the psalms of LI were not genuine liturgical compositions but spiritual poems written in imitation of those actually used in worship services. Though there may be cases of literary imitation of a liturgical form (e.g. Psalms 25; 39 and 143), I follow Gerstenberger (*Psalms*, I, pp. 27, 119-21, 165-68) in assuming that the benefit of the doubt should favor liturgical usage.

rituals is never mentioned as a reason to consult the classical prophets. In biblical texts, the value of prophetic intervention is found in their personal relationship with the healing deity.[102]

The silence of the biblical record regarding the classical prophets extends to two other groups sometimes associated with the composition and performance of laments. These include cultic singers and prophets. The classical prophets were conscious of another group of prophetic functionaries with whom they were often in conflict (e.g. 1 Kings 22; Jer. 6.13-14; 14.13; 23.16-17; 28.1-10; Mic. 3.5, 11).[103] These cult prophets were generally associated with a sanctuary, although like the Babylonian *āšipu*, they also had connections with the palace and gave advice to royalty, especially on military campaigns.[104] Therefore, like the Mesopotamian *āšipu*, cult prophets belonged to large group institutions and they could operate outside the temple precincts. But biblical evidence for cult prophets identifies them primarily as givers of oracles and ecstatic performances.[105]

Sigmund Mowinckel had the opinion that the individual laments were cultic poetry, composed by expert temple singers.[106] His opinion was shaped by the thesis that many psalms with complaint in the first person singular were actually communal laments. However, Mowinckel also allowed for the existence of personal laments.[107] But there is a problem in identifying the performers of lament exclusively with temple singers. The locale for LI could vary from settings in the home to services in the temple precincts.[108] It is not clear how temple singers would participate in healing liturgies outside sacred space.

Robert Culley has demonstrated that many psalms show signs of dependency on oral formulaic language. His findings led him to conclude that there must have been a period of oral composition of both complaints and hymns in ancient Israel. According to Culley, 'the bearers of this tradition were probably 'professional' poets, well trained in the craft, whose function it was to offer psalms on behalf of people who desired a psalm to be offered'.[109]

---

102. Avalos, *Illness and Health Care*, pp. 275-76.

103. Ringgren, *Israelite Religion*, pp. 212-13.

104. Koch, *Prophets*, I, pp. 25-29.

105. Ringgren, *Israelite Religion*, pp. 212-16.

106. Sigmund Mowinckel, *The Psalms in Israel's Worship* (Biblical Resource Series; Grand Rapids: Eerdmans, 2004; original translation 1962), II, pp. 18-25, 90-91.

107. Mowinckel, *Psalms in Israel's Worship*, II, pp. 16-18.

108. Gerstenberger and Schrage, *Suffering*, p. 40. For example, Psalm 5 seems to presuppose that the petitioner is standing beside his offering (Gunkel and Begrich, *Introduction to the Psalms*, p. 124), but Psalm 42–43 laments that the poet is unable to visit the temple.

109. Robert C. Culley, *Oral Formulaic Language in the Biblical Psalms* (Near and Middle

In Culley's opinion, such language is commensurate with cultic origins for the psalms. But his example of a guild of oral poets that can compose poems for others is not cultic. His appeals to Russian oral poets suggest a similar institution to that described by Parry and Lord in Yugoslavia: a professional poet class that was able to perform on request ceremonial poetry and narrative epics. The ceremonial poetry consisted largely of chants used at peasant weddings and funerals. While almost every Russian woman could compose a lament for the dead in the traditional way, often a professional poet was called in to perform the task.[110]

What kind of synthesis is possible from the various perspectives on the performance of healing cures and psalmic composition presented above? Above all, one must take the evidence that the psalms of lament were composed by a circle of experts seriously. This is suggested by both the Mesopotamian parallels adduced by Gerstenberger and the evidence of oral composition set out by Culley.[111] However, one must also keep in mind the relationship between individual complaint prayer and formulas of everyday speech. This means that the expert poets involved in composing lament, certainly in the stage of oral tradition, could have been skilled lay persons as well as identifiable functionaries of the religion of the large group such as temple singers or prophets.

Gerstenberger suggests that, 'we cannot conclude that the psalmists formed a homogeneous group'.[112] This opinion holds for the composition of the poetry of lament. During the oral phase of individual complaint psalms, performances could have been rendered by expert poets familiar with the formula for argumentative prayer who had various relationships with the cult (including lay persons). But at some point, the psalms of lament were consigned to writing. Thereafter, the poetry of complaint came under the aegis of a scribal elite associated with the cult.

A model from the ancient Near East that bears some attention concerns the origins of the class of *kalû*-priests, whose expertise was the chanting of lamentations (discussed in more detail in the next chapter). This group of professional chanters only became an elite group in the temple system after some time. In the early period, they seem to have been composed of lower class individuals with secular occupations distinct from other kinds of professional temple singers.[113] The following section adduces evidence

Eastern Studies, 4; Toronto: University Press, 1967), p. 113.

110. Culley, *Oral Formulaic Language*, pp. 113, 129-31.

111. Aejmeleaus, *Traditional Prayer*, pp. 102-103.

112. Gerstenberger, *Psalms*, I, p. 31.

113. Paul W. Ferris, *The Genre of Communal Lament in the Bible and the Ancient Near East* (SBLDS, 127; Atlanta: Scholars Press, 1992), pp. 80-81.

for the contention that the poetic tradition of individual lament was gradually subsumed by the Jerusalem cult.

3.4.3. *Centralization of the Psalms of LI*

Rainer Albertz has established a number of distinctions between the outlook of psalms of LI and laments for the community. One of the most salient is variation in expressions of trust. Community laments usually refer to YHWH's past history with the people (e.g. Pss. 44.2-8; 80.9-12; 89.20-38) or to his status as creator of the cosmos (e.g. 74.12-17). These motifs seldom enter the confessions of trust in LI. In fact, out of 39 poems, historical memory as an argument for divine intervention occurs only in Pss. 22.4-6 and 143.5. Psalms of LI emphasize God's status as personal creator (e.g. Pss. 22.10-11; 71.6) and personal protector (e.g. Pss. 3.4; 27.1-5; 31.4, 15; 54.6; 57.2; 59.10-11). This distinct variation in relationship is also conveyed by the use of pronouns: 41 times in 24 psalms, the deity addressed by an individual lament is given a possessive pronoun, 'my God', etc. But there is no corresponding usage in psalms of community lament.[114] According to Albertz, the trust the individual feels for his personal creator and protector is analogous to the feelings that a child has for its mother or father.[115] Since God is held to have made the psalmist, cared and looked after him since birth, there is an intimate and personal relationship between the individual and his God.[116]

But Albertz's observations do not tell us about the origins of the psalms that are actually in the Psalter. There is a tension between his observations about the nature of the relationship between the petitioner and YHWH and the vocabulary of that relationship. The preferred social designations for the deity and the suppliant in the psalms of LI identify God as *'ădônāy* ('my Lord')[117] to which corresponds the role of *'abdĕkā* ('your servant').[118] This is not the vocabulary of family relationships; it is political terminology. In fact, throughout the Hebrew Bible the phrase 'your servant' is not used by a son with reference to his parents.[119] The *'adôn/ 'ebed* terminology designates a number of social relationships in which a

114. Albertz, *Persönliche Frömmlichkeit*, p. 33.
115. Albertz, *Persönliche Frömmigkeit*, pp. 37, 42.
116. Albertz, *Persönliche Frömmigkeit*, pp. 28-38.
117. Pss. 22.31; 35.17, 22, 23; 38.10, 16, 23; 39.8; 40.18; 51.17; 55.10; 57.10; 59.12; 71.5, 16; 86.3, 4, 5, 8, 9, 12, 15; 109.21; 140.8; 141.8.
118. Pss. 27.9; 31.17; 69.18; 86.2, 4, 16; 109.28 and 143.2, 12.
119. The one exception proves the rule. In 2 Sam. 13.24 Absalom makes a request of his father, King David: 'Behold, your servant has sheepshearers; pray let the king and his servants go with your servant'. Absalom's self-designation of himself as servant recognizes that his father is king. It is David who asserts the family relationship in his reply: 'No, my son...' (v. 25).

person feels himself to be in a position of social inferiority and dependence on another. Most often implicated in the Hebrew Bible are relationships with royalty. In the psalms of LI, God is called 'judge' (7.12) and 'my king' (5.3). These epithets place the relationship between the suppliant and the deity in the political arena.

In the last chapter, I observed that the liturgical functionaries involved in complaint against God for the community and for individuals could be the same by the later monarchical period (cf. the stories of Elijah and Elisha). This observation can apply to the variation of trust motifs in complaint psalms. The same experts could have composed both community and individual complaints on the understanding that YHWH related differently to each category of petitioner. What is to be contrasted is not cultic versus non-cultic usage, but the cultic practices of two different groups.[120] On one side stands the official cult of the large group with calls to public complaint ceremonies including proclamations of fasts and set worship times. On the other side stands the liturgical services conducted on an *ad hoc* basis for individuals in need.

Albertz's thesis uses confession of trust material to place the origins of lamenting practice in the home or family.[121] In fact, he wants to make more sweeping claims about the original nature of the religion of what he calls 'the small group' as opposed to the religion of the 'large group', i.e. the nation or state. Such claims have not gone unchallenged.[122] But, at least as far as lament is concerned, Albertz's distinction has merit. The last chapter established a practice of informal lay lament for individuals that was distinct from that for the community. There is evidence in the confession of trust motifs of LI to suggest a sphere of life separate from the cultic institutions of the large group. It is logical to assume that small groups would be able to lament using their own theological terms of reference.[123] But the present relational language of the psalms of LI suggests some process of integration between the religion of the large group and the small group in the psalms we now possess.

In other words, a somewhat heterogeneous situation with regard to the composition and performance of LI became increasingly standardized as the monarchical period developed. During the oral phase of the lament psalm formula, various poetic experts could have composed formal

---

120. See Albertz, *Persönliche Frömmigkeit*, p. 27.

121. Rainer Albertz, *A History of Israelite Religion in the Old Testament Period* (OTL; 2 vols.; Louisville, KY: Westminster John Knox, 1994), I, p. 100.

122. See Reventlow, *Gebet im Alten Testament*, p. 87.

123. Like Albertz, Fuchs (*Die Klage als Gebet*, p. 303) regards individual lament as originally not oriented towards the cultic centres; he regards the deity to whom individual lament was addressed as a protecting deity of everyday life.

complaint prayers in cultic and non-cultic venues. But the development of the state had a profound effect on many dimensions of traditional religious life, especially as its institutions became more and more centralized. The dramatic proposals for realigning Israel's traditional cultic life in Deuteronomy 12; 14–16 provide good examples of the lengths that centralizing tendencies were ready to go in order to reform venerable practices.[124] There are several indications that the psalms of LI, as now preserved in the Psalter, have the Jerusalem temple as their point of reference.[125] One of these has already been mentioned: the description of the personal relationship of the petitioner and the deity into political terms. In addition, there are extensive cultic references in the psalms of LI and the character of the book of Psalms as a scribal product.

References to cultic practices in the psalms of LI provide a good indication of their point of orientation. In fact, the psalms of LI contain numerous references to temple precincts (e.g. 3.5; 5.8; 26.8; 27.4; 28.2; 42.5; 43.4; 55.15; 69.10), cultic singing (e.g. 7.18; 13.6; 26.7; 27.6; 42.5) and other actions commensurate with temple rituals (e.g. 4.6; 17.15; 26.6; 27.6; 54.8; 56.13; 141.2). These references indicate that the extant psalms of LI assume participation in temple worship as a normative expression of individual piety.

Engagement with the religion of the large group is also indicated by the larger liturgical context that the psalms of LI assume: the lament-thanksgiving cycle. Following a successful recovery or relief from the experience of distress, the affected person would arrange for a thanksgiving feast to which family and friends would be invited.[126] Many LI anticipate performing the thanksgiving rite (e.g. Pss. 7.18, 13.6; 27.6; 35.27-28; 54.8-9; 57.10; 61.9; 69.31).[127] Some look forward to holding the thanksgiving ceremony in the 'great congregation' (Pss. 22.26; 35.18; 40.10-11).

A Jerusalem provenance is also indicated by the composition of the book of Psalms in which the poems of LI now appear. The psalms of LI were incorporated into small collections and eventually into a large scroll (a scribal product) that forms the basis for the book we now find in our Bibles.[128]How did scribes for a large group institution get these poems if they were not also involved at some point in their composition and use?

---

124. William S. Morrow, *Scribing the Center: Organization and Redaction in Deuteronomy 14.1--17.13* (SBLMS, 49; Atlanta: Scholars Press, 1995), pp. 26-27.

125. Emphasized by Day, *Psalms*, p. 15.

126. Albertz, *History of Israelite Religion*, I, p. 101. A number of psalms are related this liturgy (e.g. Psalms 30; 32; 34; 116 and 138). There is a description of the thanksgiving sacrifice in Gunkel and Begrich, *Introduction to the Psalms*, pp. 199-200

127. Day, *Psalms*, p. 45.

128. Various accounts of this process exist; see, e.g. Day, *Psalms*, pp. 109-21; Gunkel

The proposal of a centralization of the use of psalms of LI,[129] is commensurate with the proposal of gradual 'prophetization' of the informal lament made in the last chapter. The prestige of the temple institution would have attracted various cultic actions into its orb of influence. In fact, one cannot conclude that individual lament psalm ceremonies did not take place outside the ambit of official cultic places even at the end of the monarchical period.[130] One can conclude, however, that the psalms of LI now preserved were preserved by way of the Jerusalem temple establishment even though the genre shows signs of heterogeneous origins. This cultic institution seems to have attracted extant compositions and influenced the composition of new ones such that it became generally assumed by the psalms of LI that rehabilitation was equivalent to participating in acts of worship at the temple.

3.5. *Use of the Psalms of LI: Summary and Conclusions*

The psalms of individual lament were prayers used when the experience of suffering required some kind of more deliberate intervention than informal lament could provide. As they stand, the complaint psalms point to a form of healing liturgy that had come under the aegis of the temple system in Jerusalem. They show signs of diagnostic distinctions that were managed by persons with cultic expertise.

The psalms of Plea are prayers for suffering persons not considered to be suffering from divine punishment. They present the enemy as the overwhelming cause of distress. These poems are directed to YHWH because it is not acceptable that divine sovereignty be compromised by the attacks of the wicked, especially if the victim was an upright servant of God. Nevertheless, there remains an underlying fear that YHWH could abandon the poet to the enemy, if the petitioner were a sinner. This possibility is suggested by three different characteristics of the psalms of Plea. First of all, there is an overlap between the theme of enemy attack and psalms of Indirect Protest. Secondly, a number of psalms of Plea emphasize the innocence of the petitioner. Finally, at least one (Psalm 130) seems to have a prophylactic intent.

The psalms of Indirect Protest express the fear of divine punishment. This is apparent in the use of the petitions in the negative Imperative. It is

---

and Begrich, *Introduction to Psalms*, pp. 333-48 and G.H. Wilson, *The Editing of the Hebrew Psalter* (SBLDS, 76; Chico, CA: Scholars Press, 1985).

129. Also suggested by Fuchs, *Die Klage als Gebet*, p. 309 and Gestenberger, *Psalms*, I, p. 32.

130. Gerstenberger, *Der bittende Mensch*, p. 153.

manifest in themes that overlap with the psalms of Plea. Indirect Protest also considers enemy attack. Psalms that affirm the innocence of the poet are fairly divided between psalms of Plea (4; 7 and 17) and Indirect Protest (26 and 27). By the same token, we should not be surprised that the psalms of Indirect Protest also include a number of compositions in which the need to avoid being classified as an enemy of God comes to the fore: 28; 40; 141 and 143.

The possibility that God will either abandon or actively afflict the poet because of sin emerges in a number of psalms of Indirect Protest. With the exception of Psalm 130, this is not a theme explicitly addressed by the psalms of Plea. Probably, complaint liturgies in ancient Israel took different forms depending on whether it had been established that the petitioner was guilty or innocent of offending the deity.[131] It is likely that psalms of Indirect Protest functioned in cases where determination of sin on the part of the petitioner had been made or was a real possibility.

By contrast, there is little allusion to sin in the psalms of Direct Protest. This should not be surprising since premature death was regarded as an appropriate punishment for sinners. Premature death would only be inappropriate if the person using the psalm had already been cleared of sin. The prospect of imminent death is presented in the psalms of Direct Protest as a condition that God is both ultimately responsible for and yet out of keeping with the divine character. But how is it possible for the divine reality to act so contrary to its own character, to be the agent of chaos and death rather than the deliverer? There is no answer to this question within the psalms. The fact is, the biblical record contains a number of indications that YHWH could act in an arbitrary, negligent and even abusive manner on occasion.[132]

One must not, however, unduly emphasize the status of the psalms of Direct Protest as expressions of pain embrace. These psalms were managed within the context of legitimate cultic structures and the permission for explicit protest against YHWH was not readily granted. The psalms of Direct Protest comprise barely 20% of the total number of LI (8/39). Explicit protest was probably only permitted to sufferers who had used up other avenues for healing and who faced a situation of prolonged hardship due to chronic disease and unanswered prayer.[133]

---

131. Gerstenberger, *Psalms*, I, p. 65.

132. Brueggemann, *Theology of the Old Testament*, p. 359. A number of biblical narratives portray God as a rather frightening and unfair presence; see David Penchansky, *What Rough Beast? Images of God in the Hebrew Bible* (Louisville, KY: Westminster John Knox, 1999).

133. Broyles, *Conflict of Faith and Experience*, p. 124.

I concur with the thesis that a sizeable number of LI in the Psalter are probably pre-exilic in origin just as there are also many that are post-exilic.[134] However, I am reluctant to date individual lament psalms. The problem can be illustrated by considering two motifs that might be considered diagnostic for identifying late (postexilic) psalms: awareness of sin and references to the large group.[135]

Use of vocabulary that often designates Israel and Judah's national enemies occurs in Pss. 54.5 (strangers); 56.8 (peoples); 59.6, 9 (nations). Here enemy imagery combines the motif of YHWH's war with chaos with holy war against Israel's foes.[136] Moreover, a substantial number of LI contain references to the large group (Pss. 3.9; 22.4-6, 23; 25.22; 26.12; 28.9; 31.24-25; 35.18; 40.10-11; 51.20; 59.14; 69.36; 102.13-17; 130.7-8). It seems implausible that all of these references can be ascribed to postexilic influences (though this is certainly the case for some, e.g. 51.20; 102.13-17). If the practice of composing LI had come under the aegis of the Jerusalem temple as a result of centralizing forces in the late monarchy, then LI were being managed by a state institution. There would be a possibility of incorporation of references to the large group already in the pre-exilic period.

It is tempting to date the composition of some of the psalms of Indirect Protest, with their heightened consciousness of sin to the postexilic period, in which there was a sense of greater distance between the individual and the deity and a spreading sense of sinfulness.[137] But an alternative explanation for the references to sin and self-conscious fear for one's personal relationship with YHWH in the psalms of LI is the diagnostic process I suggest above. Such a process need not be confined to the postexilic period.

Probably most of the extant pre-exilic examples of LI were in use during the late monarchy and may stem from that time. A significant argument for this position is the provenance of the book of Psalms itself. Though some linguistic evidence has been adduced to discover Israelite (as opposed to the southern kingdom) origins for a few psalms of LI, the data is meager.[138] More compelling is the editorial traditions that accompany the psalms in their present form. Most of the psalms of LI are identified either as Davidic compositions or those of his cultic personnel

---

134. Day, *Psalms*, p. 16.

135. Fuchs, *Die Klage als Gebet*, p. 325.

136. Dhanaraj, *Theological Significance of the Motif of Enemies*, p. 279.

137. Albertz, *History of Israelite Religion*, II, p. 511.

138. Gary A. Rendsburg [*Linguistic Evidence for the Northern Origin of Selected Psalms* (SBLMS, 43; Atlanta: Scholars Press, 1990), p. 103] lists Pss. 42–43, 88, 140 and 141 in the corpus I am using. But he admits (*ibid.*, p. 104) that that his criteria cannot be used to fix a date before 721 BCE.

(Korah, see 2 Chron. 20.19). These editorial comments strongly suggest that the collections of psalms that made up the Psalter had associations with Jerusalem.

A determination that the genre of LI fell under the aegis of the Jerusalem temple in the late pre-exilic era has implications for the history of lament. As with the case for informal laments, the biblical corpus provides both usable data and an ideal picture. A reconstruction of the history of the psalms of LI suggests that the liturgical experts who composed and used them were originally somewhat varied. Nevertheless, the tradition of LI as a whole and its basic theology seem to have been institutionalized in the temple establishment by the end of the monarchical period. Moreover, centralizing tendencies would continue to assert themselves in the reorganization of Jewish life after the destruction of Jerusalem. It follows that shifts in cultic organization and theology would have an affect on the composition of psalms of LI and their use. The subsequent history of biblical religion bears this out.

Chapter 4

THE PROTEST AGAINST GOD IN COMMUNITY COMPLAINTS

Argumentative prayer was a typical form of communal supplication in pre-exilic times. Collective protest against God became especially prominent after the unprecedented destruction of Jerusalem and exile by the Neo-Babylonian empire. As the conditions of exile continued into the postexilic period, certain motifs of the tradition of LI were incorporated into protests of ongoing community distress.

The first section of this chapter discusses problems of defining the category of communal lament (§4.1). The chapter then examines generic relationships among poems containing complaint against God because of national defeat by a foreign power (§4.2). There are two reasons for beginning with protests against national defeat. First, they are primary to most discussions about the genre of community lament. Second, other collective protests are best studied in the light of conclusions about the origins and nature of the protests of national defeat. The third section (§4.3) will discuss the dating of the protests of national defeat and §4.4 will address the question of their origins. The chapter ends with study of other collective complaint prayers in Israelite religion (§4.5).

4.1. *Psalms of Collective Protest in Biblical Literature*

Identification of psalms of community lament is disputed. Definition of the category is beset by difficulties in discerning a common structure or content and arguments about which elements are properly diagnostic. There is a strong consensus for including Psalms 44; 60; 74; 79; 80; 83 and 89,[1] but there are disagreements as to why these psalms form a unity and what other compositions should be associated with them. Claus Westermann's classical study listed Isa. 63.7–64.11; Jeremiah 14; Habakkuk 1; Psalms 44; 60; 74; 79; 80; 83; 89 and Lamentations 5 as representatives of

---

1.   See the survey in Walter C. Bouzard, *We Have Heard with Our Ears, O God: Sources of the Communal Laments in the Psalms* (SBLDS, 159; Atlanta: Scholars Press, 1997), p. 102.

the genre.[2] Recent scholarship on Jeremiah 14, however, suggests this text has a complex literary history.[3] It is not obvious that Jeremiah 14 is a psalm-like composition, although it cites complaint material. Its witness to the communal complaint genre is discussed below in §4.2.2.1. Habakkuk 1 has affinities with community lament, but I prefer to identify it as a prayer of the prophetic mediator; it was discussed in §2.2.1.

Walter Bouzard wants to restrict the category of community lament to Psalms 44; 60; 74; 79; 80; 83 and 89. They are described as a unity due to a combination of shared stylistic and thematic traits. Stylistic traits include common use of the first person plural ('we/us') to refer to the complaining community and the second person singular pronominal suffix ('your') to remind of the deity of his relationship with Israel. Thematic elements include accusatory statements and questions directed at God and evocations of the community's previous experience of divine salvation in contrast with YHWH's present silence.[4]

But Bouzard's stylistic grouping also lacks homogeneity:

- Psalm 60 stands out because it alone contains an oracle of salvation (vv. 8-10);
- Psalm 79 stands out because it alone contains a penitential motif (vv. 8-9);
- Psalm 83 stands out because it contains no direct complaint against God; its complaint is confined to indirect protest (v. 2);
- Psalm 89 is peculiar because of the lengthy hymnic rehearsal of past salvation history (vv. 2-38).

Moreover, it seems like special pleading for Bouzard to exclude Isa. 63.7–64.11. While he admits the poem contains all the stylistic and thematic markers common to Psalms 44; 60; 74; 79; 80; 83 and 89, Isa. 63.7–64.11 is eliminated because it contains penitential motifs (but cf. Ps. 79.8-9) and its introduction implies that the first person plural references are subsumed by a single speaker (but cf. Ps. 44.5, 7, 16 where first person singular references alternate with plural references).[5]

2.   Claus Westermann, *Praise and Lament in the Psalms* (Atlanta: John Knox Press, 1981), pp. 173-75.

3.   Jenö Kiss, *Die Klage Gottes und des Propheten: Ihre Rolle in der Komposition und Redaktion von Jer 11–12, 14–15 und 18* (WMANT, 99; Neukirchen–Vluyn: Neukirchener Verlag, 2003), pp. 209-11.

4.   Bouzard, *We Have Heard*, pp. 114-15. Bouzard bases himself on the work of Murray J. Haar, 'The God–Israel Relationship in the Community Lament Psalms' (PhD Dissertation, Union Theological Seminary, 1985). I have omitted the sole structural element in Haar's typology, Imperative prayer, because this is a common form of petition in the psalms.

5.   Cf. Bouzard, *We Have Heard*, pp. 118-19.

Michael Emmendörffer's recent study concludes that that no single form or structure of the national lament exists. Though the poetry of communal lament shows stock elements such as address, lament, and petition, there is no overarching generic formula that can be extracted or considered binding on all relevant texts. Emmendörffer's claim is conditioned, however, by the fact that he lists as 'undisputed' members of the genre Isa. 63.7–64.11; Psalms 44; 60/108; 74; 79; 80; 83; 85; 89; 137; Lamentations 2 and 5.[6] This collection of poems clearly does not share a common structure.

Rainer Albertz identifies relationships between Isa. 63.7–64.11; Psalms 44; 60; 74; 79; 80; 83; 85; 89 and Lamentations 5 on the basis of the following shared elements: address, lament (God, we, the enemy), reference to God's earlier acts (retrospect), petition, and double wish.[7] Identification of the 'double wish' as a separate element is debatable. Essentially, this is a refinement of the element of petition, which recognizes the presence of third person petitions for Israel and against the enemy. Nevertheless, by noting the four elements of address, lament, retrospect and petition it is possible to set some limits on the category of community lament.[8]

Genre identification often depends on perceptions of stereotypical contents. Indications of collective distress have been regarded as important signifiers of community lament, sometimes more significant than structural similarities. For example, Gerstenberger identifies Psalms 25; 44; 60; 74; 79; 80; 83; 85; 89; 94; 108; 123 and 137 as 'communal complaints'.[9] Gunkel would also include in this category royal prayers such as Psalms 20 and 144.[10] Sigmund Mowinckel would add a number of psalms with first person singular references that the previous chapter identified as psalms of LI.[11]

6.   Michael Emmendörffer, *Der ferne Gott: Eine Untersuchung der alttestamentlichen Volksklagelieder vor dem Hintergrund der mesopotamischen Literatur* (Forschungen zum Alten Testament, 21; Tübingen: Mohr–Siebeck, 1998), pp. 15, 290.

7.   Rainer Albertz, *Israel in Exile: The History and Literature of the Sixth Century B.C.E.* (Studies in Biblical Literature, 3; Atlanta: Society of Biblical Literature, 2003), p. 148.

8.   Albertz, *Israel in Exile*, p. 151. Albertz's list is agreement with Westermann's with the exceptions of Jeremiah 14 and Habakkuk 1.

9.   Erhard S. Gerstenberger, *Psalms: I-II* (FOTL, 14–15; Grand Rapids: Eerdmans, 1988, 2001).

10.   Hermann Gunkel and Joachim Begrich, *Introduction to the Psalms: The Genres of the Religious Lyric of Israel* (Mercer Library of Biblical Studies; Macon, GA: Mercer University Press, 1998; 4th German edn, 1985), p. 82.

11.   Sigmund Mowinckel, *The Psalms in Israel's Worship* (Biblical Resource Series; Grand Rapids: Eerdman's, 2004; original translation 1962), I, pp. 225-27. Examples of LI identified by Mowinckel as communal lament include Psalms 3; 7; 22; 27; 42–43; 56; 59 and 102.

I have attempted to circumvent the problem of assuming genre as a starting point for discussing psalms of collective lament by using a single formal criterion to identify possible candidates for study. The biblical poetry that directly concerns this chapter includes all those compositions that contain complaint against God on behalf of the community. As noted in the last chapter, there are three categories of God-complaint: accusatory questions, accusatory statements, and indirect protest in the form of negated Imperative petitions. They are distributed over the following biblical poems:

Table 3. *Collective Complaint against God in Biblical Poems.*

Psalm	Accusatory Questions			Accus. Statements	Ind. Pro.
	Why?	How Long?	Other		
9–10	10.1, 13				10.12
44	24, 25			10-15, 20	24
60			12	3-6	
74	1, 11	10			19, 23
77			8-10	5	
79	10	5			8
80	13	5		6-7	
83					2
85			6, 7		
89		47	50	39-41, 43-46	
90		13		8, 15	
94		3			
108			12		
115	2				
Isa. 63.7–64.11	63.17		63.11-12, 15 64.11	64.4, 6	64.8
Lam. 5	20			22[12]	

Table 3 only surveys complete biblical poems expressing complaint against God on behalf of the community. Fragments of community protest in anonymous citations of complaints against God will be discussed below (§4.2.2.1). Criteria for selection in the chart above were kept as formal as possible. 'Why?' and 'how long?' questions are regarded as

12.   The syntax of Lam. 5.22 is difficult; various solutions are surveyed by Tod Linafelt ('The Refusal of a Conclusion in the Book of Lamentations', *JBL* 120 [2001], pp. 340-43). Linafelt regards the verse as a conditional sentence in which the apodosis is left unstated. The rules of Hebrew syntax support his translation of vv. 21-22, which suggest a deliberate 'nonending' to the book: 'Take us back, YHWH, to yourself and we will come back. Renew our days as of old. For if truly you have rejected us, raging bitterly against us —'. Even so, the verbs of v. 22 describe divine action against the community.

complaints against God regardless of the subject of the verb. The same is true for 'where?' questions (Isa. 63.11-12, 15; Ps. 89.50), which Chapter Two established as an expression of complaint against God. Other questions were considered complaints against God only if God was the subject of the verb. Accusatory statements describe actions done by God against the community or its representatives. Indirect protest involves second person negated Imperatives directed to God.

Discussion about the category of communal complaint inevitably draws on content as well as formal indicators. Biblical poetry with collective protest can be sorted into two broad categories on the basis of content. A number of poems are written in the shadows of national destruction or military defeat by a foreign power: Isa. 63.7–64.11; Psalms 44; 60; 74; 79; 80; 89 and Lamentations 5. Related, but less clearly a member of this group, is Psalm 83, which would not be included if it were not for the use of indirect protest in its address to YHWH. Isa. 63.7–64.11 is accepted as a member of this group for the reasons given above against Bouzard's decision to exclude it. But in view of the disputed connections of Lamentations 5 with the psalms in this category,[13] the relationship of Lamentations 5 to this group will be revisited in the discussion of the historical development of Lamentations in Chapter Five. Therefore, §4.2 will concern itself with virtually the same group identified by Albertz: Isa 63.7–64.11; Psalms 44; 60; 74; 79; 80; 83 and 89.

A second group of poems containing collective protest consists of Psalms 9–10; 77; 85; 90; 94; 108 and 115. This group is not a thematic unity and manifests significant variations in structure. In one case, a complaint motif motivates hymnic praise (115.2). Psalm 77 stands out because its questions about divine actions are in the third person. Some of these poems (e.g. Psalm 9–10; 77; 108) show the influence of various motifs found in LI (see §4.5). The major characteristic of this second group, therefore, is that its collective complaints against God do not belong to the category of protests of national defeat.

The poems in both groups have thematic connections with other poems describing community distress that do not have motifs of God-complaint: e.g. Psalms 12; 123; 126; 137 and 144. That is, there are a number of psalms which make petitions on behalf of the community and its chief representative, the king. Some of these express collective distress (e.g. Psalm 137), but there is an absence of complaint against God. As in the case of individual lament psalms, therefore, there is validity to making a distinction between collective psalms of protest and psalms of plea.[14]

---

13. Included, e.g. by Albertz (*Israel in Exile*, p. 141) and Emmendörffer (*Der ferne Gott*, p. 15) but excluded by Bouzard (*We Have Heard*, pp. 117-118).

14. See Craig C. Broyles, *The Conflict of Faith and Experience in the Psalms: A*

Consequently, psalms addressing community distress can be organized into three groups on the basis of their complaint against God. Since Psalms 44; 60; 74; 79; 80; 83; 89 and Isa. 63.7–64.11 contain protest against God in the context of national defeat, this group will be designated 'protests of national defeat'. Psalms 9–10; 77; 85; 90; 94; 108 and 115 contain protest against God about other kinds of national distress; this group will be called 'protests of community distress'. A third group does not contain complaint against God, and will be designated as 'congregational pleas' (e.g. Psalms 12; 123; 126; 137; 144).

4.2. *Biblical Communal Lament and Mesopotamian Lamentations*

The Mesopotamian city-laments comprise a significant body of poetry that is often compared to the biblical genre of communal lament.[15] One important indicator is the presence of protests against divine action. Parallels can be found to accusatory questions,[16] accusatory

---

Form-Critical and Theological Study (JSOTSup, 52; Sheffield: JSOT Press, 1989), pp. 35-53. Albertz (*Israel in Exile*, p. 141) also distinguishes the genre of community complaints from congregational prayers.

15.   See, e.g. Bouzard, *We Have Heard*, pp. 199-200; F.W. Dobbs-Allsopp, *Weep, O Daughter of Zion: A Study of the City-Lament Genre in the Hebrew Bible* (BibOr, 44; Rome: Pontifical Biblical Institute, 1993), pp. 155-56; Paul W. Ferris, *The Genre of Communal Lament in the Bible and the Ancient Near East* (SBLDS, 127; Atlanta: Scholars Press, 1992), pp. 174-75; Hans U. Steymans, 'Traces of Liturgies in the Psalter: The Communal Laments, Psalms 79, 80, 83, 89 in Context', in D.J Human and C.J.A. Vos (eds.), *Psalms and Liturgy* (JSOTSup, 410; London: T. & T. Clark, 2004), pp. 168-234; Claus Westermann, *Lamentations: Issues and Interpretation* (Minneapolis: Fortress Press, 1994), pp. 15-16. There are also interesting comparative lists in Geo Widengren, *The Accadian and Hebrew Psalms of Lamentation as Religious Documents: A Comparative Study* (Uppsala: Almqvist & Wiksell, 1936), but these are not useful because Widengren (p. 16) restricts the definition of lament to cases of individual lament.

16.   Examples of 'why?' questions are found in M.W. Green, 'The Uruk Lament', *JAOS* 104 (1984), p. 266, l.19; Piotr Michalowski, *The Lamentation over the Destruction of Sumer and Ur* (Mesopotamian Civilizations, 1; Winona Lake, IN: Eisenbrauns, 1989), p. 57, ll. 341-42; Mark E. Cohen, *The Canonical Lamentations of Ancient Mesopotamia* (2 vols.; Potomac, MD: Capital Decisions Ltd, 1988), pp. 58, ll. 28-38; 109, ll. 90-98; 292, ll. 29-33.

Examples of 'how long?' questions are found in Thorkild Jacobsen, 'The Lament for Ur', *The Harps That Once…Sumerian Poetry in Translation* (New Haven: Yale University Press, 1987), p. 472, l. 374; Michalowski, *Destruction of Sumer and Ur*, pp. 61, l. 398; 65, l. 451; Cohen, *Canonical Lamentations*, pp. 59, l. 62; 112, l. 195; 166, ll. 24-29; 193, ll. 73-74; 382, ll. 33-36; 410, l. 36.

Parallel to 'how long?' are questions asking 'when?' Examples are found in 'The Lament for Nibru', in Oxford University Oriental Institute (ed.), *The Electronic Text Corpus of Sumerian Literature* (July 29, 1999; cited 14 August 2005; http.//www-etcsl. orient.ox.ac.uk/section2/tr224.htm), ll. 1-11; Cohen, *Canonical Lamentations*, pp. 70,

statements,[17] and the use of indirect protest.[18] The similarities in accusatory expressions are reinforced by the fact that the Mesopotamian poems
are often directed towards a high god, Enlil. While the actual destruction
of the city is carried out by enemies, Enlil is regarded as the one who sets
the storm of destruction in motion. In the biblical protests of national
defeat, a similar role is played by YHWH. Both bodies of literature also
regard abandonment by the tutelary god(s) as a necessary condition for
enemy attack. Therefore, it is not surprising to find indirect protest
against divine abandonment in both sets of poems.

Parallels between expressions of divine protest and the Mesopotamian
city-laments raise two issues of particular concern for this study. First, it
is necessary to determine if there is a case for direct influence on the
composition of the protests of national defeat by the Mesopotamian city
laments, which often antedate biblical literature (§4.2.1). Second, F.W.
Dobbs-Allsopp has claimed that the Mesopotamian parallels indicate the
probability that, besides the protests of national defeat, biblical religion
knew of a pre-exilic tradition of city-lament presupposed by the book of
Lamentations (§4.2.2).

4.2.1. *Temporal Relationships between Mesopotamian Laments and Israel's Complaints*

Collective lamentation in Mesopotamia includes at least three different
kinds of poems.[19] The earliest are the group of Sumerian city-laments composed after the destruction of the Ur III empire. Of the six compositions in
this category, only the *Lament over Ur*, the *Lament over the Destruction of Ur
and Sumer* and the *Nippur Lament* have been transmitted in a fairly complete fashion.[20] These poems were written for recitation in ceremonies

---

ll. 1-14; 85, l. 46; 171, ll. 247-57); Mark E. Cohen, *Sumerian Hymnology: The Eršemma*
(HUCA Supplements, 2; Cincinnati: Hebrew Union College–Jewish Institute of Religion,
1981), pp. 120, ll. 1-14; 129, l. 36).

Examples of 'where?' questions are found in M.W. Green, 'The Eridu Lament', *JCS* 30
(1978), p. 139, ll. 7-8; Jacobsen, 'Lament for Ur', p. 471, l. 372; Cohen, *Canonical Lamentations*, p. 59, l. 65.

17.   Examples are found in Jacobsen, 'Lament for Ur', p. 472, ll. 376-77; Cohen,
Canonical Lamentations, pp. 138, ll. 67-68, 79-101; 166, l. 30; 261-62, ll. 41-44; 340, ll. 9-13;
Cohen, *Eršemma*, p. 129, ll. 33-34.

18.   Examples are found in Cohen, *Canonical Lamentations*, pp. 110, ll. 108-28; 167, ll.
84-92; Cohen, *Eršemma*, p. 138, ll. 30-31.

19.   I omit discussion of the *eršahunga*. This word seems to designate a form of
individual lament, but there are also resemblances to the *eršemma*; see Ferris, *Genre of
Communal Lament*, pp. 67-68.

20.   Michalowski, *Destruction of Sumer and Ur*, p. 5. There are fragments of laments
over Uruk, Eridu and Ekimar.

marking the restoration of ruins after a major disaster. Their liturgical usage was limited, however; after they had fulfilled the purpose for which they were written, they were preserved as *belles lettres* in the scribal curriculum.[21] There are indications that some of these poems functioned as a form of legitimation for the new dynasty built on the ruins of the Ur III kingdom.[22] These early city laments are found in scribal copies from the Old Babylonian period.

In addition, there are two genres of collective lament attested from Old Babylonian times down to the Seleucid era in the first millennium: *balag*-compositions and the genre of liturgical poetry called the *eršemma*. The *balag*-compositions appear to be derived from the older Sumerian city-laments and emulate them both in form and content. Nevertheless, the *balag* constitutes a separate genre from the Sumerian city-laments for three reasons. Unlike the older city-laments, historical references in the *balag*-poems are not specific. Secondly, *balag*-poems are written in the Sumerian dialect called *emesal*, whereas the older city laments mostly use the main dialect. Finally, the *balag*-laments were composed for recurrent use, specifically for the liturgies of the *kalû*-priesthood. They were used to placate the wrath of the gods when sacred structures were demolished and renovated. During the first millennium they were also used in liturgies for certain days of the month, festivals (including the *akītu*) and apotropaic rituals.[23]

Like the *balag*, *eršemma*-poems were written in *emesal*. The *eršemma*-poems were originally a genre distinct from the *balag*. The *eršemma*-poems are much shorter than *balag*-poems, which typically run into hundreds of lines consisting of long sections with little connection to each other. But *eršemma*-poems concern a single topic and originally were used for hymnic themes as well as laments. From the perspective of length and the fact that they typically address a single theme, the *eršemma*-poems are much closer to the conventions of Hebrew psalmody. Nevertheless, connections between the *eršemma* and the *balag* are well documented. Some *eršemma*-poems were taken over as sections of *balag*-compositions; and in Middle Babylonian times and later it became customary to end every *balag* with an *eršemma*.[24]

Among recent scholars, Bouzard, Dobbs-Allsopp and Emmendörffer agree that the ancient Jewish lament tradition came under the influence of Mesopotamian exemplars in the pre-exilic period. Bouzard's argument

21. Raphael Kutscher, *Oh Angry Sea (a-ab-ba hu-luh-ha): The History of a Sumerian Congregational Lament* (New Haven: Yale University Press, 1975), p. 6.

22. Michalowski, *Destruction of Sumer and Ur*, pp. 6-7.

23. Cohen, *Canonical Lamentations*, pp. 33-44; Ferris, *Genre of Communal Lament*, pp. 38-43.

24. Cohen, *Eršemma*, pp. 18-28; Ferris, *Genre of Communal Lament*, pp. 43-47.

assumes cultural continuity between late Bronze Age Canaan and Iron
Age Israel in terms of cuneiform traditions. Scribes of various late Bronze
Age city-states in the region (including Jerusalem) used Akkadian in dip-
lomatic correspondence and show familiarity with some types of Akkadian
literature. Bouzard assumes that this knowledge influenced the religious
compositions of ancient Israel. In addition, various cultural contacts
between Mesopotamia, Israel and Judah during the first millennium provided other opportunities for the influence of the Mesopotamian lamentation tradition on Israelite religion.[25]

Dobbs-Allsopp believes that the Mesopotamian lament tradition stands
behind the origins of an Israelite genre of city-lament. This tradition was
internalized in ancient Judaism and sustained a native development from
approximately the eighth to the sixth centuries BCE. There are indications,
however, that it emerged in ancient Israel prior to the time of Amos.
Dobbs-Allsopp does not specify how this Mesopotamian tradition became
rooted in Israel's culture.[26] Emmendörffer, however, thinks that priestly
circles would have been familiar with the Mesopotamian laments throughout the Neo-Assyrian and Neo-Babylonian eras.[27]

J.H. Tigay has recently examined criteria for assessing claims regarding
literary borrowings in ancient Near Eastern literature. Two forms of evidence must combine. First, there must be a reasonable degree of probability that borrowing has taken place: the fewer differences and the more
similarities there are, the more convincing the claim. Second, one must
consider the circumstantial evidence: the likelihood of a particular author
being familiar with motifs of a foreign provenance. In other words, there
must be a probable channel of transmission.[28]

It is not evident that there was a channel of transmission that could
bring the Mesopotamian lament tradition into the awareness of Israel's or
Judah's intellectuals prior to the exile. Elsewhere I have discussed problems with the assumption that knowledge of cuneiform literature was
transmitted from Bronze Age Canaan to Iron Age Israel and Judah. Here I
will only communicate the results of that study. It does not appear that

    25.   Bouzard, *We Have Heard*, pp. 154-55, 201-11. For earlier scholarship with similar
opinions, see the discussions in Ferris, *Genre of Communal Lament*, pp. 167-74 and
Delbert R. Hillers, *Lamentations* (AB, 7A; Garden City, NY: Doubleday, 1972), pp.
xxviii-xxx.

    26.   F.W. Dobbs-Allsopp, 'Darwinism, Genre Theory, and City Laments', *JAOS* 120
(2000), pp. 626-27.

    27.   Emmendörffer, *Der ferne Gott*, pp. 17-38, 294.

    28.   J.H. Tigay, 'On Evaluating Claims of Literary Borrowing', in M.E. Cohen *et al.*
(eds.), *The Tablet and the Scroll: Near Eastern Studies in Honor of William W. Hallo*
(Bethesda, MD: Capital Decisions, 1993), p. 255.

cuneiform literacy survived in the Levant after the beginning of the Iron Age. Consequently, any reading knowledge of cuneiform texts would have to be acquired *de novo* by scribes in the monarchical era. There is a case for the transmission of some Akkadian literature to Iron Age Judah. The most likely candidates are royal inscriptions, omen and incantation texts, and the Neo-Assyrian loyalty oath. But an argument even for this limited amount of cuneiform knowledge is built on a liberal interpretation of meagre evidence. During the Iron Age, familiarity with Akkadian in the native states of western Syria and the Levant seems to have been marginal at best. Available indicators of Mesopotamian cultural influence in Iron Age Judah suggest that it was primarily Neo-Assyrian technology (including divination techniques) and instruments of statecraft that impressed Jerusalem's elite. The second category would include both royal inscriptions and the Neo-Assyrian loyalty oath.[29]

The situation changes, of course, in the period when much of Jerusalem's cultural leadership was exiled to Babylon, a region where the lamentation tradition native to Mesopotamia continued to be practised into Seleucid times. But, even in the exilic era, influence would be dependent on the familiarity of Judah's intellectuals with the language of traditional scholarship, as the Mesopotamian lament tradition is primarily attested in Sumerian.[30] Such cultural knowledge would require time both to develop and assimilate. It is difficult to imagine, therefore, that the poetry of the *balag* and *eršemma* could have affected the liturgies of Judah in the first generation of exile (i.e. before c. 570). Consequently, the thesis of Mesopotamian influence can only be seriously entertained in cases of community lament that are judged to be later exilic or postexilic in origin.

4.2.2. *A Pre-exilic Genre of City-Lament in Ancient Judaism?*

Dobbs-Allsopp has attempted to show that there was a native tradition of city-lament in pre-exilic Israelite religion to which the (exilic) poems in Lamentations are related.[31] His argument relies on motifs in biblical oracles against the nations and a number of prophetic indictments of

---

29. William S. Morrow, 'Cuneiform Literacy and Deuteronomic Composition', *BO* 62 (2005), pp. 204-213.

30. There is limited evidence for an Akkadian lament tradition, see Ferris, *Genre of Communal Lament*, pp. 26-27. Emmendörffer (*Der ferne Gott*, p. 294) identifies the *balag* UDAM KI AMUS ('It Touches the Earth like a Storm') as a possible missing link between the poetry and Lamentations and the early Sumerian city laments. On the one hand, this Mesopotamian poem lifts whole lines out of the Sumerian 'Lamentation over Ur', on the other hand it is attested in a bilingual Akkadian-Sumerian version. However, the *balag*-tradition was clearly performed in Sumerian. The existence of an Akkadian translation was probably furnished for the purposes of study only.

31. Dobbs-Allsopp, *Weep, O Daughter*, pp. 7-8.

Israel or Judah. Significant characteristics of the city-lament motif shared between Mesopotamian and biblical witnesses are supposed to include subject matter (e.g. images of the destroyed city), poetic techniques (e.g. the motif of the impartial observer) and personification of the city or country as a weeping woman.[32]

If one follows the logic of Dobbs-Allsopp's thesis, there were two forms of community lament native to pre-exilic and exilic Israel: the protests of national defeat and the city-lament. Two features particularly distinguish the city-laments of Lamentations from the protests of national defeat: the appearance of the weeping woman motif and the use of the *qînâ* metre. Some control over Dobbs-Allsopp's thesis can be obtained by searching for citations of community-laments in prophetic contexts, the source of his comparative materials (§4.2.2.1). If there is evidence of a genre of city-lament in the *qînâ* metre in which the weeping woman motif is prominent, one might expect it to appear in such citations.

4.2.2.1. *Fragmentary Citations of Corporate Complaint in Prophetic Sources.*
Biblical references are mainly derived from Gunkel's catalogue.[33] My list is limited to citations with complaint elements (Gunkel's list also contains other texts without complaining material). Citations with penitential motifs but without complaint against God will be reserved for Chapter Seven, as this category does not seem to be important in either the corpus of biblical community complaints or in the Mesopotamian lament tradition.[34]

First Person Singular References
A number of complaints use the first person singular. It is often unclear who the speaker is. Although the personified city or land may be indicated, in other cases it is more likely to be the prophet, and in some cases the speaker could be God.[35] The absence of two texts from this list warrants comment. The list of I-complaints does not include the first person observations in the prophecy over Moab's destruction in Isa. 15.5; 16.9-11. These texts report the reactions of an observer, who is not a participant in the communal suffering they record. There are similarities between the

---

32.   Dobbs-Allsopp (*Weep, O Daughter*, pp. 30-96) has nine categories of matching generic features: subject and mood, structure and poetic technique (including authorial point of view), divine abandonment, assignment of responsibility, the divine agent of destruction, descriptions of destruction, the weeping goddess, lamentation and restoration of the city (including return of the gods).

33.   Gunkel and Begrich, *Introduction to the Psalms*, p. 82.

34.   Bouzard, *We Have Heard*, pp. 143-44.

35.   In the case of lament by God, see, e.g. the analysis of Jer. 12.7-12; 15.5-9 and 18.13-17 in Kiss, *Die Klage Gottes*, pp. 199-208. I have not used Kiss's work here, because these are not citations of communal lament.

first person narrative voice in Isaiah 15–16 and the motif of the poet as internal observer in Lamentations and in the Mesopotamian lament tradition.[36] But the narrative voice is not the voice of the suffering city or people.

Isa. 40.27. Jacob's statement that 'my way is hid from YHWH' is a complaint about divine absence.

Isa. 49.14. God-complaint in the form of an accusatory statement appears in Zion's lament, 'YHWH has forsaken me'.

Isa. 49.21. Zion cites her personal distress of bereavement and abandonment in the exile (I-complaint).[37]

Jer. 3.4aβ.b-5a. The quotation with accusatory questions is found inside a lawsuit form (*rîb*) that the prophet speaks in YHWH's name to indict Israel.[38] The context of the people's complaint appears to be a drought.[39] The claim 'my father, you are the friend of my youth' makes this a complaint with a first person singular reference.

Jer. 4.19-21. The land of Judah or the city of Jerusalem are the most fitting subjects of the complaint in vv. 19-21. Verse 22 has been added as a gloss to explain why the destruction took place (because of the people's wickedness).[40] The personified city describes its distress at imminent attack from the enemy in I-complaint. The passage contains complaint against God because of the 'how long?' question in v. 21.

Jer. 4.31. The text represents Zion bemoaning her distress at being attacked using I-complaint.

Jer 10.19-20. The text contains I-complaint that represents the response of the city or the community to the disaster hinted at in vv. 17-18. Verse 21 has been secondarily added as an explanation for the disaster.[41]

Jer. 51.34-35. According to the *qĕrē'* Jerusalem is the first person singular speaker, complaining about her experiences at the hands of the Babylonians. But the *kĕtîb* for many of the references to Jerusalem in v. 34 is in the first person plural. A divine response follows in vv. 36-37.[42]

Mic. 7.1-4a. Micah 7 is a prophetic composition that imitates liturgical poetry.[43] Verses 8-10 appear to be a speech by the suffering people;

36. Dobbs-Allsopp, *Weep, O Daughter*, p. 168.

37. Anton Schoors, *I Am God Your Savior: A Form-Critical Study of the Main Genres in Is. XL–LV* (VTSup, 24; Leiden: E.J. Brill, 1973), p. 107.

38. William L. Holladay, *Jeremiah* (Hermeneia; 2 vols.; Philadelphia: Fortress Press, 1986, 1989), I, p. 73.

39. John Bright, *Jeremiah* (AB, 21; Garden City, NY: Doubleday, 1965), p. 23; Robert P. Carroll, *Jeremiah* (OTL; London: SCM Press, 1986), p. 143.

40. Carroll, *Jeremiah*, p. 167.

41. Carroll, *Jeremiah*, p. 261; Holladay, *Jeremiah*, I, p. 342.

42. Carroll, *Jeremiah*, p. 847.

43. Francis I. Andersen and David N. Freedman, *Micah* (AB, 24E; New York:

vv. 11-13 contain an announcement of salvation by a prophetic voice. Following is petitionary material in vv. 14-17 and a section of praise in vv. 18-20.[44] One need not assume that all of these sections originally belonged to the same poem. Material in vv. 1-7 has affinities with the complaints of LI, but there is a problem in accounting for its unity: vv. 1-4a seem to represent the voice of the community, but vv. 4b-5 contain second person address. The answer to these problems is to see that the voice of the prophet is intermingled with the voice of the community in Micah 7. The prophet is exhorting the nation as well as speaking on its behalf.[45] The theme of the I-complaint in vv. 1-4a is social disintegration.

First Person Plural References
Isa. 26.13a, 16-18. Isa. 26.7-18 appears to be an imitation of liturgical genres. There is an admixture of complaint psalm elements and wisdom motifs.[46] This text is followed by two oracles of salvation in vv. 19 and 20-21. Another indication of the composite nature of this text is the odd placement of the assurance of being heard (v. 12).[47] The complaint in vv. 13a, 16-18 is mainly in the first person plural; the community is lamenting its powerlessness.

Isa. 58.3a. This is an accusation of divine inaction using 'why?' in the first person plural.[48]

Jer. 8.19aβ, 20. Jer. 8.18-23 alternates speakers; it was previously discussed in §2.2.1.3. The personified community or city speaks in vv. 19aβ, 20 (we-complaint). An explanatory gloss has been added in v. 19b to explain the reason for the destruction (the people's idolatry). The questions about God in v. 19aβ are rhetorical, not complaining. The condition the people lament in v. 20 appears to be drought.[49]

Jer. 9.18. Verse 18 is a citation of we-complaint. The people have been forced to leave the land and abandon all that is dear to them.[50]

Jer. 14.7-9, 19-22. The complexities of Jer. 14.1-15.4 have been previously discussed in §2.2.2.2. Here, the task is to decide if community complaint

Doubleday, 2000), p. 563; Delbert R. Hillers, *Micah* (Hermeneia; Philadelphia: Fortress Press, 1984). p. 89; Schoors, *I Am God Your Savior*, p. 36.

44.   Hillers, *Micah*, p. 89; Schoors, *I Am God Your Savior*, p. 36.

45.   Andersen and Freedman, *Micah*, p. 563.

46.   Joseph Blenkinsopp, *Isaiah 1–39* (AB, 19; New York: Doubleday, 2000), p. 368.

47.   The JPSV solves the problem by translating v. 12 as a petition; but see Otto Kaiser, *Isaiah 1–39* (OTL; Philadelphia: Westminster Press, 1974), p. 210.

48.   R.N. Whybray, *Isaiah 40–66* (NCB; Grand Rapids: Eerdmans, 1987; original edn, 1978), p. 213; Claus Westermann, *Isaiah 40–66* (OTL; Philadelphia: Westminster Press, 1969), p. 335.

49.   Carroll, *Jeremiah*, pp. 235-37.

50.   Holladay, *Jeremiah*, I, p. 313.

citations include more than vv. 7-9; 19-22. Some commentators also read vv. 2-6 as complaint.[51] But vv. 2-6 and vv. 7-9 are best read as two different poems.[52] It is not clear that the speaker of vv. 2-6 is the speaker of vv. 7-9.[53] Verses 2-6 can be read as a description of the disastrous drought that occasions the lament, rather than as complaint proper.[54] Therefore, identification of lament is limited to vv. 7-9 and 19-22.[55]

Jer. 14.7-9 contain why-questions that challenge divine activity. The passage ends with petition in the negative Imperative, a form of indirect protest of YHWH's abandonment of his people, 'do not leave us'.

Jer. 14.19-22 also protests divine abandonment. There are accusatory questions in v. 19 and indirect protest in v. 21.

Jer. 51.51. A fragment of we-complaint from the survivors of the destruction of Jerusalem is preserved in the judgment against Babylon.

Joel 1.16-18. There are citations of complaint material in Joel 1, but scholars are divided as to how to identify them. An exhortation to lament is found in vv. 5-14. The cry 'alas for the day' in v.15 is difficult to assess. According to Hans W. Wolff, the prophet is not interested in accurately portraying a complaint liturgy but has interwoven fragments of complaint with other materials in order to describe the devastations of the locust attack. A fragment of we-complaint is found in vv. 16-18.[56]

Third person references

Isa. 33.7-9. There is general agreement that there is collective lament in v. 2 followed by an oracle of salvation in vv. 3-6.[57] Commentators are also generally agreed that vv. 7-13 have the pattern of lament followed by

51. For example, Schoors (*I Am God Your Savior*, p. 37) sees vv. 2-6 as the people's complaint; Henning G. Reventlow (*Gebet Im Alten Testament* [Stuttgart: Kohlhammer, 1986], p. 259) views these verses as the words of Jeremiah, interceding for the people.

52. Holladay, *Jeremiah*, I, p. 424.

53. W.A.M. Beuken and H.W.M. van Grol ('Jeremiah 14,1–15,9: A Situation of Distress and its Hermeneutics. Unity and Diversity of Form—Dramatic Development', in P.M. Bogaert (ed.), *Le Livre de Jérémie: Le prophète et son milieu, les oracles et leur transmission* [BETL, 54; Leuven: Peeters, 1981], p. 313) think the speaker of vv. 2-6 is YHWH.

54. Carroll, *Jeremiah*, p. 309.

55. Moshe Greenberg, *Biblical Prose Prayer as a Window to the Popular Religion of Ancient Israel* (The Taubman Lectures in Jewish Studies, Sixth Series; Berkeley: University of California Press, 1983), p. 60; Carroll, *Jeremiah*, pp. 310, 317.

56. Hans W. Wolff, *Joel and Amos* (Hermeneia; Philadelphia: Fortress Press, 1975), pp. 21-23. In contrast to vv. 16-18, which I have analysed as a citation of the community's lament, vv. 19-20 were identified as a prayer of the prophetic mediator in Chapter Two.

57. For example, Blenkinsopp, *Isaiah 1–39*, p. 436; Kaiser, *Isaiah 1–39*, pp. 339-40; Schoors, *I Am God Your Savior*, p. 36; Hans Wildberger, *Isaiah 28–39* (Continental Commentary; Minneapolis: Fortress Press, 2002), p. 270.

oracular response.[58] Only vv. 7-9 contain a complaint element in the strict sense. The identity of the ones uttering the complaint is uncertain. Emendation of the difficult *'er'ellām* in v. 7 yields a reference to the 'people of Ariel', an epithet for Jerusalem.[59] The lament, therefore, is likely a complaint by the city. It appears that the region has been afflicted by drought (v. 9).

Isa. 49.24. Westermann interprets v. 24 as enemy-complaint.[60] This complaint is in the form of question but the verbs are not explicitly directed at divine actions.

Joel 2.17. The citation consists of two petitions for YHWH to act motivated by a complaint in the form of an accusatory question, 'Why should they say among the peoples, "Where is their God?"' A similar protest appears in Pss. 79.10a and 115.2.

One of the motivations for listing the sources in §4.2.2.1 was to test citations of community complaints against the prophetic materials that Dobbs-Allsopp identifies as parallels to motifs of city-lament in Mesopotamia. Outside the book of Jeremiah, there is no overlap.[61] Another important observation concerns the connection between complaint texts cited in prophetic sources and the *qînâ* metre, which Dobbs-Allsopps identifies as an important marker of poetic technique in the Israelite city-lament.[62] None of the examples in §4.2.2.1, including those in Jeremiah, are written in *qînâ* metre.

Comparison of the themes found in citations of laments with first person singular and plural elements is instructive. Both kinds of citations protest divine abandonment (cf. Isa. 40.27; 49.14 and Jer. 14.7-9, 19-22)

---

58.   For example, R.E. Clements, *Isaiah 1–39* (NCB; Grand Rapids: Eerdmans, 1980), p. 266; Kaiser, *Isaiah 1–39*, p. 340; Schoors, *I Am God Your Savior*, p. 36; Wildeberger, *Isaiah 28–39*, p. 281.

59.   Wildberger, *Isaiah 28–39*, p. 283. See also the translation in *JPSV*.

60.   See Schoors, *I Am God Your Savior*, p. 120; Westermann, *Isaiah 40-66*, p. 218.

61.   Prophetic oracles held by Dobbs-Allsopp (*Weep, O Daughter*, pp. 100-54) to contain parallels to motifs in Lamentations and the Mesopotamian laments include,

Oracles against the Nations:

> Isa. 13.1-22; 14.28-32; 15.1–16.14; 23.1-14; 47.1-15; Jer. 46.3-12, 14-24; 47.1-7; 48.1-47; 49.1-6, 23-27; 50.1–51.58; Ezek. 26.15-18; 27.1-11, 26-36; 32.1-16; Nah. 2.4-14; 3.1-7, 8-11; Zeph. 2.13-15.

Oracles against Israel and Judah:

Isa. 1.7-9, 21-26; 3.25–4.1; 22.1-14; 52.1-2; Jeremiah 4–6; 8–10; 14.17; Amos 5.1-3, 16-17, 18-21; Mic. 1.2-16; 4.9-10; Zeph. 3.14-20.

62.   Dobbs-Allsopp, *Weep, O Daughter*, pp. 42-43, 170.

and complain of agricultural disasters (cf. Jer. 3.4aβ.b-5a and Jer. 8.19aβ, 20; Joel 1.16-18) as well as military defeat. But the Mesopotamian city-lament genre never bewails agricultural disasters outside the context of military defeat and the poems in Lamentations which contain the personified voice of the weeping woman do not contain direct protest against God (cf. Lamentations 1–2 and 4).[63] There is evidence that a form related to LI could be used by community representatives to pray on behalf of the community (see §4.4). Therefore, the appearance of I-complaint, by itself, is not a sufficient indication of a city-lament genre separate from the form of argumentative prayer.

The texts in Jeremiah require additional comment because they belong to sections of prophetic discourse that Dobbs-Allsopp identifies as under the influence of the city-lament genre. The significant cases are the complaints uttered by the personified city in Jer. 3.4aβ.b-5a; 4.19-21, 31; 10.19-20; 51.34-35. First person singular references, however, can be used for community protests. Though the motif is not well attested in the protests of national defeat (cf. Isa. 63.7; Ps. 44.16), allusions to the singular the community occur in Isa. 40.27 and 49.14. Neither is identified by Dobbs-Allsopp as representative of the city-lament genre. Jer. 3.4aβ.b-5a is a citation of lament on behalf of the community in the context of a drought; it cannot be a citation of city-lament, because city-laments assume destruction by military power. The *kĕtîb* in the case of Jer. 51.34 shows that this passage is connected to the rhetoric of the protests of national complaint, because it is in the first person plural.

The texts of Jer. 4.19-21, 31; 10.19-20, therefore, are the most suggestive for comparisons with the Mesopotamian city-lament genre. However, Dobbs-Allsopps does not believe the prophetic references to city-lament in biblical contexts imply cultic performance.[64] This can only mean that the prophet himself is imagining the sufferings of Zion and articulating them. On what basis would he do so? There are similarities between the city destruction imagery articulated in Jer. 4.19-21, 31; 10.19-20 and Jer. 9.18, which is a we-complaint, a typical motif of the protests of national defeat. Their distinction from Dobbs-Allsopp's reconstructed city-lament is demonstrated by the fact that none is in *qînâ* metre.

In addition to the reasoning of the last three paragraphs, the general absence of complaint in Dobbs-Allsopp's biblical citations is a significant argument against the thesis that there was a native city-lament genre in Israel. Westermann thought prophetic texts of the kind cited by Dobbs-Allsopp adapted motifs belonging to the dirge to oracles of judgment

---

63. Cf. Dobbs-Allsopp, *Weep, O Daughter*, pp. 178-81.
64. Dobbs-Allsopp, *Weep, O Daughter*, p. 162.

against Israel, Judah and the nations.[65] In the absence of indications of a distinct genre of complaint on the city-lament model which was native to ancient Israel, I accept Westermann's analysis of the composition of the prophetic texts of judgment. I conclude that pre-exilic Israel did not know of a genre of city-lament in addition to the form used for protests of national defeat. Implications of this conclusion for the origins of the book of Lamentations will be explored in the next chapter. For the present, focus will remain on the protests of national defeat.

Dobbs-Allsopp also wants to bring the protests against national defeat in Psalms 44; 60; 74; 79; 80 and 83 into his discussion.[66] By and large the purpose of Mesopotamian laments is to appease an offended deity.[67] But there is no indication (i.e. no parallel to the 'heart-pacification motif' common in Mesopotamian laments) that the purpose of the protests of national defeat is appeasement of an angry god. Though YHWH is often depicted as wrathful, the major appeal of the biblical poems is to YHWH's sense of reason: the situations they protest are contradictory to the conditions that bind YHWH and Israel in their relationship together. The structural elements in the protests of national defeat point to an argumentative cast that is absent from the Mesopotamian laments.[68]

The theological focus of the protests of national defeat provides an important reason for refusing to derive them or equate them with the Mesopotamian city-lament genre. The particular modes of argumentation reflected in the extant biblical protests of national defeat arose out of unprecedented national catastrophe. Whether Israel had sinned or not does not appear to have been a principle concern to the writers of these poems. Rather these psalms spring out of a primary conviction that YHWH has an obligation to act in order to protect the God-Israel relationship.[69] This presumption of divine obligation is missing in the Mesopotamian lamentations.

The primacy of the God-Israel relationship is revealed in at least two features. First, throughout the protests of national defeat God is considered the major perpetrator of Israel's misfortunes. It is YHWH who has caused

---

65. A number of the prophetic texts that Dobbs-Allsopp identifies as witnesses to the city-lament genre appear in the list of prophetic allusions to the dirge-form set out by Westermann (*Lamentations*, p. 6): Isa 1.21-23; 14.4-21; 23.1-14; Jer. 9.9, 16-21; Ezek. 19.1-9, 10-14; 26.17-18; 27.2-36; 28.11-19; 32.12-16; Amos 5.2. If there is a linkage with these texts and the complaint tradition, it belongs to the protests of national defeat. Note that Jer. 9.16-17 suggests that the impetus for the prophet's calling for a dirge is the we-complaint in Jer. 9.18.

66. Dobbs-Allsopp, *Weep, O Daughter*, pp. 155-56.

67. Cohen, *Eršemma*, pp. 49-50.

68. Albertz, *Israel in Exile*, p. 149.

69. Haar, 'The God-Israel Relationship', p. 129.

the people to lose, sold them to their military opponents, exiled them and delivered them to unspeakable suffering.[70] It is YHWH who is chiefly responsible for their continuing desperate straits by virtue of his inactivity. The second indicator can be found in the petitions of these poems. All but absent are imprecations or cursing prayers against the enemy.[71] The enemy do not act on their own initiative; YHWH's own decisions are always prior to whatever Israel's external enemies are able to do. Consequently, throughout the protests of national defeat, it is YHWH's actions which are the decisive factor, both in creating the community's distress and also relieving it.

The fact that YHWH is regarded as having primary responsibility for the welfare of the community is directly related to the prominence of the complaint against God in protests of national defeat. But what motivates the conviction that YHWH has an obligation to act in the community's favour even when its distress is analysed as a result of sin (e.g. 79.8-9)? An easy answer would be to appeal to a covenantal theology. But the psalms of national defeat do not often invoke covenant terminology (cf. 44.18; 74.20; 89.4). Much more important is that YHWH is thought to have authored Israel's history (Isa. 63.7-14; Pss. 44.2-9; 60.8-10; 74.2; 80.9-12; 83.10-13; 89.20-38) and created all of its fundamental institutions, including covenant, kingship, and temple. It is a contradiction in terms that Israel should disappear, or that its institutions should be destroyed. By the very virtue of creating them, of calling Israel into being, YHWH has a responsibility to ensure their continuity. *Noblesse oblige.*

4.3. *Dating the Protests of National Defeat*

Since influence by Mesopotamian lament traditions on Israel's laments can be no earlier than the second generation of the exile (§4.2.1), the major interest of this section is to establish the probability that some of the protests against national defeat stem from the early exilic period or before.

There are grounds for considering that Psalm 80 or its core stem from the eighth century BCE. The primary evidence is v. 18, which presupposes the presence of a king. Psalm 80 combines traditions from the northern (vv. 2-3) and southern (vv. 12, 18) kingdoms. It is likely that the psalm was a lament for the fall of the northern kingdom composed and sung in the south with fugitives from Israel participating.[72] While either the time

---

70. Rainer Albertz, *Persönliche Frömmigkeit und offizielle Religion: Religionsinterner Pluralismus in Israel und Babylon* (Calwer Theologische Monographien Reihe A, Bibelwissenschaft 9; Stuttgart: Calwer Verlag, 1978), p. 38.
71. Albertz, *Persönliche Frömmigkeit*, p. 43.
72. Albertz, *Israel in Exile*, p. 150.

of Hezekiah or Josiah has been suggested, the work of Thomas Hieke makes a good case for a date not far after 722 BCE.[73]

Once it is admitted that one of the protests of national defeat comes from the eighth century, it is tempting to see if there are any other candidates. Following the work of Hieke, Beat Weber has suggested that Psalm 74 can be dated to the same time period. Weber reads the reference to Mt. Zion in Ps. 74.2c as the dwelling from which YHWH is called to come in order to survey the ruins of other cult places. These sanctuaries are the 'meeting places of God' mentioned in v. 8. Psalm 74 has in mind the destruction of Israel's holy places by Assyrian troops and the subsequent installation of their own cult-symbols when the northern kingdom was destroyed.[74]

The best cases for compositions from the early exilic period are Psalms 44 and 79. In its present form, Psalm 44 refers to the trauma of exile.[75] Indicators include the accusation that YHWH has scattered the community among the nations (v.12) and sold them for no gain (v. 13, thus fulfilling the curse of Deut. 32.30).[76] There are also resonances with the poetry of the Second Isaiah, particularly with the motif of waking the sleeping God in Isa. 51.9-11 (cf. Ps. 44.24).[77] A reason for dating Psalm 44 early in the exilic period is the absence of complaint about the duration of national distress. The thrust of Psalm 44 is simply to protest that YHWH has been the instigator of Israel's military defeat. The psalmist argues that the people had a legitimate expectation that the divine warrior who was victorious in the past would prevail over their enemies. Instead there has been a reversal that feels like betrayal, given its cruelty and apparent lack of motivation.[78]

---

73. Thomas Hieke, *Psalm 80 – Praxis eines Methoden-Programms: Eine literaturwissenschaftliche Untersuchung mit einem gattungskritischen Beitrag zum Klagelied des Volkes* (Arbeiten zu Text und Sprache im Alten Testament, 55; St Ottilien: EOS Verlag, 1997), pp. 422-23; see Beat Weber, 'Zur Datierung der Asaph-Psalmen 74 und 79', *Bib* 81 (2000), p. 522.

74. Weber, Zur Datierung der Asaph-Psalmen 74 und 79', pp. 530-31; Bouzard (*We Have Heard*, pp. 174-76) also offers some cogent arguments for dating Psalm 74 prior to the Josianic centralization of sacrificial worship.

75. Psalm 44 may draw on pre-exilic tradition in vv. 2-9; see Walter Beyerlin, 'Innerbiblische Aktualisierungsversuche: Schichten im 44. Psalm', *ZTK* 73 (1976), pp. 447.

76. Beyerlin, 'Schichten im 44. Psalm', pp. 456-57; Loren D. Crow, 'The Rhetoric of Psalm 44', *ZAW* 104 (1992), p. 397.

77. Bernard F. Batto, 'The Sleeping God: An Ancient Near Eastern Motif of Divine Sovereignty', *Bib* 68 (1987), pp. 168-70. Crow ('Rhetoric of Psalm 44', p. 337) points to a community of thought between Ps. 44.13 and Isa. 50.1.

78. Broyles, *Conflict of Faith and Experience*, pp. 140-44.

Psalm 79 also has a claim as an early exilic composition because of its explicit geographical references to Jerusalem (vv. 1, 3) and its description of the wholesale slaughter of its inhabitants.[79] These details are commensurate with what is known about the conquest of Jerusalem in 587 BCE. The first Babylonian conquest took place in March of 597. The Babylonian Chronicle suggests that after a short siege, the city was captured, heavily plundered and its monarch exiled. A second rebellion under the substitute king, Zedekiah, led to a two-year siege of Jerusalem in the late 580s. By its end, there was famine in the city. A few weeks after Jerusalem was captured, the temple, royal palace and homes of the aristocracy were burned to the ground. The city walls were torn down. Some surviving royal and temple officials, military commanders and provincial leaders were rounded up and summarily executed. There was also wide-ranging destruction in the countryside, particularly affecting the fortress towns, which were pillaged and despoiled. There is no way to estimate the casualties, but it is safe to assume that a fair percentage of Judah's manpower and leadership was killed off.[80]

The other psalms of national defeat are either exilic or early postexilic compositions. Psalm 60 is preoccupied with maintaining a claim on the central hill-country. References to conflict with Edom point to late monarchical conditions at the earliest. But these appear in an oracle of salvation that has been reused to motivate complaint (vv. 8-10). This re-appropriation points to exilic or postexilic conditions.[81]

It is likely that the oppressive neighbours listed in Ps. 83.7-9 do not reflect a single historical situation. They are a synthesis of traditions made in the exilic or postexilic era.[82]

Psalm 89 presupposes the continuity of promises to the Davidic dynasty. But this ideal is brought into sharp contrast by analysis of the present situation, which is either the exilic or postexilic era.[83] Evidence for literary borrowings can be found in resemblances to Deuteronomistic texts such as 2 Samuel 7 and material in the Second Isaiah and Lamentations.[84]

---

79. Weber (Zur Datierung der Asaph-Psalmen 74 und 79", p. 531) regards Psalm 79 as a exilic derivative of the earlier Psalm 74.

80. J.M. Miller, and J.H. Hayes. *A History of Ancient Israel and Judah* (Philadelphia: Westminster Press, 1986), pp. 408-16).

81. Gerstenberger, *Psalms*, I, p. 240; Albertz, *Israel in Exile*, p. 142.

82. Gerstenberger, *Psalms*, II, p. 121; Emmendörffer (*Der Ferne Gott*, p. 195) thinks that Psalm 83 represents a late stage in the development of the community complaints he discusses.

83. For example, Albertz favours an exilic date (*Israel in Exile*, pp. 144-54); Emmendörffer (*Der ferne Gott*, pp. 230-31) advocates a postexilic date.

84. Gerstenberger, *Psalms*, II, p. 151.

Dating Isa. 63.7–64.11 is disputed; but the argument is limited to whether the poem is best assigned to the exilic or postexilic era.[85] A date at the end of the exilic period is suggested by the confession of sin in Isa. 64.4, which has an unusual form: divine wrath is not the consequence of sin but its cause; the fact that the community is not conforming to divine standards is attributed to prior abandonment by YHWH. The complaint against God is due to unrealized hopes for the full restoration of the community of faith despite their return to Judah after exile. The discouraged returnees have to deal with opposition and ethical failings in the community,[86] which is also the subject of communal lament in Isa. 59.9-13 (another text from Trito-Isaiah). Since the Temple remains are described as consumed by fire (64.10), this protest prayer might be connected to services for rebuilding the temple c. 520 BCE.

4.4. *Origins of the Protests of National Defeat*

I see no reason not to date Psalms 44 and 79 to shortly after the destruction of Jerusalem in 587 BCE, i.e. in the first generation of the exile. These poems are formally related to Psalms 74 and 80, which can be dated to the eighth century. The dating of these poems indicates that the genre of protests of national defeat is native to ancient Judaism. Its origins cannot be due to influence by Mesopotamian models. The value of the Mesopotamian parallels, therefore, is analogical. There are a number of shared motifs that point to a common culture of argumentative prayer in the Near East that ancient Jewish and Mesopotamian poets drew on in various ways.[87]

As in the case of psalms of LI, the biblical material is not rich enough to indicate how the form of argumentative prayer represented by the protests of national defeat first arose in ancient Israelite religion. Among recent scholars, Emmendörffer has made a strong case for the derivation of the protests of national defeat from the psalms of LI. But each of his major arguments can be rebutted:

- The use of the question 'why' as opposed to 'how long' (cf. Pss. 44.24-25; 74.1) is a mark of influence from LI.[88] But accusatory

---

85. For example, Westermann (*Isaiah 40-66*, 386) dates the poem not long after the fall of Jerusalem in 587; Albertz (*Israel in Exile*, pp. 145-46) prefers a late exilic date; while Emmendörffer (*Der ferne Gott*, pp. 266-67) prefers to read the psalm as postexilic composition.

86. Robert Carroll, *When Prophecy Failed* (New York: Seabury, 1979), pp. 152-53.

87. Steymans, 'Traces of Liturgies in the Psalter', pp. 214-15.

88. Emmendörffer, *Der ferne Gott*, pp. 83, 118.

questions in the Mesopotamian city lament tradition include 'why' as well as 'how long' and 'until when' (§4.2.1.2). Therefore, they are appropriate to expressions of community complaint.

- The concatenation of motifs of rejection, the wrath of YHWH and the divine storm in Ps. 74.1 have their original context in LI.[89] But all of these motifs are attested in Mesopotamian city-lament traditions,[90] which is a form of corporate complaint.

- The call to YHWH to 'rise up' in Ps. 74.3, 22 is language derived from the traditions of LI.[91] But Emmendörffer does not consider the possibility that this is holy war language (cf. Num 10.35) which may have influenced both LI and protests of national defeat.[92]

- Citation of the enemy's words in Pss. 74.8; 79.10 and 83.5 is a stylistic mark of LI.[93] There can be no doubt that quoting enemy speech is characteristic of psalms of LI,[94] so the presence of this feature in the protests of national defeat calls for an explanation. However, citation of enemy speech is also attested in prophetic discourse describing national destructions, e.g. Isa. 10. 8-11. 13-14; 14.13-14; Jer. 6.4a, 5; 16.19; 30.17. Moreover, plurivocality is common in the Mesopotamian lament tradition. So, the citation of the enemy's words is not unexpected in national laments.

One argument of Emmendörffer's requires more comment. This is the observation that the form and tone of the petitions in Ps. 89.48-49 resemble that of petitions in LI. The first person singular is used as a corporate reference for the community.[95] The use of the first person singular as a symbol of the community has been discussed by other scholars, most notably Mowinckel who insisted that many of the psalms of LI were actually communal laments. The position taken in Chapter Three was to dismiss this claim except when there were clear indications in the text that the community was meant. This decision limits the number of cases in which I-complaint indicates the sufferings of the community, but it

89. Emmendörffer, *Der ferne Gott*, p. 84.
90. Dobbs-Allsopp, *Weep, O Daughter*, pp. 171-75.
91. Emmendörffer, *Der ferne Gott*, p. 101.
92. Ee Kon Kim, 'A Study of the Rapid Change of Mood in the Lament Psalms' (PhD Dissertation; Union Theological Seminary, 1984), p. 219.
93. Emmendörffer, *Der ferne Gott*, pp. 90, 97, 197. Westermann (*Praise and Lament*, p. 174) has observed that, although Psalm 83 is completely dominated by references to the enemy, this is an enemy that has not yet attacked but only threatens to do so. Elsewhere in the psalms, such a depiction of the enemy is only visible in LI.
94. Gunkel and Begrich, *Introduction to the Psalms*, pp. 142-43.
95. Emmendörffer, *Der ferne Gott*, pp. 237-38.

does not eliminate them. Along with Isa. 63.7; Pss. 44.16; 89.2-3, 48, one should also note the use of first person singular references in Isa. 40.27; 49.14, 21; Jer. 3.4aβ.b-5a; 4.19-21, 31; 10.19-20; 51.34-35.

In the monarchical period, it is fairly clear that kings functioned as intercessors for the state by using the complaint form (cf. Psalms 18 and 144). Commentators are divided about how to date either psalm and there is a case for assuming that both, in their present forms, are post-exilic compositions. Even so, Psalms 18 and 144 reflect older traditions in which kings used the lament-thanksgiving cycle as prayers for their welfare,[96] which was connected to the welfare of the state. The presence of royal figures interceding for the nation is well attested in biblical tradition (e.g. 2 Sam. 24.17; 1 Kgs 8.22-53; 2 Kgs 19.15-19). Royal connections with the lament tradition are also indicated by attributions of laments to David. Aside from the editorial superscriptions over many psalms of LI, note David's informal lament in 2 Sam. 24.17 and that a version of Psalm 18 is attributed to David is 2 Samuel 22.

There are also relationships between the protests of national defeat and royal ideology. Most obviously, Psalm 89 complains about YHWH's desertion of the king. In addition, there is an allusion to royal ideology in the image of the 'man of your right hand' in Ps. 80.18.[97] Evidently, there was a tradition of collective lament associated with the monarchy in pre-exilic times.

One may assume, therefore, that there was a pre-exilic tradition of offering prayers for the welfare of the state in a form related to LI. This would explain the occasional appearance of references in the first person singular in the protests of national defeat observed by Emmendörffer. An extra-biblical indication of this custom appears in the Aramaic Zakir stele in which the king depicts himself as the recipient of a favourable oracle of salvation after a personal lament during a siege.[98] But Emmendörffer's thesis demands that one come to the conclusion that the protests of national defeat represent a new form of the complaint genre. Was the emergence of a form of argumentative prayer characterized by we-complaint an innovation in the lament tradition?

---

96. On the form of Psalm 18, see Gerstenberger, *Psalms*, I, p 100; on Psalm 144, see A.A. Anderson, *Psalms* (NCB; 2 vols.; Grand Rapids: Eerdmans, 1989, original edn, 1972), II, pp. 930-31.

97. Less certain is the thesis of Beyerlin ('Schichten im 44. Psalm', pp. 453-54) that Psalm 44 may be composite, with its present form built on a pre-existing royal prayer now preserved in Ps. 44.2-9. Others would defend the unity of the psalm, e.g. Crow, 'The Rhetoric of Psalm 44', p. 400; Gerstenberger, *Psalms*, I, p. 183.

98. *KAI* 202.

I have already noted alteration between I- and we-complaint attested in the protests of national defeat (cf. Isa. 63.7–64.11; Psalms 44; 74). Though unusual, there are also we-complaint passages in the Mesopotamian city-lament tradition.[99] A shift between first person singular and plural references seems a likely rhetorical trope in prayers uttered by a representative on behalf of the community. Since one of the oldest of the Psalter's protests on national defeat typically refers to the community in the first person plural (Psalm 80). I conclude that the we-lament was firmly anchored in the traditions of Israel's collective prayers in the pre-exilic period.

While argumentative prayer was probably the typical form for community supplications in the pre-exilic period, it is not the case that the complaint against God would always have been prominent. There was a tradition of lamenting supplication in biblical culture involving a set of ritual actions that included adopting a posture of mourning (ripping clothes, covering one's head with ashes, wearing sackcloth), prolonged and pronounced weeping, fasting, and seeking out a sacred place to perform such actions and make various kinds of offerings.[100] It is instructive to note that this kind of ritual activity accompanied a number of different types of prayer. Elements of this ritual pattern are attested for community complaints against God (e.g. Josh. 7.6; Judg. 21.2-4), obtaining an oracle (e.g. Judg. 20.23, 26-27), news of approaching destruction (e.g. Jer. 6.26; Amos 5.16-17; Jon. 3.5-9) or its consequences (e.g. Isa. 15.2-5; 32.9-14; Jer. 4.8; Joel 1.13-14; Mic. 1.8-16), and as preliminary acts to supplication or prayers for help (e.g. Ezra 8.21; 2 Chron. 20.3). Similar actions accompany penitential rituals and prayers (e.g. Jer. 3.21; Zech. 7.3). In other words, fasting and mourning rites were indicated in Israel in the face of various communal troubles including natural and political calamities, apotropaic rites, and penitential services.[101]

Although many of the references in the previous paragraph come from exilic texts (or later), the evidence can be extrapolated in order to imagine what would have been typical practice in the monarchical period. Gunkel already proposed that the form of lament in ancient Israel would vary depending on the needs of the occasion and how the disaster was analysed. There would be penitence in a situation understood as divine punishment (e.g. Hos. 6.1; 14.3); but in other situations different emphases might come to the fore. Such concerns would include supplication (e.g.

---

99. Examples are found in Michalowski, *Destruction of Sumer and Ur*, pp. 51, ll. 229-33, 241-42; 61, ll. 400-402; Cohen, *Canonical Lamentations*, pp. 58, ll. 38-41; 333, l. 127; 398, l. 204; 719, ll. 21-22.

100. Gunkel and Begrich, *Introduction to the Psalms*, pp. 82-84.

101. Ferris, *Genre of Communal Lament*, pp. 105-108.

2 Kgs 19.15-19; 2 Chron. 20.6-12), seeking for an oracle (e.g. Judg. 20.23, 26-27) or complaint (e.g. Joel 2.17).[102] The complaint against God is prominent in two circumstances in particular: national defeat and agricultural disasters (e.g. drought).

A liturgical difference between the administration of the psalms of LI and the protests of national defeat can be discerned in the fact that the element of assurance of being heard/the vow of praise is usually missing in the latter (exceptions are Pss. 60.14 and 79.13). But one can discern a functional equivalent to the assurance of being heard in the oracles of salvation that became attached to community complaints. This element is not visible in the psalms; but among the texts surveyed in §4.2.2.1 examples of salvation oracles occur in Isa. 26.19, 20-21; 33.10-13; 58.3-7; Jer. 9.19-23; 51.36-37 and Mic. 7.11-13.[103] These passages are not all contemporary with the complaints they respond to, but they point to a common practice.

The *locus classicus* of the oracle of salvation is Isaiah 40–55. These poems often contain oracles and proclamations of salvation in response to community complaints (either in the form of individual or collective lament) to which the poetry of the Second Isaiah alludes.[104] Because it is common there, I suggest that the oracle of salvation represents typical liturgical practice associated with protests of national defeat. There is no assurance of being heard in most protests of national defeat because the element was provided by a priestly or prophetic functionary.

Recent study suggests that the oracle of salvation enjoyed its *floruit* during the exilic era.[105] But the oracle of salvation is derived from responses to individual laments and prayers by officials such as kings, military commanders and prophets in the pre-exilic period.[106] Probably, when a community representative used the argumentative prayer form in the pre-exilic period, the prayer would be answered by a salvation oracle (cf. the Zakir stele). Therefore, the form of the protests of national defeat (with absence of the vow of praise) may represent a traditional form of argumentative prayer used by community representatives, because it was expected that such prayers would be answered by a prophetic message of assurance.

The national character of the protests of national defeat helps to identify the circle responsible for their composition and performance. Some biblical

---

102. Gunkel and Begrich, *Introduction to the Psalms*, pp. 84, 88.

103. For a fuller list of biblical examples, see Schoors, *I Am God Your Savior*, pp. 36-37.

104. Schoors, *I and God Your Savior*, pp. 45-46; Norman K. Gottwald, *The Hebrew Bible: A Socio-Literary Introduction* (Philadelphia: Fortress Press, 1985), pp. 493-94.

105. Albertz, *Israel in Exile*, pp. 178-79.

106. Albertz, *Israel in Exile*, pp. 170-71.

references to lament and mourning practices point to the engagement of trained lay persons (e.g. Amos 5.16-17).[107] Moreover, the last chapter suggested that the psalms LI reflect a tradition of oral composition by expert poets that was only gradually integrated into the cult. But such data cannot be extrapolated to the composition of the protests of national defeat. Their references to the temple locate them under the aegis of the Jerusalem cult. In all probability, they were composed by expert cultic poets associated with the temple establishment. The postexilic context of Joel suggests that both prophet (1.19-20) and priest (2.17) might participate in the articulation of public lament. Although Joel probably is a postexilic document, the cooperation of prophet and priest is also indicated for late monarchical times (e.g. Jer. 2.8; 6.13; 8.10; 14.18; 23.11). But a number of citations in the prophetic corpus suggest another voice than the prophet's own. This is apparent in the citations of community lament in Isa. 40.27 and 49.14 as well as some of the passages in Jeremiah (e.g. Jer. 3.4aβ.b-5a; 14.7-9, 19-22). It is possible the protests of national defeat were composed and performed by a guild of temple singers.[108]

4.5. *The Development of the Protests of Community Distress*

As historical conditions shifted, the poetry of national protest changed as well. Protests against the fact of defeat became protests over the duration of national distress as the exile continued (Isa. 63.7–64.11; Psalm 60) into the postexilic period (Psalm 83). A general scholarly opinion connects the protests of national defeat with the proclamation of a public fast.[109] On this model, ceremonies involving these poems were episodic and *ad hoc* in nature. But they may have also been used in regular services of lament in the exilic and postexilic period.[110] One of these is mentioned in Zech 7.3, 5; 8.19 as the fast of the fifth month. This regular ceremony commemorated the day of the first temple's destruction.[111]

---

107. There were professional mourners guilds in both ancient Israel and Mesopotamia, see Ferris, *Genre of Communal Lament*, pp. 74-75, 80-81.

108. See Mowinckel, *Psalms in Israels Worship*, II, pp. 91-92.

109. Broyles, *Conflict of Faith and Experience*, p. 20.

110. Steymans ('Traces of Liturgy in the Psalter', pp. 226-27) thinks that Psalms 79–83 constitute a liturgy for a single day of New Year's celebrations. Although he cautiously suggests that this liturgy could be dated to the eighth century, he ignores the probability that Weber's work (on which he relies) indicates that Psalm 79 is an exilic derivative of the earlier Psalm 74. Steyman's allows, however, for the possibility that such a liturgy could also be a postexilic creation and this suggestion fits better with the dating of both Psalms 79 and 83.

111. John Day, *Psalms* (OTG; Sheffield: Academic Press, 1992), p. 33.

Besides occasions for protests of national defeat, one must also account for the protests of community distress attested by Psalms 9–10; 77; 85; 90; 94; 108 and 115. These psalms seem to reflect postexilic conditions; many of them also show influence of the LI genre. According to Albertz, such innovations were necessary to compensate for a loss of confidence in the historical intervention of Yhwh. Israel could rediscover itself in the fate of the individual sufferer. As a result, petitions for Israel, Zion or the congregation could be articulated in models originally used for the suffering of the individual.[112]

A second explanation for the influence of LI proceeds from the suggestion that it is likely that psalms of LI were incorporated into public worship in the exilic and postexilic period.[113] This led to the creation of mixed genres such as the community intercession (cf. Psalms 90 and 115). This type of community intercession differs from the older model of community complaint in that an historical dimension is almost completely lacking.[114] Another kind of mixed genre can be seen in the parallelism between Psalms 60 and 108. Ps. 108.7-14 repeats Ps. 60.7-14, but in place of the introductory complaint in Ps. 60.3-6, Ps 108.2-6 repeats motifs of trust found in Ps. 57.8-12. Good examples of the influence of the LI genre occur in the cases of Psalms 9–10; 77; 90 and 94:

Psalms 9–10. Though the speaker appears to be an individual, his concern is a corporate one. The complaint is expressed mostly clearly in Psalm 10: the arrogant, blasphemous wicked are hunting down (vv. 2, 7-10) the oppressed and unfortunate (vv. 12, 17-18). Such abstract descriptions recall the terminology used in psalms of LI.[115] But this observation must be coupled with the fact that the same malefactors are described as *gôyim*, a word which often designates non-Israelite peoples (Pss. 9.6; 16, 18, 20; 10.16). Gerstenberger believes that the poem may be directed at protesting the predations of both external rulers and the rich members of the community who are cooperating with them.[116] Whoever they are, these enemies are not regarded as God's instruments of judgement.[117] They appear, therefore, to belong to that category of enemy, so well known in the psalms of LI, who attack the divine order through their own wilful perversity.

112. Rainer Albertz, *A History of Israelite Religion in the Old Testament Period* (OTL; 2 vols.; Louisville, KY: Westminster/John Knox, 1994), II, pp. 509-510.

113. Albertz, *History of Israelite Religion*, II, p. 402.

114. Albertz, *History of Israelite Religion*, II, p. 510. See also Westermann, *Praise and Lament*, p. 55.

115. Lea Jakobzen, 'The Individual's Suffering in Psalms and in Mesopotamian Narratives [Modern Hebrew]', *Bet Miqra* 168 (2001), p. 45.

116. Gestenberger, *Psalms*, I, p. 75.

117. Broyles, *Conflict between Faith and Experience*, p. 136.

The complaint against God is found in the accusatory questions in 10.1 and 13. YHWH is not reproached for causing such affliction but for allowing it to continue unchecked while the wicked prosper. In support of the charge of divine idleness, the psalmist gives more attention to a description of the wicked then to depicting the innocent and needy.[118] Unlike most psalms of national defeat, the poem ends with a note of praise and an affirmation of divine justice (vv. 16-18).

Psalm 77. Psalm 77 is unusual in a number of ways. First, though the source of distress is national, the anxiety it expresses is personal. Secondly, the complaining questions against God in vv. 8-10 are about God, not to God. But the deity is directly addressed by an accusatory statement in v. 5 and expressions of praise beginning in v. 13.

The psalm seems to contain a mixture of motifs of LI and collective protest. Recently, Gregory Stevenson has made the case for assigning Psalm 77 to the category of LI. But his arguments actually support the other case more convincingly. Stevenson notes that Ps. 77.8 'directly questions an assertion of Exod 15.13' and 77.9-10 seem to challenge the depiction of the divine character found in Exod. 34.6.[119] Moreover, the poet invokes the memory of the Exodus not only in the concluding hymn (77.12-21) but also to describe himself: 'Just as the Israelites were greatly oppressed (Exod 1.11-14; 2.23; 3.9), the psalmist is greatly oppressed. During his 'distress' he 'groans' and finds no comfort (77.2-4). Just as the Israelites cry out...to God for help (Exod 3.7, 9; 14.10, 15) the psalmist cries out...to God for help (77.1)'.[120]

Why does the poet compare himself to a slave of the Exodus story and invoke other texts alluding to this national event? It is reasonable to assume that the saving deeds the poet wants YHWH to perform are those of the Exodus story. Since these wonders were performed for the nation as a whole, it is likely that the complaint is not about a personal problem, but concerns God's apparent neglect of his people.[121] One may read Psalm 77, therefore, as a complaint about the continuing debasement of Israel, in many ways not significantly changed in the postexilic era.

Psalm 90. It may seem that, like Psalms 39 and 102, Psalm 90 complains about the brevity of human life. But the petitions in vv. 14-17 suggest that the real issue is quality of life not its length. Evidently the community has lived under the effects of divine punishment for a long time (v.15), so much so that an entire human life span only experiences 'toil and trouble'

---

118. Broyles, *Conflict between Faith and Experience*, pp. 136-37.

119. Gregory M. Stevenson, 'Communal Imagery and the Individual Lament: Exodus Typology in Psalm 77', *Restoration Quarterly* 39 (1997), p. 220.

120. Stevenson, 'Communal Imagery and the Individual Lament', p. 218.

121. Gerstenberger, *Psalms*, II, p. 89.

(v. 10). God is considered the sole cause of the community's distress. Wrath has come upon it because of sin (vv. 7-9), but the purpose of the psalm is not penitential. Rather the poet expresses disappointment that God should be so overly preoccupied with venting his anger. Neither the intensity of divine punishment (vv. 7-8) nor its duration (vv. 13, 15) are warranted.[122] For these reasons, the poem uses an accusatory question to reinforce the petitions in v.13: 'Return, YHWH! How long? Have pity on your servants!'

It is tempting to view Psalm 90 as protesting prolonged conditions of affliction unalleviated in the postexilic period. Other collective protests probably lament this situation (e.g. Psalms 83 and 85). In its use of accusations against God (vv. 13 and 15) and its protest about the duration of divine anger, Psalm 90 resembles Psalms 74; 79; 80.

Psalm 94. Psalm 94 hints at national enemies when it mentions 'a throne of ruin' in v. 20; but they appear only as allies of the ones who are considered to be the opponents of the 'righteous'. Gerstenberger seems to be correct, therefore, in his description of the social conflict as basically internal to the community.[123] The social situation is probably close to that of Psalms 9–10. Opponents of the worshippers are allied with foreign powers and use their wealth and status to oppress their poorer relations (94.5-7). As in Psalms 9–10, the poet uses motifs of individual complaint to take their part against the wicked. Note, e.g. the confession of Trust in God as personal protector (94.22-23; cf. Pss. 9.10 and 59.17).

There is no indication that the congregation is suffering because of divine actions. The wicked have risen against the righteous for no reason. Despite the unjustified nature of this attack, God has not yet acted. For that reason, accusatory questions are directed against YHWH in 94.3: '...how long shall the wicked exult?' Like Psalm 9–10, Psalm 94 also ends with a statement of confidence in divine justice (vv. 22-23).

Changes to the expression of collective protest came about because of shifts in the political conditions of the postexilic period and new patterns of worship. Influences from the genre of LI on the expression of collective protest were motivated by a need to appropriate motifs of YHWH's care for suffering individuals to shore up failing confidence in traditional affirmations of Israel's relationship with its God. There is evidence that the community experienced hardship at the hands of its oppressive overlords in the postexilic period. Moreover, some of its wealthiest members (the

---

122. Gerstenberger, *Psalm*, II, p. 175.
123. Gerstenberger, *Psalms*, II, p. 180.

'wicked' rich) no doubt benefited from collaboration with imperial authorities in oppressing their less powerful *confrères* (the 'poor' righteous).[124] The situation parallels that of individuals suffering from the predations of those more powerful than they. Such innovations show the influence not only of sociology but also of theology on the generation of forms of complaint. In fact, theological trends arising in the exilic and postexilic would have a profound effect on the practice of argumentative prayer, as the next two chapters seek to demonstrate.

124. Cf. Nehemiah 5. See Gerstenberger, *Psalms*, II, pp. 75, 180-81.

Chapter 5

EXILIC CRITIQUE OF THE PROTEST AGAINST GOD

Chapter Four discussed the use of community protests during exilic times (597–520 BCE). Use of argumentative prayer as a means to digest the immense suffering of the destruction of Judah and Jerusalem was not without opposition, however. A vocal minority of Israel's prophets had been predicting the collapse of the nation for some time. Traditions about their visionary experiences suggest that they had come to the opinion that complaint against God for impending national devastation was unwarranted. Illustrations include material from Jeremiah and Ezekiel surveyed in Chapter Two.

Although Jer. 14.1–15.4 probably contains material that goes back to Jeremiah himself, the present form of the chapter is due to later revision.[1] Jer. 14.7-9 cites a lament of the people searching for the cause of their distress. Jer. 14.10-16 has the form of a dialogue between the prophet Jeremiah and God in which the national distress is interpreted as divine judgment and prophetic acts of intercession are rejected. Jer. 14.19-22 also contains national lament. But again prophetic intercession is rejected in 15.1-2. Even in its current form, the text seems to reflect a critical development in Jeremiah's consciousness. Jeremiah came to realize that divine judgment on Jerusalem was inescapable and that he had become the announcer of the judgment rather than intercessor for the people. God would not allow him another role.[2]

Another prophet who experienced the refusal of intercession was Ezekiel. There are complaining intercessions in his vision of the destruction of Jerusalem (Ezek. 9.8 and 11.13). Ezekiel's prayers on behalf of the

---

1. Jenö Kiss, *Die Klage Gottes und des Propheten: Ihre Rolle in der Komposition und Redaktion von Jer 11–12, 14–15 und 18* (WMANT, 99: Neukirchen–Vluyn: Neukirchener Verlag, 2003), p. 213.

2. W.A.M. Beuken and H.W.M. van Grol, 'Jeremiah 14,1–15,9: A Situation of Distress and its Hermeneutics. Unity and Diversity of Form—Dramatic Development', in P.M. Bogaert (ed.), *Le livre de Jérémie: Le prophète et son milieu, les oracles et leur transmission* (BETL, 54; Leuven: Peeters, 1981), pp. 326, 341.

populace of Jerusalem are denied, though hope is held out for those who have already been deported to Mesopotamia.

Although the protests of national defeat show no signs of assimilating the prophetic critique, other literary products from the exilic era do. Three important bodies of literature will be surveyed here including the book of Lamentations (§5.1), the poetry of Isaiah 40–55 (§5.2) and the Deuteronomistic History (§5.3). Each has indications of critical attitudes towards the tradition of lament. These works reveal trends that would affect future approaches to argumentative prayer in early Judaism (§5.4).

5.1. *Lamentations and the Logic of Complaint*

Many commentators assume a close connection between the poetry of Lamentations and the destruction of Jerusalem.[3] Some, however, have claimed that there are no historical references in the book to make such an association certain.[4] Lamentations is a highly structured literary composition, whose motifs are applicable to a plurality of communal catastrophes, such that it is still read today by contemporary Jews to mourn the destruction of both the first and the second Temples. Nevertheless, there are grounds for associating a core of the poems in Lamentations with the catastrophe of the Babylonian conquest.[5] Engagement with the poems of Lamentations occurs in the late exilic prophecy of the Second Isaiah.[6] For example, Isa. 51.17-23 contains allusions to Lam. 2.13-19,[7] and Lam. 4.1.[8] Inter-textual references between Lamentations and the Second Isaiah reinforce the impression that the poetry of Lamentations is associated with the destruction of Jerusalem.

I agree with the thesis that the poetry of Lamentations represents the development of a new genre in biblical literature.[9] What forces were instrumental in this literary development? I will suggest that one of the primary

---

3. See the survey of literature in Delbert R. Hillers, *Lamentations* (AB, 7A; Garden City: Doubleday, 1972), pp. xviii-xix.

4. E.g. Iain Provan, *Lamentations* (NCB; Grand Rapids: Eerdmans, 1991).

5. Rainer Albertz, *Israel in Exile: The History and Literature of the Sixth Century B.C.E.* (Studies in Biblical Literature, 3; Atlanta: Society of Biblical Literature, 2003), pp. 158-59.

6. Tod Linafelt, *Surviving Lamentations: Catastrophe, Lament, and Protest in the Afterlife of a Biblical Book* (Chicago: Chicago University Press, 2000), pp. 62-79.

7. Benjamin D. Sommer, *A Prophet Reads Scripture: Allusion in Isaiah 40-66* (Contraversions, Jews and Other Differences; Stanford: Stanford University Press, 1998), pp. 128-30.

8. Anton Schoors, *I Am God Your Savior: A Form-Critical Study of the Main Genres in Is. Xl-LV* (VTSup, 24; Leiden: E.J. Brill, 1973), p. 129.

9. Albertz, *Israel in Exile*, pp. 155-56.

motives in the composition of Lamentations was to accommodate the prophetic account for Jerusalem's destruction with the community's complaints. Among other techniques, the prophetic judgments against Judah adapted the dirge form to announce the nation's doom (see §4.2.2). The laments in Lamentations mix the dirge and the complaint forms.[10] This literary technique reflects a characteristic of the theology of Lamentations, which mixes admission of guilt with the nation's complaints of excess suffering.

The mixture of dirge and complaint also marks the Mesopotamian lament tradition.[11] Scholarship remains divided on the question as to whether the poetry of Lamentations was written under the influence of the Mesopotamian lament tradition or not. Studies that relied heavily on the Sumerian city-laments from the Ur III period have been rightly criticized by Thomas McDaniel for the improbability of direct literary influence.[12] However, Claus Westermann has faulted McDaniel's study for failing to note the significance of the shared literary tactic of mixing complaint and dirge motifs.[13] A number of scholars have responded to the problem of positing dependence on the early Sumerian city-laments by pointing to the continuation of the Mesopotamian lament tradition through the poetry of the *balag* and *eršemma* compositions, which remained in use right through to Seleucid times in Babylonia.[14] Nevertheless, results continue to be ambiguous. Besides the mixture of dirge and complaint, there are significant shared features including the poet as internal observer (Lam. 2.11, 13-19) and the weeping city motif (Lam. 1.11c-22; 2.20-22).[15] But Paul Ferris points out some surprising omissions if there was real literary dependency, including absence of motifs of the evil storm, the

---

10. Linafelt, *Surviving Lamentations*, pp. 36-43.

11. See Claus Westermann, *Lamentations: Issues and Interpretation* (Minneapolis: Fortress Press, 1994), pp. 9-10, 15-16.

12. Thomas F. McDaniel, 'The Alleged Sumerian Influence upon Lamentations', *VT* 18 (1968), pp. 198-209.

13. Westermann, *Lamentations*, p. 22.

14. E.g. William C. Gwaltney, 'The Biblical Book of Lamentations in the Context of Near Eastern Lament Literature' in W.W. Hallo, J.C. Moyer and L.G. Perdue (eds), *Scripture in Context. II. More essays on the comparative method* (Winona Lake, IN: Eisenbrauns, 1983), pp. 191-211; F.W. Dobbs-Allsopp, *Weep, O Daughter of Zion: A Study of the City-Lament Genre in the Hebrew Bible* (BibOr, 44; Rome: Pontifical Biblical Institute, 1993), pp. 167-82; Michael Emmendörffer, *Der ferne Gott: Eine Untersuchung der alttestamentlichen Volksklagelieder vor dem Hintergrund der mesopotamischen Literatur* (Forschungen zum Alten Testament, 21; Tübingen: Mohr Siebeck, 1998), pp. 17-38.

15. For references to the Mesopotamian parallels, see Dobbs-Allsopp, *Weep, O Daughter*, pp. 168, 178-81.

abandoned sheepfold, the divine flood and petitions for heart pacification.[16] Caution is required.[17]

Theories of literary borrowing from Mesopotamian literature must address the problems of time and provenance. In fact, neither concern is a barrier to the possibility of Babylonian influence. In §4.2.1, I made the claim that one should allow about a generation from the beginning of the exile (597 BCE) for Judean intellectuals deported to Babylon to acquire knowledge of the specialized literature of Mesopotamian lament. There are good reasons to date the poetry of Lamentations to the early or middle years of the exilic period.[18] A mid-exilic date corresponds to c. 550, well within the timeframe necessary for Jerusalem's deported intelligentsia to have acquired familiarity with the Sumerian texts of lament.

The problem of provenance is somewhat more difficult, but by no means insuperable. Exposure to the Mesopotamian lament tradition depends, in my opinion, on an encounter with this material in the Babylonian diaspora. I do not think such familiarity would have been possible among those poets who stayed in the environs of Jerusalem because of the specialized conditions under which the Babylonian laments were performed and studied. Westermann's survey of past scholarship notes almost unanimity on the assumption that the poems in Lamentations originated in Jerusalem; but a few voices have wanted to keep open the possibility of composition in the Babylonian diaspora.[19] Recently, both Delbert Hillers and Erhard Gerstenberger have equivocated on whether the poems of Lamentations were composed in Jerusalem or Babylon.[20]

---

16. Paul W. Ferris, *The Genre of Communal Lament in the Bible and the Ancient Near East* (SBLDS, 127. Atlanta: Scholars Press, 1992), p. 173.

17. A case in point is evaluation of the meaning of the acrostic form that organizes the poems in Lamentations 1–4. Delbert R. Hillers ('Lamentations, Book of', *ABD*, IV, p. 139) suggests it is likely that acrostic composition of the kind displayed by the poetry of Lamentations owes its origin to Mesopotamian models. But biblical acrostic poetry does not model the Mesopotamian form. Mesopotamian acrostics typically encode names or some sort of message. This is not the purpose of Biblical Hebrew acrostics. Moreover, ancient Egyptian literature had its own form of acrostic composition based on the order of numbers. This is a significant parallel, because the Hebrew letters can also stand for numbers. See Moshe Garsiel, 'Studies on the Names of the Letters of the Alphabet in Acrostic Literary Units in the Bible [Modern Hebrew]', *Bet Miqra* 139 (1994), pp. 325-26.

18. Albertz, *Israel in Exile*, p. 156. Westermann (*Lamentations*, pp. 104-105) thinks it is possible that Lamentations 1; 2; 4 and 5 were all composed between c. 587 and 550, when he believes the Second Isaiah became active and had knowledge of the poetry of Lamentations.

19. Westermann, *Lamentations*, p. 55.

20. Erhard S. Gerstenberger, *Psalms: Part 2 and Lamentations* (FOTL, 15; Grand Rapids: Eerdmans, 2001), p. 474; Hillers, 'Lamentations, Book of', p. 139.

If neither date nor provenance of Lamentations rules out the possibility of Mesopotamian influence, neither do these elements prove it. I think the opportunity for cultural sharing was high in the Babylonian diaspora and I see no real barrier to placing the composition of Lamentations in that context. But borrowing from one culture to another requires motivation as well as opportunity. The mere presence of a parallel form does not mean that it will be taken from the prestige culture and incorporated into native literature.[21]

Westermann points to a likely motivation indicated by the fact that both Lamentations and the Mesopotamian tradition of collectiive lament mix the complaint genre and the dirge. On the other hand, there remain significant divergences from the Sumerian poetry of lament. Unlike the Mesopotamian examples, the poetry that most clearly mixes dirge and complaint elements (Lamentations 1–2 and 4) does not allow for protest against God. Direct complaint against God is found in material that is formally associated with the native Israelite protests of national defeat (Lam. 3.42-45; 5.20). Besides the absence of God-complaint, there is no praise of YHWH in Lamentations 1–2 and 4. Hymnic praise of the deity is a well-attested element of Mesopotamian city-laments.[22] Where praise of YHWH occurs in Lamentations, there are relationships to the tradition of argumentative prayer. The confession of trust element in Lamentations 3 can be ascribed to the influence of the genre of LI,[23] and the brief praise in Lam. 5.19 occurs in a poetic form connected to the protests of national defeat. In my opinion, the possibility that a Babylonian literature which mixed complaint and dirge inspired the writers of Lamentations 1–2 and 4 appears unlikely, but it should be subject to further research.

Theologically, Lamentations 1–2 and 4 show appropriation of perspectives on the destruction of Jerusalem that reflect those of the critical prophetic viewpoint. This is an important motivation for their adaptation of the complaint form. The aim of Lamentations 1 is to present Zion's

---

21. This claim can be illustrated from the literature of Ugarit. Dennis Pardee ('Ugaritic Science', in P.M.M. Daviau *et al.* (eds.), *The World of the Aramaeans* [Festschrift P.E. Dion; 3 vols.; Sheffield: Sheffield Academic Press, 2002, 2003], III, pp. 233-34) has surveyed the Ugaritic texts that transmitted the 'scientific' lore of the times, mainly types of omen literature, medical texts, and lexical lists. In his summary, Pardee registers his surprise at the degree to which these texts show independence from Akkadian parallels both in lexicon and syntax. While it has been assumed that these Ugaritic documents were translations of unattested Akkadian originals, it is necessary to conclude that they reflect a West Semitic tradition that was neither eclipsed nor augmented by the flow of textual data pouring out of Mesopotamia.

22. Ferris, *Genre of Communal Complaint*, p. 42.

23. Albertz, *Israel in Exile*, p. 163.

suffering and YHWH's anger as punishment for sins, while acknowledging that YHWH was in the right (v. 18). This is close to the message of the prophets, especially Jeremiah. Lamentations 2 shows the influence of Jeremianic thought by distancing itself from the illusory prophets of salvation (Lam. 2.14, cf. Jer. 14.13-16). Similarly, Lam. 4.13 singles out Jerusalem's priests and prophets of salvation to blame for the city's demise.[24]

Structurally, Lamentations 1–5 can be divided into three groups: chs. 1–2 and 4; 3; 5. Despite its peculiarities, Lamentations 5 belongs to the class of protests of national defeat treated in the last chapter. Unusual structural features include the lengthy we-complaint in vv. 2-18 (there is a single accusatory question directed to God in v. 20) and the truncated confession of trust or retrospect in v. 19. Reasons for its inclusion with Lamentations 1–4 will be adduced below.

Lamentations 1–2 and 4 have quite a different form than the protests of national defeat. Each of these poems is written in acrostic form that can be broken into three sections. In Lamentations 1, narrative description of the city's suffering (vv. 1-11) gives way to Zion's own voice (the weeping city motif) in vv. 12-16. A third section of lament and petition by Zion occurs in vv. 18-22. Lam. 2.1-10 narrates the destruction of the city and the mournful response of its leaders. A first person voice appears in v. 11, which subsequently addresses Zion as a person (vv. 13-19). The poem ends with petition to YHWH to take notice of what has happened (vv. 20-22). Unlike Lamentations 1 and 2, the poem in Lamentations 4 has no petitions. Lam. 4.1-10 describes the suffering of the population after the conquest of the city; vv. 11-16 give reasons for the destruction (divine punishment); a third section of lament with first person plural references ends with promises of expiation for Zion and punishment for Edom (vv. 17-22). In each of these chapters the last two sections of the poem are more closely connected than the first, so it is also possible to describe the structure of these poems as one in which the acrostic poem breaks into two at about the tenth or eleventh verse.[25]

Lamentations 3 has a different form of organization than chapters 1–2 and 4. The structure of this poem is complex and disputed.[26] The poem shows a fusion of the genres of LI (vv. 1-39) and protest of national defeat (vv. 42-53), including complaints of non-forgiveness (v. 42) and other accusatory statements against God (vv. 43-45). Despite its variety, the poem is unified by the acrostic form of composition. I agree with Kathleen O'Connor that this arrangement is too complex to have been imposed

---

24. Albertz, *Israel in Exile*, p. 157.
25. Albertz, *Israel in Exile*, p. 151.
26. Gerstenberger, *Psalms*, II, p. 492.

secondarily. Consequently, the poem's imagery and message must be presumed to possess some sort of unity.[27]

The perception of a unified composition is an important indicator of the identity of the unnamed male sufferer whose voice opens the poem. Readers of the preceding two chapters in Lamentations are not prepared for the appearance of a solitary male voice (v. 1) as the emblematic sufferer, nor for the confessions of confidence in vv. 21-39. Later the poem shows an alternation between singular and plural references in vv. 47-48. It is possible to see the suffering community behind the singular references in the poem.[28]

I follow Westermann in his observation that the intent of Lamentations 3 can be recognized by starting from the central position given to the affirmation of confidence (vv. 21-39). Here the writer calls for a humble perseverance in suffering, an acknowledgement of one's own sins and a return to YHWH.[29] Structurally, this penitential posture precedes petition that is motivated by complaint. Lam. 3.26-41 admonishes the community to bear its suffering in silence, to turn away from sin and towards YHWH. According to Westermann, these motifs are marks of the influence of the theological perspective of Deuteronomy.[30] So, as with the case of Lamentations 1–2 and 4, there are indications that ch. 3 has accommodated itself to a prophetic perspective on Jerusalem's suffering.

Despite the fact that the book consists of five distinct poems, a number of commentators have insisted that Lamentations ought to be read as a literary whole.[31] There are relationships between chapters that should be described and developed.[32] In the discussion below, I will argue for relationships on the basis of the distribution of complaint and associated petitions. The last chapter showed how assumptions of the God-Israel relationship generated the poetry of collective protests. Interpretations of

27. Kathleen M. O'Connor, *Lamentations and the Tears of the World* (Maryknoll, NY: Orbis Books, 2002), p. 46.

28. Gerstenberger, *Psalms*, II, p. 493. Westermann's (*Lamentations*, pp. 68-72) identification of the predominant voice of Lamentations 3 as an individual rests on the perception of an amalgam of poetry in which the genre of individual lament predominates. Provan (*Lamentations*, pp. 80-81) also dismisses the idea that the solitary voice is a representative of the community. He identifies the main speaker in Lamentations 3 with the narrator, whose voice is already heard in Lamentations 1–2. But this narratorial voice speaks to the people and also speaks for the people (Lam. 3.47-48). The switch between first person singular and plural references is visible in other community complaints, e.g. Ps. 44.15-17.

29. Westermann, *Lamentations*, p. 193.

30. Westermann, *Lamentations*, p. 180.

31. See the survey in O'Connor, *Lamentations*, p. 13.

32. Provan, *Lamentations*, p. 29.

the God-Israel relationship are also operative in the poetry of Lamentations.

Lamentations 1 assigns the responsibility for Judah and Jerusalem's misfortunes to YHWH. Though enemies may be the immediate agents, YHWH has been the effective cause (cf. vv. 5, 12-17). There are also complaints against the enemy (vv. 10, 21) and extensive descriptions about Zion's own miserable condition (vv. 1-6, 9, 11, 20). The poem is punctuated by petitions. There are calls on YHWH to pay attention to how the enemy has behaved (v. 9), to look and see how the city is despised (v. 11) and suffering (v. 20). The poem ends with a curse against the enemies in v. 22.

How is the God-Israel relationship analyzed according to the perspective of Lamentations 1? The poem is clear that YHWH has been justified in punishing the community for its sins (vv. 8 and 18). Apparently, an acceptable punishment was the exile (forcible deportation) of its young men and women (v. 18). What is lamented is a fundamental violation of the city's sanctity against YHWH's command (v. 10).[33] Evidently, the city has been raped and desolated by an enemy who exceeded the punitive power that YHWH had the right to exercise. For that reason YHWH has an obligation to the community to put things right; hence the call for divine attention and the curse against the enemy (vv. 20-22).

Lamentations 2 is particularly full in ascribing the destruction of the city to divine action (vv. 1-9, 17). The desolate condition of the community is described in detail (vv. 9-14). By contrast, less is said about the enemy (vv. 15-16). Petition to YHWH occurs only in v. 20. But the petition is telling in terms of where the discrepancy in the God-Israel relationship lies: 'Look, YHWH, and see! With whom have you dealt thus?' What follows is a description of women eating their own children and priest and prophet slain in the sanctuary. The destruction has grown to encompass persons whom the writer believes YHWH ought to have protected. YHWH has to take responsibility for the fact that the catastrophe has grown excessive.[34] Though it was YHWH who brought the enemy on the community (v. 22) to punish sin (v. 14), the destruction has reached a point where it is counter to YHWH's values rather than commensurate with them. This reasoning is similar to that of Lamentations 1.

Though structurally different from Lamentations 1–2 (and probably later), Lamentations 3 can be considered as the compositional centre of the whole book.[35] Lamentations 3 lays out in explicit fashion the logic of complaint that characterizes the units of thought in Lamentations. In

33. O'Connor, *Lamentations*, p. 34;
34. O'Connor, *Lamentations*, pp. 42-43.
35. Albertz, *Israel in Exile*, p. 161.

Lamentations 1 and 2 there was acceptance of a certain level of community suffering as justifiable punishment for sin, and then complaint about excess affliction. This same pattern is visible in Lamentations 3: resigned acceptance (vv. 25-34) of legitimate God-caused suffering (vv. 1-18) as a result of sin (vv. 40-42) precedes complaint that leads to petition. While God remains ultimately responsible for the distress of the community (vv. 43-45), enemies have maliciously attacked the community without cause (vv. 52, 59-60). For this reason, the poem ends with petitions to YHWH to deal with Jerusalem's enemies (vv. 64-66).

Lamentations 4 falls outside the pattern established by the first three poems in the book, for it contains no petitions. There is overlap in this poem's imagery with Lamentations 1–2. YHWH's wrath is identified as the cause of the city's suffering (4.11, 16) and this destructive experience is seen as punishment for sin (vv. 6, 13). But sources of complaint in Lamentations 1 and 2 are registered without objection in Lamentations 4. The starvation of the people objected to in 1.11 is recorded without comment in 4.4; the cannibalism complained of in 2.20 is merely mentioned in 4.10.

An argument can be made, however, that Lamentations 4 also participates in the pattern discerned in Lamentations 1–3. This pattern emerges when Lamentations 4 and 5 are taken together as a unit of discourse.[36] Lamentations 5 is also anomalous in terms of the structure of Lamentations. Though it has 22 verses, these verses do not reflect the order of the Hebrew alphabet. Moreover, unlike the poetry in Lamentations 1–3, Lamentations 5 begins with petition.

It is tempting to conclude that Lamentations 5 begins with the petition that one should expect Lamentations 4 to end with. If Lamentations 5 is read as a continuation of the discourse begun in Lamentations 4, these two chapters reflect the same logic visible in Lamentations 1–3. A certain amount of suffering is accepted as the just desserts of sin, an additional amount is subject to petition. In the case of Lamentations 4, the poem ends by indicating that Zion's punishment has been fulfilled (v. 22): that is, the desperate state of the inhabitants of Jerusalem described in Lam. 4.1-20 is considered to be the wages of sin. This includes the predations of the enemy (vv. 18-20). The enemy also figures prominently in Lamentations 5, but now their actions are the object of complaint. Sin is again prominent as an explanation for the origin of this state of affairs (vv. 7, 16), but the poem laments the continued enslavement of the people by foreigners (vv. 2-4, 8, 12-13). In other words, Lamentations 4 accepts the

---

36. There are discourse relationships over the chapter boundary elsewhere in Lamentations. Note, e.g. the way Lam. 3.1 presupposes 2.22; see Provan, *Lamentations*, pp. 80-81.

destruction of the city as divine punishment, while Lamentations 5 protests its continued slavery to aliens. The sin was committed by a previous generation but the present community is bearing its consequences (v. 7). Lamentations 5 does not complain of the destruction of the city, but its continuing desolation (v. 18). It is not YHWH's punishing acts which are protested, but his enduring absence (v. 20).

This is not to claim that Lamentations 4 and Lamentations 5 form an original literary unit. The connection was created by the writer who assembled the poetry of Lamentations into something like its current literary form. Ascription of such authorial purpose is bolstered by the recognition that the acrostic form of Lamentations 1–4 suggests written, as opposed to, oral composition.[37] Moreover, scholars have recognized that, although Lamentations 5 has connections with the protests of national defeat, the lengthy we-complaint in vv. 2-18 indicates that the form of collective complaint has been adapted to accord with other chapters in Lamentations.[38] Despite their different structures, the petitions in Lamentations 1–3 also have associations with complaint psalms.[39] However, the petitions of Lamentations only occur after acknowledging the legitimacy of divine wrath at the sins of the nation.

The pattern of theological thinking uncovered in Lamentations 1; 2; 3; 4–5 shows both similarities and differences. On the one hand, the logic of these four units of thought is the same: resignation to legitimate punishment precedes petition. This is the paradigm of Lamentations 3. On the other hand, the poems differ as to what point in the destruction of Jerusalem acquiescence is no longer acceptable. Lamentations 1 draws the line at the desecration of the temple, but it accepts the exile of Jerusalem's elite. Lamentations 2 accepts the destruction of the city, but it complains when the rape of the city becomes so extreme that mothers are driven to cannibalism and consecrated people are slain in sacred space. The logic is similar to Lamentations 1: once the enemy violates an important symbol of holiness, complaint is justified. Lamentations 4–5 display a different point of protest. Lamentations 4 accepts the complete destruction of the city as the fulfillment of Jerusalem's punishment. What is unacceptable is the continuing enslavement of city and people to the enemy (Lamentations 5).

The logic of complaint in Lamentations has similarities and differences with the protests of national defeat. On the one hand, complaint is motivated in all cases by perceptions of discrepancies in the God–Israel relationship. On the other hand, lament is not conditioned by penitence and

---

37. O'Connor, *Lamentations*, pp. 12-13.
38. Hillers, *Lamentations*, p. 102; Westermann, *Praise and Lament*, pp. 174-75.
39. Albertz, *Israel in Exile*, p. 154.

the acceptance of a necessary degree of punishment in the protests of national defeat. What has happened that resignation to justified punishment is considered *de rigueur* in Lamentations prior to complaints about excess suffering? There are two answers to this question. They are not mutually exclusive. First, one can discern in Lamentations' complaints a psychological dilemma that is characteristic of victims of violence. Second, there is also a pattern of theological reasoning influenced by prophetic thought.

There is a psychological conflict that is typical of victims of violence: they are torn between the desire to deny the horrible events that overcame them and the desire to proclaim them aloud.[40] This conflict is reflected in the pattern of prayer found in Lamentations. There is a profound ambivalence in the way Lamentations describes the sufferings of Jerusalem: there is both resignation to a certain level of violence and complaint of its excess; there is both compassion for Zion as victim and justification for her punishment.[41]

Trauma can be defined as (violent) stress that is sudden, unexpected, or non-normative, exceeds the individual's perceived ability to meet its demands, and disrupts various psychological needs.[42] There is little doubt that the destruction of the First Temple with the captivity and exile of the inhabitants of Jerusalem qualifies as trauma under this definition. In view of the long tradition of the inviolability of Zion, it was certainly non-normative. It was an event that exceeded the capacity of many to encompass within the perspective of continuing faith in Israel's deity. Among various psychological needs, those for self-esteem, independence and a coherent worldview were injured.[43]

When the experience of violence conflicts with prior beliefs, the victim is often less able to reconcile the violating event and recovery is more difficult. For example, among victims of rape, it is the woman who thought she was particularly invulnerable or safe who usually has more difficulty recovering than others.[44] It is significant that rape imagery is found in

40. Judith Herman, *Trauma and Recovery* (New York: BasicBooks, rev. edn, 1997), p. 1.

41. Hugh S. Pyper, 'Reading Lamentations', *JSOT* 95 (2001), p. 56.

42. I.L. McCann and L.A. Pearlman, *Psychological Trauma and the Adult Survivor: Theory, Therapy, and Transformation* (Brunner/Mazal Psychosocial Stress Series, 21; New York: Brunner/Mazal, 1990), p. 10.

43. For a discussion of the psychological injuries entailed by Jerusalem's destruction, see William S. Morrow, 'Comfort for Jerusalem: The Second Isaiah as Counselor to Refugees', *BTB* 34 (2004), pp. 80-86. O'Connor (*Lamentations*, p. 29) also describes Zion as a victim of trauma.

44. Donald Meichenbaum, *A Clinical Handbook/Practical Therapist Manual for Assessing and Treating Adults with Post-Traumatic Stress Disorder* (Waterloo, ON: Institute Press, 1994), p. 73.

descriptions of the devastation of Jerusalem (e.g. Ezekiel 16; 23; Lamentations 1).[45] Biblical records attest to an exaggerated sense of confidence held by the population of Jerusalem about the safety and inviolability of the city due to the presence of the temple (cf. Jeremiah 7). It is not surprising if the faith community that counted on divine protection was overwhelmed by the experience of profound violation.

One effect of various kinds of abuse involves identification with the perpetrator, resulting in agreement that the violence was justified. This dynamic has been identified in Lamentations by the psychoanalytically trained Alice Miller. In the course of her discussion about recovery from child abuse, Miller discovers the cry of a victim of domestic violence in the Bible. Though she relies on a pre-critical connection between the words of Jeremiah and the poems of Lamentations, her psychological insights remain provocative. Miller's comments stem from her perception of a high degree of self-blame in the poetry of Lamentations 3. Here the poet rebels against the cruelty he and his people have experienced in the manner of a battered child. He seeks comfort in the thought that torture is no more than just punishment for his own misdemeanors. He desperately seeks consolation, finding it in his own apparent guilt, his own wickedness. This gives him hope. This child refuses to believe that the same parents who speak of love and loyalty are capable of a pitiless massacre — though this is what the truth is.[46]

Readers may object that Lamentations 1–2 and 4 present multiple images of Zion as a kind of *mater dolorosa*, as a widow violently bereft of her children, or alternately as a kind of ravished virgin daughter. But there is abundant evidence for similarity between the psychological damage of child abuse, domestic violence and the effects of war.[47] Recently, attention had been paid to pathological consequences that accompany the prophetic decision to portray Israel as the wife of YHWH.[48] The discourse of domestic violence found its first theological expression in Hosea. In writings

45. For a discussion of rape imagery in Lamentations see F.W. Dobbs-Allsopp and Tod Linafelt, 'The Rape of Zion in Thr 1,10', *ZAW* 113 (2001), pp. 77-81.

46. Alice Miller, *Breaking Down the Wall of Silence: The Liberating Experience of Facing Painful Truth* (New York: Meridian, 1993), p. 123.

47. Herman, *Trauma and Recovery*, pp. 2-4.

48. See, e.g. Deryn Guest, 'Hiding Behind the Naked Woman in Lamentations: A Recriminative Response', *BibInt* 7 (1999), pp. 413-48; F. Rachel Magdalene, 'Ancient Near Eastern Treaty-Curses and the Ultimate Texts of Terror: A Study of the Language of Divine Sexual Abuse in the Prophetic Corpus', in A. Brenner (ed.), *The Feminist Companion to the Latter Prophets* (Feminist Companion to the Bible, 8; Sheffield: Sheffield Academic Press, 1995), pp. 326-52; and Renita J. Weems, *Battered Love: Marriage, Sex, and Violence in the Hebrew Prophets* (Overtures to Biblical Theology; Minneapolis: Fortress Press, 1995), pp. 35-67.

associated with this eighth century seer, the reader encounters images of
God as the outraged husband forced to discipline his wayward wife (Hos.
2.4-15) and as the offended father compelled to chastise his rebellious son
(Hos. 11.1-9). It is likely that the prophet seized upon these images in
order to solve a problem implicit in the theological thinking of the times.
By portraying national disaster as correction within the family, Hosea
was able to affirm the possibility of a continuing relationship between
God and God's people even if the terms of the covenant were broken.[49]
The book of Jeremiah also has discipline imagery including both marital
(Jer. 2.20-37) and filial symbols (Jer. 31.18-20).

The concepts of structure legitimation and pain embrace can also contribute to an understanding of the dynamics of the complaint in Lamentations. It is a matter of record that the pain embrace authorized by the
biblical tradition is circumscribed. The Bible's mythology of Exodus and
Conquest affirms that the social and religious experiment called Israel was
meant to protect small autonomous units of agrarian production against
encroachment by larger concentrations of political power.[50] Various passages in biblical law (e.g. Exod. 21.12-17; Deut. 21.18-21) and Proverbs
suggest that there was little or no permission in Israel's founding traditions to question asymmetries in the distribution of power within the
social unit biblical mythology was meant to protect: the land-owning,
patriarchal family. Only those concentrations of power above it (i.e. the
state or monarchy) are commonly the objects of the Bible's revolutionary
protest. By the same token, it is noteworthy that complaint psalms never
portray the petitioners in domestic terms. If God is named through cultural metaphors, the reference is to the deity as ruler: king and shepherd.[51]
If we compare such motifs with the poems that make up Lamentations,
there are noteworthy differences. God is not explicitly called king (though
there may be an allusion to his royal status in 5.19) and the plethora of
references to Zion as (virgin) daughter and mother in Lamentations 1–2,
and 4 brings the reader into a world of domestic imagery.

In the light of the domestic imagery that dominates Lamentations, it is
important to note shifts related to the accusation against God. In comparison to the protests of national defeat, accusatory statements about YHWH's
destructive actions are found only in Lam. 3.42-45; 5.20. Lamentations 1–2

---

49. Donald E. Gowan, *Theology of the Prophetic Books: The Death and Resurrection of
Israel* (Louisville: Westminster John Knox, 1998), pp 46-50.

50. William Dever, 'Archaeology and the Israelite "Conquest" ', *ABD*, III, pp. 550-51.

51. A list of epithets used of God in community complaints can be found in Claus
Westermann, *Praise and Lament in the Psalms* (Atlanta: John Knox, 1981), p. 58. The only
poem in the protests of national defeat which calls God 'father' is Isa. 63.7-64.11 (63.16;
64.7).

and 4 prefer descriptions of divinely ordained destruction in the third person. These depictions of divine actions are balanced by images of the suffering and disgrace of the city (we-complaint). The significance of the we-complaint is visible in the lengthy sections given over to describing the desolation of the city (cf. 1.1-15; 2.9-12, 21; 4.1-15; 5.2-18). Not only has the we-complaint become predominant in Lamentations, it has been transformed into extensive depictions of affliction that are less actual complaint than descriptions of what is lamented.[52] This transformation reflects the ambiguity that the poems of Lamentations have towards the city's misfortunes. These terrible images demand a certain of degree of acceptance, of resignation to YHWH's terrible wrath, as well as protest. The impetus for this shift is partly to be explained by the psychology of trauma: lowered self-esteem and heightened self-blame are characteristics of victims of violence. Nevertheless, prophetic theology also played a part in rationalizing the disaster. YHWH was entitled to exercise abusive violence towards a community perceived as wayward child and adulterous wife.

So far, nothing has been said about the identity of the writer(s) of the poems in Lamentations. One of the best clues is the inclusion of Lamentations 5. This poem has a form related to the protests of national defeat but which has been adapted to the perspective of the other poems in the book. Chapter Four suggested that the identity of the writers of the protests of national defeat could not be fixed with too much precision; but it was safe to conclude that these poems were composed by expert cultic poets. A similar viewpoint is warranted for the origin of Lamentations. Moreover, Lamentations 5 gives reason to assume that the same circles that composed the protests of national defeat could also have composed another kind of complaint poetry that accommodated itself to the prophetic critique of monarchical religion. This suggestion might appear to be a contradiction in terms until it is examined in the light of the psychology of grieving. Studies in grief show that a person can experience a gamut of emotions within a short span of time. Application of grief theory to Lamentations helps explain how its poetry can vacillate between depression and hope, anger and sadness.[53] The inclusion of Lamentations 5 suggests a people torn between self-recrimination and anger against God. These same characteristics can be observed in the community addressed by the Second Isaiah.

---

52. Westermann, *Praise and Lament*, pp. 176-80.

53. Paul Joyce, 'Lamentations and the Grief Process: A Psychological Reading', *BibInt* 1 (1993), pp. 312-13.

5.2. *The Second Isaiah and the Transformation of Complaint*[54]

According to 2 Kings 25, there were deportations in both 597 and 587 BCE. Jeremiah 52 suggests a third deportation in 582. While there are discrepancies in the biblical record, by any account, thousands of inhabitants of Judah and Jerusalem were transported to Mesopotamia.[55] Jewish victims of the Babylonian deportations were settled in regions south of Babylon. Most were reduced to the status of peasants who farmed plots of land assigned to them by the state.[56] Under those circumstances they experienced both privation and prophetic intervention.

This section is concerned with the activity of the anonymous prophet known to scholarship as 'the Second Isaiah'. The poetry he (or is it she?)[57] composed is now found in Isaiah 40–55. Active in the last decade of the Neo-Babylonian empire (c. 547–539),[58] the Second Isaiah's message of imminent deliverance was not met with open arms. Indications are that, by the mid-540s, the exiles were becoming thoroughly discouraged with their religious identity as Israel. Theirs was a story of defeat and rejection by God.

We may infer that exiled Israel's trauma story loomed large in its religious consciousness because the engagement of the Second Isaiah with the nation's laments is extensive. This function is discernible in all the major genres of the prophet's poetry. There are two major genres of

---

54. Much of the material in this section is digested from my articles, 'Comfort for Jerusalem' and 'Post-Traumatic Stress Disorder and Vicarious Atonement in the Second Isaiah', in H.J. Ellens and W.G. Rollins (eds.), *Psychology and the Bible: A New Way to Read the Scriptures* (4 vols.; Westport, CT: Greenwood-Praeger Publishers), I, pp. 167-83.

55. J.M. Miller and J.H. Hayes. *A History of Ancient Israel and Judah* (Philadelphia: Westminster, 1986), pp. 417-20. In making this claim, I align myself with those who dispute the 'myth of the empty land'. For a review of archaeological and textual evidence that supports the biblical view of massive deportations after the Babylonian conquest, see Oded Bustenay, 'The Exile—Myth or History? The Origin of the Assyrian and the Babylonian Exile [Modern Hebrew]', *Bet Miqra* 176 (2003), pp. 103-25.

56. Niels P. Lemche, *Ancient Israel: A New History of Israelite Society* (Sheffield: JSOT Press, 1988), pp. 179-80.

57. For the possibility that Second Isaiah was a woman, see Sean McEvenue, 'Who Was the Second Isaiah?', in J.T. van Ruiten and M. Vervenne (eds.), *Studies in the Book of Isaiah: Festschrift Willem A.M. Beuken* (Leuven: Leuven University Press, 1997), pp. 213-22. Along with McEvenue and most of the scholars mentioned in this section, I assume the poetry of Isaiah 40–55 is basically the product of a single person. For a different model, see Albertz, *Israel in Exile*, pp. 380-81.

58. P.E. Dion, 'Les chants du serviteur de Yahweh et quelques passages apparentés d'Is 40–55', *Bib* 51 (1970), p. 18.

poems promising deliverance: 'oracles of salvation' and 'proclamations of salvation'.[59] The oracles of salvation are addressed to Israel as a personified singular and presuppose an individual complaint psalm; the proclamations of salvation are formulated as responses to collective laments voiced by the people.[60] The interaction between these poems and Israel's liturgies of complaint is evident from the large amount of shared vocabulary and imagery.[61]

The Second Isaiah's poetry also includes argumentative genres meant to defend the validity of the prophet's message. They comprise 'trial speeches' and 'disputations'.[62] The prophet's need to reject accusations against God is prominent in both.[63] The preoccupation with Israel's complaints throughout the poetry of the Second Isaiah suggests that complaint against God was perceived by the prophet as a pervasive characteristic of the community and that it represented an obstacle to the message of an imminent and glorious salvation.

The second generation of exiles in Babylon had various institutions of religious observances, including public prayers and fasts.[64] Evidently, liturgies of communal lament were part of these ceremonies. The rich number of allusions to community lament in the poetry of the Second Isaiah suggests that various kinds of complaining rhetoric were current among the people, including the poetry of Lamentations. One may infer that memories of the violence done to Jerusalem in the previous generation were continually reinforced by these complaint liturgies. The result was not only anger but also self-recrimination and despair. In the Babylonian exile, a combination of extreme shame, guilt, grief, inchoate rage and scapegoating can be observed. Israel had become appalling to itself: accounted as plagued, smitten and afflicted by God (cf. Isa. 52.14; 53.4).

The exiles' complaint against God had three different emphases. One was that YHWH's actions had resulted in permanent abandonment of his

---

59. Following Schoors, (*I Am God Your Savior*), oracles of salvation include Isa. 41.8-13, 14-16; 43.1-7; 44.1-5; 54.4-6; proclamations of salvation comprise 41.17-20; 42.14-17; 43.16-21; 49.7-13, 14-26; 51.9-16, 17-23; 54.7-10, 11-17; 55.1-5.

60. Norman K. Gottwald, *The Hebrew Bible: A Socio-Literary Introduction* (Philadelphia: Fortress Press, 1985), p. 493.

61. Schoors, *I Am God Your Savior*, pp. 45-46; Westermann, *Praise and Lament*, p. 178.

62. Following Schoors (*I Am God Your Savior*), trial speeches occur in Isa. 41.1-5, 21-29; 42.18-25; 43.8-13, 22-28; 44.6-8; 45.18-25; 50.1-3 and disputations in 40.12-31; 44.24-28; 45.9-13; 46.5-11; 48.1-11, 12-15; 55.8-13.

63. Gottwald, *The Hebrew Bible*, p. 494.

64. James D. Purvis, 'Exile and Return: From the Babylonian Destruction to the Reconstruction of the Jewish State', in Hershel Shanks (ed.), *Ancient Israel: From Abraham to the Roman Destruction of the Temple* (Washington: Biblical Archaeology Society, rev. edn, 1999), p. 212.

servant, Israel. A second was that the hegemony of imperial Babylon was unbreakable, even by YHWH. A third arose from the fact that most of the exiled community was composed of the sons and daughters of those who had actually suffered the humiliation of defeat and exile. There was resentment that the children were paying the price for their parents' sins.

The perception of divine abandonment is conveyed in citations or allusions to the complaints of the community (e.g. 40.27; 49.14; 50.1). Another indicator that the faith community thought itself as rejected by God can be derived from the observation that the Second Isaiah's poetry alludes to material found in the book of Jeremiah. Of particular relevance are passages in which Jeremiah's oracles of doom against Judah and Jerusalem are reversed, including 42.10-16 (cf. Jer. 14.2-9) and 54.1-5 (cf. Jer. 10.17-25).[65] These allusions would make little sense unless the community also knew of Jeremiah's prophecies and was thereby conscious of itself as the object of YHWH's wrath. Another illustration of the reversal of the complaint of abandonment can be seen in the description of Zion in Isa. 49.14-26. A key theme is the return of the children of Zion. With allusions to the complaints of Lamentations, the Second Isaiah promises the restoration of Zion's captive citizens, the children of whom she was bereaved (cf. 49.20).[66]

The captive community also showed signs of despair because its prayers were not being answered. Basically, the liturgy of lament is a call for help.[67] But considerable pessimism about the efficacy of this traditional appeal to Israel's deity seems to have developed. One can infer this by noting the main themes of the genre of the Second Isaiah's poems called disputations. They point to those aspects of the prophet's message most resisted by a discouraged Israel. In the disputations, the Second Isaiah asserts YHWH's creative power and his dominion over history (e.g. 40.22-24; 44.24-26 and 48.12-14). Other deities are powerless (e.g. 46.5-11 and 48.3-8) as are the nations who trust in them (e.g. 45.20). Moreover, YHWH's coming salvation will be realized by Cyrus (e.g. 45.1-3; 48.12-15), who is described in messianic terms.[68]

The presence of such arguments implies that the exiles were losing faith in YHWH's capacity to control either nature or history. Moreover, they could not discern in the changing political scene evidence of YHWH's hand. The lack of a visible response by YHWH to the exiles' liturgies of lament left the faith community with the sense that Israel had no control over its destiny: YHWH was either no match for Babylon and its deities or

---

65. Sommer, *A Prophet Reads Scripture*, pp. 38-40, 43-45.

66. Linafelt, *Surviving Lamentations*, pp. 72-79.

67. Patrick D. Miller, *They Cried to the Lord: The Form and Theology of Biblical Prayer* (Minneapolis: Fortress Press, 1994), p. 55.

68. Schoors, *I Am God Your Savior*, pp. 294-95.

determined to permanently reject Israel. This perception was not altered in their eyes by a changing political reality that suggested an imminent collapse of Babylonian rule through the agency of Cyrus. The replacement of one foreign rule by another would hardly have been perceived as evidence of YHWH's hand.

The Second Isaiah also had to address the complaint that the experience of the exile was unfair. This was a common sentiment among the exiles, who felt that they were being punished for their ancestors' sins. Jer. 31.29-30 and Ezek. 18.2 both show that this complaint was current during the exilic period. The famous poem about the suffering servant in Isaiah 52.13–53.12 was an important and innovative response to the charge of divine injustice. For the sake of discussion, I will refer to this poem as 'Isaiah 53'.

It is a matter of intense and ongoing debate whether the servant of Isaiah 53 is an individual or a collective referent.[69] Nevertheless, there is strong support for the traditional Jewish interpretation that the servant refers, in the first place, to Israel.[70] This argument does not necessarily rule out an individual identification of the servant. A representative of the community can be identified with that collective persona as well as speak for it. There are grounds for assuming, therefore, that Israel in the servant songs can represent both the people and the prophet.[71]

The exiled community perceived its plight as unfair. The Second Isaiah's position on this question is ambivalent. On the one hand, the violence of the exile is defended in trial disputations such 42.18-25 and 43.22-28. On the other hand, there is admission that the exile has been excessive. This is most notable in Isa. 40.2, 'Speak tenderly to Jerusalem and cry to her that her time of service is over, that her iniquity is pardoned; that she has received from YHWH's hand double for all her sins'. Various scholars have sought to ward off any implication of injustice on the part of YHWH. A common tactic is to suppose that the word

69. See references to past scholarship in R.J. Clifford, 'Isaiah, Book of (Second Isaiah)', *ABD*, III, pp. 490-501 and Gowan, *Theology of the Prophetic Books*, pp. 160-61.

70. Dion, 'Les chants du serviteur', p. 35; Yehezkel Kaufmann, *The Babylonian Captivity and Deutero-Isaiah* (Histroy of the Religion of Israel 4.1-2; New York: Union of American Hebrew Congregations, 1970), pp. 148-49; C.R. North, *The Second Isaiah: Introduction, Translation, and Commentary to Chapters XL–LV* (Oxford: Clarendon Press, 1964), pp. 20-22. An indicator that the servant can be taken collectively may be derived from the usage of the term in the Second Isaiah. Altogether there are twenty references to the servant in Isaiah 40-55. According to Clifford ('Second Isaiah', p. 499), there is general agreement that the thirteen occurrences outside the four 'servant songs' in 42.1-4; 49.1-6; 50.4-9; 52.13-53.12 refer to the community as servant.

71. W.H. Robinson, *Corporate Personality in Ancient Israel* (Philadelphia: Fortress Press, rev. edn, 1980), pp. 41-42.

'double' in this context really means 'equivalence' and that the proclamation of YHWH's forgiveness is commensurate with Jerusalem's punishment.[72] But this attempt to exculpate YHWH will not do. The Hebrew word translated as 'double' in 40.2 means 'twice as much' elsewhere in Biblical and Rabbinic Hebrew. Behind the opening words of comfort in 40.1-2 lies the perception that an innocent generation was now paying the price for the sins of its ancestors.[73]

Isaiah 53 addresses this accusation by an innovative use of the imagery of vicarious atonement to describe the vocation of the suffering servant. The idea of vicarious atonement has two references in the Hebrew Bible. First, it can refer to the fact that people pay juridical penalties for the crimes of others. Second, vicarious atonement occurs through the concept of sacrificial substitution.[74] The juridical and cultic meanings of vicarious suffering come together in Isaiah 53. The servant suffers on account of the sins of others (v. 5); this is a juridical concept. But it is also stated that the servant effects a cultic offering as a compensation for sin in v. 10.[75] In both cases, the community's sufferings are revealed as having an expiatory significance.

Isaiah 53, therefore, offered to the community a process of rationalization whereby it could accept the possibility of coming salvation without denying the painfulness of its perceptions of the past. The poem reframes the perception that the suffering of the exile was unjust by offering a new interpretation of the violence experienced by the exiles as servant Israel.[76]

72. See discussion and history of scholarship in Klaus Baltzer, *Deutero-Isaiah: A Commentary on Isaiah 40–55* (Hermeneia; Minneapolis: Fortress Press, 2001), p. 52.

73. North, *Second Isaiah*, p. 73; Anthony Phillips, 'Double for All her Sins', *ZAW* 94 (1982), p. 132.

74. Kaufmann, *Deutero-Isaiah*, pp. 142-45.

75. Baltzer, *Deutero-Isaiah*, p. 421.

76. The association of the servant with Israel suggests that the Second Isaiah wrote the servant songs, though this conclusion is not universally accepted (Clifford, 'Second Isaiah', p. 499). The question of authorship is most vexed in connection with Isaiah 53 (North, *Second Isaiah*, p. 20). Dion ('Les chants du serviteur', pp. 35-36) is of the opinion that, while the first three poems are compositions of the Second Isaiah, Isaiah 53 was likely written by a disciple of the prophet. This is debate reflects an opinion that the servant songs seem slightly later than the other genres of the Second Isaiah's poetry (North, *Second Isaiah*, p. 188) with Isaiah 53 the latest of all (Dion, 'Les chants du serviteur', p. 36). Since the Second Isaiah probably operated among the exiled community in Babylon for most of a decade, it is possible that Isaiah 53 comes at the very end of that period. But, even if Dion is correct to assign its composition to a disciple of the Second Isaiah, Isaiah 53 still meditates on the effect of the prophet's message on the community. My discussion is not substantially affected by the assumption that Isaiah 53 was written by an immediate disciple of the Second Isaiah.

The servant continues to serve, even in the midst of the exile, as a compensation for sin. But it is not the sins of the past or the present that the exilic community's sufferings affect. The superfluous violence of that experience has an atoning value that will benefit future generations (53.10-11). This was YHWH's will. The result is that servant Israel has a future with God, just as he had a past. This gives an unrecognized dignity to the suffering of the second-generation survivors of the exile. They are actually suffering so others will not have to. Though exiled Israel makes its grave (figuratively speaking) with rich Babylon (cf. 53.9), as YHWH's servant the Babylonian diaspora will be the means so that future generations will prosper.[77]

The purpose of the Second Isaiah's various kinds of poetry was to refuse the continuation of the complaint against God as an appropriate response to the situation of the exiles. The Second Isaiah disputed accusations of divine abandonment and impotence with claims that deliverance with more than adequate forgiveness (40.1-2) by a universally powerfully deity (45.5-8) is promised to servant Israel who has an exalted destiny in the divine economy (41.8-13; 42.1-4). As a result, displaced persons from Judah and Jerusalem were called upon to embrace the opportunity of a new Exodus (43.1-7). Babylon will be defeated (47.1-15); a political messiah is at hand (45.1-6) and the journey home will not be arduous (42.12-20). Positive aspects of being God's servant people are brought to the fore. Their suffering bore a hidden meaning that will benefit future generations (53.9). The time for punishment is past, and a glorious future is promised (52.1-12).

5.3. *Complaint against God in the Deuteronomistic History*

I assume that the bulk of the DtrH was either completed or composed in the exilic period.[78] Timo Veijola has observed that the DtrH projects exilic practices of lament onto earlier eras of Israelite history. Both the book of Lamentations and the protests of national defeat show that collective complaint was important in the exilic period. Contemporary sources mention Bethel (Zech. 7.2-7) and Mizpah (Jer. 41.4-6) as cities of note. These two locales are identified in the DtrH as places of national lament. References to Bethel include Judg. 2.1-5; 20.18, 23, 26-28. References to Mizpah include Judg. 20.1, 3; 21.1, 5, 8 and 1 Sam. 7.5-11.[79]

---

77. Phillips, 'Double for All her Sins', p. 132.
78. See Albertz, *Israel in Exile*, pp. 273-80 and my discussion in §2.2.
79. Timo Veijola, 'Das Klagegebet in Literatur und Leben der Exilsgeneration am Beispiel eigenen Prosatexte', in J.A. Emerton (ed.), *Congress Volume: Salamanca 1983* (Leiden: E.J. Brill, 1985), p. 306,

The Achan legend in Joshua 7 is especially instructive with respect to the attitude towards complaint in the DtrH. Against the thesis that the lament in Josh. 7.7-9 represents early tradition,[80] Veijola has observed that the prayer in v. 7 opens with a formula typical in the exilic period: *'hh 'dny* YHWH (cf. Jer. 4.10; 32.17; Ezek. 9.8; 11.13; 21.5).[81] In addition, the lament is rejected because of the sin of the people (Josh. 7.10-15). This pattern is also observable in exilic or early postexilic contexts including Isa 58.3-7; Jer 14.7-12 and Ezek 9.8-10. But the rejection is not permanent. Once the sin is confessed and dealt with, YHWH works to deliver the people (Joshua 8).[82]

Joshua 7 is a kind of narrative theology, therefore, that comments on the conditions of the exile. Israel's defeat because of Achan's infraction served as an analogy for exilic theologians, who considered their era one when the nation was living under YHWH's wrath. But there was a solution. Confession of sin was a precondition for divine answer to lamenting prayer. A similar logic appears elsewhere in the DtrH. The pattern imposed on the stories of Judges points to the importance of repentance from apostasy as a condition for YHWH to hear the cries of Israel in captivity and respond.[83] Solomon's prayer in 1 Kings 8.31-53 shows a consistent relationship between forgiveness and divine response to pleas uttered in distress. Underlying this prayer is a Deuteronomistic theology which holds that if people seek forgiveness and walk in God's paths, YHWH will hear their prayers, forgive them and act on their behalf.[84]

The importance of these observations for the present discussion lies in the recognition that the sin-consciousness of the exilic period did not suppress the tradition of protest prayer so much as qualify it. A text such as Joshua 7 shows that exilic theologians regarded complaint prayer and

---

80. See, e.g. Dankwart Kirchener, 'Gruppendynamische Untersuchung zu Struktur und Geschichte der Klage im Alten Testament', *TLZ* 114 (1989), col. 790; Henning G. Reventlow, *Gebet im Alten Testament* (Stuttgart: Kohlhammer, 1986), pp. 96-97; Westermann, *Praise and Lament*, p. 197.

81. Veijola, 'Klagegebet', pp. 299-300.

82. Mark J. Boda (*Praying the Tradition. The Origin and Use of Tradition in Nehemiah 9* [BZAW, 277; Berlin: W. de Gruyter, 1999], pp. 59-61) points to the possibility of priestly influences in Joshua 7, but he does not determine whether this implies a priestly source used by the writer of the DtrH or a later priestly redactor. These priestly influences are not found in the prayer of Josh. 7.7-9. Therefore, I assume that Josh. 7.7-9 is a product of a DtrH writer; see Samuel E. Balentine, *Prayer in the Hebrew Bible: The Drama of Divine–Human Dialogue* (Overtures to Biblical Theology; Minneapolis: Fortress Press, 1993), pp. 118-19.

83. Bernhard W. Anderson, *Understanding the Old Testament* (Englewood Cliffs, NJ: Prentice Hall, 4th edn, 1986), p. 184.

84. Balentine, *Prayer in the Hebrew Bible*, pp. 83-87.

confession of sin as compatible. Both had a role to play in relieving the distress of the nation.[85]

5.4. *Protest against God in the Exile*

This chapter and Chapter Four have now surveyed four different bodies of exilic literature related to the tradition of argumentative prayer: the protests of national defeat, the book of Lamentations, the DtrH and the poetry of the Second Isaiah. Taken together, these works of literature reveal a faith community deeply divided between a sense of betrayal by its deity and self-blame: a contradictory set of emotions characteristic of victims of violence. Moreover, there is reason to think that the same community might be capable of producing expressions of both contrition and protest before God. This is implied in the layout of Lamentations and in the intertextual references of the Second Isaiah, which allude both to Lamentations and the rhetoric of the protests of national defeat.

Although late pre-exilic and early exilic prophets resisted the impulse of the community to protest, on the assumption that this terrible disaster was YHWH's righteous punishment on the errant nation, clearly the complaint tradition was not suppressed. But it was controlled and compromised by accommodation to the prophetic critique of the Jerusalem cult in various exilic writings. The three bodies of literature surveyed in this chapter show different attitudes in their toleration of the lament tradition. But all bear out the conclusions of earlier chapters: shifts in theology would affect the practice of protest against God.

The book of Lamentations and the DtrH agree in their overall strategies towards containing protest against God. Both works reveal a theology that allows for complaint only after some amount of suffering is acknowledged as legitimate punishment for national apostasy. In the case of Lamentations this is conveyed by the organization of its poetic units. The result is a structure which controls even the context in which the poem most obviously related to the protests of national defeat is set. While Lamentations 5 ends with a stark complaint against God, such an expression is only permitted after a certain amount of national suffering is accepted as divinely ordained judgment (ch. 4). The DtrH also allows for complaint prayer directed at God, but typically only after the nation acknowledges its sin against YHWH and repents.

The Second Isaiah is less tolerant of the complaint against God than either the book of Lamentations or the DtrH. The poetry of this anonymous prophet of the Babylonian diaspora means to answer complaint

85. Veijola, 'Klagegebet', p. 305.

prayer by oracles and proclamations of an imminent and glorious salvation. The Second Isaiah does not so much dismiss the value of national lament as proclaim that the practice is no longer needed due to historical changes initiated by YHWH. The answer to the exiles' complaint is notable for introducing a new concept of suffering. The Second Isaiah introduces a theory of redemptive/vicarious suffering that appears to be unprecedented in the Hebrew Bible.[86] This innovation undermines the perception of the community that its suffering was unfair by proclaiming that the misfortunes of exiled Israel had a redemptive quality that would benefit future generations. Though the Second Isaiah does not deny that God caused the servant to suffer, the lament tradition is effectively vitiated because the theory of redemptive/vicarious suffering shows that the God-Israel relationship remains intact in spite of the exile.

Both the qualification of the protest against God by the demand for prior contrition and the substitution of a theology of redemptive/vicarious suffering for the pain embrace of the argumentative prayer tradition presage important trends in the history of communal lament. The impact of these trends for the expression of collective complaint will be taken up in Chapter Seven. It is not the case, however, that exilic theology under the influence of the prophetic critique of Israelite religion was simply opposed to complaint against God. It was still permitted, albeit conditionally, in Lamentations and the DtrH. Nevertheless, it is clear that expressions of protest against God went into eclipse as Judaism developed in the postexilic period. Some other influence had to have been at work besides the domination of a prophetic perspective that analysed national disaster as punishment for sin. The identification of this additional factor will be the subject of discussion in the next chapter.

---

86. The redemptive or vicarious pattern is described in Balentine, *Prayer in the Hebrew Bible*, p. 191. Besides passages from the Second Isaiah (Isa. 50.4-11 and Isaiah 53), Balentine points to texts from Job as examples of the redemptive theory of suffering. However, Job is best considered a postexilic work and subsequent to the Second Isaiah (see Chapter Six).

Chapter 6

PROTEST AGAINST GOD IN THE AXIAL AGE

The book of Job invites its readers to reflect on the relationship between Job's faith and his humiliation (Job 1.11; 2.5). It confronts its readers with the paradox that faces all those who refer their existence to a single and righteous deity: the experience of unjust suffering in a world made by a God supposed to love justice. The book allows for multiple interpretations of its theological tensions and their resolution.[1] Recent scholarship has explored themes such as unmerited suffering,[2] theodicy,[3] and the nature of faith.[4] These various topics are not mutually exclusive. Here I wish to highlight another layer of interpretation in this dense and difficult book. The book of Job is responding to a crisis in the liturgical economy of early Judaism: the complaint against God became theologically problematic in the postexilic era.

A number of literary problems emerge when readers encounter the book of Job. The odd mixture of narrative and poetry, the organization of the speeches in Job 22–27, the appearance of a previously unmentioned speaker (Elihu) in Job 32–37, and difficulties in the cohesion of the YHWH

---

1. See, e.g. K. Fullerton, 'The Original Conclusion of the Book of Job', *ZAW* 42 (1924), pp. 130-35; William S. Morrow, 'Consolation, Rejection, and Repentance in Job 42.6', *JBL* 105 (1986), pp. 224-25; Dale Patrick and Allen Scult, *Rhetoric and Biblical Interpretation* (JSOTSup, 82; Bible and Literature, 26; Sheffield: Almond Press, 1990), pp. 82-83; Carol A. Newsom, 'Cultural Politics and the Reading of Job', *BibInt* 1 (1993), pp. 136-37; Kevin Snapp, 'A Curious Ring in the Ears: Ambiguity and Ambivalence in the Conclusion of the Book of Job', *Conservative Judaism* 53.1 (2000), pp. 34-35.

2. For example, Burton Z. Cooper, 'Why God? A Tale of Two Sufferers', *TTod* 42 (1986), pp. 423-24; Stanley E. Porter, 'The Message of the Book of Job: Job 42.7b as Key to Interpretation', *EvQ* 63 (1991), p. 302.

3. For example, T.W. Tilley, 'God and the Silencing of Job', *Modern Theology* 5 (1989), pp. 267-68; Yair Hoffman, 'The Creativity of Theodicy', in Henning G. Reventlow and Yair Hoffman (eds.), *Justice and Righteousness: Biblical Themes and their Influence* (JSOTSup, 137; Sheffield: Sheffield Academic Press, 1992), pp. 117-30.

4. For example, Daniel E. Fleming, 'Job: The Tale of Patient Faith and the Book of God's Dilemma', *VT* 44 (1994), p. 469; Andrew E. Steinmann, 'The Structure and Message of the Book of Job', *VT* 46 (1996), pp. 95-96.

speeches in Job 38–41 are a few of its significant puzzles.[5] Some of these difficulties are resolved by supposing that the book was altered over time. A thorough discussion of the literary history of Job extends beyond the scope of this study and is, in any case, open to controversy. I accept common opinions that the book of Job has been subject to two substantial additions. One of these is the poem on wisdom in Job 28.[6] A second entails the Elihu speeches in Job 32–37.[7] These texts probably entered the book of Job as a result of perceptions that a previous version provided an unsatisfactory answer to problems the book raises.

But the task still remains to explain the book of Job as a meaningful communication in its final form.[8] The insertion of substantial additions into a shorter original gives the impression that the book as it now stands ought to be read as an anthology of reflections and possible solutions to the problem of divine justice and human suffering.[9] In other words, the final form of Job presents a collection of responses to Job's dilemma. This

5. See the list in Steinmann, 'The Structure and Message of the Book of Job', pp. 87-89.

6. Yair Hoffman, *A Blemished Perfection: The Book of Job in Context* (JSOTSup, 213; Sheffield: Sheffield Academic Press, 1996), pp. 281-84 and Leo. G. Perdue, *Wisdom in Revolt: Metaphorical Theology in the Book of Job* (JSOTSup, 112; Bible and Literature, 29; Sheffield: JSOT Press, Almond Press 1991), pp. 82-83.

7. Hoffman, *A Blemished Perfection*, pp. 289-93; Perdue, *Wisdom in Revolt*, pp. 80-82. Recently, the original unity of the Elihu speeches with Job 1-27; 29–31; 38–42 has been defended in the thesis of F. Rachel Magdalene, 'On the Scales of Righteousness: Law and Story in the Book of Job' (PhD Dissertation, The Iliff School of Theology and University of Denver, 2003). Magdalene provides an innovative approach to the legal language that permeates the book of Job by a comparative study with approximately 250 Neo-Babylonian litigation records. According to Magdalene, during the Neo-Babylonian period, convictions typically required a second accusation against the defendant in order to obtain a conviction. In Job 1-2, the śāṭān brings a substantive legal charge against Job for having the mind of a blasphemer while Job counterclaims against God on a charge of abuse of authority. Elihu provides the critical second accusation against Job on the blasphemy charge, against which Job cannot muster a counterclaim. At present, however, I am not convinced that Elihu's intervention belongs to the same literary stratum as the dialogues. If either Job or God are on trial, it is only metaphorically. The legal scenario breaks down if it is applied literally; e.g. there is no suggestion that Job is required to make his case in a place customary for legal decisions such as a city-gate or palace. Most importantly, Job is vindicated by YHWH against his accusers in 42.7. Nevertheless, Magdalene's thesis deserves careful study by anyone interested in the legal background of the book of Job or ancient Near Eastern law. She has discovered a plausible literary trope to connect the later insertion of the Elihu speeches with the legal metaphors that the book plays with.

8. C.R. Seitz, 'Job: Full Structure, Movement and Interpretation', *Int* 43 (1989), p. 10; D.J.A. Clines, *Job 1–20* (WBC, 17; Dallas, TX: Word Books, 1989), p. lix.

9. Hoffman, 'The Creativity of Theodicy', pp. 127-28.

chapter will examine them more or less in canonical order, beginning with the dialogues where the basic dilemma is presented through the language of disputation (§6.1). The dialogues are the presenting symptom of a paradigmatic shift in Israel's religious imagination brought on by its entry into the Axial Age (§6.2). Various responses to Job's rhetoric of complaint are surveyed in §6.3. These involve Job 28, the speeches of Elihu (Job 32–37) and Job 38–42, including the speeches of YHWH and the prose epilogue in 42.7-17. All indicate the effects of a profound transformation in the conceptualization of Israel's deity.

6.1. *Dialogue and Complaint in Job 3–27; 29–31*

Job begins the dialogue with a soliloquy in the form of a self-curse and two complaints. The themes expressed are: 'I wish I had never been born' (3.3-10); 'Death is better than life' (3.11-19); 'What meaning can life possibly have in the face of my suffering?' (3.20-26). As in Jer. 20.7-18, disappointment with the protection of a personal God has reached the point of cursing the day of birth.[10]

After Job 3, the positions of Job and his friends are set out in three cycles of poetic speeches: Job 4–14; 15–21; 22–27. The third speech cycle is not complete. Most commentators believe that its contents are distorted and disorganized, likely due to an error in transmission.[11] Therefore, my analysis of the dynamics of the dialogue between Job and his comforters relies only on the first two speech cycles (Job 4–21).

Throughout the dialogue both Job and his friends assume that God is primarily responsible for Job's predicament. At stake is whether Job's suffering is justified or an exercise of divine power that can be challenged. In his speeches, Job continually protests the assumption that his suffering is deserved. The speech cycles end with another soliloquy by Job in which he affirms his innocence (Job 29–31). This affirmation takes a dramatic

---

10. Scholars are divided on the question as to whether Job 3 is dependent on Jer. 20.7-18 or *vice versa*; e.g. Perdue (*Wisdom in Revolt*, p. 101) thinks that Jer 20.14-18 is dependent on Job 3; the opposite position is maintained in Pieter van der Lugt, *Rhetorical Criticism and the Poetry of the Book of Job* (OTS, 32; Leiden: E.J. Brill, 1995), p. 58. But Job is to be dated to the postexilic period (see note 16). If Jer. 20.7-18 stems from the prophet or his exilic tradents, then it is probable that Job 3 is dependent on the passage from Jeremiah.

11. See Hoffman, *A Blemished Perfection*, pp. 276-86. Though Hoffman acknowledges the majority position, he demurs and suggests the third speech cycle was simply never finished. Recently, van der Lugt (*Rhetorical Criticism*, pp. 515-17) has defended the thesis that there are only two speech cycles in the book, the second being Job 15–26. But van der Lugt's opinion depends on the perception of a chiastic scheme that is not complete. Hence, the impression that something is missing or distorted in Job 22-27 remains.

turn when Job assumes the posture of a person on trial who takes an oath daring God to punish him if his testimony is false (31.5-40).

The position of Job's erstwhile friends is that God acts justly, treating persons as they deserve.[12] Protests like Job's lose their force if God's sovereignty is so secure that all suffering can be ascribed to divine retribution. The theological perspective of Job's friends was common in educated circles of the Ancient Near East. It is associated with the ideology of wisdom. Wisdom thinking often endorsed a doctrine of divine retribution in which there was a predictable cause and effect relationship between order and chaos, justice and suffering. In other words, the wisdom of Job's erstwhile comforters is a form of structure legitimation.

The most prominent genre in the book of Job is the argumentative rhetoric of disputation (debate).[13] This is the style used by Job and the three comforters, Eliphaz, Bildad and Zophar when they advance their positions. While he engages in dispute with his comforters, Job's speeches also address God (Job 7; 10; 13.17–14.22; 17.3-4). Throughout his speeches, Job complains in categories similar to those found in individual complaint psalms. This includes examples of.[14]

I-complaint	6.2-4, 11-13; 7.3-6; 9.25-28; 10.1; 16.16-17; 17.6-7; 19.13-20
God-complaint	7.11-21; 9.17-18, 22-24; 10.2-7, 13-17; 16.7-14; 19.6-12
Enemy-complaint	6.14-27; 12.2-6; 16.2-5; 17.12; 19.2-5; 21.34

The overlap of complaint elements between disputations directed to the friends and to God should not be surprising. After all, the complaint psalm itself is a kind of argument urging the divine judge to act (§3.2.1). Once, however, Job's direct address to God parodies a psalm of individual complaint (Job 10). The context of this pseudo-psalm is telling. It follows on some of the harshest and most pointed accusations against God that Job makes in the book (Job 9).

Job begins his speech in Job 9 by apparently assenting to the wisdom teaching of his friends about the justice of the all-powerful Creator (vv. 1-12). The universal monotheism of the Second Isaiah echoes in the midst of this expression of praise (cf. Job 9.8 and Isa 44.24).[15] Previously, Eliphaz invoked a similar exaltation of divine power to support an equation

---

12. Carol A. Newsom, 'Job', in Carol A. Newsom and Sharon H. Ringe (eds.), *The Women's Bible Commentary* (Louisville, KY: Westminster John Knox, 1992), p. 132.

13. Perdue, *Wisdom in Revolt*, p. 79.

14. This list is based on John E. Hartley, 'The Genres and Message of the Book of Job', in Roy B. Zuck (ed.), *Sitting with Job: Selected Studies on the Book of Job* (Grand Rapids: Baker, 1992), pp. 68-69.

15. Edouard Dhorme, *A Commentary of the Book of Job* (London: Thomas Nelson & Sons, 1967), p. clvii.

between sin and suffering (4.17-21). But the praise of the almighty God is subverted in Job's hands. Job proceeds to show how the concept of omnipotence makes the justice of God capricious and arbitrary (9.13-20). In fact, it releases God from having to be just at all (9.22-24). The wisdom of Job's friends amounts to dogma without comfort or correction: the all-powerful God is free to act with impunity.

The thrust of this theological indictment continues in Job 10. The pseudo-psalm of Job 10 is reminiscent of psalms labeled in Chapter Three as 'Direct Protest of Divine Affliction' (§3.3.3.2). This speech can be broken down into the typical elements of the complaint psalm:

I-Complaint	I loathe my life	10.1a
Address	I will say to God,	10. 2a
Petition	Do not condemn me. Let me know why you contend against me ...	10.2b
God-Complaint	Accusatory questions	10.3-7
Trust	God as personal creator	10.8-12
God-Complaint	But you hunt me down like a lion	10.13-17
	Why did you let me be born?	10.18a
Petitions	Would that I had died	10.18b-19
	Leave me alone	10.20-22

Ordinarily in complaint psalms there are three categories of distress: the personal distress of the poet, the absence of God and the attacks of the enemy. In Job 10, God *is* the enemy. Job contends that God betrays the divine vocation of Creator by attacking him (10.8-17). Better not to be born than to endure such capricious and arbitrary treatment (10.18-19). The poem ends with a remarkable twist on the petitions for salvation that typify psalms of individual complaint. Where the psalmists plead for God's presence, rescue and help, Job pleads to be left alone. In effect, divine abandonment becomes Job's hope, not his despair.

By the end of the second speech cycle, the confrontation between Job and his dialogue partners has reached an impasse. Both parties are entrenched in their theological positions. Job's resolute posture of protest remains undiminished. Eliphaz, Bildad and Zophar are just as adamant in demanding that Job accept his suffering as punishment for sin. This situation stands in contrast to the social effects of complaint rhetoric in the Psalms. There, the language of complaint and affirmation of innocence were tactics used by ostracized people to win support from a hostile or indifferent community. In other words, protest against undeserved suffering functioned to rehabilitate individuals into their local support group. What has happened to make Job's theologically motivated protest so ineffective? And why does the accompanying assertion of innocence not move Job's former support group to accept him?

6.2. *Job and the Emergence of Israel's Axial Age*

My response to the questions raised above assumes that the book of Job is a postexilic composition likely composed sometime in the fifth or fourth century BCE.[16] Previous scholarship has perceived that Job registers a spiritual crisis related to that historical context.[17] Most obviously, the destruction of the First Temple by the Babylonians plunged the religion of Israel into great theological turmoil. Restoration of the Second Temple (dedicated in 515) brought with it numerous problems about the (re-) organization of religious life.[18]

As a result, it is sometimes thought that the character of Job personifies suffering Israel. Job's protests, therefore, would symbolize the quandaries of the nation struggling to make theological sense of the loss of the Temple during the exilic period and the difficulties of national reconstruction after the return to Judah in the late 6th century. Support for a collective interpretation of Job notes two developments in exilic and postexilic writings: the use of individual complaint imagery to represent the voice of the community (e.g. Lamentations 3) and the emergence of a literature that reacts to the destruction of Judah and Jerusalem by the Babylonians.[19]

I find, however, no grounds for interpreting Job as a symbol of national distress. Job's language resonates most clearly with the language of individual complaint, in particular with psalms emphasizing the innocence of the petitioner (cf. Job 6.28-30; 16.16-17; 23.10-12; 27.2-6 with Pss. 17.3-5; 26.2-7).[20] Particularly significant is the use of an oath formula in Job 29–31, in effect calling on God to curse the poet if his righteousness is not established (cf. Job 31.5-22 and Pss. 7.4-6). Such a procedure would have been

---

16. This is a common scholarly opinion, see, e.g. James L. Crenshaw, 'Job, Book of', *ABD*, III, pp. 863-64; Anson Laytner, *Arguing with God: A Jewish Tradition* (Northvale NJ: Jason Aronson, 1990), p. 34.

17. See, e.g. James L. Crenshaw, *Old Testament Wisdom: An Introduction* (Louisville, KY: Westminster John Knox, rev. edn, 1998), pp. 103-104; Leo G. Perdue, *Wisdom and Creation: The Theology of Wisdom Literature* (Nashville: Abingdon Press, 1994), p. 124. René Girard (*Job, the Victim of his People* [London: Athlone Press, 1987], p. 83) refers to the religious dilemma addressed by the book of Job as a 'sacrificial crisis'.

18. Rainer Albertz, *A History of Israelite Religion in the Old Testament Period* (OTL; 2 vols.; Louisville, KY: Westminster John Knox, 1994), II, pp. 458-64.

19. Laytner, *Arguing with God*, pp. 34-37. David Wolfers (*Deep Things out of Darkness: The Book of Job. Essays and a New English Translation* [Grand Rapids: Eerdmans, 1995], pp. 70-73) also proposes a collective interpretation of Job, dating the book to c. 701 in the wake of the Assyrian conquest of Judah.

20. John E. Hartley, 'From Lament to Oath: A Study of Progression in the Speeches of Job', in W.A.M. Beuken (ed.), *The Book of Job* (BETL, 114; Leuven: Leuven University Press, 1994), pp. 90-91.

considered highly risky unless the guiltlessness of the afflicted party was beyond doubt.[21] But much exilic literature assumes the guilt of Israel. A second feature is the description of Job's God as personal creator in 10.8-12 (cf. Ps. 22.10-11). Appeals to God as personal creator and protector mark the genre of individual complaint as distinct from community prayers.[22]

In the postexilic period, protests of community distress were composed under the influence of the LI genre (§4.5). But these poems also have a system of collective references that establish their community focus. There are simply no unambiguous references to national catastrophe in Job. This absence sets the book apart from other exilic and postexilic literature that explicitly wrestles with the destruction and exile of Jerusalem and Judah.

The absence of allusions to the catastrophe of the Neo-Babylonian conquest and subsequent exile means that one must look elsewhere for an explanation of the eclipse of LI in the postexilic era. It is my opinion that the spiritual crisis underlying the Joban dialogues reflects social, political and theological shifts in Israelite religion that came about as biblical faith entered the 'Axial Age'. According to the philosopher Karl Jaspers, the Axial Age encompassed 800–200 BCE with a center at approximately 500 BCE.[23] Jaspers used the epithet 'Axial' because this epoch heralded fundamental and revolutionary changes in human social, religious and intellectual history. Many civilizations were affected including those of ancient Israel, Greece, Iran, China and India.

According to sociologist S.N. Eisenstadt, Axial Age civilizations perceived a large degree of tension between the transcendental and mundane orders of reality. This tension emerged and was expressed in ways that distinguish these societies from their predecessors. Human societies typically perceive the divine or spiritual realm as somewhat different, usually higher and more powerful, than everyday reality. In pre-Axial Age civilizations, this higher world was symbolically structured according to principles very similar to the mundane or lower one. In other words, the two worlds were thought to operate by similar principles and accessed by similar means. By contrast, in the Axial Age there developed the perception of a sharp disjunction between the everyday and transcendent worlds. The divine reality was no longer simply human reality writ large.

21. Erhard S. Gerstenberger, *Psalms: Part 1 with an Introduction to Cultic Poetry* (FOTL, 14; Grand Rapids: Eerdmans, 1988), p. 65.

22. Rainer Albertz, *Persönliche Frömmigkeit und offizielle Religion: Religionsinterner Pluralismus in Israel und Babylon* (Calwer Theologische Monographien Reihe A, Bibelwissenschaft 9; Stuttgart: Calwer, 1978), pp. 37-38.

23. Karl Jaspers, *Vom Ursprung und Ziel der Geschichte* (Zürich: Artemis-Verlag, 1949), p. 19.

Such a distinction created numerous problems in the construction of social institutions with respect to the cosmic order.[24]

Axial Age social, political, religious and intellectual processes were closely connected with the emergence of new social elites. Examples include the Jewish prophets, Greek philosophers, the Chinese scholar-class and Buddhist monks. They created new institutions and practices to manage the perceived tension between the transcendental and mundane orders. These new types of thinkers differed from the elites that had been ritual, magical and sacred specialists prior to their society's Axial Age revolution.[25] Radical changes in the nature of knowledge partly account for the rise and influence of these new religious specialists. The Axial Age did not simply involve transformations in social structures; it portended significant changes in the conceptual worlds of human beings. In fact, these new elites produced the first true ideologies in that they offered comprehensive views of the world and how people should live in it.[26]

What does the Axial Age have to do with the composition of the book of Job and the questions it poses? The postexilic era is dated from the foundation of the Second Temple (520 BCE). By the end of the sixth cetury, the process of reconstructing a society around the temple had begun. Chronologically, therefore, the postexilic era can be located within the emergence of the Axial Age in human intellectual history.

Postexilic Israel also experienced the influences of intellectual development. The emergence of ancient Israel into the Axial Age is associated with the development of its monotheistic faith into a universal religious claim.[27] Though there are antecedents, the late exilic prophet called the Second Isaiah (Isaiah 40–55) can be considered the endpoint of the evolution of an unambiguous and universal monotheism in Israel.[28] Second Isaiah proclaimed YHWH not only sovereign over Israel, but the sole existing deity whose sway was universal (Isa. 45.14-25). Moreover, YHWH was immeasurable, unteachable and incomparable (e.g. Isa. 40.12-18).[29]

---

24. S.N. Eisenstadt, 'The Axial Age Breakthroughs—Their Characteristics and Origins', in S.N. Eisenstadt (ed.), *The Origins and Diversity of Axial Age Civilizations* (SUNY Series in Near Eastern Studies; Albany: State University of New York, 1986), pp. 1-3.

25. Eisenstadt, 'The Axial Age Breakthroughs', pp. 4-6.

26. Peter Machinist, 'On Self-Consciousness in Mesopotamia', in Eisenstadt, *Origins and Diversity of Axial Age Civilizations*, p. 183.

27. S.N. Eisenstadt, 'The Axial Age Breakthrough in Ancient Israel', in Eisenstadt, *Origins and Diversity of Axial Age Civilizations*, pp. 128-29.

28. Benjamin Uffenheimer, 'Myth and Reality in Ancient Israel', in Eisenstadt, *Origins and Diversity of Axial Age Civilizations*, p. 168; John J. Scullion, 'God in the OT', *ABD*, II, pp. 1042-43.

29. Scullion, 'God in the OT', p. 1043.

These characteristics suggest a sharp distinction between transcendent reality and the human world.

This theology was the product of a history of intellectual speculation that had been taking place among Israel's prophetic elite.[30] One has only to compare the more anthropomorphic picture of YHWH in Isa. 6.1-3 (mid-eighth century) with that of Ezek. 1.22-28 (early sixth century) to realize that a belief in a more transcendent deity, less amenable to the human imagination had been developing for some time. The prophets were responsible for taking the God of a small independent state and making him into a universal deity. They did so under the pressure of, and partly in reaction to, imperial imagery and claims made by Israel and Judah's overlords and conquerors: the empires of Assyria, Babylon, and Persia.[31] In this triangular process, the common object of desire of both Israelite and ancient Near Eastern intellectuals was a deity competent to control history. The politics of empire was an impetus for the emergence of the Axial Age and the need to envision a sufficiently transcendent order to comprehend this new international reality.[32]

The result was a deity more transcendent and more powerful than that envisaged in the complaint psalm tradition, an imperial deity, king not only of Israel, but unmatched emperor of the universe. The faith tradition reflected in complaint psalms accepted the possibility of inexplicable and even arbitrary absences of the divine presence.[33] But Israel's religious imagination required the construction of a less compromised God in the Axial Age. To a certain extent, in the Axial Age YHWH's absence was structured into the universe because of his greater transcendence. But as an imperial deity, ruler of the universe, YHWH had to be portrayed as

30. Karen Armstrong (*A History of God: The 4,000-Year Quest of Judaism, Christianity and Islam* [New York: Ballantine Books, 1993], pp. 41-45) connects the emergence of the Axial Age in ancient Israel with the 8th century prophets. I would argue, however, that they set in motion a process of intellectual and theological innovation that did not reach its fruition until the articulation of the monotheistic vision of the Second Isaiah and the reorganization of Israel's religious institutions in the early postexilic period.

31. Moshe Weinfeld, 'The Protest against Imperialism in Ancient Israelite Prophecy', in Eisenstadt, *Origins and Diversity of Axial Age Civilizations*, pp. 178-81.

32. Marcel Gauchet, *The Disenchantment of the World: A Political History of Religion* (New French Thought; Princeton: University Press, 1997), p. 41. By contrast, Armstrong (*History of God*, p. 27) emphasizes the rise of market capitalism as a stimulus for the emergence of the Axial Age. But the development of monotheism in Israel appears to have been more closely tied to changing political circumstances. Besides the thesis of Gauchet, see Baruch A. Levine, "Ah, Assyria! Rod of My Rage' (Isa 10.15) — Biblical Monotheism as Seen in International Perspective: A Prolegomenen [Modern Hebrew]', *Eretz Israel* 27 (2003), pp. 136-37.

33. Samuel E. Balentine, *The Hidden God: The Hiding of the Face of God in the Old Testament* (Oxford: University Press, 1983), p. 166.

completely sovereign. Consequently, all of YHWH's absences must be defensible; such a deity's actions were not to be subject to criticism by mere mortals.

At first glance, ascribing this process of theological development to prophetic thought contradicts earlier chapters in this book. For example, Chapter Two connected prophetic functionaries with the complaint against God as it appeared in informal lament on behalf of the nation. Chapter Three left open the possibility that prophetic functionaries were involved in the use of LI as healing rituals. But it stands to reason that this same movement would also be the first to feel discomfort with protest against God as it developed a theology that could not include it. The last chapter noted how prophetic thought inhibited the articulation of community complaint during the exile. It is no coincidence that the Second Isaiah, who articulated the monotheistic vision operative as Israel entered the Axial Age, also developed a theology of redemptive/vicarious suffering that undermined the legitimacy of protest among the Babylonian exiles.

Though the so-called writing prophets represented a minority view in the pre-exilic period, the destruction of the monarchy and temple that they had predicted validated their views and brought them to prominence after the exile. We should not be surprised that the domination of the prophetic elite influenced the popular religious imagination in postexilic times. This prophetic movement represented the destruction of Jerusalem and subsequent exile as the punishment for sin. But at the same time it was involved in a revision of Israel's religious imagination in order to justify divine action. This movement can be seen in the emphasis on divine holiness present in Ezekiel's vision of the ideal temple (Ezekiel 40–48) as well as in the transcendent perspective of the Second Isaiah.

The intransigent refusal of Job's comforters to entertain the force of his complaint against God and his declarations of innocence points to their engagement with Axial Age influences. In the pre-exilic period, wisdom discourse as well as complaint rhetoric existed in Israel.[34] It is the assertion of wisdom theology to the exclusion of complaint rhetoric by Job's comforters that marks a theological turning point in the history of biblical thought.

Wisdom discourse is particularly suitable for speaking about a transcendent God. Walter Brueggemann points out that Israel's core testimony about God uses active verbs: Israel sees and knows God directly in the midst of its life. But there is a strong and crucial counter claim that maintains that the God of Israel is hidden. A key text appears in the Second Isaiah: 'Truly, you are a God who hides himself...' (Isa 45.15). The

---

34. For example, cf. the collections in Proverbs 10–29; see Norman K. Gottwald, *The Hebrew Bible: A Socio-Literary Introduction* (Philadelphia: Fortress Press, 1985), p. 571.

testimony of wisdom is that in much of life YHWH's actions are not direct and visible, but concealed in ongoing processes.[35] The application of wisdom thinking to justify the ways of divine transcendence is a logical development in the Axial Age.

The wisdom of Job's friends claims divine mono-causality in connection with human suffering. There are biblical parallels to this viewpoint. For example, YHWH is said to be the single cause of all that happens in Deut. 32.39; 1 Sam. 2.6-7; Isa. 14.24-27; 45.7 and Dan. 4.31-32. Brueggemann opposes the idea that these statements are to be taken as sources for a theology that makes God the cause of everything.[36] But the book of Job suggests that some Axial Age thinkers were prepared to make such a claim when the alternative was to assent to a theology of complaint, which permitted protest against a God who could act in arbitrary and unpredictable ways.

6.3 *Responses to Job's Dilemma*

Eliphaz, Bildad and Zophar reject Job's right to protest against God. How does his complaint fare in other answers to the Joban dilemma? Job 28; 32–37 and 38–42 also make claims about the nature of divine providence. Not all belong to the same edition of the book. None defends Israel's tradition of protest prayer.

6.3.1. *The Wisdom Poem in Job 28*
Job 28 places an emphasis on the distance between the divine and human realities that is characteristic of Axial Age theology. Nothing in creation knows the way to wisdom, not even the preternatural realms of death and the grave (28.20-22). As for human beings, not only has wisdom remained undiscovered, but it is so much beyond their attainment that they are not even able to assess it properly (28.16-19). Such distancing dissolves any analogy between human and divine wisdom. From the point of view of Job 28, it is category confusion to talk of human and divine wisdom as if they were the same thing. A subtle detail in vocabulary

---

35. Walter Brueggemann, *Theology of the Old Testament: Testimony, Dispute, Advocacy* (Minneapolis: Fortress Press, 1997), pp. 333-35.

36. Brueggemann, *Theology of the Old Testament*: pp. 354-55. In Brueggemann's opinion, affirmations of YHWH's omni-causality are best understood as disputatious claims that oppose the following ideas:

(i)   gods alternative to YHWH have reality (Deut. 32.39)
(ii) people are hopelessly fated to their circumstances (1 Sam. 2.6-7)
(iii) human autonomy can proceed as it wants (Dan. 4.32)
(iv) counter-political powers can resist YHWH (Isa. 14.24-27).

helps to convey this impression. It is wisdom with a definite article ('the wisdom', i.e. Wisdom) that God possesses in 28.12, 20. It is a less definite wisdom with no article ('wisdom') that is accessible to humanity. The content of these two sorts of wisdom is different. In the case of human beings, wisdom is the fear of YHWH; it is not ultimate knowledge about the nature of creation.[37]

What does Job 28 say to Job's practice of protest prayer? Complaint prayer theology assumes the validity of analogical thinking. The farther the distance between the divine and human realities, between the everyday world and the way things look *sub specie aeternitatis*, the less certain human beings can be that God looks at their world the way they do. The psalms of individual complaint are filled with pleas to God to see, take notice, pay attention and hear. But though human beings may search and see the hidden gems of the earth (28.10), wisdom is beyond their powers of perception (28.13). A sharp distinction is raised between divine and human perspectives. By contrast, argumentative prayer rests on a confidence that God will act as soon as he sees things the way the psalmists do. Ordinary language is sorely stretched in the distance between God and humanity depicted in Job 28.

6.3.2. *The Elihu Speeches*
The Elihu speeches in Job 32–37 appear to compete with the YHWH speeches of Job 38-41 as an answer to Job's dilemma.[38] We need not think that the same hand responsible for Job 28 also composed the Elihu speeches. But as in Job 28, Elihu's speeches presuppose an Axial Age theology that rejects the human analogies on which protest prayer is based.

Elihu begins with a remarkable claim in Job 32.6-9: wisdom is not simply a benefit of age but is a possession of any human being in whom God's spirit dwells. It is characteristic of the Axial Age that new elites emerged, who were not defined by the same categories used by their predecessors. Elihu rejects a traditional equation between age and wisdom and makes a claim for an exception from ordinary processes of social validation. The wise person is the God-inspired person who speaks the truth, a claim that later will be made in Wis. 4.7-9.[39]

Contrary to Job's claim that God does not speak, Elihu sets out two ways in which God makes his ways known: through dreams and through physical affliction which brings one close to death (33.12-22). The worldview of the psalms of individual complaint would have little problem

---

37. See the discussion in Hoffman, *Blemished Perfection*, pp. 278-81.
38. Seitz, 'Job', pp. 12-13.
39. Perdue, *Wisdom in Revolt*, pp. 248-49.

with these claims. What distinguishes Elihu's analysis from that found in the psalms is that he regards both dreams and sickness only as means for explaining suffering as a punitive experience.

In addition, Elihu introduces the idea of a mediating angel (following the translation tradition represented by the NRSV) between God and suffering humans as an agency of deliverance (33.23-26). Angelic figures as emissaries of God appear elsewhere in scripture (e.g. Num. 22.31; Judg. 2.1; 13.6 and 2 Sam. 24.16). What distinguishes Elihu's conception is the dual role of the angelic figure as both revealing the reason for the petitioner's illness and interceding for him before God.[40] Nowhere in the psalms of individual complaint does the psalmist imply he is without direct access to YHWH. The intercessory role of angels is typical of the angelology of postexilic Judaism.[41] Such emphasis on divine transcendence is characteristic of the Axial Age. A mediator is needed in Elihu's religious imagination to narrow the gap between the divine and human realities.

Behind the imagery of Elihu's angelic intermediary, scholars have detected the shadow of a ritual expert who oversaw an individual healing liturgy. He would have disclosed to the petitioner the cause of his illness and led the liturgy for deliverance. Alongside ritual actions, the prayer mandated by Elihu required both praise of God and confession of sin. In other words, a form of prayer related to the function of the complaint psalm liturgy was still permitted, but it was purchased at the price of expunging any claim to innocence by the petitioner.[42]

Beginning in Job 34, Elihu turns to Job's charges of divine injustice. God is supremely righteous and chastises those who have become estranged from him and who have oppressed others (34.21-30). God's transcendence is such that God is not touched by human sin or human acts of goodness; wickedness and righteousness mainly have to do with the treatment of fellow persons (35.1-8). Many of the oppressed are not liberated, however, because they themselves rail against God and do not turn to him (35.9-15). In fact, God is great and righteous, rewarding people according to their works. Misfortune is but an instrument in the hands of God to save the guilty (36.5-16). Elihu ends with lengthy praise to this exalted and ever righteous deity. He concludes that God is not within human reach. By reason of his power and righteousness, God is to be feared and reverenced. The divine being has no accounts to render to human beings (37.19-24).[43]

---

40. James F. Ross, 'Job 33.14-30: The Phenomenology of Lament', *JBL* 94 (1975), p. 43.

41. Carol A. Newsom, 'Angels, Old Testament', *ABD*, I, p. 252.

42. Erhard S. Gerstenberger, *Der bittende Mensch: Bittritual und Klagelied des Einzelnen im Alten Testament* (WMANT, 51; Neukirchen–Vluyn: Neukirchener Verlag, 1980), pp. 138-39.

43. Dhorme, *Commentary on the Book of Job*, p. lvii.

Elihu's reasoning essentially represents the positions of Job's friends in the dialogue. But he offers a more sophisticated theological defense for the rejection of the protest prayer tradition. He reaffirms the thesis that God is always righteous and human suffering is connected to wrongdoing.[44] Elihu allows that human suffering can be inflicted by one person on another. But if God fails to intervene, then the sufferer has faults which the affliction should make clear. Obviously, protests or doubts in connection with divine faithfulness or justice cannot be entertained in such a worldview.

6.3.3. *The YHWH Speeches*

The YHWH speeches belong to an older edition of Job that essentially included Job 1–27; 29–31; 38–42. Though there has been much discussion about their literary integrity, they can be read as transmitted.[45] A vexed interpretive problem concerns the connection between the prose prologue and epilogue in Job 1–2; 42.7-17 and the poetic speeches in Job. Probably the author of Job took over a traditional folktale about an exemplary person who patiently endured the trials and tribulations of life.[46] But he adapted it to suit his own needs. There are other ancient Near Eastern books with a prose prologue and epilogue framing an extensive section of poetic dialogue. Therefore, one can assume some meaningful relationship between the discourse in the dialogues and the prose frame. For example, the prose prologue sets up verbal criteria for apostasy: Job must curse God to his face (1.11; 2.5). Job can actually be quite critical of the divine character without crossing this line.[47] Moreover, the prose epilogue identifies the use of right speech as the criterion by which Job is approved and Eliphaz and the others censured (42.7).

Job 42.7 is quite ambiguous. Unlike Eliphaz, Job is commended for speaking correctly about God. But what has Job said right? Has he been correct to use the language of complaint, despite reservations about its appropriateness by Israel's Axial Age theologians? Or was Job right to maintain his innocence when religious logic said that he had sinned? Or is he right because he finally admitted his ignorance about the nature of God (42.2-6), displaying a humility uncharacteristic of his dialogue partners? The reader does not know; one can only guess.

---

44. Claus Westermann, *The Structure of the Book of Job: A Form-Critical Analysis* (Philadelphia: Fortress Press, 1981), p. 147.

45. Westermann, *Structure of the Book of Job*, p. 108; Perdue, *Wisdom in Revolt*, p. 83.

46. Crenshaw, 'Job', p. 863.

47. Yair Hoffman, 'Ancient Near Eastern Literary Conventions and the Restoration of the Book of Job', *ZAW* 103 (1991), p. 410.

The difficulty in interpreting 42.7 suggests that there is a lack of resolution in the end of Job which has been intentionally created by the author. Further evidence for deliberate ambiguity in the YHWH speeches appears in the long tradition of commentary on their meaning. Prominent suggestions include:[48]

a.   The YHWH speeches serve to maintain God's freedom in a world of chaos.

b.   The presence of paradox in creation is emphasized in order to undermine the logic of retribution theology.

c.   Nature is shown not to be organized by moral categories, exposing a fundamental error of Job and his friends.

d.   God's power is actually revealed as limited, and evil cannot be completely eliminated from the world.

e.   Divine wisdom and righteousness are beyond human understanding: attempts to cast aspersions on divine justice are foolish.

f.   The YHWH speeches uphold the view of God as Creator and Lord of history. Confession and praise are proper responses to God, even for suffering persons, not accusatory questions and disputational rhetoric.

The perspectives listed above are not all compatible. There are various details in the YHWH speeches which can be used to support each of them.

Equally puzzling is the meaning of Job's response to YHWH's revelation (42.2-6). Scholars have variously suggest that Job is humbled by the divine response; that he gives up his position of protest in favor of repentance or praise; or, more minimally, that Job receives enough satisfaction from YHWH's appearance to abandon his former intellectual and/or physical posture.[49] These ambiguities continue to assert themselves as readers choose to emphasize or ignore various contradictory details in YHWH's revelation to interpret Job's reply.[50] They are important data in any attempt at resolving to the dilemma posed by the book of Job.

48. This list is based on the survey in Perdue, *Wisdom in Revolt*, pp. 197-98. However, I have omitted 'Promethean' interpretations which seem to me to be distinctly modern and unlikely expressions of ancient reader-responses.

49. Scholarship holding these various possibilities is summarized in Morrow, 'Consolation, Rejection and Repentance', pp. 217-23. See also the surveys in Perdue, *Wisdom in Revolt*, pp. 232-38 and Ellen van Wolde, 'Job 42,1-6: The Reversal of Job', in Beuken, *Book of Job*, pp. 242-50.

50. Van Wolde ('Job 42,1-6: The Reversal of Job', p. 247) rejects my thesis that this ambiguity is a deliberate tactic of the Joban author. She believes that a full command of the Hebrew language, the context and the text linguistic organization of Job 42.2-6 can resolve apparent ambiguities. But see Hoffman's remarks in *Blemished Perfection*, pp. 296-97: 'It makes no sense for someone to express full repentance in such evasive

Overall, the YHWH speeches suggest that neither the position of Job nor his comforters is entirely supported. Despite, or perhaps because of, their imperious tone, they force Job (and the reader) to take stock of reality in a new way, to look seriously at the world which God as creator brought into being.[51]

On the one hand, YHWH's description of creation undoes key premises of wisdom's theology of divine retribution:

1. The conventional wisdom thinking which appears in the dialogues is based on the notion that the cosmos operates with human inter-ests at its center. The YHWH speeches challenge this idea. In the natural world, human-centered moral categories are not operative. Neither the weather (38.25-27) nor the wild animals (39.5-18) reflect human values.[52] Though a non-anthropocentric vision of creation might be upsetting to a religious person in Job's culture, it possesses therapeutic potential. A view of the cosmos that does not have humanity at its center relieves suffering persons from having to interpret every situation as a potentially blameworthy response to their own actions.[53]

2. Job's dialogue partners assume that the created world perfectly reflects the character of God, thereby repressing any moral ambi-guity in the cosmos. This supposition is refuted in the YHWH speeches.[54] Texts such as 38.13, 15 and 40.8-14 confront Job with a world where the unjust thrive as well as the just.[55] Their misdeeds do not make them simply (unwitting) agents of divine retribution.

On the other hand, the YHWH speeches also undo assumptions made by the lament tradition:

language'. I continue to maintain that this enigmatic speech is a deliberate ploy by the writer of Job to let readers' response to the YHWH speeches inform their understanding of Job's final words. For other suggestions that the book of Job is structured by deliberate ambiguity, see the references in note 1 to this chapter.

51. Matitiahu Tsevat, 'The Meaning of the Book of Job', *HUCA*, 37 (1966), p. 100. See also Norman C. Habel, *The Book of Job* (OTL; London: SCM Press, 1985), p. 535; Fredrik Lindström, *God and the Origin of Evil: A Contextual Analysis of Alleged Monistic Evidence in the Old Testament* (ConBOT, 21; Lund: C.W.K. Gleerup, 1983), pp. 156-57.

52. Newsom, 'Job', p. 135; Tsevat, 'Meaning of the Book of Job', pp. 100, 102.

53. For a fuller discussion of the therapeutic value of the YHWH speeches, see William S. Morrow, 'Toxic Religion and the Daughters of Job', *SR* 27 (1998), pp. 272-74.

54. P.W. Nimmo, 'Sin, Evil and Job: Monotheism as a Psychological and Pastoral Problem', *Pastoral Psychology* 42 (1994), pp. 436-37.

55. Tsevat, 'The Meaning of the Book of Job', p. 99.

1.   Like wisdom thinking, complaint theology relies on an opposition between chaos and order. One of the central metaphors for chaos was the wild, untamed natural world. This imagery is used to describe enemies in the individual complaint psalms (e.g. Pss. 7.3; 17.12; 22.14; 35.17; 57.5; 59.7). Another symbol of chaos and suffering in the psalms is deep and raging water (e.g. Pss. 42.8; 69.2-3; 88.18; 130.1) The contrast between chaos and order can be maintained only by repressing the knowledge that 'chaos creatures' are also the creations of God. The YHWH speeches force Job to reevaluate conventional images of chaos. These include various manifestations of water in 38.8-38 and wild animals in 38.39–39.30. Both categories of wildness are claimed as products of the creative activity of God. Finally, Job is challenged to contemplate the huge water monsters thought to occupy creation (Job 40–41), praised as pinnacles of YHWH's creative power.[56]

2.   Earlier chapters have noted the dialogical nature of protest prayer. But YHWH's revelation to Job does not promote dialogue; it ends it. Job's first response is clear in this regard: 'I have spoken once, and I will not answer twice' (40.5). The exact nuance of Job's second response to the divine revelation is quite ambiguous. Nevertheless, there also one can see some kind of repudiation of Job's previous words, not their continuation (42.3). This effect stands in contrast with the visionary experiences of some of Israel's prophets where the revelatory moment becomes the occasion for complaint (e.g. 1 Kgs 19.10; Isa. 6.11; Ezek. 9.8; 11.13; Amos 7.2, 5).

YHWH's transcendence, a typical Axial Age doctrine, is affirmed in Job 38–41 by increasing his distance from the created world. The pre-Axial traditions of Israel's wisdom and complaint theologies were both anthropocentric in their outlook. But both perspectives on human suffering are undermined by the YHWH speeches. The deity they reveal is not simply a human being writ large. His creatures and his actions are often unfathomable according to human categories. The moral order and the natural order are distinguished in a way that neither pre-Axial wisdom or complaint theologies envisaged.

At least one detail in the prose epilogue seems to respond to YHWH's revelation. The endowment of Job's daughters with a share of inheritance along with their brothers has no precedent in the biblical record (42.15). Moreover, the daughters of Job are named, whereas their brothers remain nameless. It has been claimed that Job's generous treatment is a mark of

---

56. Tsevat, 'The Meaning of the Book of Job', p. 100. See also Athalya Brenner, 'God's Answer to Job', *VT* 31 (1981), pp. 133-34.

moral growth and deepened insight into the human condition, undermining patriarchal conventions because of its clear deviations from biblical
norms.[57] But this liberating effect can be discounted by observing that a
thoroughly patriarchal value seems to be responsible for their new status.
It is not because Job's daughters are said to be equal to their brothers, but
because of their outstanding beauty that they are given inheritance.[58]
Here again, we encounter ambiguity in the ending of Job.

Nevertheless, even a reading that identifies the sexual power of Job's
daughters as the reason for their inheritance indicates the transformative
impact of the divine revelation. Both (pro)creative power and power to
do evil are distributed by the YHWH speeches to diverse creatures in the
cosmos. Therefore, a positive reevaluation of female agency (usually feared
as chaotic in ancient Near Eastern cultures) is an appropriate response on
Job's part.[59] In fact, the YHWH speeches contain a number of motifs which
have analogues with concerns expressed in modern feminist theology.
They suggest an image of God 'as a power for life, balancing the needs of
all creatures, not just humans, cherishing freedom, full of fierce love and
delight for each thing without regard to its utility, acknowledging the
deep interconnectedness of death and life, restraining and nurturing each
element in the ecology of all creation'.[60]

In my opinion, the writer Job 1–27; 29–31 and 38–42 did not intend to
resolve questions regarding the propriety of protest as a response to affliction in Israel's Axial Age. The original version of Job worked as a vehicle
to express and experience tensions between traditional theologies of suffering and newer conceptions of divine transcendence. Readers were left
to infer their own solutions to the dilemma. Carol Newsom has observed
that the book of Job not only ruptures the ideological closure of retribution thinking but that its structure actually resists all closure and all resolution of contradiction.[61] I follow that observation here. The YHWH
speeches support neither the tradition of complaint prayer nor retribution
theology. But they refrain from articulating a vision to take the place of
either theological construct. The ambiguity and lack of clarity of Job
38–42 may well have been the reason why later hands added the Elihu
speeches and the poem to divine wisdom in Job 28.

57. See, for example, F.C. Clark, 'Job, or the Suffering of God', *Judaism* 42 (1993), p.
223; Ilana Pardes, *Countertraditions in the Bible: A Feminist Approach* (Cambridge, MA:
Harvard University, 1992), p. 153.

58. Clines, *Job 1-20*, p. 1; J.T. Wilcox, *The Bitterness of Job: A Philosophical Reading*
(Ann Arbor, MI: University of Michigan Press, 1989), pp. 222-23.

59. Morrow, 'Toxic Religion and the Daughters of Job', pp. 275-76.

60. Newsom, 'Job', p. 136.

61. Newsom, 'Cultural Politics and the Reading of Job', p. 136.

Chapter 7

COMMUNITY COMPLAINT IN SECOND TEMPLE LITERATURE

Chapter Six concluded that the book of Job was registering theological difficulties encountered by the tradition of individual lament (LI) in the postexilic period. This chapter will demonstrate that similar conclusions are warranted for the liturgical poetry of collective protest. Axial Age innovations contributed to the eclipse of the complaint against God in communal prayers during the Second Temple period.

The chapter begins by identifying categories of congregational pleas and laments attested in extra-biblical Second Temple literature (§7.1). These are surveyed for forms of complaint against God (§7.2). The results of these surveys bring into prominence two features of Second Temple prayers touching on the scriptural tradition of argumentative prayer. First, poems protesting the conditions of national defeat and exile were superseded by the penitential prayer tradition (§7.3). Second, there is evidence of a tendency to discourage protests against God in informal prayer (§7.4). A separate section will discuss evidence for collective complaint against God in the New Testament (§7.5). Summary remarks will indicate the status of collective protest prayer at the end of the Second Temple period (§7.6).

Critical scholarship has concluded that the earlier part of the Second Temple period witnessed the redaction of most of the books of the Hebrew Bible into their traditional form. The process of biblical composition overlapped with the creation of other literary works important to Second Temple Judaism. For example, the book of Daniel reached its canonical form in the second century BCE, roughly the same time Sirach (Ecclesiasticus) was also composed.

It is a subject of continuing debate when the biblical canon became closed and no longer open to new collections of prayers and other literature from postexilic Jewish communities. But, by any account, there is a sizeable body of literature from Second Temple times that was either not accepted for inclusion in the scriptures or was composed after the various canonical writings achieved some kind of normative status. These writings are found in collections of the Apocrypha and the Pseudepigrapha. Here I refer to this material by the more general epithet 'extra-biblical Second Temple literature' in order to include references to the Dead Sea Scrolls. The term indicates a range of Jewish texts composed in Aramaic, Hebrew and Greek roughly between 200 BCE and 135 CE, as determined by scholarly consensus.[1]

Many prayers are conserved in the large body of extra-biblical Second Temple literature. This chapter proposes to survey this material for evidence about the status of the lament tradition in prayers for the community. The following chapter will examine the same body of literature for the complaint against God in prayers for individuals. But the distinction between community and individual prayers is not always clearly made. A mark of extra-biblical Second Temple prayers is that the fate of the community and of individuals were considered closely entwined.[2] Some cases discussed below contain both prayers for the petitioner and the nation (e.g. Add. Est. 14.3-19; Jdt. 9.2-14). These are considered here, rather than in the next chapter, because they contain at least one petition on behalf of the community.

A methodological problem arises from the recognition that a significant number of the examples classified in §7.1 occur in prose narrative contexts. It was common for ancient storytellers and historiographers to compose speeches and prayers appropriate to the circumstances of the narrative. Therefore, what can it mean to talk about the liturgical practice of prayer as opposed to literary imitations in Second Temple texts? Drawing conclusions about liturgical practice from written documentation in Second Temple times involves considerable speculation.[3] David Flusser is helpful when he suggests that, although some of the prayers and hymns preserved in Second Temple literature were actual liturgical texts, even merely literary prayers may serve as witnesses for liturgical forms in this era of Jewish history.[4] This means that literary witnesses may reflect patterns of prayers in use at the time of writing.

A second problem emerges with the need to generalize. Unfortunately, there is little reason to think that a standard liturgy existed in the Second

---

1.   Dating of extra-biblical sources follows opinions found in the *Anchor Bible Dictionary* and introductory articles in J.H. Charlesworth (ed.), *The Old Testament Pseudepigrapha* (2 vols.; Garden City, NY: Doubleday, 1983, 1985).

2.   Bilhah Nitzan, *Qumran Prayer and Religious Poetry* (STDJ, 12; Leiden: E.J. Brill, 1994), p. 83.

3.   Eileen Schuller, 'Petitionary Prayer and the Religion of Qumran', in J.J. Collins and R.A. Kruger (eds.), *Religion in the Dead Sea Scrolls* (Grand Rapids: Eerdmans, 2000), p. 45.

4.   David Flusser, 'Psalms, Hymns, and Prayers', in Michael E. Stone (ed.), *Jewish Writings of the Second Temple Period* (CRINT, 2; Assen: Van Gorcum, 1984), p. 551.

Temple period.[5] There were, however, standard texts used in certain Jewish circles for specific occasions.[6] This difficulty can also be (at least partially) overcome by looking for patterns of prayer rather than trying to focus on texts that might be specific only to a particular Jewish group. A case in point is the sect responsible for the preservation of the Dead Sea Scrolls. Some of this material is probably specific to the Qumran community, but other texts seem to have a prior history so they cannot be identified as sectarian compositions. The fact that there is overlap, e.g. in categories such as penitential prayers (§7.1.3) or imitations of Lamentations (§7.1.4), between material in the Dead Sea Scrolls and other Second Temple compositions suggests that there were common patterns of prayer in use by various Jewish groups at the time, even if the texts were different.

The benefit of appealing to patterns of prayer also overcomes difficult problems in distinguishing between actual liturgical texts and literary models. For example, some penitential prayers show signs of composition prior to their present context (e.g. Neh. 9.5-37 and Prayer of Azariah 3-22).[7] But it is not clear whether these prayers are records of actual liturgical texts or literary models that informed extemporaneous prayers uttered in liturgical situations. In fact, it is probable that, like early rabbinic authorities,[8] Second Temple Jewish leaders were experts at formulating prayers *ex tempore*. Consequently, the discussion that follows is mainly concerned with identifying patterns of prayer. Historical inferences drawn from the distribution of these patterns inform a discussion of the fate of complaint prayer in Second Temple times.

7.1. *Extra-biblical Second Temple Community Pleas and Laments*

To date, the most thorough approach to the description of lament in extra-biblical Second Temple prayers remains that of Claus Westermann.[9]

---

5. Richard S. Sarason, 'Communal Prayer at Qumran and among the Rabbis: Certainties and Uncertainties', in Esther G. Chazon (ed.), *Liturgical Perspectives: Prayer and Poetry in the Light of the Dead Sea Scrolls* (STDJ, 48; Leiden: E.J. Brill, 2003), pp. 152-54. According to Sarason (p. 168), post-70 CE rabbinic sources also point to only partial formalization of communal prayers.

6. Stefan C. Reif, 'The Second Temple Period, Qumran Research, and Rabbinic Liturgy: Some Contextual and Linguistic Comparisons', in Chazon, *Liturgical Perspectives*, p. 149.

7. Mark J. Boda, *Praying the Tradition. The Origin and Use of Tradition in Nehemiah 9* (BZAW 277; Berlin: W. de Gruyter, 1999), pp. 189-90; Carey A. Moore, 'Daniel, Additions to', *ABD*, II, p. 19.

8. See Sarason, 'Communal Prayer at Qumran and among the Rabbis', p. 170.

9. Claus Westermann, *Praise and Lament in the Psalms* (Atlanta: John Knox, 1981), pp. 201-13.

Though I interact with Westermann's account, I also modify his system of classification. This is required for a number of reasons. First, Westermann's evidence can be supplemented by material not fully available to him, particularly from Qumran. Second, his discussion does not distinguish witnesses for collective complaint from those for individual laments because he believed that the lament genre suffered the same fate whether used for individuals or the community. Finally, and connected with the second point, Westermann missed the fact that an informal tradition of collective complaint prayer persisted during the Second Temple period.

7.1.1. Laments like those in the Psalter

A number of prayers have a structure similar to biblical laments. That is, they contain Address, elements of Complaint, Confession of Trust/Retrospect and Petitions. They can be divided into two categories: prayers with petitions only for the community (§7.1.1.1) and prayers mixing petitions for the community and the intercessor (§7.1.1.2).

7.1.1.1. Laments with Petitions for the Community.

Add. Est. 13.9-17:

9a	Address
9b-11	Confession of Trust/Praise
12-14	Declaration of Innocence
15-17	Petitions, including Enemy-complaint motif (v.15b)

3 Macc. 2.2-20:[10]

2a	Address
2b	Petition, including We-complaint motif
3-12	Confession of Trust/Retrospect
13	Petition, including Confession of Sin and We-complaint motifs
14-16	Enemy-complaint, including Trust motif
17-20	Petitions

3 Macc. 6.2-15:[11]

2	Address
3	Petition, including We-complaint motif
4-8	Confession of Trust/Retrospect
9	Petition, including Trust and We-complaint motifs
10-15	Petitions, including Enemy-complaint (v. 12) and Trust motifs (vv. 12-13)

---

10. Identified in Westermann, *Praise and Lament*, pp. 203-204.
11. Identified in Westermann, *Praise and Lament*, pp. 203-204.

Prayer of Azariah 3-22:[12]

3	Address
4-9	Confession of Sin, including justification of divine righteousness
10	We-Complaint
11-13	Petitions, including Retrospect motif
14-15	We-complaint
16-22	Petitions, including Trust motif

7.1.1.2. Laments mixing Collective and Individual Petitions. The presence of motifs of LI was noted in the protests of community distress (§4.5). But the prayers in §7.1.1.2 are more like prayers of the covenant mediator or community leader which combine personal and collective concerns. It is difficult to find biblical examples that combine petitions for personal and national concerns in the same way. The best parallel is probably Neh. 1.5-11, in which Nehemiah prays for help in order to intercede for the ruined nation. The fact that Neh. 1.5-11 is connected to the penitential prayer genre (see §7.1.3) is significant. It suggests that the texts listed in §7.1.1.2 are connected to a penitential theology that explains personal suffering as participation in the afflictions of the nation. Although Add. Est. 13.9-17 was listed in §7.1.1.1 because it contains no individual petitions, it is related to this group by virtue of its declaration of innocence.

Add. Est. 14.3-19:[13]

3a	Address
3b-4	Personal petition, including I-complaint and Trust motifs
5	Confession of Trust/Retrospect
6-7	Confession of Sin, including justification of divine righteousness
8-10	Enemy-complaint
11-14	Petitions
	11 Imprecations against the enemy
12-13a	Personal petitions, including Trust motif
	13b Petition for the king
	14a Petition for the nation
	14b Personal petition, including I-complaint motif
15-18	Declaration of Innocence
19a	Collective Petitions
	19b Personal petition

---

12. Identified in Westermann *Praise and Lament*, p. 202.
13. Identified in Westermann. *Praise and Lament*, p. 202.

Jdt. 9.2-14:[14]

2	Address
2b-4a	Retrospect
4b	Petition
5-6	Confession of Trust
7	Enemy-complaint
8-10	Petitions
	8-9a	Imprecations against the enemy
	9b-10	Personal petitions
11	Confession of Trust
12-14	Petitions
	12-13	Personal petitions
	14	Petition for the nation

7.1.2. *Communal Prayers for Help*

As in the Hebrew Bible, there are other prayers for help in times of national distress besides those written in lament form. Examples include 2 *Bar.* 48.2-24; 2 *Esd.* 8.20-36; 1 *Macc.* 4.30-33; 2 *Macc.* 1.24-29; 15.22-24; *Psalms of Solomon* 5; 7; 18 and Sir. 36.1-22 (17). The fragmentary 4Q509 col. I, frag. 1-2 may mention the word 'complaint' in describing an act of prayer. Unfortunately, the context does not indicate the nature of the complaint although col. III refers to the sufferings of those in exile.[15]

7.1.3. *Penitential Prayers*

A significant feature of Second Temple liturgical practice is the emergence of a genre known as the 'Penitential Prayer'. Biblical witnesses to this genre include Dan. 9.4-19; Ezra 9.6-15; Neh. 1.5-11; 9.5-37.[16] Penitential prayer is more easily identified by stereotypical contents than structure.

14. Identified in Westerman, *Praise and Lament*, p. 204.

15. See F.G. Martínez, and E.J.C. Tigchelaar. *The Dead Sea Scrolls Study Edition* (2 vols.; Leiden: E.J. Brill, 2000), II, pp. 1022-25.

16. Samuel E. Balentine, *Prayer in the Hebrew Bible: The Drama of Divine–Human Dialogue* (Overtures to Biblical Theology; Minneapolis: Fortress Press, 1993), p. 103; Rodney A. Werline, *Penitential Prayer in Second Temple Judaism: The Development of a Religious Institution* (Early Judaism and its Literature, 13; Atlanta: Scholars Press, 1998), pp. 45-64. Psalm 106, in which confession of sin is also prominent is not considered part of this genre by Westermann (*Praise and Lament*, p. 206), cf. also the list of Werline, *Penitential Prayer*, p. 1 and the remarks of Richard J. Bautch, *Developments in Genre between Post-Exilic Penitential Prayers and the Psalms of Communal Lament* (Academia biblica, 7; Atlanta: Society of Biblical Literature, 2003), p. 160. For a contrary view on Psalm 106 see Boda, *Praying the Tradition*, pp. 66-68. I have not included a discussion of the penitential liturgy in 1QS 1.16–2.18 since this is not a prayer text *per se*. For a discussion of penitential theology in the Rule of the Community, see Werline, *Penitential Prayer*, pp. 135-38.

Traits of penitential prayer include an emphasis on divine sovereignty, mercy and justice, the influence of Deuteronomic theology and rhetoric, and expressions of confession of sin and contrition.[17] Extra-biblical examples include Bar. 1.15–3.8;[18] 1 Esd. 8.74-90;[19] and *Psalms of Solomon* 2; 8; 9.[20] Prayer of Azariah 3-22 listed in §7.1.1.1 can be also associated with this group.[21] Fragments of the same genre are probably also attested in the Dead Scrolls: 4Q393 (*4QCommunal Confession*) and 4Q481c (*4QPrayer for Mercy*).[22]

7.1.4. *Imitations of Lamentations*

Westermann has a category of extra-biblical Second Temple texts he calls 'the exclusion of the lament from prayer'. A prime example is Bar. 4.9-16 where he discerns a pattern also found in Lamentations: a dirge form merged with complaint. Parallels with Lamentations are quite close: a female voice portrays herself both as a mother deprived of her children (Bar. 4.10) and a widow (Bar. 4.12); moreover, the destruction has been brought on Zion by divine agency (Bar. 4.9-10, 14-15). The fact that this lament is cited in a larger text (Bar. 3.9–5.9) leads Westermann to conclude that the lament over Israel's misfortunes was often separated from prayer in Second Temple times.[23]

There is evidence, however, that Bar. 4.9-16 alludes to a genre of communal laments with relationships to Lamentations that continued to be composed and performed long after the destruction of the First Temple. Another lament over the destroyed city appears in *2 Bar.* 10.6–12.4. Examples from Qumran include 4Q179 (4QapLam[a]), 4Q282 (formerly 4Q241),

---

17. Balentine, *Prayer in the Hebrew Bible*, pp. 103-104; Werline, *Penitential Prayer*, pp. 1-2.

18. Westermann, *Praise and Lament*, p. 206.

19. Westermann, *Praise and Lament*, p. 206. 1 Esd. 8.74-90 is a paraphrase of Ezra 9.6-15.

20. Westerman (*Praise and Lament*, p. 206) identifies *Psalms of Solomon* 9 as a genuine prayer of repentance. Werline (*Penitential Prayer*, pp. 185-88) perceives *Psalms of Solomon* 1; 2 and 8 as written under the influence of penitential theology. Here I include *Psalms of Solomon* 2 and 8 as examples of the penitential psalm genre because both explicitly justify God while confessing the sins of Jerusalem.

21. Moore, 'Daniel, Additions to', p. 19.

22. Esther G. Chazon, 'Hymns and Prayers in the Dead Sea Scrolls' in P.W. Flint and J.C. VanderKam (eds.), *The Dead Sea Scrolls after Fifty Years: A Comprehensive Assessment* (2 vols.; Leiden: E.J. Brill, 1999), I, p. 259. Penitence and confession of sin loomed large in the consciousness of the sectarians of Qumran. 4Q504–506 (*4QWords of the Heavenly Luminaries*) is a collection of daily prayers that includes among their elements confessions of Israel's sins; see Werline, *Penitential Prayer*, pp. 147-59.

23. Westerman, *Praise and Lament*, p. 207.

4Q445 (*4QLament A*), 4Q453 (*4QLament B*) and 4Q501 (*4QapLam*[b]). In addition, there is a first person singular lament that seems to bewail the fate of the nation: 4Q439 (*4QLament by a Leader*).[24]

The liturgical tradition represented by Lamentations has had a long life in Jewish worship.[25] The Dead Sea Scrolls show new compositions written in the same idiom. The Qumran material creates a larger context for evaluating other Second Temple prayers that resemble the rhetoric of Lamentations. The texts include Bar. 4.6-16; *2 Bar.* 10.9–12.4 and also the fragmentary 1 Macc. 3.45. Although this latter text is said to have been a prayer before battle, the complaint is entirely in the we-complaint mode that dominates Lamentations.[26] Second Temple Jews seem to have used the stock forms of Lamentations to lament contemporary experiences of suffering.[27]

7.1.5. *Informal Laments*
Besides 1 Macc. 3.45, there are two citations of prayers that are not well-formed in that they lack both address and petition elements: 1 Macc. 2.7-13; 3.50-53. Chapter Two noted that the biblical tradition of self-contained complaint was modeled on forms of implied request between persons. Examples of this form in human conversation occur in *2 Baruch*. The people protest the departure of Baruch:

> Where are going from us, Baruch, and do you leave us as a father who leaves his children as orphans and goes away from them? (*2 Bar.* 32.9).[28]

A complaint in similar form is uttered by the people in *2 Bar.* 46.1-3 to protest the announcement of Baruch's impending death.

An example of the self-contained lament form in a prayer occurs in 1 Macc. 2.7-13. There is no address to God, but the speech is bracketed by two why-questions:

> Alas! Why was I born to see this, the ruin of my people, the ruin of the holy city, and to dwell there when it was given over to the enemy, the sanctuary given over to aliens? (v. 7) … Why should we live any longer? (v. 13)

The speaker is the priest Matthias, father of the Maccabees. The prayer is spoken in the presence of Matthias's sons who, together with their

---

24.   Listed in Adele Berlin, 'Qumran Laments and the Study of Lament Literature', in Chazon (ed.), *Liturgical Perspectives*, p. 1. The article treats 4Q179 and 4Q501 in detail.

25.   Erhard S. Gerstenberger, *Psalms: Part 2 and Lamentations* (FOTL, 15; Grand Rapids: Eerdmans, 2001), p. 474.

26.   Westermann, *Praise and Lament*, p. 179.

27.   Berlin, 'Qumran Laments', pp. 16-17.

28.   A.F.J. Klijn, '2 (Syriac Apocalypse of) Baruch', in Charlesworth, *Old Testament Pseudepigrapha*, I, p. 631.

father, tear their clothes and don sackcloth in mourning after Matthias has uttered his lament. Westermann regards this utterance as influenced by the literary model of the Bible's individual lament.[29] But in view of its collective reference in v. 13 and the fact that the chief object of sorrow is the temple, this complaint can be viewed as a lament of the covenant mediator. Compare, e.g. Hab. 1.2-4, which is simultaneously a personal lament of the covenant mediator and a complaint on behalf of the nation. The narrative in 1 Maccabees 2 indicates a spontaneous act of prayer, which accords with the circumstances under which informal lament is often uttered in biblical contexts.

1 Macc. 3.50-53 probably contains a fragment of community lament. It is difficult to determine who utters this prayer, although the circumstances have similarities to 1 Macc. 2.7-13. The priestly family of the Maccabees is prominent in a position of leadership (v. 55) and the prayer is accompanied by mourning rituals (v. 47). As in 1 Macc. 2.7-13, the lament is framed with questions directed towards God (vv. 50, 53). In between the frame of questions, there is complaint about the desolation of the sanctuary (v. 51) and the threats of the enemy (v. 52). The questions are entirely in the first person plural and the circumstances suggest deliberate ritual action.

Westermann considered the complaints of Ezra in 2 Esdras and of Baruch in *2 Baruch* as examples of the severance of lament from prayer.[30] But these books contain prayers in conformity with the definition adopted in Chapter Two: a speech in which a person or community brings a concern before God (§2.2). The significance of Westermann's description of lament excluded from prayer will be addressed in §7.4.

Characteristic of the prayers of *2 Baruch* and 2 Esdras is their use of the rhetoric of disputation. This is a technique encountered previously in the book of Job and there are parallels in other biblical prayers. Prayers of disputation contain questions directed at God seeking information and response that can spill over into complaint (cf. Job 7.17-21; 10.2-7). Prose examples include Abraham's prayer on behalf of Sodom (Gen. 18.23-32) and Moses' prayer as covenant mediator in Num. 11.11-15. The rhetoric of disputation can also be found in psalms of communal lament (e.g. Pss. 77.8-10; 85.6-7; 94.20).

The prayers in *2 Baruch* and 2 Esdras are informal laments by a covenant mediator. This is indicated by their non-liturgical context and the fact that at least three of them do not end with explicit petitions. The same

---

29. Westerman, *Praise and Lament*, pp. 207-208.
30. Westerman, *Praise and Lament*, pp. 209-12.

rhetoric is also found in dialogue between God (or a divine representative) and Ezra. For example, Ezra's speeches to Uriel contain rhetorical questions or requests for information in interrogative form. Some of these questions are genuine complaints, e.g.

> How long and when will these things be? Why are our years few and evil?
> (2 Esd. 4.33)

The connection between the language of prayer and conversation in visionary circumstances was made previously in §2.2, cf. also *2 Bar.* 5.1; 2 Esd. 4.23-25.

2 Esd. 3.4-36; 5.23-30; 6.38-59, *2 Bar.* 3.1-9 resemble prayers of the covenant mediator; *2 Bar.* 3.1-9 mixes elements of LI with disputation on behalf of the community (cf. §7.1.1.2).

2 Esd. 3.4-36:

4a	Address	
4b-27	Confession of Trust/Retrospect	
28-36	Disputation	
	30-31	God-complaint
	33	We-complaint
	34	Petition/Challenge

2 Esd. 5.23-30:

23a	Address	
23b-27	Confession of Trust/Praise	
28-30	Disputation	
	28	God-complaint
	29	Enemy-complaint

2 Esd. 6.38-59:

38a	Address	
38b-54	Retrospect	
55-59	Disputation	
	57	Enemy-complaint
	58	We-complaint
	59	God-complaint

2 Bar. 3.1-9:

1a	Address	
1b	I-complaint	
2	Petition	
3	I-complaint	
4-9	Disputation	
	9	God-complaint

7.1.6. *Paraphrases of the Biblical Tradition*

Extra-biblical Second Temple Literature includes retellings of the biblical story. Within these 'parabiblical texts' are re-castings of biblical prayers as well as new petitionary material meant to fill out gaps in the scriptural narrative. For example, *Jubilees* 1 fills out the story of the revelation of the law on Sinai with conversation between Moses and God while Moses was on the mountain for forty days and forty nights. *Jub.* 1.19-21 contains a prayer of Moses for mercy on the people after being informed that they will not keep the Torah that God has just revealed.

Most interesting for this study is the retelling of the biblical story in *Pseudo-Philo*. Where prayers of Moses are paraphrased, the disputation form is prominent (cf. *Ps.-Philo* 12.8-9; 15.7; 19.8-9). The writer of *Pseudo-Philo* also created prayers of lament with no biblical precedent. In the paraphrase of Judg. 20.19-28, the people led by Phineas, the priest, pray after their defeat at the hand of Benjamin:

> What is this deceit by which you have led us astray, LORD? If what the sons of Benjamin have done is right in your eyes, why have you not told us so we might consider it? But if it did not please you, why have you allowed us to fall before them? (46.4)[31]

Another unprecedented complaint occurs in the search for a new leader during the time when Eli was high priest at Shiloh. No one is willing to exercise leadership even after the sacred lot has identified Elkanah as a candidate. The people complain to God:

> LORD God of Israel, why have you abandoned your people in the victory of your enemies, and in the time of distress why have you neglected your inheritance ... (49.6)[32]

In both cases the people's accusatory questions to God are answered by divine speech. *Ps.-Philo* 47.3-8 advances a sin-punishment explanation for the apparent divine failure in the case of the Benjaminites' initial victory: the people were discomfited because the previous sin of Micah's idolatry (Judges 17) had to be expiated. Elkanah's refusal is explained as a part of divine plan that will see the leadership fall on his son, the great prophet Samuel (*Ps.-Philo* 49.7-8).

---

31. D.J. Harrrington, 'Pseudo-Philo', in Charlesworth, *Old Testament Pseudepigrapha*, II, p. 361.
32. Harrington, 'Pseudo-Philo', p. 363.

7.2. Complaints against God in Second Temple Literature

As with biblical examples, it is possible to classify complaint against God in terms of direct and indirect expressions of protest. But Second Temple literature reveals a reversal of the distribution of the complaint against God as it was described in Chapter Four. There it was shown that community laments favored direct protest (accusatory questions and statements) and that indirect protest (negated Imperatives addressed to God) was less common (see Table Three). Not only is indirect protest the rule rather than exception in Second Temple communal laments (§7.2.1), but it is necessary to create a second category of indirect complaint against God unknown in biblical prayers outside of penitential compositions: the justification of divine action (7.2.2). Since expressions of indirect protest/complaint constitute the larger category in Second Temple literature, they will be surveyed first, followed by a list of examples of direct protest (§7.2.3).

7.2.1. Petitions of Indirect Protest
Petitions asking God not to act in a certain way are a mark of biblical lament.[33] But unlike the Psalms, in which negative Imperative petitions are virtually confined to the complaint form, apotropaic petitions are found in a wide range of extra-biblical literature.[34] They often cluster around common themes:

a. Turning aside wrath and punishment:

> Have pity on us and do not hold against us the iniquities of the forefathers... (4Q504 Frag. 4.5-6)[35]

> Do not weigh down your hand upon us, lest under duress we sin. (*Ps. Sol.* 5.6)[36]

See also Add Est. 13.17; Bar. 3.5; 2 *Bar.* 48.14; 2 Esd. 8.26-30; 3 *Macc.* 2.17; *Ps.-Philo* 12.9.

b. Against divine abandonment:

> Do not abandon your people... (*Jub.* 1.19)[37]

---

33. Werline, *Penitential Prayer*, p. 172-73.
34. See also the examples in David Flusser, 'Qumrân and Jewish Apotropaic Prayers', *IEJ* 16 (1966), p. 202.
35. Martínez and Tigchelaar, *Dead Sea Scrolls Study Edition*, II, p. 1011.
36. R.B. Wright, 'Psalms of Solomon', in Charlesworth, *Old Testament Pseudepigrapha*, II, p. 657
37. O.S. Wintermude, 'Jubilees', in Charlesworth, *Old Testament Pseudepigrapha*, II, p. 53.

> Do not forsake your people and your inheritance... (4Q393 Frag. 3.3)[38]

See also Add. Est. 13.16; Prayer of Azariah 11-12, 19; *Pss. Sol.* 7.1; 8.30; 9.8; 4Q393 Frag. 1-2, col. ii, 7; Frag. 3.3-5 (cf. Neh. 9.32).

c. Against being handed over to the enemy:

> Do not give our inheritance to foreigners, nor our produce to the sons of foreigners. (4Q501.1)[39]

See also Add. Est. 14.11; *Jub.* 1.19-20; *Ps. Sol.* 7.2-3.

d. Against the delay of help:

> ...do not take away the hope of our people and do not make short the times of our help. (*2 Bar.* 48.19)[40]

See also *Ps. Sol.* 2.25 (cf. Dan. 9.19).

7.2.2. *Justification of Divine Righteousness*

One of the characteristics of penitential prayer is justification of divine actions that have created the conditions of distress from which the community seeks relief. This motif is common in biblical examples from Ezra, Nehemiah and Daniel.[41] It may be considered as a form of indirect complaint because the confession of divine righteousness usually qualifies a description of the straits the community finds itself in because of divine punishment.[42] An extra-biblical example is found in Prayer of Azariah 8-9:

> So all that you have brought upon us, and all you that you have done to us, you have done in true judgment. You have given us into the hands of lawless enemies, most hateful rebels, and to an unjust king, the most wicked in all the world.

By the principles used in the analysis of the protests of national defeat in Chapter Four, the statement of what God has done to the people in v. 9 ought to be analyzed as direct protest against God. But its qualification in v. 8 justifies the divine action as 'true judgment'. The justification of divine righteousness turns an accusatory statement into a form of indirect protest. Other cases occur in Add. Est. 14.6-7; Bar. 1.15-20; 2.6-10; Prayer of Azariah 4-5; *Pss. Sol.* 2.15-21; 8.7-17; 9.1-2.[43]

---

38. Martínez and Tigchelaar, *Dead Sea Scrolls Study Edition*, II, p. 789.
39. Martínez and Tigchelaar, *Dead Sea Scrolls Study Edition*, II, p. 993.
40. Klijn, '2 Baruch', p. 636.
41. Patrick D. Miller, *They Cried to the Lord: The Form and Theology of Biblical Prayer* (Minneapolis: Fortress Press, 1994), pp. 257-58; cf. Dan. 9.7, 14; Ezra 9.15; Neh. 9.33.
42. Westermann, *Praise and Lament*, p. 202.
43. Identified in Westermann, *Praise and Lament*, p. 203. The justification of divine

7.2.3. *Direct Complaint against God*

Direct complaint against God is mainly found in questions in Second Temple prayers:

'Why?'

> If the world has indeed been created for us, why do we not possess our world as an inheritance? (2 Esd. 6.59)

Other cases occur in 2 Esd. 4.23-24, 33; 5.28; 1 Macc. 2.7, 13; *Ps.-Philo* 46.4; 49.6.

'How long?' (2 Esd. 4.33; 6.59)

'Where?'[44] (1 Macc. 3.50)

> And where is all that which you said to Moses about us?[45] (2 Bar. 3.9)

Other accusatory questions (*Ps.-Philo* 46.4):

> And what have you done to your great name?[46] (2 Bar. 5.1)
> O Lord, how have you borne it? (2 Bar. 11.4)[47]

There is an accusatory statement in 2 Esd. 3.30-31:

> I have seen how you endure those who sin, and have spared those who act wickedly, and have destroyed your people, and have preserved your enemies.

righteousness by the suffering people is a common theme of the *Psalms of Solomon*, see Werline, *Penitential Prayer*, pp. 186-88.

44. Another possible candidate for a complaining question against God using 'where?' occurs in 4Q393 Frg. 3, 'Where is strength? And upon whom shall you shine your face?' (Martínez and Tigchelaar, *Dead Sea Scrolls Study Edition*, II, p. 791). But the text uses the questions as a motif to reinforce petitions against the man who walks with 'stubbornness in his heart'. The questions are rhetorical rather than complaining, therefore, because they reinforce the assertion that the wicked will not be purified and sanctified.

45. Klijn, '2 Baruch', p. 621.

46. Klijn, '2 Baruch', p. 622.

47. Westermann (*Praise and Lament*, 209) finds evidence of all three forms of complaint in *2 Bar.* 10.6–12.4, including we-complaint in 10.6-19 and enemy-complaint in 11.1-3. But, as in the case of Lamentations 1–2, the we-complaint in *2 Baruch* 10 is mixed with dirge-like elements including the summons to mourn (10.8), a comparison of the former with the present state of affairs (10.6-7; cf. 11.1-2), a description of the mourner's pain (10.15-16) and questions expressing bewilderment about what has happened (10.10-15); cf. the typology of the dirge in Claus Westermann, *Lamentations: Issues and Interpretation* (Minneapolis: Fortress Press, 1994), p. 7. I do not agree with Westermann that there is enemy-complaint in 11.1-3; this is direct address to Babylon warning of its punishment in due time (cf. Lam. 4.21).

7.3. *The Eclipse of Collective Protest by Penitential Prayer*

The surveys in the last two sections show both continuities and discontinuities with biblical traditions. There are laments with a structure similar to protests of national defeat, including Address, Complaint, Confession of Trust/Retrospect and Petitions (§7.1.1). There are also echoes of the poetry in Lamentations (§7.1.4). Chapter Five concluded that both forms of communal lament were probably composed by similar groups of cultic singers/poets (§5.1). Evidently, their successors continued to compose community pleas and lamentations in the Second Temple era. But, in comparison with biblical tradition, there is also a notable absence. While there is evidence for complaint against God in extra-biblical Second Temple texts (§7.2.3), no motifs of direct protest are found in the poems that most formally resemble the protests of national defeat.

In his classic study on the history of lament, Claus Westermann explains the disappearance of protests against God in Second Temple prayers as due to a separation of lament from prayer. In effect, the complaint against God was silenced by the constantly repeated statement that everything that had happened to the community was justified. What had once been the occasion for lament became an opportunity for praising the righteous God. Therefore the polarity between lament and praise, so characteristic of biblical psalms, was abolished.[48]

The Prayer of Azariah provides a good illustration of this phenomenon. Internal details suggest a provenance associated with the persecution of Antiochus Epiphanes, although it was not inserted into Daniel at that time.[49] Despite its structural similarities with protests of national defeat, there is no direct complaint against God. Both types of indirect protest are attested, including the justification of divine righteousness (vv. 4-5, 8-9) and negative Imperatives (vv. 11-12, 19). But this is as close to protest against God as this text can come, despite the fact it was written as a prayer for the suffering righteous in a time of persecution.

The praise of divine justice in lieu of lament is especially prominent in penitential prayers (§7.1.3). It is typical to account for the origins of the penitential prayer genre in terms of a transformation of the protests of national defeat.[50] Reasons given for this transformation usually appeal to a combination of historical and psychological conditions that impinged

---

48. Westermann, *Praise and Lament*, pp. 202-203.
49. Moore, 'Daniel, Additions to', p. 19; Werline, *Penitential Prayer*, pp. 174, 178-79.
50. E,g. Bautch, *Developments in Genre*, pp. 23, 143; Boda, *Praying the Tradition*, pp. 25-26; Miller, *They Cried to the Lord*, p. 256; Westermann, *Praise and Lament*, p. 206.

on early Judaism as a result of the exile.[51] But it would be just as true to suggest that penitential prayer acts as a substitute for protest prayer as to say that the former is a transformation of the latter.[52] A typology of the common elements of penitential prayer includes Praise, Supplication, Confession of Sin, Historical Retrospective, Themes (covenant, land, law) and Statement of Purpose.[53] These stereotypical contents do not reflect the argumentative prayer genre; note the absence of an element of complaint. In fact, only one extra-biblical penitential prayer has a form common to psalms of collective protest, Prayer of Azariah 3-22.

No less than protests of national defeat and community distress, however, penitential prayers were intended for a people in crisis.[54] What has happened that prayers for the community in distress should often adopt a penitential rhetoric, while extra-biblical examples of argumentative prayer on behalf of the community eschew protest against God? Other scholars are producing extensive and useful studies on the nature of development of the penitential prayer genre in Second Temple Judaism.[55] The purpose of this section is not to duplicate those efforts but to complement them. I do not challenge the general opinion that historical and psychological conditions favoured the development of penitential prayer in the post-exilic period. I want to contribute to current scholarship on the rise of penitential prayer and the corresponding eclipse of communal protest, however, by suggesting that Judaism's entry into the Axial Age was a contributing factor to these developments.

Undoubtedly the practices of penitential prayer and collective protest overlapped for some time in the postexilic era, because there are indications that the psalms of collective protest complain about postexilic conditions (e.g. Psalms 9–10; 77; 90 and 94). But Judaism's entry into the Axial

---

51.   E.g. Rainer Albertz, *A History of Israelite Religion in the Old Testament Period* (OTL; 2 vols.; Louisville, KY: Westminster John Knox, 1994), II, pp. 508-11; Bautch, *Developments in Genre*, p. 172; Boda, *Praying the Tradition*, pp. 189-95; Meinrad Limbeck, 'Die Klage — Eine verschwundene Gebetsgattung', *TQ* 157 (1977), p. 11; Timo Veijola, 'Das Klagegebet in Literatur und Leben der Exilsgeneration am Beispiel eigenen Prosatexte', in J.A. Emerton (ed.), *Congress Volume: Salamanca 1983* (VTSup, 36; Leiden: E.J. Brill, 1985), pp. 304-305.

52.   It is significant that Werline (*Penitential Prayer*, pp. 62-64) does not trace the origins of biblical penitential prayer to the psalms but to the theology of Deuteronomy and Trito-Isaiah.

53.   Based on Boda, *Praying the Tradition*, p. 28.

54.   See Werline, *Penitential Prayer*, p. 194.

55.   E.g. Bautch (*Developments in Genre*), Boda (*Praying the Tradition*) and Werline (*Penitential Prayer*), all of whom were associated with the 'Consultation on Penitential Prayer, Origin, Development and Impact' at the annual meeting of the Society of Biblical Literature, 2003–2005.

Age favoured the development of penitential prayer and inhibited the continuity of lament. The argument below highlights a number of features of biblical penitential prayers that indicate this fundamental shift in the religious imagination of early Judaism. These diagnostic traits include the use of the motif of divine righteousness (§7.3.1), scriptural awareness in historical retrospectives and communal confessions of sin (§7.3.2) and the influence of a priestly elite in generating the theological perspective that penitential prayers assume (§7.3.3). The valorization of divine righteousness reinforced by a written record of divine commandments was commensurate with an exalted vision of transcendence that put the Holy One beyond question.

7.3.1. *Reversal of the Rhetoric of the God-Israel Relationship*
Chapter Four underscored theological assumptions governing the God–Israel relationship that were operative in the biblical poetry of collective protest. Protests of national defeat assume that it is a contradiction in terms if Israel should disappear or its institutions should be destroyed. By the very virtue of creating them, of calling Israel into being, YHWH has a responsibility to ensure their continuity.

The presuppositions of the God–Israel relationship are altered in biblical penitential prayers. In particular, the righteous party in the God–Israel relationship is redefined. According to Richard Bautch, this is apparent in three different ways: the use of the historical retrospect, the function of the confession of sin and the reference value of the binary pair, 'righteous and wicked'. Neh. 9.5-37 furnishes a good illustration of these traits. Whereas historical retrospect is used in communal laments to remind YHWH of the God–Israel relationship, its function in the penitential prayers is to motivate the people to confess their infidelity and recognize their dependency on divine grace. By the same token, the confession of sin becomes a motivating element for petitions for help and deliverance. This is not the confession of sin's function in community laments, where it is all but absent. A related reversal is manifested in the use of the binary pair, 'the righteous' and 'the wicked'. The tone of the communal laments implies that the people are righteous, while it is YHWH who is culpably indifferent to the people's plight. Neh. 9.33 is a key text in demonstrating how that logic is reversed in the penitential psalms. The people penitently assert their wickedness while imputing all justice to God.[56]

This transformation can be associated with the Axial Age theology articulated in the Elihu speeches that undermine Job's right to complain

---

56. Bautch, *Developments in Genre*, pp. 109-21.

against God. The last chapter observed that, according to Elihu, by virtue of his power and righteousness God has no accounts to render to human beings (Job 37.19-24). Similarly, in the biblical penitential prayers, divine sovereignty and righteousness are beyond question: YHWH is 'the great and awesome God' (Dan. 9.4; Neh. 1.5; 9.32),[57] who is in the right to afflict his people (Dan. 9.7, 14; Ezra 9.15; Neh. 9.33).[58] See also Bar. 1.15; *Pss. Sol.* 2.15-16; 9.2.

7.3.2. Scriptural Allusions in Penitential Prayers

There are two shifts in perspective between the protests of national defeat and biblical penitential prayers that are diagnostic of Axial Age thinking. These occur in the historical retrospectives and confessions of sin. They are connected through their emphasis on scripture. The transformation of ancient Judaism into a scriptural religion reflects the dynamics of the Axial Age.[59]

Historical retrospectives occur in a number of protests of national defeat: Isa. 63.7-14; Pss. 44.2-4; 60.8-10; 74.2; 80.9-12; 83.10-13; 89.20-38. They also occur in Dan. 9.7-15; Ezra 9.7-13; Neh. 1.7-9; 9.6-31. A comparison of the two groups shows that retrospects in the protests of national defeat emphasize the experience of Exodus, conquest of the land of promise and the gift of the Davidic dynasty. There is no mention of the bestowal of divine commandments on the nation as part of the descriptions of salvation history. The closest to this theme is the retrospect in Ps. 89.20-38, which mentions the precepts and laws given to the Davidic dynasty (v. 31). In contrast, the historical retrospects of biblical penitential prayers all mention the gift of commandments and divine instruction to the nation in its early history (Dan. 9.10; Ezra 9.10-11; Neh. 1.7; 9.14).

The emphasis on disobedience to divine commandments also stands in contrast to confessions of sin that belong to the late pre-exilic or exilic period. Witnesses to community confessions from these eras can be obtained from material in the DtrH and prophetic citations: Judg. 10.10, 15;[60] Isa. 59.9-15a;[61] Jer. 3.22b-25;[62] 14.7-9, 19-22. Such texts confess idolatry

---

57. Balentine, *Prayer in the Hebrew Bible*, p. 104.

58. Miller, *They Cried to the Lord*, pp. 257-58.

59. Michael E. Stone, 'Eschatology, Remythologization, and Cosmic Aporia', in S.N. Eisenstadt (ed.), *The Origins and Diversity of Axial Age Civilizations* (SUNY Series in Near Eastern Studies; Albany, NY: State University of New York, 1986), p. 244.

60. This text is recognized as an interpretative passage bearing the perspective of the Deuteronomistic History, see Norman K. Gottwald, *The Hebrew Bible: A Socio-Literary Introduction* (Philadelphia: Fortress Press, 1985), p. 242. It appears to be one of a number of passages in the DtrH reflecting exilic practice (see Veijola, 'Klagegebet', p. 306).

and rebellion against Yhwh; but they fail to make mention of a specific body of commandments. The confessions of sin in the postexilic penitential prayers, however, are closely connected with their historical retrospectives: both suggest that the nation possessed a body of scriptural instruction it deviated from.[63] This perspective sets the confessions of sin in Daniel 9; Ezra 9; Nehemiah 1; 9 apart from earlier expressions of communal contrition. Evidently, some kind of theological development has taken place by time the postexilic prayers of communal repentance were composed.

As the last chapter noted, the appearance of the Axial Age was closely connected with the rise of new social elites. They created new institutions to manage the perceived tension between the transcendental and mundane orders and offered comprehensive views of the world and how people should live in it. One of these institutions was scripture. Wilfred Cantwell Smith observes that there was a qualitative difference between the motives for composing scriptural writings in Israel and earlier models of authoritative texts in the ancient Near East. The idea of scripture attests to a transition from using writing to fix the status quo to setting out the manifesto of a group less interested in recording the past than on propounding its viewpoint in the present.[64] Creation and dissemination of a comprehensive religious and social program in written form was characteristic of the elite that dominated Persian-era Yehud.[65]

The scriptural context of the confessions of sin in penitential prayers and their associated historical retrospectives shows a new form of self-awareness in the community. The theology of penitential prayers suggest that a self-evident sense of belonging to the community has been lost; in its place one finds indications of a sense of belonging that is conscious

---

61. The dimensions of this text are disputed. Anton Schoors (*I Am God your Savior: A Form-Critical Study of the Main Genres in Is. Xl-LV* [VTSup, 24; Leiden: E.J. Brill, 1973], p. 37) identifies vv. 15b-20 as an oracular response to a community lament in vv. 9-15a. Claus Westermann (*Isaiah 40-66* [OTL; Philadelphia: Westminster Press, 1969], pp. 345-50) regards several portions of Isaiah 59 as belonging to a lament that underwent expansion. In his view, the original text included vv. 1, 9-11 and 15b-20, which portrays the longed-for divine epiphany. But there is no petition to link vv. 15b-20 to the preceding complaint, therefore, vv. 15b-20 are best considered as the prophet's answer to the people's complaint.

62. The text cites a communal lament that is followed by an oracular response in Jeremiah 4, see Schoors, *I Am God Your Savior*, p. 37.

63. Werline, *Penitential Prayer*, p. 64.

64. W.C. Smith, *What Is Scripture? A Comparative Approach* (Minneapolis: Fortress Press, 1993), p. 62

65. Ehud Ben Zvi, *Micah* (FOTL, 21B; Grand Rapids: Eerdmans, 2000), pp. 9-11.

and reflected.[66] Such deliberate and self-critical processes are marks of Axial Age civilizations.[67]

7.3.3. *Priestly Influences in the Emergence of Penitential Prayer*

Although Israel Knohl's dating of the Priestly movement is controversial, his characterization of P's reforms of Israel's cultic space remains valid, '...the cultic relation between humans and the dimension of God represented by the name Yahweh is detached from all aspects of mutual dependence. Instead, two principles are at the heart of the ideal cultic system—holiness and commandment'.[68] Publication of the Torah in a written form was part of an agenda to combine holiness and morality in a way that would encompass the people as a whole. This program of extending the limits of the sacred to include national morality can be viewed as an Axial Age transformation.[69]

The principles of holiness and commandment are both assumed in postexilic penitential prayer. Emphasis on commandment in the penitential prayers is obvious from the historical retrospectives and confessions of sin discussed in §7.3.2. Connections with holiness thinking have been disputed.[70] However, references to holy categories are attested in penitential prayers, cf. 'holy mountain' (Dan. 9.16), 'holy place' (Ezra 9.8), 'holy Sabbath' (Neh. 9.14), 'Israel your holy one' (Prayer of Azariah 12) and multiple occurrences in 4Q504.[71] Terminology related to holiness thinking includes allusions to uncleanness and pollution (1 Esd. 8.87; *Pss. Sol.* 2.3, 13; 8.11-12, 22) as well as to cleansing and purification (*Ps. Sol.* 9.6; 4Q393 Frg. 3.5).

The equation of national morality with holiness reinforced perceptions that Israel's (mis)fortunes were tied to its covenant (in)fidelity. The recent study of Neh. 9.5-37 by Mark Boda has underscored the engagement of

---

66. Balentine, *Prayer in the Hebrew Bible*, pp. 116-17.

67. Yehuda Elkana, 'The Emergence of Second-Order Thinking in Classical Greece' in Eisenstadt, *Origins and Diversity of Axial Age Civilizations*, pp. 63-64.

68. Israel Knohl, *The Sanctuary of Silence: The Priestly Torah and the Holiness School* (Minneapolis: Fortress Press, 1995), p. 149. Knohl dates writings in the P-style to both the pre-exilic period and postexilic era (p. 201). Here, I assume the dominance of P in the postexilic era following the consensus of critical scholarship.

69. Israel Knohl, 'Axial Transformations within Ancient Israelite Priesthood', in J.P. Árnason, S.N. Eisenstadt and Björn Wittrock (eds.), *Axial Civilizations and World History* (Jerusalem Studies in Religion and Culture, 4; Leiden: E.J. Brill, 2005), pp. 213-15, 221.

70. Werline (*Penitential Prayer*, pp. 193-94) de-emphasizes the influence of Levitical thought on the formation of penititential prayer. For the opposite point of view, see Boda, *Praying the Tradition*, pp. 196-97.

71. Conceded by Werline (*Penitential Prayer*, p. 193) who acknowledges levitical vocabulary in Ezra 9 and allusions to the Day of Atonement in 4Q504.

Priestly as well as Deuteronomistic theology in the generation of the prayers of community repentance.[72] Holiness thinking is also visible in the penitential prayer of Ezra 9, which emphasizes the uncleanness and impurity of the people in its allusion to the Deuteronomic instructions about mixed marriages. In fact, the vocabulary of 'abomination' is not used by Deuteronomy in connection with mixed marriages. Its appearance in Ezra 9.11 establishes an exegetical bridge between the marriage instructions in Deut. 7.1-3; 23.3-7 and Leviticus 18, an instruction on impurity and defilement. According to Lev. 18.26-30, the peoples cut off from the land were abominators. This link authorizes the exclusion of those who persist in the practice of mixed marriages lamented by Ezra 9.[73]

Additional evidence for the allergy of holiness thinking towards the complaint tradition can be seen in the fact that the P portions of the Pentateuchal narrative do not multiply the record of Israel's protests in the wilderness. The tables of references to prayers containing complaint against God which appear in Chapter Two show an absence of P material. The same is true for citations of complaints against God and Moses by the people in the wilderness. According to traditional Pentateuchal source divisions, the protests in Exod. 17.2-3; Num. 11.20; 14.2-3 and 21.5 likely belong to J-E. Critical consensus is divided only about the origins of the complaint against God in Exod. 16.3. If Exod. 16.3 comes from P,[74] the purpose of P's story of the manna in the wilderness is clearly to undercut the legitimacy of the people's lament. One may conclude that there is no approval of complaint against God in P and little acknowledgement even of the practice of a protest prayer.

Holiness thinking, therefore, reinforces the kind of theological reasoning that analyzes the distress of the people as due to their willful negligence of scriptural commands. The actions of God in bringing disaster upon his people are not arbitrary according to this construction, but a result of 'evil deeds and…great guilt' (Ezra 9.13). That Israel continues to survive at all is an expression of divine benevolence (v. 15). A theology that emphasizes divine transcendence and holiness while affirming the presence of a body of revealed instructions accessible and known to the community undermines the perception that experiences of divine absence or affliction are exercises in arbitrary power. The only conclusion that the community can draw from such a theology is that it has itself to blame for

---

72. Boda, *Praying the Tradition*, pp. 186-87.
73. Bautch, *Developments in Genre*, pp. 88-89.
74. John Van Seters (*The Life of Moses: The Yahwist as Historian in Exodus–Numbers* [Louisville, KY: Westminster John Knox Press, 1994], pp. 181-88) thinks that the core of Exodus 16 (including v. 3) belongs to a story by J that was merged with P's manna story.

its misfortunes because of its failures to obey the divine commandments; its deity remains in the right even when the nation fails to prosper. In such circumstances, protest gives way to penitence.

7.4. *Protest Prayer in Second Temple Sources*

I have already mentioned Westermann's opinion that lament became separated from prayer in later Second Temple times. He cites as evidence of the exclusion of lament from prayer four different types of examples: the lamentation in Bar. 4.9-16; the apparently free-standing complaints in 1 Macc. 2.7-13; 3.50-53; *Psalms of Solomon* 2 and 8; and complaints appearing the apocalyptic books of *2 Baruch* and *2 Esdras*.[75]

These texts, however, can be explained differently. Section 7.1.4 made the case for a continuing tradition of composition in the style of Lamentations to which Bar. 4.9-16 belonged. Chapter Five observed that the poetry of Lamentations represented a form of community complaint that had accommodated the prophetic critique to the need to lament the destruction of Israel. Evidently, poetry continued to be composed in this vein to provide a vehicle for community supplications. Even if Bar. 4.9-16 is a literary imitation of this genre, there is reason to believe that Lamentations-type prayers were being composed in the Second Temple era. *Psalms of Solomon* 2 and 8 belong to the genre of penitential prayers (§7.1.3). It is not surprising that these poems do not contain direct complaint against God, because this genre does not normally do so.

Westermann interprets 1 Macc. 2.7-13 and 3.50-53 as examples of free-standing lament because the element of supplication is not evident. However, this explanation seems to forget the fact that informal lament containing complaint against God is attested in the biblical record (see Chapter Two). As an appropriation of a conversational strategy for making requests, informal lament could have continued as a form of prayer as long as the conversational trope itself was in use. Section 7.1.5 points to the presence of complaining requests in speech in *2 Baruch*. 1 Macc. 2.7-13 can be analyzed as an extra-biblical example of informal lament by a covenant mediator.

1 Macc. 3.50-53 alludes to a ceremony of lamenting supplication. If one allows for the possibility that prayers could be spontaneously produced by cultic experts, there is little reason to dismiss 1 Macc. 3.50-53 as a witness to a tradition of prayer that persisted in the Maccabean era. Along with 1 Macc. 2.7-13, the text in 1 Macc. 3.50-53 points to the practice of protest prayer by recognized leaders of the community in extreme

75. Westerman, *Praise and Lament*, pp. 206-12.

circumstances that symbolize a breach in the God–Israel relationship. Both texts are uttered in the wake of the desecration of the Second Temple by Antiochus Epiphanes and prior to its liberation (1 Maccabees 4).

There are connections between the practice of protest prayer represented by 1 Macc. 2.7-13; 3.50-53 and intercessions by covenant mediators using protest prayer in biblical texts. Most of the biblical examples are uttered by prophetic types, but there was a synthesis of priestly and prophetic traditions in the postexilic period.[76] An indicator of this synthesis is that references to community mediators in Second Temple narratives favour priests as intercessors. Ezra, e.g. intercedes for the people in Ezra 9. He also vociferously complains on behalf of the people in 2 Esdras. Judah Maccabee comes from a priestly family and he prays for the people (e.g. 1 Macc. 4.30; 2 Macc. 15.22) as does his father (1 Macc. 2.7). According to 2 Macc. 1.23, priests offer prayer while the people and Nehemiah respond. In 3 *Macc.* 2.1 it is the high priest Simon who prays for the protection of the community from King Ptolemy's persecution, while the distinguished priest Eleazar prays on behalf of the people in 3 *Macc.* 6.1. Moreover, when the writer of *Ps.-Philo* 46.4 inserts an unprecedented complaint into the paraphrase of Judg. 20.26-28, the narrative specifies that the prayer is led by 'Phineas, the son of Eleazar, the priest'.

I assume, therefore, it is probable that behind the fragmentary prayer of 1 Macc. 3.50-53 stands a priestly figure, perhaps Judah the Maccabee who is mentioned in 3.55. There is a connection, therefore, between the status of the petitioners in 1 Macc. 2.7-13 and 3.50-53 as well as in the form of these prayers and the *ad hoc* circumstances in which they appear in the narrative. These two prayers are similar in form: both are framed by complaining questions that enclose lament over the destroyed temple. Evidently, the author of 1 Maccabees thought these texts were an appropriate form of prayer for the national crisis of the time.

It would be hardly surprising that such a monumental catastrophe as the loss of the Temple would generate accusations that Israel's deity was unfaithful to the conditions of the God–Israel relationship. Such outbursts would have been fed by the scriptural record itself. If the library of Qumran is any indicator, the large number of Psalm-scrolls discovered there points to the usage and importance of the Psalms in the community's liturgical life. Therefore, the community's worship must have included the many psalms of lament with their petitions for help and deliverance.[77] The same conclusion is valid for other communities in Second Temple Judaism. For example, Ps. 79.2-3 is quoted in 1 Macc. 7.17 and there are

---

76. Boda, *Praying the Tradition*, pp. 189-95; Benjamin D. Sommer, 'Did Prophecy Cease? Evaluating a Reevaluation', *JBL* 115 (1996), pp. 41-42.
77. Schuller, 'Petitionary Prayer and the Religion of Qumran', pp. 44-45.

likely allusions to the same psalm in 1 Macc. 1.16-40; 2.7-13 and 2 Macc. 8.2-4.[78] We may assume that the biblical laments continued to be read in services of worship. They remained a powerful witness to the God–Israel relationship. In times of extreme stress the logic of this theology and its perception of divine responsibility would have asserted itself, even if normative practice denied protest against God expression in worship.

Indications are that the protests in 1 Macc. 2.7-13 and 3.50-53 reflect spontaneous protest prayer uttered in extraordinary circumstances. Both take place at a time of almost total breakdown of the worship system, when the temple itself was inoperative due to its defilement. There are other indications that complaint emerged in such extreme conditions (cf. the 'how long?' questions in Dan. 8.13 and 12.6). These conditions correspond, in fact, to the conditions under which the biblical protests of national defeat were also composed. Direct protest was articulated at the moment of a profound breakdown in the prevailing theological paradigm.

The form of the informal prayer of distress uttered by the community representative in 1 Macc. 2.7-13 remained part of liturgical practice into the Mishnaic period. Evidence is best for prayers in times of drought, but there are also indications of spontaneous informal laments in times of siege and political crisis.[79] Most striking is Levi's prayer in *b. Ta'an.* 25a:

> Master of the universe, you have ascended and taken your seat on high, but you are not showing mercy on your children![80]

Like a number of biblical informal laments on behalf of the community, the prayer is motivated by complaint against God with no explicit petition (cf. §2.2.1.1). The text from *b. Ta'an.* 25a, therefore, reveals continuity in the use of informal lament as a form of intercession for the community. Such prayers were permitted only to especially righteous persons and only in extreme situations when other means had failed.[81] But they do show the persistence of a spontaneous tradition of complaint prayer for the people *in extremis*.

78. Gerstenberger, *Psalms*, II, p. 102.

79. Joseph Heinemann, *Prayer in the Talmud: Forms and Patterns* (SJ, 9; Berlin: W. de Gruyter, 1977), p. 201. Law court prayers for drought are discussed at length in Anson Laytner, *Arguing with God: A Jewish Tradition* (Northvale, NJ: Jason Aronson, 1990), pp. 87-101. I would analyze some of Laytner's examples differently, however. For example, what he labels as petition in the case of Hanina b. Dosa is an informal lament which implies petition, 'Master of the universe, the whole world is at ease while Hanina is in distress!' (p. 91; *b. Ta'an.*24b; *b. Yom.*53b).

80. My translation of the Hebrew text published in Heinemann, *Prayer in the Talmud*, p. 292; Heinemann's translation is on p. 209.

81. Laytner, *Arguing with God*, pp. 100-101.

Therefore, I cannot accept Westermann's judgment that the pattern of prayer in 1 Macc. 2.7-13; 3.50-53 represents the exclusion of lament from prayer. On the contrary, these prayers suggest a continuity of the biblical informal lament tradition identified previously. As in the biblical examples of informal collective complaint, the prayers are uttered by recognized intermediaries. But what distinguishes the biblical from the extra-biblical material is not only the relatively small number of examples of informal lament in the latter, but also indications that the practice was not sanctioned by the scribal elites responsible for much of Second Temple literature.

Protest prayer is resisted in other Second Temple literature that reflects community crisis. One of the most significant indicators of a theological shift is that the various destructions of the Second Temple (including the attacks of Antiochus Epiphanes and Pompey) did not generate a significant collection of poetry like the protests of national defeat. It is significant that no direct complaint against God occurs in a lengthy or well-formed composition of prayer (i.e. with elements of Address and Petition). A good illustration is found in the so-called *Psalms of Solomon*. Composed in the wake of Pompey's desecration of the temple,[82] these poems do not imitate the psalms of national defeat but prefer to echo penitential themes. Another indicator is found in the poetry of Qumran. There is not a single expression of direct protest against God at Qumran.[83]

In addition, the various complaints found in 2 *Baruch* and 2 *Esdras* appear to be compositions by authors whose main intent was to silence complaint against God after the destruction of the Second Temple.[84] The complaints in both books are systematically refuted by divine revelations. The protest against God, therefore, in these apocalyptic works is a literary device. A similar motif appears with respect to the complaints composed in the parabiblical book of *Pseudo-Philo* from roughly the same time period.[85] The author invents complaints of the people in 46.4 and 49.6 only to have them definitively refuted by the divine voice.

There are resemblances between the informal laments found in 2 *Baruch* and 2 *Esdras* (§7.1.5) and texts found in aggadic literature, identified by Joseph Heinemann as prayers in the 'law court pattern'. Disputational

82. Wright, 'Psalms of Solomon', pp. 640-41.
83. For the identification of penitential prayers in Qumran as crisis literature, see Werline, *Penitential Prayer*, p. 194.
84. See Westermann, *Praise and Lament*, pp. 209-12.
85. Harrington ('Pseudo-Philo', p. 229) dates *Pseudo-Philo* to about 100 CE, roughly the same time in which both 2 *Baruch* and the Jewish apocalypse in 2 Esdras 3–14 were composed, see Michael E. Stone, 'Esdras, Second Book of', *ABD*, II, p. 612 and Klijn, 'Second Baruch', p. 617.

rhetoric is prominent in all of these cases. Examples are found in *Lev. R.* 10.1,[86] *Exod. R.* 5.22;[87] *Lam. R.* Proem 24;[88] 5.19.[89] An example of a prayer of the covenant mediator which retains its focus as a prayer of individual lament occurs in *Deut. R.* 11.20.[90]

There is no indication that the prayers preserved in aggadic literature were used in liturgical contexts.[91] This observation reinforces the suggestion made above that the prayers in *2 Baruch* and *2 Esdras* are literary compositions. Both *2 Baruch* and *2 Esdras* were written about a generation after the destruction of the Second Temple (with the possibility that *2 Baruch* is slightly later and dependent on *2 Esdras*). The force of the silencing of complaint against God in *2 Baruch* and *2 Esdras* is underscored by the status of the covenant mediators whose protest is refused. The literary symbols of Ezra and Baruch are community representatives of unquestioned piety and authority. But the prayers and disputations of Baruch and Ezra are only recorded so that they can be explained away by divine revelation.

These apocalyptic works interpret national suffering as a symptom of the approach of the final judgment of the world by Israel's deity. This theology is manifested in more than one way. *2 Esdras* argues that the only reasonable explanation for the severity of the current sufferings of Judaism is that they are the final, most painful birth pangs of salvation. In contrast to *2 Esdras*, *2 Baruch* explains that Zion has been removed so the evil world at large may be properly punished. Suffering is neither necessary punishment nor rejection, it is fallout from the emergence of the messianic age.[92]

Such explanations recall the redemptive/vicarious theory of suffering articulated by the Second Isaiah (§5.4). This prophet also attempted to silence complaint by denying that the social disasters the exilic community was suffering meant that the God–Israel relationship was dysfunctional. The community complaints of the diaspora in Babylon were discounted by the proclamation of a future salvation that was prepared for by present

---

86. Also found in *Gen. R.* 39.6 without the element of address, see Heinemann, *Prayer in the Talmud*, pp. 215-16. This prayer is analyzed in Laytner, *Arguing with God*, pp. 45-46, but Laytner is incorrect to suggest that this text contains the element of petition.

87. See Laytner, *Arguing with God*, pp. 49-50.

88. Heinemann, *Prayer in the Talmud*, p. 215.

89. See Laytner, *Arguing with God*, p. 75.

90. See Heinemann, *Prayer in the Talmud*, p. 216; discussed in Laytner, *Arguing with God*, p. 65.

91. Laytner, *Arguing with God*, p. 100.

92. David Kraemer, *Responses to Suffering in Classical Rabbinic Literature* (New York: Oxford University, 1995), pp. 41-44.

suffering (cf. Isaiah 53). This theory reasserted itself in Second Temple apocalyptic works that acknowledged the complaints of the people even as they attempted to explain them away.

But there is a vital difference between the complaints alluded to in the Second Isaiah and those in 2 *Baruch* and 2 Esdras. The Second Isaiah cites fragments of liturgical poetry with lamenting formulas. This is not the case in 2 *Baruch* and 2 Esdras. The absence of allusion to a living liturgical background is telling. In all probability there was a practice of informal protest prayer after the destruction of Jerusalem's temple in 70 CE. The spontaneous complaint tradition doubtless asserted itself in the wake of the terrible catastrophe that was the loss of the Second Temple. The disputational prayers of 2 *Baruch* and 2 Esdras indirectly witness to this practice. But the intent of these apocalyptic works is to undermine the legitimacy of such actions, in other words: to exclude lament from prayer.

Therefore, where Westermann sees a *fait accompli*, I see a *Tendenz* in the patterns of extra-biblical prayer. There does appear to be an interest in excluding the complaint against God from prayer in Second Temple times, but it was not completely successful. All categories of well-formed prayer exclude protest against God. One may infer that the tradition of argumentative prayer was not ordinarily used in community worship. However, moments of extreme crisis involving loss of access to the temple revived spontaneous and informal prayers of protest. Most strange, given the biblical data, is the resistance to the complaint against God after the destruction of the Second Temple. The refutation of the protests of community representatives of the utmost probity found in 2 *Baruch* and 2 Esdras suggest awareness of sentiment in the community that called into question divine providence. Subsequent Jewish authorities would also work to suppress the voice of complaint. In the face of a long and interminable exile, the Rabbis of the Amoraic period (c. 200–500 CE) were anxious to avoid a rhetoric that called divine justice into question. As a result, complaint against God was deemed inadmissible in public statuatory prayers.[93] But protest prayer would continue to assert itself in key moments of the Jewish experience (see §9.2).

7.5. *Collective Protest in the New Testament*

There are three possible texts of community lament in the New Testament. They include Jesus' lament over Jerusalem, the Lord's Prayer, and the protests of the martyred saints in Revelations. Only the last one meets the formal criteria used in this study, however. Mt. 23.37-39 (= Lk. 13.34-35) is

93. Laytner, *Arguing with God*, p. 110.

a lament in the sense that it is a prophetic announcement of judgment, perhaps ending with a call to repentance.[94] Therefore, it resembles prophetic oracles of judgment which adapt the dirge form to proclaim the coming fate of the nation (e.g. Isa. 1.21-23; 14.4-21; 23.1-14; Jer. 9.16-21). The Lord's Prayer (Mt. 6.9-13 = Lk. 11.2-4) is a prayer in the first person plural that contains as one of its petitions 'lead us not into temptation'. This is a form of indirect protest, consisting of a negative Imperative directed at God.[95] Its membership, however, is with a group of personal prayers that occasionally use apotropaic sentences.[96] One of the traits of Second Temple prayers is the widespread use of apotropaic sentences beyond the lament form proper (see §7.2.1).

Conversational strategies for communicating requests indicate the potential for informal collective lament. Faced with the prospect of death at sea, the disciples appeal to Jesus with a complaint implying a request for help in Mk 4.38 (= Lk. 8.24; cf. Mt. 8.25 where the request is explicit). The only community complaint prayer in the New Testament also uses the conversational strategy of implicit request motivated by complaint:

> O Sovereign Lord, holy and true, how long before you will judge and avenge our blood on those who dwell upon the earth? (Rev. 6.10)

The first person plural reference indicates that this is a communal lament. Its form is typical of prayers in which the request for help is implied by a complaint. The question places the responsibility for the continuity of the community's suffering onto God. There are two possible models for explaining the background to the inclusion of this prayer in the Apocalypse of John. One is that the prayer represents a literary allusion to pre-existing biblical models. The other is that the text attests to a convention still in use in Jewish circles. I suggest that both explanations are necessary to explain the presence of Rev. 6.10.

Commentators on Rev. 6.10 typically point to biblical parallels to the question 'how long?' in the Psalms and in prophetic texts.[97] There is no doubt that there are biblical models for the form of Rev. 6.9-11. Parallels

---

94. Warren Carter, 'Matthew 23.37-39', *Int* 54 (2000), p. 66; H. van der Kwaak, 'Die Klage über Jerusalem (Matt. XXIII 37-39)', *NovT* 8 (1966), p. 170.

95. Unfortunately, the modern translation of the Lord's Prayer used in many English-speaking denominations obscures this relationship. The petition 'save us from the time of trial' (copyright 1988, by the English Language Liturgical Consultation) is a paraphrase which severs the connection between the indirect protest 'lead us not into temptation' and the traditions of lament

96. Flusser, 'Qumrân and Jewish Apotropaic Prayers', p. 202.

97. E.g. G.K. Beale, *The Book of Revelation* (NIGTC; Grand Rapids: Eerdmans, 1999), pp. 392-93; R.P. Mounce, *The Book of Revelation* (NICNT, 17; Grand Rapids: Eerdmans, 1977), p. 159.

occur in Hab. 1.2-4; Zech. 1.12; Dan. 8.13 and 12.6 where prayers with the question 'how long' are met with divine answers.

The examples from Daniel belong to its Hebrew portions, which are generally associated with Jewish apocalyptic. The texts of 2 *Baruch* and 2 *Esdras* also show the eruption of questions to God in apocalyptic contexts (§7.2.3). In fact, Rev. 6.9-11 has a number of points of contact with Second Temple apocalypses. These include:

v. 9   The motif of the souls under the altar.[98]
v. 10   The expectation that martyrdom should be a cause for divine judgment.[99] The question 'how long?' has a close parallel in 2 Esdras 4.35 where it is put into the mouths of the souls of the righteous.[100]
v. 11   The idea that the end cannot come before the full number of martyrs is reached (cf. *1 En.* 47.4; 2 Esd. 2.41; 4.36).[101]

Rev. 6.10 is an example of the tradition of spontaneous complaint prayer described in §7.4. Apart from Rev. 6.10, the few allusions to collective complaint against God in the New Testament are of a piece with the dominant attitude of Second Temple Judaism, which rejects the legitimacy of protest against God. Paul, e.g. turns aside complaints against divine justice in Rom. 9.19-21 because God has hardened the hearts of Jews so that Gentiles may come into the covenant. There are indications in the book of Hebrews that members of a persecuted community of early Christians have become disaffected with their new faith. But the goal of the writer is clearly to challenge and rebuke those whose faith is weakening.[102] It would appear that early Christian leadership was prone to adopt the viewpoint of the divine respondents in 2 Esdras and 2 *Baruch*: the old order is passing away and apparently unjust suffering is necessary as the birth pangs for a new reality. A similar position was articulated by the writer of Hebrews (cf. 12.1-3) and the divine voice in Rev. 6.11. Nevertheless, in an extreme situation such as the persecution reflected in Revelations, the tradition of spontaneous complaint prayer in Second Temple Judaism found an expression in early Christian literature.

98. J. Massyngberde Ford, *Revelation* (AB, 38; Garden City, NY: Doubleday, 1975), p. 110.

99. Beale, *Revelation*, p. 393. The idea that martyrdom ought to arouse divine vengeance was current in Second Temple Judaism; see J.A. Goldstein, *1 Maccabees* (AB, 41; Garden City, NY: Doubleday, 1976), p. 40.

100. Jürgen Roloff, *The Revelation of John* (Continental Commentary; Minneapolis: Augsburg Fortress Press, 1993), p. 89.

101. Roloff, *Revelation*, p. 89; Mounce, *Revelation*, p. 160.

102. Harold W. Attridge, 'Hebrews, Epistle to', *ABD*, III, p. 100.

7.6. *Summary and Conclusions*

The composition of lament psalms did not end with the return to Jerusalem and the beginning of the Second Temple era. There is evidence of postexilic communal laments in the Psalter (e.g. Psalms 85 and 90). In fact, liturgical poems following the structure of protests of national defeat continued to be written in Second Temple Jewish communities. Nevertheless, it is characteristic of extra-biblical Second Temple prayers on behalf of the faith community that, where the lament form is used, the complaint against God is absent or indirect.

Direct complaint against God did not entirely disappear, however. It asserted itself in moments of extreme distress connected with the cessation of temple services. Especially devout leaders of the community did voice the people's complaint to God in extemporaneous prayers, and there are witnesses to this practice both in 1 Maccabees and the apocalyptic tradition. But as an expression of Second Temple Jewish piety, spontaneous protest prayer had to contend with barriers besides the institutionalization of protest against God built into biblical tradition. Chapter Five pointed out the psychological impact of the devastations of the Babylonian conquest. The nation collectively lost some of its self-esteem in the presence of God and its relationship with the deity was considered less certain. As a result, the confidence in its rights as a covenant-partner in the God–Israel was severely shaken. At the same time, there was the impact of Deuteronomistic thinking among Israel's intellectuals (prophets), who denied the suitability of the complaint tradition as a response to national catastrophe. This prophetic response became merged with a priestly theology under the influence of the Axial Age, with its emphasis on a synthesis of public morality and holiness.

One result of this nexus of influences was the rise of penitential prayer. The theology of penitential prayer undermines the protest against God by its insistence on national disaster as the just penalty for sin. But it would be truer to the literature of Second Temple Judaism to claim that the rhetoric of collective protest was eclipsed rather than replaced in penitential prayer. Indirect complaint against God continued to be expressed. It is attested both in the use of petitions in the negated imperative and in the praise of divine righteousness in penitential compositions. Even while justifying divine punishment, penitential prayer catalogues the suffering of the people.

Unlike biblical literature, there is no sizeable body of Second Temple liturgical poetry comparable to the biblical protests of national defeat. The non-normative nature of the complaint against God in Second Temple times is borne out by the patterns of informal prayer that contain direct protest. These prayers are connected with extreme exigencies involving the loss of the temple during the time of the persecutions of Antiochus Epiphanes and after 70 CE. Some development can be detected, however, with respect to the attitude of Jewish religious leadership towards protest prayer in these two time periods. The impetus of the times was towards the exclusion of lament from prayer. While spontaneous protests by pious covenant mediators were given some sanction in the narratives of 1 Maccabees, the apocalyptic works of 2 *Baruch* and 2 Esdras refuse the complaints against God uttered by even the most reputable of community representatives. A similar treatment of protest against God appears in other contemporary Second Temple literature including the parabiblical book of *Pseudo-Philo* and Revelations. Nevertheless, the tradition of informal lament persisted into Talmudic times, though rabbinic authorities sought to prevent the articulation of protest against God in public worship.

Chapter 8

PRAYERS FOR INDIVIDUALS IN EXTRA-BIBLICAL SECOND TEMPLE LITERATURE

Direct complaint against God is uncommon in extra-biblical Second Temple prayers with petitions only for individuals — even more uncommon than in community prayers. The goal of this chapter is to account for this situation. First, relevant examples of prayers for individuals will be identified (§8.1). As in Chapter Seven, examples are taken from extra-biblical Jewish compositions of the Second Temple period according to scholarly consensus.[1] Expressions of complaint against God are classified in §8.2. The evidence of these two sections indicates a shift in function for the form of individual lament (LI) in Second Temple times (§8.3). This shift is also indicated by the forms of prayer used against demonic attack (§8.4). New Testament usage suggests a similar picture to that obtained from other groups of early Jewish texts (§8.5). Observations will be synthesized in order to establish at what point in the Second Temple period the poetry of LI lost its original function (§8.6).

8.1. Parallels to LI in Extra-Biblical Second Temple Literature

8.1.1. Laments like those in the Psalter

The following prayers have a structure reminiscent of individual complaint prayers in the Psalter:

1 En. 84.2-6

2a	Address
2b-3	Confession of Trust/Praise
4a	Enemy-complaint
4b	God-complaint (statement)
5-6	Petitions

---

1.   Dating of extra-biblical sources follows opinions found in the *Anchor Bible Dictionary* and introductory articles in J.H. Charlesworth (ed.), *The Old Testament Pseudepigrapha* (2 vols.; Garden City, NY: Doubleday, 1983, 1985).

Joseph and Aseneth 12

Joseph and Aseneth 12–13 contains the text of a long prayer of repentance and conversion by Aseneth. Though the pattern is not visible in the continuation of Aseneth's prayer, ch. 12 contains many elements common to the individual complaint prayer:

1	Address
1b-2	Confession of Trust/Praise
3	Confession of Sin
4-5a	Petitions, including motifs of Confession of Sin
5b-6	I-complaint, including Confession of Trust motif
7	Petition
8	Confession of Trust
9-10	Enemy-complaint and I-complaint
11-12	Petitions, including Enemy-complaint motif
13	I-complaint
14-16	Petitions, including Confession of Trust motif.

Jub. 10.3-6:

3a	Address
3b	Confession of Trust/Retrospect
3c-6	Petitions, including Enemy-complaint motif

Prayer of Manasseh:[2]

This prayer of individual confession of sin and contrition was apparently written to supply the text of King Manasseh's repentance described in 2 Chron. 33.12-13. The text of this prayer is preserved in the Septuagint and Syriac translations of the Hebrew Bible. A second, fragmentary prayer of Manasseh is preserved in 4Q381 (*4QNon-Canonical Psalms B*) Frag. 33–35.8-11 but no elements of complaint are extant. The parallel provides additional support for the assumption that the Prayer of Manasseh stems from Jewish circles before the turn of the era.[3]

1	Address
2-8	Confession of Trust/Praise
9-10	I-complaint
11-12	Confession of Sin
13-14	Petitions, including Confession of Trust motif
15	Vow of Praise

Psalm 152

Several non-canonical psalms have been transmitted in the Septuagint and the Syriac versions of the Hebrew Bible. The Dead Sea Scrolls also

2. Identified by Claus Westermann, *Praise and Lament in the Psalms* (Atlanta: John Knox Press, 1981), p. 202.

3. See J.H. Charlesworth, 'Prayer of Manasseh', in Charlesworth, *Old Testament Pseudepigrapha*, II, p. 627.

attest to the composition of extra-biblical psalms (cf. Psalms 151A; 151B; 154; 155). Psalm 152 is attested only in Syriac; nevertheless, it shows indications of a similar origin to non-canonical psalms attested at Qumran.[4]

1	Address and Petition
2-3	Enemy-complaint
4-6	Petitions, including a Vow of Praise motif (vv. 4-5)

Ps.-Philo 18.4

Balaam replies to God's request for information with a complaint unprecedented in the biblical parallel (cf. Num. 22.9-10):

Address
God-complaint ('why?')
Confession of Trust
Petition

Ps.-Philo 50.4 (paraphrase of 1 Sam. 1.11):

Address
Disputation
Petition, including Confession of Trust motif

Tob. 3.2-6.[5]

2a	Address
2	Confession of Trust/Praise
3a	Petitions
3b-5	Confession of Sin, including justification of divine righteousness
6a, 6c	Petitions
6b, 6d	I-complaint

Tob. 3.11-15.[6]

11-12	Address and Praise
13	Petition, including I-complaint motif
14-15a	Declaration of Innocence
15b	I-complaint and God-complaint ('why?')
15c	Petition

Wis. 9.1-18 (paraphrase of 1 Kings 3.6-9):

1a	Address
1b-3	Confession of Trust/Praise
4	Petitions
5-6	I-Complaint

---

4. J.H. Charlesworth and J.A. Sanders, 'More Psalms of David', in Charlesworth, *Old Testament Pseudepigrapha*, II, p. 615.
5. Identified by Westermann, *Praise and Lament*, p. 204.
6. Identified by Westermann, *Praise and Lament*, p. 204.

7-9	Confession of Trust/Retrospect
10	Petition
11-12	Confession of Trust
13-18	Praise (in disputation form)

4Q372 (4QApocJos^b) Frag. 1.16-31:[7]

16	Address
16-17	Petitions
17-19	Confession of Trust
19-21	Enemy-complaint
22-31	Vow of Praise

8.1.2. *Informal Lament*

There is one individual complaint prayer similar to the self-contained lament form described in Chapter Two:

Susanna 42–43

There are indications that the story of Susanna was originally written in either Hebrew or Aramaic. The story of Susanna is preserved in both the Septuagint and the Greek translation of Theodotian; however, this speech of Susanna is preserved only in the version of Theodotian. The petition in Susanna's prayer is implied by the elements of complaint. Its structure includes:

42a	Address
42b	Confession of Trust
43a	Enemy-complaint
43b	I-complaint, including a Declaration of Innocence

8.2. *Complaints against God in Second Temple LI*

All three categories of God-complaint noted in §7.2 are found in extra-biblical individual laments.

8.2.1. *Petitions of Indirect Protest*

There are three categories of apotropaic petitions:

a. Turning aside wrath and punishment: *1 En.* 84.5-6; Pr. Man. 13; Tob. 3.3.
b. Against divine abandonment: Tob. 3.6; Wis. 9.4; 4Q372 Frag. 1.16.
c. Against being handed over to the enemy: *Jub.* 10.3, 5-6.

---

7. Identified by Esther G. Chazon, 'Hymns and Prayers in the Dead Sea Scrolls', in P.W. Flint and J.C. VanderKam (eds.), *The Dead Sea Scrolls after Fifty Years: A Comprehensive Assessment* (2 vols.; Leiden: E.J. Brill, 1999), I, p. 268.

As in the case of Second Temple communal laments, apotropaic petitions occur in other types of prayers besides the LI form (e.g.1 QH^a 8.26;[8] 4Q381 Frag. 45 and 79; Psalm 155).

8.2.2. *Justification of Divine Righteousness*
Chapter 7 noted a second class of indirect protest involving the justifications of divine righteousness associated with descriptions of national suffering as a result of punishment for sin (§7.2.2). This category also appears in Tob. 3.5, where Tobit connects his personal suffering with the suffering of the nation inflicted by a righteous God on account of sin.

8.2.3. *Direct Complaint against God*
Question:

> Why should I live? Tob. 3.15

Cf. *Ps.-Philo* 18.4

Statement:

> The angels of your heavens are now committing sin (upon the earth) and your wrath shall rest upon the flesh of the people until (the arrival of) the great day of judgment.[9] (*1 En.* 84.4)

This is a prayer for the salvation of those that remained righteous before the deluge. Enoch assigns the ultimate responsibility for the pre-deluge situation to God. The corruption of all flesh has angered God, whose destructive wrath is anticipated (vv. 5-6). Verse 4 complains of the sin of the angels in the pre-flood generations, alluding to Gen. 6.1-6. But they are 'angels of your heavens' and the calamity of divine wrath is a problem which requires relief.

8.3. *Functional Shifts in Second Temple LI*

The goal of this discussion is not to deny that prayers in the form of LI could be uttered by individuals in Second Temple Judaism. There are several reasons to think that the form of LI might continue in use. First, there are multiple attestations of the structural formula used in psalms of LI in §8.1.1 Second, there is a case of informal lament in §8.1.2, which Chapter

---

8.   Eileen Schuller, 'Petitionary Prayer and the Religion of Qumran', in J.J. Collins and R.A. Kugler (eds.), *Religion in the Dead Sea Scrolls* (Grand Rapids: Eerdmans, 2000), p. 40. Schuller cites this references as 8.36.

9.   E. Isaac, '1 (Ethiopic Apocalypse of) Enoch', in Charlesworth, *Old Testament Pseudepigrapha*, I, p. 62.

Two concluded would be a prime locus for the practice of argumentative prayer in lay circles. Third, the lament tradition has a logic to it which makes it a natural form of prayer, one which was not necessarily confined to Judaism in the Second Temple era. Note, e.g. the prayer of Lucius to Isis in Apuleius's Hellenistic novel, *The Golden Ass*. After a lengthy address to Isis using a number or praising epithets, Lucius prays for relief from his affliction (he was turned into an donkey) in petitions that contain I-complaint motifs.[10]

The intention of this discussion is rather to provide reasonable grounds for concluding that the LI as a form of prayer had lost its status as a therapeutic tactic administered by liturgical experts in Second Temple Judaism. And the right of worshipping individuals to protest against God under the aegis of religious institutions vanishes with it. Three lines of evidence contribute to this argument. First, there are indications of a shift away from a cultic point of reference in the prayers themselves (§8.3.1). Second, Second Temple prayers of LI shows signs of scriptural influence (§8.3.2). Finally, there are indications that the disputational rhetoric characteristic of the LI form has been appropriated for exegetical purposes (§8.3.3).

8.3.1. *Absence of Cultic References in Second Temple LI*
One reason for connecting the biblical psalms of LI with therapeutic practices associated with the cult was the relative abundance of references to temple-based activities including pilgrimages to the sanctuary, sacrifice and cultic singing. It may be argued that such evidence is irrelevant in Second Temple times when the Jewish diaspora was widespread and access to the temple was limited. Nevertheless, the extra-biblical LI of Second Temple Jews do not complain about being excluded from participation in the cult or of being ostracized by the worshipping community.

Evidence of a shift in theological perspective is visible in the descriptions of personal suffering (I-complaint) in the prayers surveyed in §8.1.1. Enemy attack is prominent. Note the emphasis on insults in Tob. 3.6 and Sarah's lament in Tob. 3.13, the threat of evil angels in *1 En*. 84.4 and demons in *Jub*. 10.4, wild animals in Ps. 152.2-3 and the danger of gentiles to Joseph and his brothers in 4Q372 Frag. 1.16, 19. Two laments focus on the need for forgiveness for sin (*Joseph and Aseneth* 12 and Prayer of Manasseh) and one for divine guidance (Wisdom 9). Chapter Three concluded that the psalms of lament were meant to address both physical

---

10. Noted in C. Burchard, 'Joseph and Aseneth', in Charlesworth, *Old Testament Pseudepigrapha*, II, p. 220. In *Metamorphoses* 11.2, Lucius ends his prayer with the request to die if no relief for his condition is possible (cf. Tob. 3.6, 15).

illness and social distress. But none of the extra-biblical texts of LI contain imagery of physical distress that might imply sickness or disease.

The discussion of the development of protests of community distress in §4.5 noted a tendency in the postexilic era to appropriate motifs of LI in order to create prayers for the suffering community. There is also some indication that community concerns affected the composition of individual complaint psalms because there are a number of references to the large group.[11] This synthetic movement continued into the post-biblical period. Both *1 En.* 84.2-6 and *Jub.* 10.3-6 are personal prayers that contain supplications for coming generations of the righteous (but neither mentions or alludes to Israel as such, therefore, they were not considered in §7.1.1.2). Although Tob. 3.2-6 contains no petitions for the nation, Tobit's personal suffering is connected with the collective affliction of the Jewish people. While Add. Est. 14.3-19 and Jud. 9.2-14 were analyzed in the last chapter because they combined personal and communal petitions, they could also be classified as prayers of LI because the bulk of their petitions have personal concerns.

The extra-biblical prayers of LI, therefore, show a typical development of Jewish spirituality, whereby the individual understands himself or herself in terms of identity with the large group. This trend is illustrated by the poetry of Qumran. Unlike biblical complaints, prayers for help at Qumran are typically concerned with national and universal religious ideas including forgiveness of transgressions, knowledge of the Torah, protection from sin, hopes for peace, complete salvation and the like. Focus on these subjects is manifest both in the petitions of the community and individuals. Bilhah Nitzan traces this change to the absorption of the needs of the individual into those of the collectivity. She considers this movement to be connected to the dominance of Deuteronomic theology during the Qumran era.[12]

Another indicator of a changed frame of reference is the absence of the element of the vow of praise/assurance of being heard in most of the examples surveyed in §8.1.1. Out of eleven prayers, this element is missing in nine. This absence contrasts with the typical form of LI in the Psalter. Though it appears as a motif in Ps. 152.4, the vow of praise stands as a distinct element only in Pr. Man. 15 and 4Q372 Frag. 1.22-31. The only vow of praise with an explicit cultic reference is 4Q372 Frag. 1.24, which mentions offering sacrifices in a broken context. Section 3.2.1 suggested that the vow of praise/assurance of being heard was an expression of the

---

11. Ottmar Fuchs, *Die Klage als Gebet: Eine theologische Besinnung am Beispiel des Psalms 22* (Munich: Kösel, 1982), p. 325.

12. Bilhah Nitzan, *Qumran Prayer and Religious Poetry* (STDJ, 12; Leiden: E.J. Brill, 1994), pp. 82-83.

confidence that caused the individual petitioner to seek divine help in the first place: a just trial with a judgment that God would free the petitioner from distress. The absence of the vow of praise/assurance of being heard suggests that the liturgical fiction of approaching the great judge is no longer operative in the administration of prayers of extra-biblical LI.

Readers might object that it is unreasonable to expect to find complete examples of the LI form in Second Temple literature, because most appear in prose contexts. In fact, this observation about form is important in itself for noting a shift in the social location of extra-biblical prayers of LI. Most extra-biblical Second Temple LI are not transmitted as poems in an anthology compiled and transmitted by expert cultic poets, unlike the Psalms. Two Second Temple parallels can be considered. First, there is the example of the long psalms scroll from Qumran, 11Q5 (11QPsª). Second, there is the collection of 18 poems in *Psalms of Solomon*.

Psalms of Solomon is an anthology of poetry that is a conscious imitation of the biblical Psalter.[13] Various genres appear including a number of psalms containing motifs of individual and community lament. *Psalms of Solomon* 2, 8 and 9 were surveyed in the last chapter, but motifs of LI also appear in this anthology despite the fact that no poem follows the form of LI exactly (cf. *Pss. Sol.* 1.1; 8.4-5; 12.1; 16.6-15). This imitative tendency, as well as the appearance of these texts in a discrete collection, indicate authorship of the *Psalms of Solomon* by some expert circle of poets.[14] If the 18 poems in *Psalms of Solomon* are surveyed in comparison with complaint motifs in the psalms of LI, one is struck by the absence of accusatory questions or statements. The absence of direct protest suggests that the theology that generated the biblical psalms is no longer operative in these imitations.[15]

11QPsª is a compilation that includes most of Psalms 101–150, although reorganized and supplemented with non-biblical prayers. 11QPsª contains a few of psalms of LI (102; 109; 130; 140; 141). But these have been appropriated for a theological agenda that is not connected to the rehabilitation of individuals but the larger group. Supplementary material in *11QPsalmsª* also shows that the LI form is not a vital factor in the collection. Two of its non-biblical poems can be considered as pleas for individuals, but neither imitates the lament structure: 11Q5 col. 19 (*Plea for Deliverance*) and the

13. R.B. Wright, 'Psalms of Solomon', in Charlesworth, *Old Testament Pseudepigrapha*, II, p. 646.

14. Identity of the social context of the writers of the *Psalms of Solomon* remains elusive, see Wright, 'Psalms of Solomon', p. 642.

15. See also Hermann Gunkel and Joachim Begrich, *Introduction to the Psalms: The Genre of the Religious Lyric of Israel* (Mercer Library of Biblical Studies. Macon, GA: Mercer University Press, 1998; 4th German edn, 1985), p. 197.

apocryphal Psalm 155 (col. 24.3-17). Towards its end, the scroll contains a summary account about David's compositions (col. 27.2-11).[16] The psalm collection in 11QPsᵃ has undergone a thorough reworking in order to heighten the relationships between the psalms and David, who is described as the author of the psalms. The historical memory of David combines with eschatological expectation so that the scroll also becomes a sort of manual for the expected Davidic messiah. It seems to be intended to make a statement on behalf of the Qumran community in opposition to the authorities in control of the Jerusalem temple. Programmatically, David and the Qumran community are connected.[17]

Finally, an indication of a changed function for prayers of LI can be found in the Hodayot. The poems in the Hodayot can be considered psalmic compositions.[18] Scholarly literature on the psalms in the Hodayot is extensive. Here I simply want to draw attention to the fact that their use of the first person singular and the emphasis on the act of thanksgiving suggest comparisons between the Hodayot psalms and the genre of individual thanksgiving psalms. As with the biblical thanksgiving psalms, there are allusions to personal afflictions experienced by the psalmist. These mainly concern attacks by the enemy (e.g. 1QHᵃ 10.10-28; 12.8-11; 13.22-32; 16.14-15), but there also images of physical distress and sickness (e.g. 12.33-35; 16.24-34). However, the authors of the poems in 1QHᵃ do not feel compelled to reproduce the biblical genre in any rigid way. For example, there are no references to a thanksgiving vow or sacrifice.[19] The fairly free model of composition shows that, in contrast to the biblical genre, the psalms of the Hodayot lack a formal model or pattern of ritual recitation.[20] Another prominent deviation from the genre of biblical thanksgiving is the strong didactic cast of the Hodayot. Besides giving an expression of religious experience, these post-biblical psalms served the function of instructing hearers in the doctrines of the Qumran sect.[21] Insofar as they may be connected to the biblical genre of individual thanksgiving psalm, the Hodayot do not give evidence that the ritualized cycle of lament

16. See the chart in Ulrich Dahmen, *Psalmen- und Psalter-Rezeption im Frühjudentum: Rekonstruktion, Textbestand, Struktur und Pragmatik der Psalmenrolle 11Psᵃ aus Qumran* (STDJ, 49; Leiden: E.J. Brill, 2003), p. 312.

17. Dahmen, *Psalmenrolle 11Psᵃ*, pp. 316-18,

18. Hartmut Stegemann, 'The Number of Psalms in *1QHodayotᵃ* and some of their Sections', in Esther G. Chazon (ed.), *Liturgical Perspectives: Prayer and Poetry in the Light of the Dead Sea Scrolls* (STDJ, 48; Leiden: E.J. Brill, 2003), pp. 191-92.

19. Schuller, 'Petitionary Prayer', pp. 28-39.

20. Nitzan, *Qumran Prayer*, p. 324.

21. Nitzan, *Qumran Prayer*, p. 342.

and thanksgiving that generated so many biblical psalms continued at Qumran.[22]

8.3.2. *Scripturalization of Second Temple LI*

The reliance on biblical themes and motifs is so extensive and programmatic in the composition of various Second Temple prayers, that Judith Newman describes this process as one of 'scripturalization'.[23] Examples of scripturalization among the poems listed in §8.1.1 include the extra-biblical prayers of David, Enoch, Manasseh and Tobit. Psalm 152 is connected to the narrative of David's early life in 1 Sam. 17.34-36. This is indicated both by the prose superscript and the references in Ps. 152.2-3.[24] No biblical psalm is connected to the context of 1 Samuel 17; Psalm 152 has been written in imitation of other psalms with superscripts referring to David's life. Enoch's prayer in *1 En.* 84.2-6 is a prayer of a covenant mediator, a type that allows for both personal and national intercession (cf. the prayers of Moses in the Pentateuch). It belongs to a series of texts that assure the reader that a righteous remnant will survive the typology of flood and final judgment.[25] In other words, it appears to offer a form of commentary on the flood narrative. Tobit's confession of sin echoes the language of community penitential prayers based on a Deuteronomistic theology. It provides a model for living the pious life while the nation continues to suffer the absence of redemption.[26] The Prayer of Manasseh parallels the confession of sin in Psalm 51.[27]

With respect to the biblical tradition of LI, scripturalization does two things. First, it creates a connection between personal prayers and biblical models. But, second, it also particularizes the tradition of LI. The scriptural allusions actually limit the reference value of the description of personal distress.[28] There is reason to believe that there is some kind of vital

22. In stating this conclusion, I do not mean to indicate that the Hodayot necessarily had no liturgical use at all. This is a vexed question; see Eileen Schuller, 'Some Reflections on the Function and Use of Poetical Texts among the Dead Sea Scrolls', in Chazon, *Liturgical Perspectives*, pp. 177-79.

23. 'Scripturalization' is defined in Judith H. Newman, *Praying by the Book: The Scripturalization of Prayer in Second Temple Judaism* (Early Judaism and its Literature, 14; Atlanta: Scholars Press, 1999), pp. 11-17.

24. Charlesworth and Sanders, 'More Psalms of David', p. 616.

25. G.W.E. Nickelsburg, 'The Bible Rewritten and Expanded', in M.E. Stone (ed.), *Jewish Writings of the Second Temple Period* (CRINT, 2; Assen: Van Gorcum, 1984), p. 95.

26. Rodney A. Werline, *Penitential Prayer in Second Temple Judaism: The Development of a Religious Institution* (Early Judaism and its Literature, 13; Atlanta: Scholars Press, 1998), pp. 162-65.

27. Charlesworth, 'Prayer of Manasseh', p. 630

28. Esther M. Menn, 'No Ordinary Lament: Relecture and the Identity of the Distressed in Psalm 22', *HTR* 93 (2000), p. 302.

relationship between literary representations of what praying persons might say and actual practice.[29] In the place of general prayers, with application to a large number of persons and afflictions, the prayer of LI in Second Temple appears to be *ad hoc*, connected to a particular person in a particular situation. Moshe Greenberg noted that extemporaneous prayers in biblical texts could follow the formal models of the psalms.[30] Extemporaneous prayers of lament in biblical times were contemporary with the tradition of psalms of LI contemporary with them. The scripturalization of prayer means, however, that extemporaneous prayer could continue to be modeled on a biblical form even when the form was no longer employed in a liturgical context.

8.3.3. *Disputation and Exegesis*

Another interest of extra-biblical prayers in Second Temple literature is to illustrate the character of the petitioner.[31] This observation has connections with the motif of scripturalization discussed above.

The use of disputation in informal complaints was identified as a literary feature in the prayers of *2 Baruch* and 2 Esdras (§7.4). Disputational rhetoric appears in extra-biblical LI for various purposes. In Wis. 9.13-18 it motivates the petition for the gift of divinely inspired wisdom (v. 10). In Ps. 152.2-3, rhetorical questions reinforce the enemy-complaint about the predation of wild animals. The prayers of Balaam and Hannah in *Pseudo-Philo* are particularly interesting because there are parallels with rabbinic exegesis in aggadic literature.

Balaam is usually evaluated quite negatively in post-biblical literature, but *Pseudo-Philo* 18 is more complimentary.[32] The text seems to indicate the Balaam was a legitimate prophet, who lost his powers only after disobeying God (*Ps.-Philo* 18.10-12). A disputational tone is present in the why-question put into the mouth of Balaam. The issue is not, as it is in the biblical psalms of LI, chronic physical or social affliction. Instead, Balaam's why-question introduces a form of confession of trust when God asks him about the identity of the men who have come from the king of Moab,

29. Newman, *Praying by the Book*, p. 208.

30. Moshe Greenberg, *Biblical Prose Prayer as a Window to the Popular Religion of Ancient Israel* (The Taubman Lectures in Jewish Studies, Sixth Series; Berkeley: University of California Press, 1983), pp. 45-46.

31. Carey A. Moore, *Tobit: A New Translation and Commentary* (AB, 40A; New York: Doubleday, 1996), p. 141.

32. Jo Ann Hackett, 'Balaam', *ABD*, I, p. 572.

Why, LORD, do you try the human race? They cannot endure it, because you know well what is to happen in the world, even before you founded it. And now enlighten your servant if it be right to go forth with them.[33] (*Ps.-Philo* 18.4)

There is a parallel to this confession of Balaam in a commentary on Cain's question to YHWH in Gen. 4.9b. According to *Num. R.* 20.6, instead of trying to deceive the deity, the exegete suggests that Cain should have replied,

Master of the universe! Both the hidden and the revealed things are evident to you, and you ask me about my brother?[34]

Joseph Heinemann classifies this form of discourse as an example of the law court pattern of prayer,[35] although it is missing the element of petition. Evidently, the tradition cited in *Numbers Rabbah* considers such a reply appropriate to the circumstances. The disputation proposed for Cain's case is actually an expression of reticence and piety.

Despite the fact that why-questions in informal laments usually indicate protest against God, the confession of trust that accompanies Balaam's 'why' in *Ps.-Philo* 18.4 suggests that this disputational question is also an expression of reticence and piety. *Ps.-Philo* 18.4 occurs in a visionary situation. As Chapter Two noted, complaining speech in response to divine questions is typical of prophetic experience in biblical sources. The informal complaint of *Balaam* is therefore an appropriate speech-act for a prophetic functionary whom Pseudo-Philo appears to evaluate somewhat positively.

Pseudo-Philo's paraphrase of Hannah's prayer (cf. 1 Sam. 1.11) omits her vow. Instead it inserts an argument with God,

Did you not, LORD, search out the heart of all generations before you formed the world? Now what womb is born opened or dies closed unless you wish it?[36] (*Ps.-Philo* 50.4)

In her later speech to Eli, Hannah defends her disturbed conduct in prayer 'because God has shut up my womb' (v. 7). Similarly, the deep structure of the questions in v. 4 places the responsibility for Hannah's barrenness on God. As the queries in v. 4 cannot easily be paraphrased by 'why?', they may viewed as rhetorical questions typical of a disputational

---

33. D.J. Harrrington, 'Pseudo-Philo', in Charlesworth, *Old Testament Pseudepigrapha*, I, p. 325.

34. My translation based on the Hebrew text in Joseph Heinemann, *Prayer in the Talmud: Forms and Patterns* (SJ, 9; Berlin: W. de Gruyter, 1977), p. 297 (no. 34).

35. Heinemann, *Prayer in the Talmud*, p. 216.

36. Harrrington, 'Pseudo-Philo', p. 364.

argument that anticipates Hannah's assertion of divine responsibility in v. 7.

The appropriateness of the disputation form in Hannah's prayer is indicated by aggadic exegesis which glosses Hannah's prayer with forms of what Heinemann calls the law court pattern. There are three different versions preserved in *b. Ber.* 31.b. Each consists of an address and a disputatious argument.[37] The permission for such a prayer emphasizes the piety of the petitioner, as rabbinic tradition restricted the legitimate use of such informal prayers only to persons of unquestionable probity.[38] The trait of piety can also explain the tone of Sarah's why-question in Tob. 3.15.[39] Biblical characters sure of their righteousness also despair of their lives using why-questions (cf. Jer. 20.18; Job 3.11).

In contrast to informal laments in biblical contexts, where complaint against God calls into question the divine character, the disputational forms discussed here act to cast light on the petitioner. There appears to be an unstated assumption that such rhetoric is only appropriate for persons of proven piety. Hence its appearance is a sign to the reader of the good character of the persons who resort to argumentative prayer in extra-biblical Second Temple literature.

8.4. *Prayers against Demonic Attack in Second Temple Sources*

One might also ask after the fate of the therapeutic impulse that generated the psalms of LI. Surely there was still a place for private or semi-public services for suffering individuals conducted by liturgical experts? In the later Second Temple period and beyond, this scenario is valid for prayers against demonic attack.

The Hebrew Bible is rather hostile towards the various classes of professional exorcist in the ancient world,[40] probably because it is opposed to magic in general.[41] Nevertheless, the psalms of LI have parallels with the form of incantations used by the Mesopotamian *āšipu* (see §3.4.2), a ritual expert who dealt with demonic attack.[42] The enemy-imagery of the psalms of LI shows that they were concerned with attack by demonic agencies as

---

37. Heinemann, *Prayer in the Talmud*, p. 215.

38. Heinemann, *Prayer in the Talmud*, pp. 199-200.

39. Analysis of the prayer of Sarah reveals its role as a literary device for depicting Sarah's character. Despite her suicidal despair, her love for her father and her faith in God are stronger, see Moore, *Tobit*, pp. 152-53.

40. Eric Sorenson, *Possession and Exorcism in the New Testament and Early Christianity* (WUNT, 2/157; Tübingen: Mohr–Siebeck, 2002), pp. 49-49, 59.

41. See Nitzan, *Qumran Prayer*, p. 227-28.

42. Sorenson, *Possession and Exorcism*, pp. 19-20.

well as by human beings.[43] There is also evidence that the motif of enemy attack gained prominence in later biblical psalms of LI.[44] Moreover, attacks by the enemy are prominent in the literary imitations of LI that characterize extra-biblical Second Temple sources (§8.3.1). But, in contrast to the biblical tradition, argumentative prayer was not favored when addressing the problem of demonic attack in post-biblical Judaism.

The goal of this section is not to present a comprehensive discussion of beliefs related to demonic affliction in Second Temple Judaism. Exorcism in the ancient world used a variety of methods and is a complex subject.[45] Prayers against demonic attack constitute one aspect of a constellation of therapeutic and cultic practices which are often loosely referred to as 'exorcism'. In this connection, it is important to distinguish two different kinds of demonic affliction. The word exorcism can apply both to remedies for attacks by demonic agency external to the sufferer and for possession, in which an evil spirit somehow takes up residence in the victim. Evidence is best for the concept of external demonic attack in Mesopotamia and in the biblical material.[46] Beliefs in both external demonic attacks and possession appear in various later Second Temple Jewish texts, including the New Testament.

Three types of compositions used to ward off demonic agencies are of particular interest to this chapter. These include psalm-like compositions, spells or incantations, and apotropaic prayers. These texts seem mainly focused on driving off demonic attacks. In that sense, they conform to the dominant biblical worldview (including the psalms of LI) that was concerned with repelling externally caused affliction rather than with the exorcism of possessed persons.

The Talmud knows of the use of two psalms for prophylactic intervention in order to ward off the danger of demonic attacks: Psalms 3 and 91.[47]

---

43. Erhard S. Gerstenberger and Wolfgang Schrage, *Suffering* (Biblical Encounters Series; Nashville: Abingdon Press, 1980), pp. 64-65. Hans-Peter Müller ('Feinde, Tiere und Dämonen: Ein kleiner Beitrag zu den Klage- und Bittpsalmen des Einzelnen', in Klaus Kiesow and Thomas Meurer [eds.], *Textarbeit: Studien zu Texten und ihrer Rezeption aus den Alten Testament und der Umwelt Israels: Festschrift Peter Weimar* [Münster: Ugarit-Verlag, 2003], p. 329) contends that demonic imagery in the psalms of LI is only metaphorical. But he documents analogies with the demonology of ancient Mesopotamia. One is still entitled, therefore, to speak of the psalms of LI as concerned with demonic agencies, though it may be debated whether the references envisage only social conflict or also allow for supernatural causes of personal distress.

44. Fuchs, *Die Klage als Gebet*, p. 344.

45. John J. Rousseau, 'Jesus, an Exorcist of a Kind', in Eugene H. Lovering (ed.), *Seminar Papers* (SBLSP, 32; Atlanta: Scholars Press, 1993), pp. 134-41.

46. Sorenson, *Possession and Exorcism*, pp. 30-31, 53-54.

47. Nitzan, *Qumran Prayer*, p. 228; see Y. 'Erub. 10.11.

The sages were insistent, however, that these psalms were not to be recited over afflicted persons, but as a preventative measure. Psalm 3, of course, is a psalm of LI. Its restriction to a preventative function is a reverse of its use in biblical times. The talmudic constriction seems to be connected to a prohibition on using the Tetragrammaton in incantations.

There are indications that other authorities allowed for more latitude in the case of Psalm 91. The use of Psalm 91 against demonic attacks is functionally connected with powers thought to inhere in the Aaronic blessing (Num. 6.24-26). Protective wording similar to the Aaronic blessing has been discovered at Kuntillat Ajrud and Khirbet el-Qôm.[48] Rabbinic commentary on Num. 6.24-26 in *Targum Pseudo-Jonathan* and *Sifre* recognizes the benefits of both the Aaronic blessing and Psalm 91 in warding off demonic attack.[49]

After recounting that David composed 3,600 psalms (*thlym*) and 446 songs, 11QPs[a] col. 27.9-10 adds 'And songs to perform over the possessed: four' (*wšyr lngn 'l hpgw'ym 'rb'h*).[50] Identification of these four songs has been debated.[51] It is not clear if a collection of such psalms has been found at Qumran, or if there was only one collection. The term *šyry pg'ym* is also attested in rabbinic literature.[52] What is certain, however, is that there are writings in the Dead Sea Scrolls that were recited to drive away evil spirits.

There are various ways of categorizing the genres of texts employed against demons at Qumran. An important distinction is between those compositions meant to prevent demonic attack and those intended to cure cases of demonic affliction.[53] 11Q11 (11QApocPs[a]) is the foremost

---

48. Émile Puech, 'Les deux derniers psaumes davidiques du rituel d'exorcisme, 11QPsAp[a] IV 4–V 14', in Devorah Dimant and Uriel Rappaport (eds.), *The Dead Sea Scrolls: Forty Years of Research* (STDJ, 10; Leiden: E.J. Brill, 1992), pp. 84-87.

49. Esther Eshel, 'Apotropaic Prayers in the Second Temple Period', in Chazon, *Liturgical Perspectives*, p. 71.

50. F.G. Martínez and E.J.C. Tigchelaar, *The Dead Sea Scrolls Study Edition* (2 vols.; Leiden: E.J. Brill, 2000), p. 1179.

51. See the review of the literature in Hermann Lichtenberger, 'Ps 91 und die Exorzismen in 11QPsAp[a]', in Armin Lange, Hermann Lichtenberger and K.F.D. Römheld (eds.), *Die Dämonen/Demons* (Tubingen: Mohr Siebeck, 2003), p. 417.

52. Esther Eshel, 'Genres of Magical Texts in the Dead Sea Scrolls', in Lange, Lichtenberger and Römheld, *Die Dämonen/Demons*, p. 411.

53. Eshel ('Magical Texts', p. 396) distinguishes between texts meant to cure demonic affliction and apotropaic psalms meant for protection. Philip S. Alexander ('The Demonology of the Dead Sea Scrolls', in Flint and VanderKam, *Dead Sea Scrolls after Fifty Years*, II, pp. 344-45) divides the Qumran material into three categories by assigning 4Q560 the status of a recipe book for amulets that 'a professional magician would have copied out and personalized for a client's use'. The songs of the Maskil are another form of apotropaic prayer. Texts such as 11Q11 were intended for use when

example of a psalmic composition meant to drive away demons who are afflicting an individual.[54] 11Q11 contains at least four poems, one of which attsts an attribution to David in a form similar to many psalms (*ldwyd*).[55] Characteristics of these incantations include direct address to demons asking for their identity, formulae of adjurations, invocations in the name of God (including frequent use of the Tetragrammaton) and threats against the demons.[56]

The collection in 11Q11 ends with a version of Psalm 91 (mentioned above) that is derived from the Masoretic text but reworked in order to adapt it for defense from demonic attack. In the form it possesses in 11Q11, Psalm 91 is the oldest Hebrew magical text known from Second Temple times. Its appropriation in 11Q11 is through its assimilation to a world-view that is dualistic in nature, occupied by both angels of light and demons.[57] Psalm 91 does not belong to the complaint psalm genre, so one cannot easily argue that such appropriation is related to the liturgical use of the lament psalms.

Apotropaic prayers or hymns were also used to ward off demonic attack;[58] they constitute a different genre of prayers against demons. There are more of these texts attested at Qumran than the incantations listed above and they fall into two groups. First, there are a number that cannot be identified as compositions of the Qumran community: 4QLev[b] (4Q213a); Plea for Deliverance (11QPs[a] col. 19); Psalm 155; *Jub.* 10.2-6 and 12.19-20. Second, there are four prayers that probably are compositions of the Qumran community: 1QH[a] Frg. 44; Q444; 4Q510–511; 6Q18. The texts indicate demons may be frightened off by reciting the praise of God.[59] Common elements in the apotropaic prayers include references to the knowledge of God and divine law, pleas for protection against sin, requests

---

demonic affliction was diagnosed. The major difference between the categories of Alexander and Eshel is in the analysis of 4Q560, a difference that does not substantially affect my argument.

54. Alexander, 'Demonology', p. 345; Eshel, 'Magical Texts', pp. 398-406.

55. Émile Puech ('Les deux derniers psaumes davidiques', p. 78) claims that at least three of the poems bear Davidic ascription, but two of these references involve restorations of missing text.

56. Eshel, 'Magic Texts', pp. 403-404. A precedent for the incantation formula found in the Dead Sea Scrolls is attested in the seventh century plaque found in Arslan Tash (see Nitzan, *Qumran Prayer*, pp. 229-30).

57. Puech, 'Les deux derniers psaumes davidiques', p. 89.

58. Alexander, 'Demonology', pp. 344-45; Eshel, 'Magical Texts', pp. 406-410.

59. Eshel, 'Apotropaic Prayers', pp. 74, 79. Eshel refers to Noah's prayer against demons as *Jub.* 6.1-7, but I follow the numbering of the version in O.S. Wintermude', Jubilees', in Charlesworth, *Old Testament Pseudepigrapha,* II, pp. 75-76.

for forgiveness, and pleas for purification. Unlike the incantations, they do not address demons directly nor do they adjure them.[60]

The apotropaic prayers also make abundant use of negative Imperatives directed at God. This form of petition is not limited to either the apotropaic prayers of Qumran or to later rabbinic equivalents, it also appears in other kinds of supplications. Cases include prayers of complaint (§§7.3.1 and 8.2.1) and the Lord's Prayer, which in common with the apotropaic prayers pleads for divine protection from the powers of sin.[61] David Flusser has suggested that Psalm 51 might be a distant ancestor of the apotropaic prayer, because the poet in Psalm 51 alternates in his search for spiritual peace and forgiveness of sins, a polarity also at work in Second Temple apotropaic prayers. But there is a basic difference: Psalm 51 does not demonize sin. The theology of the apotropaic prayer shows signs of a development of a dualism beyond its biblical roots.[62]

The fact that various kinds prayers could be used to the same end warns against viewing all acts of exorcism as ritual performances that required expert mediation. Of the various groups of prayers against mentioned above, incantations for victims of demonic affliction were most likely to have been administered to suffering persons by recognized liturgical experts. For example, *Pseudo-Philo* 60 contains the text of a song David was supposed to have played so that the evil spirit might depart from Saul. This seems to be a literary imitation of an incantation against demonic attack rather than a citation from actual practice because of the reference made to David's progeny (i.e. Solomon) as the one who will rule over the demons. The fame of Solomon as a composer of incantations to master demons is attested in the story of the exorcist Eliezer at Vespasian's court told by Josephus.[63] References to the *maskîl* in 4Q510-511 also suggest expert mediation.[64] However, the widespread use of apotropaic petitions cautions against the assumption that the apotropaic prayers as a group were always reserved for recitation by liturgical experts.

Attacks by demonic agency link the religious concerns of later Second Temple Judaism with biblical religion. Their common interests also manifest themselves in the fact that one of the apotropaic prayers against

---

60. There are other differences also, see Eshel, 'Apotropaic Prayers', pp. 87-88.

61. David Flusser, 'Qumrân and Jewish Apotropaic Prayers', *IEJ* 16 (1966), pp. 197-202.

62. Flusser, 'Qumrân and Jewish Apotropaic Prayers', pp. 203-204.

63. Nitzan, *Quman Prayer*, p. 228; *Ant.* 8.45.

64. Alexander, 'Demonology', p. 344. Bilhah Nitzan ('Hymns from Qumran—510-511', in Diamant and Rappaport, *Dead Sea Scrolls*, pp. 63-64) describes the *maskîl* as a sort of magician.

demonic attack in the book of Jubilees is written in the LI form: *Jub.* 10.2-6 (§8.1.1). However, the LI form is uncharacteristic of prayers against demons in post-biblical Judaism. For the most part, the biblical genre for warding off demonic attacks is not used in extra-biblical Second Temple exorcistic texts.

The eclipse of the psalms of LI as a tool against demonic attack corresponds to a shift in worldview which was much more explicit about the existence of a demonic realm in conflict with the divine than the biblical tradition. Later Second Temple Judaism shows evidence of a dualistic worldview with an elaborated angelology and demonology that is not directly derived from the biblical material. Reasons for the emergence of this aspect of the Jewish religious imagination in the Persian and Hellenistic periods are not entirely understood.[65] But such a development is appropriate to a theological need to rid God of the suspicion that he may be capable of arbitrary or demonic actions (e.g. Exod. 4.24; 2 Sam. 24.1). Psalms of LI belong to a world in which YHWH sometimes seems to act against his best interests (e.g. Psalms 6; 88). A more sharply dualistic world with a demonic adversary allows for a deity free of evil.[66] In that sense, prayers of exorcism support a worldview that requires a more completely righteous God than the theology of the psalms of LI could provide.

8.5. *Prayers of the Righteous Sufferer in the New Testament*

There are no prayers in the New Testament which conform to the structure of psalms of LI in the Hebrew Bible.[67] There is some evidence for the use of complaint to motivate an individual request between persons (Mt. 9.18; 15.22; 17.15) including communication in which the request remains implicit (Mt. 8.6). Therefore, conditions were in place for the articulation of informal lament. However, there is no indication that a therapeutic practice of formal lament practice existed alongside the potential for spontaneous *ad hoc* complaint prayer.

As in other chapters, lament prayer is only identified in texts which contain an explicit element of complaint. This rules out texts of supplication such as Jesus' prayer in the garden of Gethsemane.[68] It is best to

---

65. Joanne K. Kuemmerlin-McLean, 'Demons: Old Testament', *ABD*, II, p.139.

66. Karl van der Toorn, 'The Theology of Demons in Mesopotamia and Israel: Popular Belief and Scholarly Speculation', in Lange, Lichtenberger and Römheld, *Die Dämonen/Demons*, p. 83.

67. New Testament prayers are listed in Donald Coggan, *The Prayers of the New Testament* (London: Hodder & Stoughton, 1967).

68. Both the Lord's Prayer (Mt. 6.9-13; Luke 11.2-4) and the synoptic traditions

regard the prayer at Gethsemane as a member of the class of *taḥănunîm* (supplications), a large but rather amorphous category of prayers for help in times of distress.[69] Explicit uses of the element of complaint in individual prayer are restricted to Jesus' words from the cross. Mt. 27.46 and the parallel in Mark 15.34 record a citation from Ps. 22.2, 'My God, My God, why have you forsaken me?'[70]

Critics are divided as to whether the attribution of Ps. 22.2 to Jesus in Mt. 27.46 (= Mk 15.34) is an accurate memory or due to the activity of the gospel storytellers.[71] Against the possibility that Jesus actually cited Ps. 22.2 is the fact that Luke uses another citation from the lament tradition (Ps. 31.6, cf. Lk. 23.46). While this historical question is too large to solve here, the discussion above noted that Jewish authorities allowed for the possibility that individuals could employ motifs of complaint against God in moments of personal crisis (§8.3). If they did so, it was as an application of the scriptural tradition to their own situation. There is no indication that such sporadic outbursts are evidence for the use of LI as a therapeutic technique mediated by a cult-related institution.

The impression that the New Testament writers operated in a milieu that was unfamiliar with the cultic use of the LI genre is reinforced by a consideration of the use of Psalm 22 in the gospel narratives. Whatever the historical plausibility for the words of Ps. 22.2 on the lips of the crucified Jesus, it is clear that Psalm 22 influenced the telling of the crucifixion story.[72] Its use points to an appropriation which is at variance with the original context of LI. The citation partakes of the phenomenon of scripturalization described above (§8.3.2).

---

containing Jesus' prayer in Gethsamane (Mt. 26.39; Mark 14.36; Luke 22.42) are identified as lament-like prayer in Kathleen D. Billman and Daniel L. Migliore, *Rachel's Cry: Prayer of Lament and Rebirth of Hope* (Cleveland: United Church Press, 1999), pp. 34-37. The Lord's Prayer was addressed above in §7.5. As a model prayer, it can be considered a prayer for individuals as well as for groups. But, despite its several petitions, it contains no element of complaint.

69. The category of *taḥănunîm* is defined in David Flusser, 'Psalms, Hymns, and Prayers' in Stone, *Jewish Writings of the Second Temple Period*, pp. 570-73.

70. Adela Yarbro Collins ('The Appropriation of the Psalms of Individual Lament by Mark', in C.M. Tuckett [ed.], *The Scriptures in the Gospels* [BETL, 131; Leuven: Leuven University Press, 1997], p. 227) finds allusions to eight different psalms of LI in Mark. But these references are not used in contexts of prayer outside the passion narratives.

71. Menn, 'No Ordinary Lament', pp. 330-31; John H. Reumann, 'Psalm 22 at the Cross', *Int* 28 (1974), pp. 55-57.

72. Reumann, 'Psalm 22 at the Cross', pp. 41-42. There are allusions to various LI in the crucifixion narrative, e.g. Ps. 69.22 in Mark 15.23, 36 and Ps. 109.25 in Mark 15.29; but these other texts do not exercise the same programmatic effect as Psalm 22; see Reumann, 'Psalm 22 at the Cross', p. 40.

There are different indicators that the use of Psalm 22 as applied to Jesus has been historicized and particularized. For example, there are striking parallels between the motifs of enemy persecution in the Septuagint translation of Psalm 22 and the mockery of Jesus.[73] The use of Psalm 22 in reference to Jesus assumes that David was not only the psalm's author, but a prophet who predicted vital events in a history yet to be fulfilled.[74] This exegetical move takes the psalm out of the present day experience of the ordinary reader and puts it into a messianic future. Finally, one may note that the death of Jesus is accompanied by apocalyptic signs emphasizing its uniqueness.[75]

The New Testament, therefore, attests to a similar pattern of scripturalization of the LI genre to that found in other extra-biblical Second Temple literature. By the same token, one can also point to the theory and therapy for sickness that is attested in the New Testament for evidence of the eclipse of the LI genre. A vital part of Jesus' ministry is exorcism. In fact, he acts as an expert healer to which various persons resort. Demons are a significant cause of sickness and affliction.[76]

Of course, exorcism is not the only strategy for healing in the New Testament. The letter of James prescribes a healing ritual by elders of the community (5.14). There are obvious lines of comparison between the appearance of the elders to conduct prayers that will rehabilitate the sufferer to the community and scenarios posited for the conduct of individual complaint liturgies in biblical times. But the effective prayers are of a different kind. The point of reference is to the intercessory prayers of Elijah (Jam. 5.17-18),[77] not to the psalms.

8.6. *The Loss of LI as Healing Liturgy*

The discussions above have identified several trends that indicate the loss of LI as healing liturgies in Second Temple times. These phenomena include the absence of indications of ritual use in the texts themselves and the way they have been transmitted, the scripturalization of extra-biblical Second Temple LI (including the New Testament) and the emergence of prayers of exorcism as a therapeutic technique for those under demonic

---

73. See Menn, 'No Ordinary Lament', pp. 332-33.

74. Menn, 'No Ordinary Lament', p. 336-37. *11QPsalms^a* col. 27.11 also regards David as a prophet.

75. Fritz Stolz, 'Alttestamentliches Reden vom Menschen und neutestamentliches Reden von Jesus', *ZTK* 77 (1980), pp. 147-48.

76. Rousseau, 'Jesus, an Exorcist of a Kind', pp. 141-42.

77. Martin C. Albl, "Are Any of You Sick?' The Health Care System in the Letter of James', *JBL* 121 (2002), pp. 136-39.

attack. How might one date the demise of the therapeutic use of liturgies LI in relation to these developments?

The book of Job indicates theological difficulties with LI in the early postexilic period. One has to allow for some time for these to percolate, although the later addition of the Elihu speeches seems to have registered the critique of LI to the point of only permitting petition for serious illness that was accompanied by confession of sin. The reference that Elihu makes to an angelic mediator (Job 33.23) points to a development in Jewish theology that is characteristic of the Persian and Hellenistic eras.

Sir. 38.9-15 also addresses the problem of sickness by recommending confession of sin accompanying sacrifice. Sin is considered to be a contra-indication of the effectiveness of the physician. Such advice assumes a Deuteronomic theory of retribution according to which illness is viewed as punishment for infidelity to the law.[78] By the same token, when the scribe performs his morning prayers, he is to 'make supplication for his sins' (39.5). Sirach was written c. 180 BCE, although the teachings represented there may have originated earlier because the book of Ben Sira seems to have been written at the end of the sage's career.[79] It would not be far amiss to suggest that Sirach represents a stream of Jewish thought based in Jerusalem about 200 BCE.

Sirach's Jerusalem temple does not seem to know the therapeutic use of LI, although Sirach contains three lamenting prayers. There is a collective plea in Sir 36.1-22 but it contains no element of complaint (§7.1.2). The personal plea for avoidance of sin in Sir. 22.27-23.6 is close to the genre of apotropaic prayers. The prayer of thanksgiving in Sir. 51.1-12 imitates biblical models and includes a citation of a prayer of lament that borrows scriptural imagery.[80] This prayer is both scripturalized and also patently autobiographical. Therefore it demonstrates the same features as other scripturalized examples of LI rhetoric from later Second Temple times.

Scripturalization also affected the transmission and interpretation of the psalms of LI themselves. Psalm 152 has already been identified as an imitation of the psalms of David. There is other evidence of an interest in David in the Second Temple period, including a growing appreciation of his status as author of the psalms. It is likely that the tradition of Davidic authorship arose in the postexilic era. For example, it is in 1 Chronicles

---

78. Patrick W. Skehan and Alexander A. Di Lella, *The Wisdom of Ben Sira* (AB, 39; New York: Doubleday, 1987), p. 442.

79. Alexander A. Di Lella, 'Wisdom of Ben-Sira', *ABD*, VI, p. 933.

80. Sir. 51.5, 'the depths of the belly of Hades', cf. Ps. 88.7; Lam. 3.55. Sir 51.7, 'there was no one to help me, etc. ', cf. Isa. 59.16; Ps. 107.12. Sir. 51.10, 'days of affliction, etc. ', cf. Zeph. 1.15. See Skehan and Di Lella, *The Wisdom of Ben Sira*, p. 506.

that David's status as patron of the temple becomes especially prominent.[81] Additional evidence for the importance of assigning Davidic authorship in Second Temple times can be seen in the fact that, while the Masoretic text of the psalms claims that 73 psalms were written by David, the Septuagint ascribes 85 psalms to David.[82] 11QPs[a] also ascribes more psalms to David than the Masoretic Text. In addition, it distributes the Davidic attributions more evenly through the Psalter.[83]

Nevertheless, these later biographical notices have an important contribution to make to the study of the history of the complaint genre. One has to inquire about the circumstances under which anonymous cultic compositions were construed as the spontaneous poetry of a single person in an identifiable situation. This interpretive shift suggests that the original liturgical function of these poems had been forgotten or was no longer important.[84] Therefore, though secondary to the composition of the poems, the historical superscriptions of the LI are by no means insignificant. Their composition may indicate the time when the living tradition of liturgical complaint for individuals had been forgotten.

Unfortunately, there is no way of dating the addition of the historical superscriptions exactly. The range of dates must begin with the date of Chronicles, but that exercise itself is controversial. Though the fourth century BCE can be considered a middle of the road suggestion, there are arguments for both earlier and later dates for 1–2 Chronicles.[85] The books of Chronicles themselves recast Davidic tradition in order to emphasize his patronage of the Temple. But they stop short of making David the author of the psalms. According to Brevard Childs, the historical notes attached to the David psalms appear to be later than the time of the Chronicler but prior to the composition of 11QPs[a] (second century BCE).[86]

---

81. James L. Mays, *Psalms* (Louisville: John Knox, 1994), p. 12. Another sign that the practice of identifying authors of the psalms is associated with the Chronicler is found in the fact that two psalms of LI are attributed to the sons of Korah: Psalms 42-43 and 88. 2 Chron. 20.19 lists the Korahites as leaders of temple singing. Louis C. Jonker ('Revisiting the Psalm Headings: Second Temple Levitical Propaganda', in D.J. Human and C.J.A. Vos [eds.], *Psalms and Liturgy* [JSOTSup, 410; London: T. & T. Clark, 2004], p. 111) suggests that some Davidic ascriptions of authorship might have been attached to the collection of Psalms 3-41, which Gerstenberger thinks originated in the exile. But Jonker (p. 112) agrees with the thesis that the superscriptions annotating the psalms with details of David's life stem from the time of Chronicles.

82. John Day, *Psalms* (OTG; Sheffield: JSOT Press, 1992), pp. 114-15.

83. G.H. Wilson, *The Editing of the Hebrew Psalter* (SBLDS, 76; Chico, CA: Scholars Press, 1985), p. 136.

84. Menn, 'No Ordinary Lament', pp. 310-14.

85. Ralph W. Klein, 'Chronicles, Book of 1–2', *ABD*, I, pp. 994-95.

86. Bervard Childs, 'Psalm Titles and Midrashic Exegesis', *JSS* 16 (1971), pp. 142-43, 148-49. For the date of 11QPs[a], see Dahmen, *Psalmenrolle 11Ps[a]*, p. 314

None of the extra-biblical Second Temple prayers surveyed either in this chapter or the last is reliably dated before 200 BCE (with the possible exception of Tobit).[87] This is about the same time as Sirach was written. The combination of angelology and penitence articulated by Elihu in a late addition to the book of Job fits well within this time period. One can assume, therefore, that the therapeutic tradition of LI had been lost by 200 BCE. This loss was probably sustained earlier given the expansion of psalm titles and superscriptions in the Septuagint. The mid-point between 400–200 is 300, early in the Hellenistic period of the Jewish experience—long enough to allow the traditions of Davidic patronage of the cult to influence the interpretation of a scriptural psalm collection that was no longer being used in its original therapeutic settings.

Corroborating arguments for such a viewpoint would recognize the beginning of the Hellenistic era as one in which the reorganization of temple life under priestly influence had already taken place. Priestly ideology did not permit many types of illness to be present at the temple, likely out of fears for impurity.[88] Such restrictions would limit the role of the temple as a resource for ill persons, although the psalms of LI indicate it played a key role by the late pre-exilic era (§3.4.3). The Priestly reorganization of sacred space had connections with Judaism's entry into the Axial Age, which undermined the theological premises of argumentative prayer (§7.3.3).[89] At the same time, the emphasis on divine righteousness and transcendence favoured the development of angelologies and demonologies in order to insulate the divine reality from the charge of arbitrary evil. This in turn opened up the way for the emergence or recrudescence of new forms of healing liturgies involving exorcism.

87. See the discussion in Moore (*Tobit*, pp. 40-42), who concludes that Tobit is to be dated no earlier than 300 BCE but prior to the Maccabean period.

88. Hector Avalos, *Illness and Health Care in the Ancient Near East: The Role of the Temple in Greece, Mesopotamia, and Israel* (HSM, 54; Atlanta: Scholars Press, 1995), pp. 318-26.

89. According to Michael E. Stone ('Eschatology, Remythologization, and Cosmic Aporia', in S.N. Eisenstadt (ed.), *The Origins and Diversity of Axial Age Civilizations* (SUNY Series in Near Eastern Studies; Albany: State University of New York, 1986), p. 246), 'In the Second Temple period, God is further removed from the ordinary world and course of events. He becomes more transcendent and his function is not discerned in the 'little happenings' of history, but in its grand, overall pattern and its crucial, pivotal events'.

Chapter 9

ECLIPSE AND RECOVERY OF PROTEST PRAYER

The preceding chapters have described the eclipse of the protest prayer tradition in early Judaism. The metaphor of 'eclipse' has been used deliberately because eclipses are only temporary, and we are now living in an era which has seen renewed interest in this ancient form of prayer. How does one account for the contemporary fascination with the lament tradition among biblical scholars and theologians? An answer to this question begins with the recognition that situations of crisis precipitated argumentative prayer, especially when such prayer involved protest against God.

I begin with a brief summary of the results of the study undertaken in the last eight chapters (§9.1). I will then note some features of the continuation of the arguing with God tradition in Judaism which has preserved, albeit on the margins of its liturgies, the capacity to engage in collective complaint against God (§9.2). Observations gleaned from these two discussions will afford commentary on what is arguably the most unexpected development in the history of complaint prayer, the recovery of individual lament in Christianity (§9.3).

9.1. *The Eclipse of Protest Prayer in Biblical Tradition*

Chapter Two concluded that informal lament uttered by individuals probably preceded appropriation of the speech-form by covenant intermediaries. There were two crises in personal life where YHWH was thought to be particularly involved: birth and death. Problematic birth situations and the prospect of premature death were typical occasions for informal lament containing protest against God.

Informal lament as protest prayer on behalf of the group was appropriated by covenant mediators of the prophetic type during the monarchical period. It is especially common in reports of their visionary experiences. These informal laments were uttered in contexts of national crisis. There is some indication that prophetic mediators also became favoured as intercessors on behalf of individuals with complaints against God as the institution of prophecy gained prestige. The preference for prophetic mediation in the case of individual protest prayer, however, may represent an ideal foisted on the biblical account of Israel's religious history. Individuals continued to employ informal lament in the postexilic period (cf. the memoirs of Nehemiah and the story of Susanna). If there are no complaints against God contained in these later prayers, the absence may be due to the bias of biblical and post-biblical writers. As long as implied requests motivated by complaint could be used as a form of prayer, complaint against God remained possible. The perceived cause of the distress, not the form itself, would dictate whether an informal lament became a prayer of protest or not. This inference is borne out by the fact that informal lament on behalf of the nation containing complaint against God is attested in extra-biblical Second Temple literature.

The biblical record is not full enough to allow for the reconstruction of an era in ancient Israelite religion which knew only of informal lament. Formal expressions of argumentative prayer probably depended on the performances of expert poets. An oral tradition probably underlies the extant psalms of LI, which have indications of centralization of the tradition on the Jerusalem temple by the late monarchical period.

Psalms of LI presuppose crisis in the lives of those who resorted to this type of healing liturgy. Nevertheless, opportunities for protest against God were not readily granted. The rhetoric of complaint differs in LI, depending on the source of the petitioner's distress. The psalms of Plea are prayers of suffering persons who present themselves as victims of baseless attack by enemies. Behind the psalms of Indirect Protest is the fear of divine punishment. It is likely that psalms of Indirect Protest functioned in cases where determination of sin on the part of the petitioner was a real possibility, one that either had to be addressed or defended against. By contrast, there is little allusion to sin in the psalms of Direct Protest. The crisis of premature death is presented in the psalms of Direct Protest as a condition that God was believed to be ultimately responsible for and yet out of keeping with the petitioner's circumstances. Psalms of Direct Protest comprise just over 20% of the total number of LI (8/39). Protest against God was probably only permitted to sufferers who had used up other avenues for healing and who faced chronic disease or imminent death.

As with the extant psalms of LI, cultic institutions are implicated in the composition and performance of psalms of collective protest. Argumentative prayer appears to have been a typical form for community petitions in the pre-exilic period. The king, as a community representative, probably used a form related to the psalms of LI. But there is no reason to suppose that forms with first person plural references are necessarily later than those with first person singular references to the community. Protest against God was particularly connected to the crises of drought and military catastrophe, both regarded as inconsistencies in the God–Israel relationship. The earliest extant protests of national defeat are probably connected to the destruction of the northern kingdom in 722 BCE (Psalms 74 and 80). Isa. 63.7–64.11; Psalms 44; 60; 79; 83 were generated by those who suffered the predations of the Neo-Babylonian empire in 587 BCE and endured the ensuing exile and its aftermath. God-complaint also appears in psalms that protest collective distress in the postexilic period. Perceptions of unrelieved exile and economic oppression drew on motifs from the psalms of LI to protest the continuing debasement of a troubled community.

The conclusions to Chapters Two–Four suggested that authorization of the argumentative prayer tradition depended on a number of related characteristics. These included assumptions about the causes of suffering, the organization of cultic institutions and a vision of a deity capable of arbitrary actions. As these conceptions began to change, the significance of complaint prayer in cultic life would shift as well. Chapters Five–Eight attempted to demonstrate such shifts. Nevertheless, protest against God would not be denied in times of extreme community crisis.

The exile marked the ascendancy of a vigorous prophetic critique of the religion of the monarchical era by schools of thought that had been minority voices in the pre-exilic period. These prophetic functionaries operated with a theology that did not regard the destruction of the nation as a violation of the God–Israel relationship. Appropriation of the prophetic perspective affected the valorization of the argumentative prayer tradition.

The poetry of Lamentations represents a new form of complaint in which elements of the dirge have been joined to the rhetoric of complaint. The acrostic form of the poems in Lamentations indicates a literate reflection on the violence sustained by Neo-Babylonian imperialism that took some time to develop. The sophisticated poems in Lamentations as well as their accommodation to the prophetic critique of pre-exilic religion probably emerged about a generation after the initial reaction to the destruction of Jerusalem represented by the protests of national defeat. But both kinds of rhetoric circulated in the same community — arguably even among the same tradents as indicated by the inclusion of Lamentations 5 with the other poems in the book. The logic of grief explains how a community could tolerate different attitudes to the exile as it vacillated between anger at God and self-loathing as a victim of divinely authorized violence.

Besides the poetry of Lamentations, two other bodies of exilic literature show the accommodation of the arguing with God tradition to prophetic viewpoints. The DtrH reveals a similar approach as Lamentations. Complaint was permitted after contrition. This theological attitude is conveyed in the books of Joshua and Judges in which aspects of the experience of the exile have been projected onto the accounts of Israel's occupation of the land of Canaan. For example, the framework of Judges shows a recurring schema in which apostasy requires repentance before YHWH answers the cries of the captive people.

The Second Isaiah has extensive allusions to the complaints of the community exiled in Babylon. The poetry of this anonymous prophet means to answer the community's protests against God by oracles and proclamations of an imminent and glorious salvation. The Second Isaiah does not so much dismiss the value of community complaint prayer as imply that the practice is no longer necessary due to historical changes initiated by YHWH. The prophet's response to the exiles' complaint is notable for introducing a new concept of suffering: the idea of redemptive/vicarious suffering as applied to national affliction. Though the Second Isaiah does not deny that God caused servant Israel to suffer, the protest prayer tradition is effectively vitiated because the theory of redemptive/vicarious suffering shows that the God–Israel relationship remains intact in spite of the exile.

While a variety of historical and psychological factors affected the collective tradition of arguing with God during the exile, the tradition of LI seems to have remained more or less intact during the same time period. In fact, its rhetoric contributed to the articulation of the protests of the community (e.g. Pss. 9–10; 77; 90; 94)). One must look for an explanation, therefore, for the demise of the tradition of individual complaint other than the catastrophic events associated with the destruction of Jerusalem and its aftermath. This is an important reason for thinking that Axial Age categories played a key role in undermining the theological underpinnings of individual lament in the postexilic period.

During the late monarchical period, the prophetic elite so influential for interpreting the meaning of the exile was developing a monotheistic vision that insisted on a quality of transcendence and consistency (righteousness) in the God of Israel that was unprecedented in Israel's religious imagination. The results of this intellectual process culminated in the monotheistic vision of the Second Isaiah in which the existence of all other deities was denied and YHWH was heralded as the sole creator and lord of human history. Such a theological development participated in a complex nexus of social change and international politics that affected not only ancient Judaism's religious imagination but also its social institutions. The result of this intellectual and social ferment was a shift in historical consciousness, religious organization and self-awareness connoted by the term, 'Axial Age'. These dynamics are registered by the book of Job.

The presenting symptom of the book of Job is the failure of LI motifs in Job's speeches and prayers to rehabilitate him to his erstwhile support group. Shifts in postexilic Judaism's religious imagination were unable to sustain the charge against God made by Job and the lament rhetoric he uses. This is apparent both from the intransigent assertion of retribution thinking by Job's comforters and also from the YHWH speeches, which seem to undermine theological foundations of both traditional wisdom and complaint. But the YHWH speeches refrain from articulating a vision to take the place of either theological construct. The ambiguity and lack of clarity of Job 38–42 may well have been the reason why later hands added the Elihu speeches in Job 32–37 and the poem to divine wisdom in Job 28. Both of these additions emphasize the distance between YHWH and human reality, a characteristic of Axial Age theology.

Prayers following the biblical formula used in generating complaint psalms are less common for individuals in extra-biblical Second Temple literature than for the nation. Where they occur, there are indications of the scripturalization and particularization of the traditions of LI. Nevertheless, there remained a strong feeling that various kinds of sickness and personal affliction could be the results of attack by demonic agencies. This exigency was allowed for by the theology and rhetoric of the psalms of LI. However, the LI form was effectively abandoned as a remedy for treating victims of demonic attack in Second Temple Judaism. Emphasis on divine righteousness and transcendence favoured the development of angelologies and demonologies in order to insulate God from the charge of arbitrary evil. This in turn opened up the way for the emergence or recrudescence of new forms of healing liturgies involving exorcism.

It is probable that the therapeutic application of psalms of LI was lost by the beginning of the Hellenistic period. Corroborating arguments for such a viewpoint recognize the beginning of the Hellenistic era as one in which the reorganization of temple life under priestly influence had already taken place. This reorganization of sacred space had connections with Judaism's entry into the Axial Age, which undermined the theological premises of protest prayer. Later Second Temple writers, such as those responsible for the New Testament, did not operate in an environment which was aware of the therapeutic use of psalms of LI.

The lines of development are not the same for collective complaint against God. There is no sizeable body of extra-biblical Second Temple liturgical poetry comparable to the biblical protests of national defeat. The impact of Deuteronomic thinking among Israel's intellectuals, who denied the suitability of the protest prayer as a response to national catastrophe, contributed to this situation. Also important was the emergence of a priestly theology reflecting the influence of Axial Age categories, with emphasis on the distance between a transcendent God (who resisted description by human categories) and ordinary experience. Along with greater transcendence, there was affirmation of divine righteousness.

One result of this nexus of influences was the rise of penitential prayer, itself another form of crisis prayer. But it would be truer to the literature of the Second Temple to claim that the rhetoric of collective protest was eclipsed rather than replaced by penitential prayer. Indirect complaint against God continued to be expressed. It is attested both in the use of petitions in the negated imperative and in the praise of divine righteousness. Even while justifying divine punishment, penitential prayer catalogues the suffering of the people.

There are no expressions of direct complaint against God in well-formed compositions (including the elements of address and petition) of extra-biblical Second Temple prayer. Protest prayers are connected to the informal lament tradition and arose in extreme exigencies involving the loss of the temple during the persecutions of Antiochus Epiphanes and after 70 CE. Therefore, it appears that the biblical practice of informal lament by covenant mediators continued in post-biblical Judaism. Some development can be detected, however, with respect to the attitude of Jewish religious leadership towards protest prayer in the Second Temple period. The impetus was towards the exclusion of lament from prayer. While spontaneous protests by pious covenant mediators were given some sanction in the narratives of 1 Maccabees, the apocalyptic works of *2 Baruch* and 2 Esdras refuse complaints against God uttered by even the most reputable of community representatives. A similar treatment of protest against God appears in other contemporary Second Temple literature including the parabiblical book of *Pseudo-Philo* and Revelations. This development set the stage for the attitude toward the arguing with God tradition shown in later Jewish liturgy.

9.2. *The Continuity of the Complaint Tradition in Judaism*

This section is not intended to provide a full survey of the arguing with God tradition in Judaism. There are other works that have discussed this material in detail.[1] The interest of my discussion is to signal that protest against God only asserted itself in Judaism's public liturgies in moments of extreme crisis after the Second Temple period.

There is no evidence for a therapeutic practice of lament directed towards individuals in later Judaism. This is to be expected since the composition of LI as cultically administered interventions for afflicted persons

---

1.   For the Talmudic period see Joseph Heinemann, *Prayer in the Talmud: Forms and Patterns* (SJ, 9; Berlin: W. de Gruyter, 1977), pp. 193-217. A comprehensive survey of the use of argumentative prayer in rabbinic Judaism and its later developments can be found in Anson Laytner, *Arguing with God: A Jewish Tradition* (Northvale, NJ: Jason Aronson, 1990).

had ceased by the beginning of the Hellenistic period. Prayers and practices related to the need to prevent or repulse demonic attack would continue in popular Jewish culture well after the Second Temple period.[2] But these instruments do not use the LI form. Jews could continue to compose prayers in the style of LI to inform their own particular circumstances, however. A good example is found in a prayer of Samuel HaNagid, which he composed and recited in the place of the afternoon service on the day of battle with the army of Seville (1039 CE).[3] This prayer, however, does not contain complaint against God.

Before the modern era, Jewish exegesis typically approached the psalms of LI by interpreting the first person references as a symbol of the nation.[4] This exegetical trend reflects the tendency, apparent in Second Temple prayers, to connect individual suffering with the suffering of the nation. It remains visible in the prayers of supplication called *taḥānûn* in the synagogue service. Psalm 6 (a psalm of Direct Protest) is prominent in both the shorter and longer forms of the *taḥānûn*. But the psalm is set in a context which conditions its reception by petitions and pleas on behalf of the nation.[5] Individuals are permitted to add personal pleas after its recitation, but these are uttered silently.[6]

The argumentative prayer tradition in rabbinic Judaism is directed to expressions of collective distress. This concurs with developments in Second Temple Judaism. A distinction must be made between expressions of the arguing with God tradition that appear in liturgy and those that remain outside the context of worship. For the most part, Judaism has kept its severest criticism of its deity apart from liturgical expression. There are pointed complaints against God in aggadic literature. The rabbinic exegesis of Lamentations is a good illustration of the arguing with God tradition by its spiritual leaders.[7] Significant protest traditions are associated

---

2.   For references, see Douglas L. Penney and Michael O. Wise. 'By the Power of Beelzebub: An Aramaic Incantation Formula from Qumran (4Q560)', *JBL* 113 (1996), p. 629.

3.   Samuel HaNagid, 'Short Prayer in Time of Battle', in T. Carmi (ed.) *The Penguin Book of Hebrew Verse* (New York: Penguin, 1981), p. 288.

4.   Rainer Albertz, *Persönliche Frömmigkeit und offizielle Religion: Religionsinterner Pluralismus in Israel und Babylon* (Calwer Theologische Monographien Reihe A, Bibelwissenschaft 9; Stuttgart: Calwer Verlag, 1978), p. 23.

5.   See Phiip Birnbaum, *Ha-Siddur Ha-Shalem* (New York: Hebrew Publishing Company, 1977), pp. 104-118.

6.   Hayim H. Donin, *To Prayer as a Jew: A Guide to the Prayer Book and the Synagogue Service* (New York: Basic Books, 1980), pp. 202-207.

7.   David Kraemer, *Responses to Suffering in Classical Rabbinic Literature* (New York: Oxford University, 1995), pp. 140-46; Tod Linafelt, *Surviving Lamentations: Catastrophe,*

with Hasidism.[8] In fact, the complaint against God can be heard in many literary creations that have been part of the Jewish response to repeated persecution in Europe over the past thousand years.[9] Voices of protest are also found in literature after the Shoah. They include such such well-known writers as Elie Wiesel, whose play, 'The Trial of God', relies on the law-court pattern of prayer for its plot.[10]

Throughout this book, I have attempted to respect the possibility that informal expressions of protest against God in prayer and speech remained current among persons identified with the religious traditions of Israel. But documenting liturgical or official permissions for complaint against God is another story. The rabbinic authorities responsible for the preservation and transformations of Judaism after the Second Temple period did not permit the voice of protest to generate regular forms of worship.[11] There are a number of reasons for this. One is that the destruction of the Second Temple was analyzed in similar theological categories to those used for accounting for the destruction of the First Temple: a penitential and retributive theology prevailed. Normative Judaism explained national suffering along the lines of Deuteronomic theology, especially as mediated by the teachings of R. Akiva.[12] A second reason for censoring expressions of protest prayer was the alignment of protest with apocalyptic expectation (illustrated, e.g. in 2 *Baruch,* 2 Esdras and Revelations 6). The rabbinic period, in view of the decisive dominance of Rome and the disastrous effects of the Jewish wars, including the defeat of Bar Kochba, could ill afford to nurture the revolutionary sentiments that apocalyptic thought engendered. Finally, one should also note the weight of tradition. It would be anachronistic to project rabbinic practice onto Second Temple Judaism where evidence for statuatory liturgies with fixed prayers is mostly absent. Nevertheless, Chapter Seven concluded that Jewish authorities sought to exclude the practice of lament from public prayer in Second Temple times. Later Jewish liturgists largely followed the same impulse.

Nevertheless, there are places in which the complaint against God breaks into liturgical forms. Most common are forms of indirect protest, but there are texts of direct protest also. Prominent contexts include prayers for the Days of Awe, the fast of *Tisha b'Av* and the medieval

Lament, and Protest in the Afterlife of a Biblical Book (Chicago: Chicago University Press, 2000), pp. 100-16.

8.   Laytner, *Arguing with God*, pp. 179-89.

9.   See, e.g. the anthology in David G. Roskies (ed.), *The Literature of Destruction: Jewish Responses to Catastrophe* (Philadelphia: Jewish Publication Society, 1989).

10.   Laytner, *Arguing with God*, pp. 218-19.

11.   Kraemer, *Responses to Suffering*, pp. 216-19.

12.   Laytner, *Arguing with God*, pp. 110-11.

piyyutîm. There are also movements in contemporary Judaism to recover the protest tradition in liturgy. They involve practices such as incorporating readings from the Holocaust into the Passover Seder and the composition of new prayers.[13] But it is beyond the scope of this discussion to document these initiatives or speculate on their long-term impact on traditional Jewish worship.

Complaint against God can be found in the penitential poems called *sĕlîḥôt*. The *sĕlîḥôt* are typically used during the days of awe leading up to Yom Kippur. They reflect a moment of crisis in the community as the year comes to an end and the Holy One must decide who will be written into the book of life. These prayers belong to the standard liturgies of the Jewish tradition.[14] They mainly contain expressions of confession of sin, contrition, repentance, and prayers for the restoration of Israel. But a minor note is sometimes sounded, however, in complaint about the continuing debasement of Israel's situation:

> Our eyes are strained as we look for deliverance. The oppressors of thy people who bow to Bel — why do they prosper morning and evening?[15]

A note of protest is also sounded in traditions associated with *Tisha b'Av*. It is customary to read the book of Lamentations, which contains poetry mourning the loss of the First Temple, and supplementary poems called *qînôt* during the fast of the ninth day of *Av*. According to tradition, this date remembers a number of profound crises in Jewish history, among them: the Babylonians destroyed the First Temple, the Romans destroyed the Second Temple and the Jews were expelled from Spain in 1492. One can hear notes of complaint in early *qînôt*. There are good examples in the poems written by Eleazar ben Kallir.[16] In general, however, these poems stop short of direct protest against God and remain conditioned by the Deuteronomic theology that influenced the poems in Lamentations.

---

13. See, e.g. the prayers in David R. Blumenthal, *Facing the Abusing God: A Theology of Protest* (Louisville, KY: Westminster John Knox, 1993), pp. 268-97. Bluementhal embraces an orthodox faith while maintaining a position of lament towards the collective evil of the Holocaust and individual experiences of child abuse. His unsettling conclusion: God is abusive but not always; faithful Jews owe God not simply praise but also protest (pp. 246-48).

14. Laytner (*Arguing with God*, pp. 115-26) discerns a number of motifs of complaint in the standard synagogue service. But he allows more examples than I do, since I insist on explicit marks of direct complaint against God in order to discover an expression of protest prayer.

15. Philip Birnbaum, *Selihoth* (New York: Hebrew Publishing Co., 1952), p. 15.

16. An analysis of some of Eleazar ben Kallir's poems can be found in Linafelt, *Surviving Lamentations*, pp. 117-32.

The *piyyutim* are poetic embellishments used to enhance the meaning of the particular holiday or prayer for which they were written. Their origins are in dispute, but it is usually agreed that the tradition of writing *piyyutim* originated during Byzantine times when the text of the standard liturgy had not become completely fixed. Though there were already standard prayers and a standard order for prayers, there was also a freedom to embellish them. Tensions emerged between rabbinic authorities anxious to fix the liturgy in standard ways and the popular tradition of supplementing the liturgy with *piyyutim*. But by the beginning of the Middle Ages a compromise had been worked out such that it was permitted for congregations to recite *piyyutim* provided that they were linked in some way to the liturgical formulas for concluding the standard prayers.[17]

The majority of *piyyutim* were intended to complement the tone of the liturgy. But there are also *piyyutim* of protest. The greatest number of these poems of complaint were attached to the penitential services of the High Holy days and the Fast Days of the Jewish calendar. The vicious slaughter of European Jews during the Crusades was perceived as a breakdown in the God–Israel relationship. A good example of a *piyyut* of protest is the poem of Isaac bar Shalom written after the massacres of Jews in Germany during the Second Crusade, 'There is none like you among the dumb'. This poem was recited on the first Shabbat after Pesach.[18]

But during the Middle Ages, rabbinic authorities such as Maimonides were critical of *piyyutim* containing theological views that, if not heretical, certainly challenged what was normative and conventional. Finally, and related to the point just made, one should note that in the nineteenth century there was a rebellion in Reform Judaism against the inclusion of *piyyutim* in the liturgy. To this day, most medieval *piyyutim*, regardless of their contents, are excluded from Reform and Conservative prayerbooks.[19]

9.3. *The Recovery of Lament in Christianity*

The surveys undertaken in the last two sections underscore the relationship between protest against God and experiences of crisis. One reason for highlighting the Jewish experience is to set it in contrast to Christianity. The Christian faith cannot point to its past and discover a similar discourse of complaint against God in its liturgies. An exception to this generalization is the African-American spiritual tradition.[20] But, by and

---

17. Laytner, *Arguing with God*, pp. 129-30.
18. Laytner, *Arguing with God*, pp. 135-38.
19. Laytner, *Arguing with God*, pp. 174-76.
20. For the complaint against God among Afro-American slaves, see David E.

large, the Christian attitude towards the arguing with God tradition has been succinctly summarized in Nicholas Wolterstorff's observation that theologians in the Christian tradition have typically called the practice of lament into question.[21] Therefore, it is all the more surprising to discover a significant body of scholarship devoted to recovering the lament tradition for the Christian church at the end of the twentieth century. How has this situation come about? Or, to ask the same question in other words: what crisis has generated the fascination with lament and its rhetoric of divine protest in contemporary Christian circles?

In assessing the attitude of the Christian tradition towards biblical complaint prayer, it is important not to engage in anachronistic speculation. The writers of the New Testament, like other groups of Second Temple Jews, had no knowledge of a living tradition of LI. Individual lament psalms had not been used in liturgical contexts for at least three centuries prior to the beginning of the Christian era. In concert with their fellow Jews, the New Testament writers were conscious that human affliction could be caused by demonic attacks, and they believed in the efficacy of exorcism. In fact, exorcism was a characteristic feature of the early Church's missionary activity in the Roman empire.[22] There can be no question, therefore, of a peculiar bias against LI in the New Testament.

Christian literature stands in contrast to Jewish lament literature because of the absence of an ecclesiastical tradition of complaint against God on behalf of the community. Why was there no corresponding tradition of complaint against God on behalf of the Church in Christian literature? There have been multiple attempts to answer this question, and it is probably the case that any explanation must acknowledge several factors. One theory needs to be discounted, however. There is little reason to point the finger at Hellenistic civilization and its suspicion of emotion as a significant cause of the demise of the lament in the Church. My study has determined that theological developments in the biblical tradition itself played a principal role in the eclipse of the arguing with God tradition.

There has been much discussion of the reasons for the absence of lament in Christian liturgy. For example, Walter Brueggemann has emphasized the non-dialogical nature of much Christian faith with its emphasis on celebration, praise and triumph.[23] This is coupled with the propensity

Goatley, *Where You There? Godforsakenness in Slave Religion* (Maryknoll, NY: Orbis Books, 1996), pp. 53, 71-72.

21. Nicholas Wolterstorff, 'If God is Good and Sovereign, Why Lament?', *Calvin Theological Journal* 36 (2001), p. 50.

22. Eric Sorenson, *Possession and Exorcism in the New Testament and Early Christianity* (WUNT, 2/157; Tübingen: Mohr–Siebeck, 2002), pp. 16-17.

23. Walter Brueggemann, 'The Costly Loss of Lament', *JSOT* 36 (1986), p. 60. See

towards a universalizing representation of God.[24] Kathleen Billman and Daniel Migliore have surveyed a number of key theologians in Christian history noting emphases on the need to turn from this world to the vision of God, on suffering as vocation and, on humility and patience in the face of providence.[25] Erich Zenger believes that early Christianity transformed itself from a morality of suffering into a morality of sin while simultaneously losing its sensitivity to time through the attenuation of the hope of the Second Coming.[26]

Common to all of these contributions is a perception that the way suffering has been characterized in normative Christian discourse has affected the Church's ability to lament.[27] According to Karl-Josef Kuschel, there have been three typical attitudes towards human suffering and moral evil in Christian theology. These include the spirituality of the cross (suffering as a redemptive vocation), a theology of recompense (structure legitimation) and a moralizing-pedagogical approach (which assumes that suffering is meant to aid character formation). All three categories of thought cut out the possibility of protest against God.[28]

The theologies of suffering that have characterized Christianity are commensurate with its engagement with Axial Age categories. In fact, the emergence of Christianity can be described as a 'secondary breakthrough' of the Axial Age. The development of Christianity is characterized by a radicalization of tendencies already evident in Second Temple Judaism. These include a universalizing predisposition which challenged definitions of religious communities by ethnic boundaries and which manifested a strong orientation towards the transcendent by redefining the land of

also Samuel E. Balentine, *Prayer in the Hebrew Bible: The Drama of Divine–Human Dialogue* (Overtures to Biblical Theology; Minneapolis: Fortress Press, 1993), p. 278.

24. Walter Brueggemann, *Theology of the Old Testament: Testimony, Dispute, Advocacy* (Minneapolis: Fortress Press, 1997), p. 327.

25. Kathleen D. Billman and Daniel L. Migliore. *Rachel's Cry: Prayer of Lament and Rebirth of Hope* (Cleveland: United Church Press, 1999), pp. 46-60.

26. Erich Zenger, *A God of Vengeance? Understanding the Psalms of Divine Wrath* (Louisville, KY: Westminster John Knox Press, 1996), pp. 75-76.

27. Belden C. Lane, 'Arguing with God: Blasphemy and the Prayer of Lament in Judaism and Other Faith Traditions', in Yehuda Bauer *et al.* (eds.), *Remembering for the Future: Working Papers and Addenda. III. The Impact of the Holocaust and Genocide on Christians and Jews* (Oxford: Pergamon Press, 1989), pp. 2549-51; Karl-Joseph Kuschel, 'Ist Gott verantwortlich für das Übel: Überlegungen zu einer Theologie der Anklagen', in G. Fuchs (ed.), *Angesichts des Leids an Gott glauben? Zur Theologie der Klage* (Frankfurt a. M.: Joseph Knecht, 1996), p. 227-28. See also the critique of traditional Christian theology and the advocacy of lament in Dorothee Soelle, *Suffering* (Philadelphia: Fortress Press, 1975), especially pp. 70-78.

28. Kuschel, 'Ist Gott verantwortlich für das Übel', p. 237.

promise as another world.[29] This other world was simultaneously found within the human heart (the law of Christ within) and in a heavenly realm yet to come.[30]

One result of such radicalization was a transformation of the theological categories available in the Bible for processing human suffering. While structure legitimation theories continued, the Christian community gravitated towards theories of suffering as redemptive/vicarious, thereby abandoning the category of lament. Such movement can be seen in the teaching about prayer in the New Testament itself. The overall attitude towards prayer in the New Testament is at odds with the assumptions of the psalms of LI. The prayer of help clearly subordinates the present distress of the petitioner to the will of God. For example, the petitions to avoid temptation and for deliverance from evil in the Lord's Prayer are subordinate to the statement 'your will be done, your kingdom come' (Mt. 6.10). Similar sentiments are found in various versions of Jesus' prayer in Gethsamene: Jesus' petition is subordinated to the will of God. The relationship between prayer and suffering has changed. This is manifest in the teaching of Paul. The appeal for help in the biblical LI 'for your name's sake' has shifted to a theology of the cross that counsels acceptance of affliction 'for the sake of Christ'.[31]

The shift to a counsel that accepts affliction as a Christian vocation echoes the kind of thinking that rejects the plea of the murdered saints in Rev. 6.10 and the questions directed at divine providence in 2 Esdras and 2 Baruch. These texts silenced the protests of the saints by setting out a vision of history in which the end cannot come until a certain amount of suffering has been sustained, and until the sins of the nations at enmity with Israel are full. In such a dispensation, the suffering of the righteous has a redemptive value; it is not to be lamented.

No doubt the survey above could be nuanced. Nevertheless, the major trends of Church teaching on the meaningfulness of human suffering clearly have been even less friendly to the lament tradition than Judaism has been. This observation ought to highlight the strangeness of the recovery of lament in the Church in the late twentieth century. Even more

29. S.N. Eisenstadt, 'The Secondary Breakthrough in Ancient Israelite Civilization—Second Temple Judaism and Christianity', in S.N. Eisenstadt (ed.), *The Origins and Diversity of Axial Age Civilizations* (SUNY Series in Near Eastern Studies; Albany, NY: State University of New York, 1986), p. 236.

30. Marcel Gauchet, *The Disenchantment of the World: A Political History of Religion* (New French Thought; Princeton: University Press, 1997), p. 117.

31. Patrick D. Miller, *They Cried to the Lord: The Form and Theology of Biblical Prayer* (Minneapolis: Fortress Press, 1994), pp. 321-24.

curious is the focus on the recovery of individual lament.[32] Individual lament under the sanction of religious institutions has not been a live therapeutic option in either Christian or Jewish circles for the past 2,300 years. What has occasioned such a momentous and unexpected shift?

The best way to approach this question is to note where and how the voice of protest prayer reasserted itself in the past, despite theological systems that were inimical to it. There is a clear relationship between the emergence of complaint against God and moments of crisis which signify breakdowns in normative theological paradigms. For example, the survival of corporate complaint in Judaism attests to the rise of protest at those moments when the theological paradigms, which typically informed the community of faith's self-understanding, seemed to be impotent. It follows that one might look for a significant breakdown in theological constructs as a way of explaining the renewed interest in lament in contemporary theology.

This line of reasoning is supported by reflection on the modern recovery of lament provided by Samuel Balentine. Biblical scholars have been well aware that the questions scholarship engages often reflect the times in which they live. Balentine notes that little attention was paid to the topic of prayer in biblical scholarship through the nineteenth century. He underscores the role of social crises of the first half of the twentieth century in promoting shifts in emphases that created both the conditions for new kinds of biblical theology and an esteem for the dialogical nature of biblical lament. It is no accident, e.g. that Claus Westermann's detailed studies of lament forms in various biblical books follow the cultural chaos and horrific suffering of the Second World War.[33]

The recovery of lament, therefore, reflects a pattern which is profoundly biblical. One resorts to the arguing with God tradition in times of crisis when relationships conventionally assumed between God and human beings seem to break down. What crisis has overcome the Church and academia such that complaint prayer recommends itself not only as an object of study but also for appropriation? I suggest that part of the

---

32. The pastoral possibilities for addressing individual suffering through the psalms of LI has been a prominent theme in contemporary Christian literature; see, e.g. Walter Brueggemann, 'The Formfulness of Grief', *Interpretation* 31 (1977): 263-75; W.W. Frerichs, *Take It to the Lord: Prayer Laments for the Afflicted* (Minneapolis: Augsburg, 1982); Ivan T. Kaufman, 'Undercut by Joy: The Sunday Lectionaries and the Psalms of Lament', in J.C. Knight and L.A. Sinclair (eds.), *The Psalms and Other Studies on the Old Testament Presented to Joseph I. Hunt* (Nashotah, WI: Nashotah House Seminary, 1990), pp. 66-78; and many of the essays in Billman and Migliore, *Rachel's Cry*; and Sally A. Brown and Patrick D. Miller (eds.), *Lament: Reclaiming Practices in Pulpit, Pew, and Public Square* (Louisville, KY: Westminster John Knox Press, 2005).

33. Balentine, *Prayer in the Hebrew Bible*, pp. 255-58.

answer lies in the fact that some of the conditions which led to the eclipse of the biblical tradition of argumentative prayer (especially individual lament) are themselves now being undone.

The Axial Age has fallen victim to modernity. It is in the context of this significant shift in worldview that contemporary theologians and biblical scholars have rediscovered lament. I have neither the space nor the competence to summarize all that accounts for the nature of modern Western culture. It is enough to note here that the Axial Age was based on some key polarities that have now become compromised if not collapsed altogether. Most important in this regard is the fate of the Axial Age's emphasis on a world of values transcendent to ordinary consciousness and superior to it.

The French political philosopher Marcel Gauchet has described the rise and the fall of the Axial Age world-view in his book, *The Disenchantment of the World: A Political History of Religion*. In relationship to pre-Axial societies, it is no accident that the Axial Age's emphasis on transcendence was simultaneous with the rise of the imperial state. In essence, political power was seen to transcend local authorities and became lodged with the rulers of great empires. Coincidental with this movement, however, was a new discovery of the individual. Mystics and philosophers discovered their own ability to transcend reality by an attention to inwardness. The Axial Age, therefore, created not only a split between ordinary reality and a higher reality of greater meaningfulness but also a split between the public person and individual consciousness.[34] Modernity, however, has profoundly affected concepts of self-identity, in part because the transcendent has lost its value as a principle of social organization.[35]

According to philosopher Stephen Erickson, Nietzsche's announcement of the death of God presaged the end of Axial Age metaphysics in the West. The 'death of God' is a pregnant phrase for signifying a shift in awareness that challenges the domination of this world by some transcendent and higher consciousness.[36] Among its various effects, the loss of transcendental categories has affected analyses of human suffering.

The conditions of modernity make it difficult to analyze human suffering on the models of either divine correction or as labor pains for the birth of a new world. That is, cultural shifts have undermined the confidence that all suffering has transcendent meaning. There is awareness of a quality of human suffering which neither a penitential nor apocalyptic theology seems able to embrace. Paradigmatic here is the *Shoah*, the

---

34. Gauchet, *Disenchantment of the World*, pp. 37-49.
35. Gauchet, *Disenchantment of the World*, pp. 166-76.
36. Stephen A. Erickson, 'The Coming Age of Thresholding: The Renewal of Mystery within Secular Culture', *Philosophy Today* 43 (Spring 1999), pp. 5-6.

calculated and industrialized destruction of one third of the Jews living at the time of the Second World War. Of course, Judaism has its own penitential traditions and messianic speculations. But since World War II a considerable literature of Jewish protest has emerged, in effect a revival of complaint, to grapple with this utterly horrific and unprecedented experience of undeserved suffering.[37]

I would like to be able to report that awareness of the Holocaust has had a significant impact on popular Christian theology. But, in my opinion, the significance of the *Shoah* for Christian practice and belief still has not been adequately addressed. Nevertheless, modernity has broken open the typical Axial Age paradigms for processing suffering in Christianity. Key here are the influences of feminism, liberation theology and psychotherapy.[38] There are forms of human suffering that cannot be comprehended either as correction for wrong-doing or as redemptive experiences.

One post-Axial development, I think, has been of particular value in fueling the interest in recovering the individual lament paradigm. This is the assertion of human rights as a category of law.[39] Its charter document is the Universal Declaration of Human Rights proclaimed by the United Nations in 1948. This was the first of a series of human rights laws that have effectively altered the balance between national sovereignty and individual rights in Western countries.[40] A key benefit of rights legislation, according to political philosopher Michael Ignatieff is that 'rights never securely legitimize the status quo; they actually make grievance legitimate ... It is largely because of rights, therefore, that ... modernity is on endless trial'.[41] Ignatieff also observes that the idea of human rights is nothing less than a residual system of entitlement that human beings have, irrespective of the states in which they may be living, 'Human rights are the rights that men and women have when all else fails them'.[42]

There are three analogies between the modern concern for human rights and the contemporary fascination with the lament paradigm. These are found in the concepts of entitlement, grievance and trial. All three are important characteristics of the tradition of argumentative prayer. In biblical times, individuals felt entitled to certain kinds of divine intervention,

---

37. For examples, see Laytner, *Arguing with God*, pp. 196-227; Roskies, *Literature of Destruction*, pp. 565-604.

38. Lane, 'Arguing with God: Blasphemy and the Prayer of Lament', pp. 2553-54.

39. For the rise in consciousness of human rights as a mark of post-Axial civilization, see Gauchet, *Disenchantment of the World*, p. 92.

40. Michael Ignatieff, *The Rights Revolution* (CBC Massey Lectures Series; Toronto: House of Anansi, 2000), p. 49.

41. Ignatieff, *The Rights Revolution*, pp. 32-33.

42. Ignatieff, *The Rights Revolution*, p. 36.

most especially orderly births and meaningful deaths. By the same token, underlying the protests of national defeat is the assumption that the God–Israel relationship required a certain consistency on the part of both parties. Inconsistencies in divine-human relationships are the subject of grievance through the liturgies of complaint.[43] The prayers of complaint themselves are stereotypical forms of disputation that rely on the metaphor of legal process.[44] In many cases, these biblical prayers represent an attempt to make a claim on a residual entitlement to life when all other supports have failed.

Arguments on behalf of human entitlement, therefore, are implicated in the argumentative prayer paradigm. It is not surprising that lament should become attractive to faith communities living and breathing the atmosphere of modern rights-based ethics in the wake of the eclipse of the Axial Age. For the ancient tradition of protest against God assumes that worshippers have rights with God as well as duties and that the Creator has obligations as well as prerogatives.

Of course, many readers will be familiar with my analysis in terms of the challenges posed by contemporary culture to the Church. Whether one wants to talk about post-modernism, post-Christendom or the death of God, significant changes in Western consciousness have been taking place. What I am describing as a general trend in the last half of the twentieth century has been analyzed by many thinkers far more adroitly than I have attempted here. I am only making one claim in the present discussion: recovery of lament in Christianity actually *depends* on the conditions of post-Christendom or post-Axial culture. This is an irony which has escaped many concerned to reappropriate the biblical tradition of protest prayer. But it follows logically from the situation as I have described it. One is most likely to recover a pre-Axial practice when the Axial Age is no longer dominant, and the explanatory value of its attendant theologies is in eclipse.[45]

Contemporary interest in the recovery of complaint prayer, therefore, is a presenting symptom of a significant challenge facing both church and synagogue. The Western world seems to have reached a turning point in

43. In the biblical tradition, the inconsistencies that give rise to lament are not perceived as discrepancies in the divine being. Complaint is directed at actions and situations that are incomprehensible to the petitioner as divine actions; see Claus Westermann 'The Complaint against God', in Tod Linafelt and T. K. Beal (eds.), *God in the Fray: A Tribute to Walter Brueggemann* (Minneapolis: Fortress Press, 1998), pp. 238-39.

44. Laytner, *Arguing with God*, pp. xvii-xviii.

45. See Ewart H. Cousins, *Christ of the 21st Century* (Rockport, MA: Element, 1992), pp. 9-10; Cousins thinks that post-Axial conditions allow for the recovery of pre-Axial traditions.

its intellectual history. This turning point amounts to something of a crisis in terms of the self-definition of both rabbinic Judaism and Christianity, because these faiths have ordinarily operated within the categories of the Axial Age. To the degree that modes of Axial Age theology continue to assert themselves, the practice of lament will no doubt continue to be inhibited in faith communities that base themselves on biblical tradition. But the contemporary fascination with protest prayer would suggest that the religious imagination of the Bible cannot be constrained by such theological categories, however much it may have been comprehended by them.

BIBLIOGRAPHY

Aejmelaeus, Anneli, *The Traditional Prayer in the Psalms* (BZAW, 167; Berlin: W. de Gruyter, 1986).

Albertz, Rainer, *Persönliche Frömmigkeit und offizielle Religion: Religionsinterner Pluralismus in Israel und Babylon* (Calwer Theologische Monographien Reihe A, Bibelwissenschaft 9; Stuttgart: Calwer Verlag, 1978).

— *A History of Israelite Religion in the Old Testament Period* (OTL; 2 vols.; Louisville, KY: Westminster John Knox, 1994).

— *Israel in Exile: The History and Literature of the Sixth Century B.C.E.* (Studies in Biblical Literature, 3; Atlanta: Society of Biblical Literature, 2003).

Albl, Martin C., ' "Are Any of You Sick?" The Health Care System in the Letter of James', *JBL* 121 (2002), pp. 123-43.

Alexander, Philip S., 'The Demonology of the Dead Sea Scrolls', in Flint and Vander-Kam, *Dead Sea Scrolls after Fifty Years,* II, pp. 331-53.

Amir, Joshua, 'Monotheistic Myth in the Bible [Modern Hebrew]', *Bet Miqra* 146 (1996), pp. 206-209.

Anbar, Moshe, 'Mari and the Bible [Modern Hebrew]', *Bet Miqra* 170 (2002), pp. 193-98.

Andersen, Francis I., and David N. Freedman, *Micah* (AB, 24E; New York: Doubleday, 2000).

Anderson, A.A., *Psalms* (NCB; 2 vols.; Grand Rapids: Eerdmans, 1989; original edition, 1972).

Anderson, Bernhard W., *Out of the Depths: The Psalms Speak for Us Today* (Philadelphia: Westminster Press, rev. edn, 1983).

— *Understanding the Old Testament* (Englewood Cliffs, NJ: Prentice Hall, 4th edn, 1986).

Anderson, Cheryl B., *Women, Ideology, and Violence: Critical Theory and the Construction of Gender in the Book of the Covenant and the Deuteronomic Law* (JSOTSup, 394; London: Continuum, 2004).

Apuleius, Lucius, *The Golden Ass* (trans. Jack Lindsay; Indiana University Greek and Latin Classics; Bloomington: Indiana University Press, 1962).

Armstrong, Karen, *A History of God: The 4000-Year Quest of Judaism, Christianity and Islam* (New York: Ballantine Books, 1993).

Attridge, Harold W., 'Hebrews, Epistle to', *ABD*, III, pp. 97-105.

Avalos, Hector, *Illness and Health Care in the Ancient Near East: The Role of the Temple in Greece, Mesopotamia, and Israel* (HSM, 54; Atlanta: Scholars Press, 1995).

Balentine, Samuel E., *The Hidden God: The Hiding of the Face of God in the Old Testament* (Oxford: University Press, 1983).

— *Prayer in the Hebrew Bible: The Drama of Divine–Human Dialogue* (Overtures to Biblical Theology. Minneapolis: Fortress Press, 1993).

Baltzer, Klaus, *Deutero-Isaiah: A Commentary on Isaiah 40–55* (Hermeneia: Minneapolis: Fortress Press, 2001).

Batto, Bernard F., 'The Sleeping God: An Ancient Near Eastern Motif of Divine Sovereignty', *Bib* 68 (1987), pp. 153-77.

— *Slaying the Dragon: Mythmaking in the Biblical Tradition* (Louisville, KY: Westminster John Knox, 1992).

Baumgartner, Walter, *Jeremiah's Poems of Lament* (Sheffield: Almond Press, 1988).

Bautch, Richard J., *Developments in Genre between Post-Exilic Penitential Prayers and the Psalms of Communal Lament* (Academia biblica, 7; Atlanta: Society of Biblical Literature, 2003).

Beale, G.K., *The Book of Revelation* (NIGTC; Grand Rapids: Eerdmans, 1999).

Ben Zvi, Ehud, *Micah* (FOTL, 21B; Grand Rapids: Eerdmans, 2000).

Benjamin, Don C., 'An Anthropology of Prophecy', *BTB* 21 (1991), pp. 135-44.

Berlin, Adele, 'Qumran Laments and the Study of Lament Literature', in Chazon, *Liturgical Perspectives*, pp. 1-17.

Beuken, W.A.M., and H.W.M. van Grol, 'Jeremiah 14,1–15,9: A Situation of Distress and its Hermeneutics. Unity and Diversity of Form — Dramatic Development', in Bogaert (ed.), *Le Livre de Jérémie*, pp. 297-342.

Beuken, W.A.M. (ed.), *The Book of Job* (BETL, 114; Leuven: Leuven University Press, 1994).

Beyerlin, Walter, 'Innerbiblische Aktualisierungsversuche: Schichten im 44. Psalm', *ZTK* 73 (1976), pp. 446-60.

Biggs, Robert D., 'Medicine, Surgery, and Public Health in Ancient Mesopotamia', *CANE*, III, pp. 1911-24.

Billman, Kathleen D., and Daniel L. Migliore, *Rachel's Cry: Prayer of Lament and Rebirth of Hope* (Cleveland: United Church Press, 1999).

Birnbaum, Philp, *Selihoth* (New York: Hebrew Publishing Co., 1952).

— *Ha-Siddur Ha-Shalem* (New York: Hebrew Publishing Company, 1977).

Blenkinsopp, Joseph, *Isaiah 1–39* (AB, 19; New York: Doubleday, 2000).

Bloom, Harold, and David Rosenberg, *The Book of J* (New York: Vintage Books, 1991).

Blumenthal, David R., *Facing the Abusing God: A Theology of Protest* (Louisville, KY: Westminster John Knox, 1993).

Boda, Mark J., *Praying the Tradition: The Origin and Use of Tradition in Nehemiah 9* (BZAW, 277; Berlin: W. de Gruyter, 1999).

— 'From Complaint to Contrition: Peering through the Liturgical Window of Jer 14,1–15,4', *ZAW* 113 (2001), pp. 186-97.

Bogaert, P.M. (ed.), *Le Livre de Jérémie: Le prophète et son milieu, les oracles et leur transmission* (BETL, 54; Leuven: Peeters, 1981).

Bouzard, Walter C., *We Have Heard with Our Ears, O God: Sources of the Communal Laments in the Psalms* (SBLDS, 159; Atlanta: Scholars Press, 1997).

Brenner, Athalya, 'God's Answer to Job', *VT* 31 (1981), pp. 129-37.

Brettler, Mark Z., *God Is King: Understanding an Israelite Metaphor* (JSOTSup, 76; Sheffield: JSOT Press, 1989).

Brichto, H.C., 'Kin, Cult, Land and Afterlife — a Biblical Complex', *HUCA* 44 (1973), pp. 1-54.

Bright, John, *Jeremiah* (AB, 21; Garden City, NY: Doubleday, 1965).

Brown, Sally A., and Patrick D. Miller (eds.), *Lament: Reclaiming Practices in Pulpit, Pew, and Public Square* (Louisville, KY: Westminster John Knox, 2005).

Broyles, Craig C., *The Conflict of Faith and Experience in the Psalms: A Form-Critical and Theological Study* (JSOTSup, 52; Sheffield: JSOT Press, 1989).

Brueggemann, Walter, 'From Hurt to Joy, from Death to Life', *Int* 28 (1974), pp. 3-19.
—'The Formfulness of Grief', *Int* 31 (1977), pp. 263-75.
—'The Costly Loss of Lament', *JSOT* 36 (1986), pp. 57-71.
—*Old Testament Theology: Essays on Structure, Theme, and Text* (Minneapolis: Fortress Press, 1992).
—*Theology of the Old Testament: Testimony, Dispute, Advocacy* (Minneapolis: Fortress Press, 1997).
Buber, Martin, 'Myth in Judaism', *Commentary* 9 (1950), pp. 562-66.
Burchard, C., 'Joseph and Aseneth', in Charlesworth, *Old Testament Pseudepigrapha*, II, pp. 177-247.
Burnett, Joel S., 'The Question of Divine Absence in Israelite and West Semitic Religion', *CBQ* 67 (2005), pp. 215-35.
Bustenay, Oded, 'The Exile—Myth or History? The Origin of the Assyrian and the Babylonian Exile [Modern Hebrew]', *Bet Miqra* 176 (2003), pp. 103-25.
Carmi, T. (ed.), *The Penguin Book of Hebrew Verse* (New York: Penguin, 1981).
Carney, Sheila, 'God Damn God: A Reflection on Expressing Anger in Prayer', *BTB* 13 (1983), pp. 116-20.
Carroll, Robert P., *When Prophecy Failed* (New York: Seabury, 1979).
—*From Chaos to Covenant: Prophecy in the Book of Jeremiah* (New York: Crossroad, 1981).
—*Jeremiah* (OTL; London: SCM Press, 1986).
Carter, Warren, 'Matthew 23.37-39', *Int* 54 (2000), pp. 66-68.
Charlesworth, J.H. (ed.), *The Old Testament Pseudepigrapha* (2 vols.; Garden City, NY: Doubleday, 1983, 1985).
—'Prayer of Manasseh', in Charlesworth, *Old Testament Pseudepigrapha*, II, pp. 625-37.
Charlesworth, J.H., and J.A. Sanders, 'More Psalms of David', in Charlesworth, *Old Testament Pseudepigrapha*, I, pp. 609-24.
Chazon, Esther G., 'Hymns and Prayers in the Dead Sea Scrolls', in Flint and Vander-Kam, *The Dead Sea Scrolls after Fifty Years*, I, pp. 244-70.
—(ed.), *Liturgical Perspectives: Prayer and Poetry in the Light of the Dead Sea Scrolls* (STDJ, 48; Leiden: E.J. Brill, 2003).
Childs, Brevard S., 'Psalm Titles and Midrashic Exegesis', *JSS* 16 (1971), pp. 137-50.
—*The Book of Exodus* (OTL; Philadelphia: Westminster Press, 1974).
Clark, F.C., 'Job, or the Suffering of God', *Judaism* 42 (1993), pp. 218-28.
Clements, R.E., *Isaiah 1–39* (NCB; Grand Rapids: Eerdmans, 1980).
Clifford, R.J., 'Isaiah, Book of (Second Isaiah)', *ABD*, III, pp. 490-501.
Clines, D.J.A., *Job 1–20* (WBC, 17; Dallas: Word Books, 1989).
Coggan, Donald, *The Prayers of the New Testament* (London: Hodder & Stoughton, 1967).
Cohen, Mark E., *Sumerian Hymnology: The Eršemma* (HUCA Supplements, 2; Cincinnati: Hebrew Union College–Jewish Institute of Religion, 1981).
—*The Canonical Lamentations of Ancient Mesopotamia* (2 vols.; Potomac, MD: Capital Decisions, 1988).
Collins, Adele Yarbro, 'The Appropriation of the Psalms of Individual Lament by Mark', in C.M. Tuckett (ed.), *The Scriptures in the Gospels* (BETL, 131; Leuven: Leuven University Press, 1997), pp. 223-41.
Cooper, Burton Z., 'Why God? A Tale of Two Sufferers', *TTod* 42 (1986), pp. 423-34.
Cousins, Ewart H., *Christ of the 21st Century* (Rockport, MA: Element, 1992).
Crenshaw, James L., 'Job, Book of', *ABD*, III, pp. 858-68.
—*Joel* (AB, 24C; New York: Doubleday, 1995).

— *Old Testament Wisdom: An Introduction* (Louisville, KY: Westminster John Knox, rev. edn, 1998).

Crow, Loren D., 'The Rhetoric of Psalm 44', *ZAW* 104 (1992), pp. 394-401.

Culley, Robert C., *Oral Formulaic Language in the Biblical Psalms* (Near and Middle Eastern Studies, 4; Toronto: University Press, 1967).

Cunningham, Graham, *'Deliver Me from Evil': Mesopotamian Incantations 2500–1500 B.C.* (Studia Pohl Series Maior, 17; Rome: Pontifical Biblical Institute, 1997).

Dahmen, Ulrich, *Psalmen- und Psalter-Rezeption im Frühjudentum: Rekonstruktion, Textbestand, Struktur und Pragmatik der Psalmenrolle 11Psᵃ aus Qumran* (STDJ, 49; Leiden: Brill, 2003).

Day, John, *Psalms* (OTG; Sheffield: JSOT Press, 1992).

Dever, William, 'Archaeology and the Israelite "Conquest"', *ABD*, III, pp. 545-58.

Dhanaraj, Dharmakkan, *Theological Significance of the Motif of Enemies in Selected Psalms of Individual Lament* (Orientalia biblica et Christiana, 4; Glückstadt: J.J. Augustin, 1992).

Dhorme, Edouard, *A Commentary on the Book of Job* (London: Thomas Nelson & Sons, 1967).

Di Lella, Alexander A., 'Wisdom of Ben-Sira', *ABD*, VI, pp. 931-45.

Diamond, A.R., *The Confessions of Jeremiah in Context: Scenes of a Prophetic Drama* (JSOTSup, 45; Sheffield: JSOT Press, 1987).

Dimant, Devorah, and Uriel Rappaport (eds.), *The Dead Sea Scrolls: Forty Years of Research* (STDJ, 10; Leiden: Brill, 1992).

Dion, P.E., 'Les chants du serviteur de Yahweh et quelques passages apparentés d'Is 40–55', *Bib* 51 (1970), pp. 17-38.

Dobbs-Allsopp, F.W., *Weep, O Daughter of Zion: A Study of the City-Lament Genre in the Hebrew Bible* (BibOr, 44; Rome: Pontifical Biblical Institute, 1993).

— 'Darwinism, Genre Theory, and City Laments', *JAOS* 120 (2000), pp. 625-30.

Dobbs-Allsopp, F.W., and Tod Linafelt, 'The Rape of Zion in Thr 1,10', *ZAW* 113 (2001), pp. 77-81.

Donin, Hayim H., *To Prayer as a Jew: A Guide to the Prayer Book and the Synagogue Service* (New York: BasicBooks, 1980).

Driver, Samuel R., *An Introduction to the Literature of the Old Testament* (Cleveland: Meridian Books, 1967).

Eisenstadt, S.N. (ed.), *The Origins and Diversity of Axial Age Civilizations* (SUNY Series in Near Eastern Studies; Albany, NY: State University of New York, 1986).

— 'The Axial Age Breakthroughs—Their Characteristics and Origins', in Eisenstadt, *Origins and Diversity of Axial Age Civilizations*, pp, 1-25.

— 'The Axial Age Breakthrough in Ancient Israel', in Eisenstadt, *Origins and Diversity of Axial Age Civilizations*, pp.127-34.

— 'The Secondary Breakthrough in Ancient Israelite Civilization—Second Temple Judaism and Christianity', in Eisenstadt, *Origins and Diversity of Axial Age Civilizations*, pp. 227-40.

Elkana, Yehuda, 'The Emergence of Second-Order Thinking in Classical Greece', in Eisenstadt, *Origins and Diversity of Axial Age Civilizations*, pp. 40-64.

Emmendörffer, Michael, *Der ferne Gott: Eine Untersuchung der alttestamentlichen Volksklagelieder vor dem Hintergrund der mesopotamischen Literatur* (Forschungen zum Alten Testament, 21; Tübingen: Mohr–Siebeck, 1998).

Erickson, Stephen A., 'The Coming Age of Thresholding: The Renewal of Mystery within Secular Culture', *Philosophy Today* 43 (Spring 1999), pp. 13-43.

Eshel, Esther, 'Genres of Magical Texts in the Dead Sea Scrolls', in Lange, Lichtenberger and Römheld, *Die Dämonen/Demons*, pp. 395-415.

—'Apotropaic Prayers in the Second Temple Period', in Chazon, *Liturgical Perspectives*, pp. 69-88.

Faber, Walter, 'Witchcraft, Magic, and Divination in Ancient Mesopotamia', *CANE*, III, pp. 1895-1909.

Falk, Ze'ev W., *Hebrew Law in Biblical Times* (Provo, UT/Winona Lake, IN: Brigham Young University/Eisenbrauns, 2nd edn, 2001).

Ferris, Paul W., *The Genre of Communal Lament in the Bible and the Ancient Near East* (SBLDS, 127; Atlanta: Scholars Press, 1992).

Fleming, Daniel E., 'Job: The Tale of Patient Faith and the Book of God's Dilemma', *VT* 44 (1994), pp. 468-82.

Flint, P.W., and J.C. VanderKam (eds.), *The Dead Sea Scrolls after Fifty Years: A Comprehensive Assessment* (2 vols.; Leiden: E.J. Brill, 1999).

Fløysvik, Ingvar, *When God Becomes My Enemy: The Theology of the Complaint Psalms* (St Louis: Concordia Press, 1997).

Flusser, David, 'Qumrân and Jewish Apotropaic Prayers', *IEJ* 16 (1966), pp. 194-205.

—'Psalms, Hymns, and Prayers', in Stone, *Jewish Writings of the Second Temple Period*, pp. 551-77.

Fohrer, Georg, *Introduction to the Old Testament* (London: SPCK, 1965).

Ford, J. Massyngberde, *Revelation* (AB, 38; Garden City, NY: Doubleday, 1975).

Frerichs, W.W., *Take It to the Lord: Prayer Laments for the Afflicted* (Minneapolis: Augsburg Fortress, 1982).

Fuchs, G. (ed.), *Angesichts des Leids an Gott glauben? Zur Theologie der Klage* (Frankfurt a. M.: Joseph Knecht, 1996).

Fuchs, Ottmar, *Die Klage als Gebet: Eine theologische Besinnung am Beispiel des Psalms 22* (Munich: Kösel, 1982).

Fullerton, K., 'The Original Conclusion of the Book of Job', *ZAW* 42 (1924), pp. 116-36.

Garsiel, Moshe, 'Studies on the Names of the Letters of the Alphabet in Acrostic Literary Units in the Bible [Modern Hebrew]', *Bet Miqra* 139 (1994), pp. 313-34.

Gauchet, Marcel, *The Disenchantment of the World: A Political History of Religion* (New French Thought; Princeton: Princeton University Press, 1997).

Gerstenberger, Erhard S., 'Jeremiah's Complaints: Observations on Jer 15.10-21', *JBL* 82 (1963), pp. 393-408.

—*Der bittende Mensch: Bittritual und Klagelied des Einzelnen im Alten Testament* (WMANT, 51; Neukirchen–Vluyn: Neukirchener Verlag, 1980).

—*Psalms: Part 1 with an Introduction to Cultic Poetry* (FOTL, 14; Grand Rapids: Eerdmans, 1988).

—*Psalms: Part 2 and Lamentations* (FOTL, 15; Grand Rapids: Eerdmans, 2001).

Gerstenberger, Erhard S., and Wolfgang Schrage, *Suffering* (Biblical Encounters Series; Nashville: Abingdon Press, 1980).

Girard, René, *Job, the Victim of his People* (London: Athlone Press, 1987).

Goatley, David E., *Where You There? Godforsakenness in Slave Religion* (Maryknoll, NY: Orbis Books, 1996).

Goldstein, J.A., *1 Maccabees* (AB, 41; Garden City, NY: Doubleday, 1976).

Gottwald, Norman K., *The Hebrew Bible: A Socio-Literary Introduction* (Philadelphia: Fortress Press, 1985).

Gowan, Donald E., *Theology of the Prophetic Books. The Death and Resurrection of Israel* (Louisville, KY: Westminster John Knox Press, 1998).

Green, M.W., 'The Eridu Lament', *JCS* 30 (1978), pp. 127-67.

—'The Uruk Lament', *JAOS* 104 (1984), pp. 253-79.

Greenberg, Moshe, *Biblical Prose Prayer as a Window to the Popular Religion of Ancient Israel* (The Taubman Lectures in Jewish Studies, Sixth Series; Berkeley: University of California Press, 1983).

Gross, Walter, 'Trifft ein Unglück die Stadt, und der Herr war nicht am Werk? Amos 3,6', in Fuchs, *Angesichts des Leids an Gott glauben?*, pp. 83-100.

Guest, Deryn, 'Hiding Behind the Naked Woman in Lamentations: A Recriminative Response', *BibInt* 7 (1999), pp. 413-48.

Gunkel, Hermann, and Joachim Begrich, *Introduction to the Psalms: The Genres of the Religious Lyric of Israel* (Mercer Library of Biblical Studies; Macon, GA: Mercer University Press, 1998; 4th German edn, 1985).

Gwaltney, William C., 'The Biblical Book of Lamentations in the Context of Near Eastern Lament Literature', in W.W. Hallo, J.C. Moyer and L.G. Perdue (eds.), *Scripture in Context. II. More Essays on the Comparative Method* (Winona Lake, IN: Eisenbrauns, 1983), pp. 191-211.

Haar, Murray J., 'The God–Israel Relationship in the Community Lament Psalms' (Ph.D. Dissertation, Union Theological Seminary, 1985).

Habel, Norman C., 'The Form and Significance of the Call Narratives', *ZAW* 77 (1965), pp. 297-323.

—*The Book of Job* (OTL; London: SCM Press, 1985).

Hackett, Jo Ann, 'Balaam', *ABD*, I, pp. 569-72.

Harrrington, D.J., 'Pseudo-Philo', in Charlesworth, *Old Testament Pseudepigrapha*, II, pp. 297-377.

Hartley, John E., 'The Genres and Message of the Book of Job', in Roy B. Zuck (ed.), *Sitting with Job: Selected Studies on the Book of Job* (Grand Rapids: Baker, 1992), pp. 65-78.

—'From Lament to Oath: A Study of Progression in the Speeches of Job', in Beuken, *The Book of Job*, pp. 79-100.

Heinemann, Joseph, *Prayer in the Talmud: Forms and Patterns* (SJ, 9; Berlin: W. de Gruyter, 1977).

Herman, Judith, *Trauma and Recovery* (New York: BasicBooks, rev. edn, 1997).

Hieke, Thomas, *Psalm 80 – Praxis eines Methoden-Programms: Eine literaturwissenschaftliche Untersuchung mit einem gattungskritischen Beitrag zum Klagelied des Volkes* (Arbeiten zu Text und Sprache im Alten Testament, 55; St Ottilien: EOS Verlag, 1997).

Hillers, Delbert R., 'Lamentations, Book of', *ABD*, IV, pp. 137-41.

—*Lamentations* (AB, 7A; Garden City, NY: Doubleday, 1972).

—*Micah* (Hermeneia; Philadelphia: Fortress Press, 1984).

Hoffman, Yair, 'Ancient Near Eastern Literary Conventions and the Restoration of the Book of Job', *ZAW* 103 (1991), pp. 399-411.

—'The Creativity of Theodicy', in Henning G. Reventlow and Yair Hoffman (eds.), *Justice and Righteousness: Biblical Themes and their Influence* (JSOTSup, 137; Sheffield: Sheffield Academic Press, 1992), pp. 117-30.

—*A Blemished Perfection: The Book of Job in Context* (JSOTSup, 213; Sheffield: Sheffield Academic Press, 1996).

Holladay, William L., *Jeremiah* (Hermeneia; 2 vols.; Philadelphia: Fortress Press, 1986, 1989).

Human, D.J., and C.J.A. Vos (eds.), *Psalms and Liturgy* (JSOTSup, 410; London: T. & T. Clark, 2004).

Ignatieff, Michael, *The Rights Revolution* (CBC Massey Lectures Series; Toronto: House of Anansi, 2000).

Isaac, E., '1 (Ethiopic Apocalypse of) Enoch', in Charlesworth, *Old Testament Pseudepigrapha*, I, pp. 5-89.

Jacobsen, Thorkild, *The Harps That Once... Sumerian Poetry in Translation* (New Haven: Yale University Press, 1987).

Jakobzen, Lea, 'The Individual's Suffering in Psalms and in Mesopotamian Narratives [Modern Hebrew]', *Bet Miqra* 168 (2001), pp. 33-56.

Jaspers, Karl, *Vom Ursprung und Ziel der Geschichte* (Zürich: Artemis-Verlag, 1949).

Jonker, Louis C., 'Revisiting the Psalm Headings: Second Temple Levitical Propaganda', in Human and Vos, *Psalms and Liturgy*, pp. 102-22.

Joyce, Paul, 'Lamentations and the Grief Process: A Psychological Reading', *BibInt* 1 (1993), pp. 304-20.

Kaiser, Otto, *Isaiah 1–39* (OTL; Philadelphia: Westminster Press, 1974).

Kaufman, Ivan T., 'Undercut by Joy: The Sunday Lectionaries and the Psalms of Lament', in J.C. Knight and L.A. Sinclair (eds.), *The Psalms and Other Studies on the Old Testament Presented to Joseph I. Hunt* (Nashotah, WI: Nashotah House Seminary, 1990), pp. 66-78.

Kaufmann, Yehezkel, *The Babylonian Captivity and Deutero-Isaiah* (History of the Religion of Israel 4.1-2; New York: Union of American Hebrew Congregations, 1970).

— *The Religion of Israel: From the Beginnings to the Babylonian Captivity* (New York: Schocken Books, 1972).

Kiesow, Klaus, and Thomas Meurer (eds.), *Textarbeit: Studien zu Texten und ihrer Rezeption aus den Alten Testament und der Umwelt Israels: Festschrift Peter Weimar* (Münster: Ugarit-Verlag, 2003).

Kim, Ee Kon, 'A Study of the Rapid Change of Mood in the Lament Psalms' (PhD Dissertation, Union Theological Seminary, 1984).

Kirchener, Dankwart, 'Gruppendynamische Untersuchung zu Struktur und Geschichte der Klage im Alten Testament', *TLZ* 114 (1989), cols. 786-96.

Kiss, Jenö, *Die Klage Gottes und des Propheten: Ihre Rolle in der Komposition und Redaktion von Jer 11–12, 14–15 und 18* (WMANT, 99; Neukirchen–Vluyn: Neukirchener Verlag, 2003).

Klein, Ralph W., 'Chronicles, Book of 1-2', *ABD*, I, pp. 991-1002.

Klijn, A.F.J., '2 (Syriac Apocalypse of) Baruch', in Charlesworth, *Old Testament Pseudepigrapha*, I, pp. 615-52.

Knohl, Israel, *The Sanctuary of Silence: The Priestly Torah and the Holiness School* (Minneapolis: Fortress Press, 1995).

— 'Axial Transformations within Ancient Israelite Priesthood', in J.P. Árnason, S. N. Eisenstadt and Björn Wittrock (eds.), *Axial Civilizations and World History* (Jerusalem Studies in Religion and Culture, 4; Leiden: E.J. Brill, 2005), pp. 201-24.

Koch, Klaus, *The Prophets* (2 vols.; Philadelphia: Fortress Press, 1983, 1984).

Kraemer, David, *Responses to Suffering in Classical Rabbinic Literature* (New York: Oxford University, 1995).

Kuemmerlin-McLean, Joanne K., 'Demons: Old Testament', *ABD*, II, pp. 138-42.

Kuschel, Karl-Joseph, 'Ist Gott verantwortlich für das Übel: Überlegungen zu einer Theologie der Anklagen', in Fuchs, *Angesichts des Leids an Gott glauben?*, pp. 227-61.

Kutscher, Raphael, *Oh Angry Sea (a-ab-ba hu-luh-ha): The History of a Sumerian Congregational Lament* (New Haven: Yale University Press, 1975).

Kwaak, H. van der, 'Die Klage über Jerusalem (Matt. XXIII 37-39)', *NovT* 8 (1966), pp. 156-70.

Lane, Belden C., 'Arguing with God: Blasphemy and the Prayer of Lament in Judaism and Other Faith Traditions', in Yehuda Bauer *et al.* (eds.), *Remembering for the Future: Working Papers and Addenda*. III. *The Impact of the Holocaust and Genocide on Christians and Jews* (Oxford: Pergamon Press, 1989), pp. 2543-57.

Lange, Armin, Hermann Lichtenberger and K.F.D. Römheld (eds.), *Die Dämonen/ Demons* (Tubingen: Mohr–Siebeck, 2003).

Laytner, Anson, *Arguing with God: A Jewish Tradition* (Northvale, NJ: Jason Aronson, 1990).

Lemche, Niels P., *Ancient Israel: A New History of Israelite Society* (Sheffield: JSOT Press, 1988).

Levenson, Jon D., *Creation and the Persistence of Evil. The Jewish Drama of Divine Omnipotence* (San Francisco: Harper & Row, 1988).

Levine, Baruch A., ' "Ah, Assyria! Rod of My Rage" (Isa 10.15) — Biblical Monotheism as Seen in International Perspective: A Prolegomenen [Modern Hebrew]', *Eretz Israel* 27 (2003), pp. 136-42

Lichtenberger, Hermann, 'Ps 91 und die Exorzismen in 11QPsApª', in Lange, Lichtenberger and Römheld, *Die Dämonen/Demons*, pp. 416-21.

Limbeck, Meinrad, 'Die Klage — Eine verschwundene Gebetsgattung', *TQ* 157 (1977), pp. 3-16.

Limburg, James, 'Psalms, Book of', *ABD*, V, pp. 522-36.

Linafelt, Tod, *Surviving Lamentations: Catastrophe, Lament, and Protest in the Afterlife of a Biblical Book* (Chicago: Chicago University Press, 2000).

—'The Refusal of a Conclusion in the Book of Lamentations', *JBL* 120 (2001), pp. 340-43.

Lindblom, J., *Prophecy in Ancient Israel* (Oxford: Basil Blackwell, 1962).

Lindström, Fredrik, *God and the Origin of Evil: A Contextual Analysis of Alleged Monistic Evidence in the Old Testament* (ConBOT, 21; Lund: C.W.K. Gleerup, 1983).

—*Suffering and Sin: Interpretations of Illness in the Individual Complaint Psalms* (ConBOT, 37; Stockhom: Almqvist & Wiksell, 1994).

Loretz, Oswald, 'Der altorientalische rechtliche Hintergrund der biblischen "Klage des Einzelnen" ', in Kiesow and Meurer, *Textarbeit*, pp. 285-307.

Lugt, Pieter van der, *Rhetorical Criticism and the Poetry of the Book of Job* (OTS, 32; Leiden: E.J. Brill, 1995).

Machinist, Peter, 'On Self-Consciousness in Mesopotamia', in Eisenstadt, *Origins and Diversity of Axial Age Civilizations*, pp. 183-202.

Magdalene, F. Rachel, 'Ancient Near Eastern Treaty-Curses and the Ultimate Texts of Terror: A Study of the Language of Divine Sexual Abuse in the Prophetic Corpus', in A. Brenner (ed.), *The Feminist Companion to the Latter Prophets* (Feminist Companion to the Bible, 8; Sheffield: Sheffield Academic Press, 1995), pp. 326-52.

—'On the Scales of Righteousness: Law and Story in the Book of Job' (PhD Dissertation, The Iliff School of Theology and University of Denver, 2003).

Martínez, F.G., and E.J.C. Tigchelaar, *The Dead Sea Scrolls Study Edition* (2 vols.; Leiden: E.J. Brill, 2000).

Mayer, Werner, *Untersuchungen zur Formensprache der babylonischen 'Gebetsbeschwörungen'* (Studia Pohl Series Maior, 5; Rome: Pontifical Biblical Institute, 1976).

Mays, James L, *Psalms* (Interpretation; Louisville: John Knox, 1994).

McCann, I.L., and L.A. Pearlman, *Psychological Trauma and the Adult Survivor: Theory, Therapy, and Transformation* (Brunner/Mazal Psychosocial Stress Series, 21; New York: Brunner/Mazal, 1990).

McDaniel, Thomas F., 'The Alleged Sumerian Influence upon Lamentations', *VT* 18 (1968), pp. 198-209.

McEvenue, Sean, 'Who Was the Second Isaiah?', in J.T. van Ruiten and M. Vervenne (eds.), *Studies in the Book of Isaiah: Festschrift Willem A.M. Beuken* (Leuven: Leuven University Press, 1997), pp. 213-22.

Meichenbaum, Donald, *A Clinical Handbook/Practical Therapist Manual for Assessing and Treating Adults with Post-Traumatic Stress Disorder* (Waterloo, ON: Institute Press, 1994).

Menn, Esther M., 'No Ordinary Lament: Relecture and the Identity of the Distressed in Psalm 22', *HTR* 93 (2000), pp. 301-41.

Michalowski, Piotr, *The Lamentation over the Destruction of Sumer and Ur* (Mesopotamian Civilizations, 1; Winona Lake, IN: Eisenbrauns, 1989).

Miller, Alice, *Breaking Down the Wall of Silence: The Liberating Experience of Facing Painful Truth* (New York: Meridian, 1993).

Miller, J.M., and J.H. Hayes, *A History of Ancient Israel and Judah* (Philadelphia: Westminster, 1986).

Miller, Patrick D., *Interpreting the Psalms* (Philadelphia: Fortress Press, 1986).

— *They Cried to the Lord: The Form and Theology of Biblical Prayer* (Minneapolis: Fortress Press, 1994).

Moore, Carey A. 'Daniel, Additions to', *ABD*, II. pp. 18-28.

— *Tobit: A New Translation and Commentary* (AB, 40A; New York: Doubleday, 1996).

Morrow, William S., 'Consolation, Rejection, and Repentance in Job 42.6', *JBL* 105 (1986), pp. 211-25.

— *Scribing the Center: Organization and Redaction in Deuteronomy 14.1–17.13* (SBLMS, 49; Atlanta: Scholars Press, 1995).

— 'Toxic Religion and the Daughters of Job', *SR* 27 (1998), pp. 263-76.

— 'Comfort for Jerusalem: The Second Isaiah as Counselor to Refugees', *BTB* 34 (Summer 2004), pp. 80-86.

— 'Post-Traumatic Stress Disorder and Vicarious Atonement in the Second Isaiah', in H.J. Ellens and W.G. Rollins (eds.), *Psychology and the Bible: A New Way to Read the Scriptures* (4 vols.; Westport, CT: Greenwood-Praeger, 2004), I, pp. 167-83.

— 'Cuneiform Literacy and Deuteronomic Composition', *BO* 62 (2005), pp. 204-13.

Mounce, R.P., *The Book of Revelation* (NICNT, 17; Grand Rapids: Eerdmans, 1977).

Mowinckel, Sigmund, *The Psalms in Israel's Worship* (Biblical Resource Series; Grand Rapids: Eerdmans, 2004; original translation, 1962).

Mullen, E. Theodore, *Ethnic Myths and Pentateuchal Foundations: A New Approach to the Formation of the Pentateuch* (Atlanta: Scholars Press, 1997).

Müller, Hans-Peter, 'Feinde, Tiere und Dämonen: Ein kleiner Beitrag zu den Klage- und Bittpsalmen des Einzelnen', in Kiesow and Meurer (eds.), *Textarbeit*, pp. 329-33.

Newman, Judith H., *Praying by the Book: The Scripturalization of Prayer in Second Temple Judaism* (Early Judaism and its Literature, 14; Atlanta: Scholars Press, 1999).

Newsom, Carol A., 'Angels, Old Testament', *ABD*, I, pp. 248-53.

— 'Job', in Carol A. Newsom and Sharon H. Ringe (eds.), *The Women's Bible Commentary* (Louisville, KY: Westminster John Knox Press, 1992), pp. 130-36.

— 'Cultural Politics and the Reading of Job', *BibInt* 1 (1993), pp. 119-38.

Nickelsburg, G.W.E., 'The Bible Rewritten and Expanded', in Stone, *Jewish Writings of the Second Temple Period*, pp. 89-156.

Nimmo, P.W., 'Sin, Evil and Job: Monotheism as a Psychological and Pastoral Problem', *Pastoral Psychology* 42 (1994), pp. 427-39.

Nitzan, Bilhah, 'Hymns from Qumran — 510–511', in Dimant and Rappaport, *Dead Sea Scrolls*, pp. 53-63.

— *Qumran Prayer and Religious Poetry* (STDJ, 12; Leiden: E.J. Brill, 1994).

North, C.R., *The Second Isaiah: Introduction, Translation, and Commentary to Chapters XL–LV* (Oxford: Clarendon Press, 1964).

O'Connor, Kathleen M., *Lamentations and the Tears of the World* (Maryknoll, NY: Orbis Books, 2002).

Oriental Institute, Oxford University (ed.), 'The Lament for Nibru', *The Electronic Text Corpus of Sumerian Literature* (July 29, 1999; accessed Aug. 14, 2005; http.//www-etcsl.orient.ox.ac.uk/section2/tr224.htm).

Pardee, Dennis, 'Ugaritic Science', in P.M.M. Daviau *et al.* (eds.), *The World of the Aramaeans* (Festschrift P.E. Dion; 3 vols.; Sheffield: Sheffield Academic Press, 2002, 2003), III, pp. 223-54.

Pardes, Ilana, *Countertraditions in the Bible: A Feminist Approach* (Cambridge, MA: Harvard University Press, 1992).

Patrick, Dale, and Allen Scult, *Rhetoric and Biblical Interpretation* (JSOTSup, 82; Bible and Literature, 26; Sheffield: Almond Press, 1990).

Penchansky, David, *What Rough Beast? Images of God in the Hebrew Bible* (Louisville, KY: Westminster John Knox, 1999).

Penney, Douglas L., and Michael O. Wise, 'By the Power of Beelzebub: An Aramaic Incantation Formula from Qumran (4Q560)', *JBL* 113 (1996), pp. 627-50.

Perdue, Leo G., *Wisdom in Revolt: Metaphorical Theology in the Book of Job* (JSOTSup, 112; Bible and Literature, 29; Sheffield: JSOT Press, Almond Press 1991).

— *Wisdom and Creation: The Theology of Wisdom Literature* (Nashville: Abingdon Press, 1994).

Phillips, Anthony, 'Double for All her Sins', *ZAW* 94 (1982), pp. 130-32.

Porter, Stanley E., 'The Message of the Book of Job: Job 42.7b as Key to Interpretation', *EvQ* 63 (1991), pp. 291-304.

Provan, Iain, *Lamentations* (NCB; Grand Rapids: Eerdmans, 1991).

Puech, Emile, 'Les deux derniers psaumes davidiques du rituel d'exorcisme, 11QpsApᵃ IV 4–V 14', in Dimant and Rappaport, *The Dead Sea Scrolls*, pp. 64-89.

Purvis, James D., 'Exile and Return: From the Babylonian Destruction to the Reconstruction of the Jewish State', in Hershel Shanks (ed.), *Ancient Israel: From Abraham to the Roman Destruction of the Temple* (Washington: Biblical Archaeology Society, rev. edn, 1999), pp. 200-29.

Pury, Albert de, 'Yahwist ('J') Source', *ABD*, VI, pp. 1012-22.

Pyper, Hugh S., 'Reading Lamentations', *JSOT* 95 (2001), pp. 55-69.

Radday, Y.T., and Haim Shore, *Genesis: An Authorship Study* (AnBib, 103; Rome: Biblical Institute Press, 1985).

Reif, Stefan C., 'The Second Temple Period, Qumran Research, and Rabbinic Liturgy: Some Contextual and Linguistic Comparisons', in Chazon, *Liturgical Perspectives*, pp. 133-49.

Rendsburg, Gary A., *Linguistic Evidence for the Northern Origin of Selected Psalms* (SBLMS, 43; Atlanta: Scholars Press, 1990).

Reumann, John H., 'Psalm 22 at the Cross', *Int* 28 (1974), pp. 39-58.

Reventlow, Henning G., *Gebet im Alten Testament* (Stuttgart: Kohlhammer, 1986).

Ringgren, Helmer, *Israelite Religion* (Philadelphia: Fortress Press, 1975).

Robinson, W.H., *Corporate Personality in Ancient Israel* (Philadelphia: Fortress Press, rev. edn, 1980).

Rofé, Alexander, *The Prophetical Stories: The Narratives about the Prophets in the Hebrew Bible, their Literary Types and History* (Publications of the Perry Foundation for Biblical Research in the Hebrew University of Jerusalem; Jerusalem: Magnes Press, 1988).

Roloff, Jürgen, *The Revelation of John* (Continental Commentary; Minneapolis: Augsburg Fortress Press, 1993).

Roskies, David G. (ed.), *The Literature of Destruction: Jewish Responses to Catastrophe* (Philadelphia: Jewish Publication Society, 1989).

Ross, James F., 'Job 33.14-30: The Phenomenology of Lament', *JBL* 94 (1975), pp. 38-46.

Rousseau, John J., 'Jesus, an Exorcist of a Kind', in Eugene H. Lovering (ed.), *Seminar Papers* (SBLSP, 32; Atlanta: Scholars Press, 1993), pp. 129-53.

Sarason, Richard S., 'Communal Prayer at Qumran and among the Rabbis: Certainties and Uncertainties', in Chazon, *Liturgical Perspectives*, pp. 151-72.

Schmitt, J.J., 'Prophecy (Preexilic Hebrew)', *ABD*, V, pp. 482-89.

Schoors, Anton, *I Am God Your Savior: A Form-Critical Study of the Main Genres in Is. XL–LV* (VTSup, 24; Leiden: E.J. Brill, 1973).

Schuller, Eileen, 'Petitionary Prayer and the Religion of Qumran', in J.J. Collins and R.A. Kruger (eds.), *Religion in the Dead Sea Scrolls* (Grand Rapids: Eerdmans, 2000), pp. 29-45.

—'Some Reflections on the Function and Use of Poetical Texts among the Dead Sea Scrolls', in Chazon, *Liturgical Perspectives*, pp. 173-89.

Scullion, John J., 'God in the OT', *ABD*, II, pp. 1041-48.

Seitz, C.R., 'Job: Full Structure, Movement and Interpretation', *Int* 43 (1989), pp. 5-17.

Seybold, K., and U.B. Mueller, *Sickness and Healing* (Biblical Encounters Series; Nashville: Abingdon Press, 1978).

Skehan, Patrick W., and Alexander A. Di Lella, *The Wisdom of Ben Sira* (AB, 39; New York: Doubleday, 1987).

Smith, Mark S., *The Laments of Jeremiah and their Contexts: A Literary and Redactional Study of Jeremiah 11–20* (SBLMS, 42; Atlanta: Scholars Press, 1990).

Smith, W.C., *What Is Scripture? A Comparative Approach* (Minneapolis: Fortress Press, 1993).

Snapp, Kevin, 'A Curious Ring in the Ears: Ambiguity and Ambivalence in the Conclusion of the Book of Job', *Conservative Judaism* 53.1 (2000), pp. 34-50.

Soelle, Dorothee, *Suffering* (Philadelphia: Fortress Press, 1975).

Soll, Will, *Psalm 119: Matrix, Form, and Setting* (CBQMS, 23; Washington: Catholic Biblical Association, 1991).

Sommer, Benjamin D., 'Did Prophecy Cease? Evaluating a Reevaluation', *JBL* 115 (1996), pp. 31-47.

—*A Prophet Reads Scripture: Allusion in Isaiah 40–66* (Contraversions, Jews and Other Differences; Stanford: Stanford University Press, 1998).

Sorenson, Eric, *Possession and Exorcism in the New Testament and Early Christianity* (WUNT, 2/157; Tübingen: Mohr–Siebeck, 2002).

Stegemann, Hartmut, 'The Number of Psalms in *1QHodayot*[a] and some of their Sections', in Chazon, *Liturgical Perspectives*, pp. 191-234.

Steinmann, Andrew E., 'The Structure and Message of the Book of Job', *VT* 46 (1986), pp. 85-100.

Stevenson, Gregory M., 'Communal Imagery and the Individual Lament: Exodus Typology in Psalm 77', *Restoration Quarterly* 39 (1997), pp. 215-29.

Steymans, Hans U., 'Traces of Liturgies in the Psalter: The Communal Laments, Psalms 79, 80, 83, 89 in Context', in Human and Vos, *Psalms and Liturgy*, pp. 168-234.

Stolz, Fritz, 'Alttestamentliches Reden vom Menschen und neutestamentliches Reden von Jesus', *ZTK* 77 (1980), pp. 129-48.

Stone, Michael E. (ed.), *Jewish Writings of the Second Temple Period* (CRINT, 2; Assen: Van Gorcum, 1984).

—'Esdras, Second Book of', *ABD*, II, pp. 611-14.

—'Eschatology, Remythologization, and Cosmic Aporia', in Eisenstadt, *Origins and Diversity of Axial Age Civilizations*, pp. 241-51.

Tigay, J.H., 'On Evaluating Claims of Literary Borrowing', in M.E. Cohen *et al.* (eds.), *The Tablet and the Scroll: Near Eastern Studies in Honor of William W. Hallo* (Bethesda, MD: Capital Decisions, 1993), pp. 250-55.

Tilley, T.W., 'God and the Silencing of Job', *Modern Theology* 5 (1989), pp. 257-70.

Toorn, Karl van der, *Sin and Sanction in Israel and Mesopotamia: A Comparative Study* (Studia semitica neerlandica; Assen: Van Gorcum, 1985).

—'The Theology of Demons in Mesopotamia and Israel: Popular Belief and Scholarly Speculation', in Lange, Lichtenberger and Römheld, *Die Dämonen/Demons*, pp. 61-83.

Tsevat, Matitiahu, 'The Meaning of the Book of Job', *HUCA* 37 (1966), pp. 73-106.

Uffenheimer, Benjamin, 'Myth and Reality in Ancient Israel', in Eisenstadt, *Origins and Diversity of Axial Age Civilizations*, pp. 135-68.

Van Seters, John, *The Pentateuch: A Social-Science Commentary* (Trajectories, 1; Sheffield: Sheffield Academic Press, 1999).

—*Abraham in History and Tradition* (New Haven, CT: Yale University, 1975).

—*The Life of Moses: The Yahwist as Historian in Exodus–Numbers* (Louisville, KY: Westminster John Knox, 1994).

Veijola, Timo, 'Das Klagegebet in Literatur und Leben der Exilsgeneration am Beispiel eigenen Prosatexte', in J.A. Emerton (ed.), *Congress Volume: Salamanca 1983* (VTSup, 36; Leiden: E.J. Brill, 1985), pp. 286-307.

—'Deuteronomismusforschung zwischen Tradition und Innovation (III)', *TRu* 68 (2003), pp. 1-44.

Vermeylen, J., 'Essai de Redaktionsgeschichte des «Confessions de Jérémie»', in Bogaert, *Le Livre de Jérémie*, pp. 239-70.

Waltke, Bruce K., and Michael P. O'Connor, *An Introduction to Biblical Hebrew Syntax* (Winona Lake, IN: Eisenbrauns, 1990).

Weber, Beat, 'Zur Datierung der Asaph-Psalmen 74 und 79', *Bib* 81 (2000), pp. 521-32.

Weems, Renita J., *Battered Love: Marriage, Sex, and Violence in the Hebrew Prophets* (Overtures to Biblical Theology; Minneapolis: Fortress Press, 1995).

Weinfeld, Moshe, 'The Protest against Imperialism in Ancient Israelite Prophecy', in Eisenstadt, *Origins and Diversity of Axial Age Civilizations*, pp. 169-82.

Wendel, Adolf, *Das freie Laiengebet im vorexilischen Israel* (Leipzig: Pfeiffer, 1931).

Werline, Rodney A., *Penitential Prayer in Second Temple Judaism: The Development of a Religious Institution* (Early Judaism and its Literature, 13; Atlanta: Scholars Press, 1998).

Westermann, Claus, 'Struktur und Geschichte der Klage im Alten Testament', *ZAW* 66.1-2 (1954), pp. 44-80 (reprinted and translated in Westermann, *Praise and Lament in the Psalms*, pp. 165-213).

— *Das Loben Gottes in den Psalmen* (Göttingen: Vandenhoeck & Ruprecht, 1954; 5th edn *Lob und Klage in den Psalmen*, 1977).

— *Isaiah 40–66* (OTL; Philadelphia: Westminster Press, 1969).

— 'The Role of the Lament in the Theology of the Old Testament', *Int* 28 (1974), pp. 20-38.

— *Praise and Lament in the Psalms* (Atlanta: John Knox Press, 1981).

— *The Structure of the Book of Job: A Form-Critical Analysis* (Philadelphia: Fortress Press, 1981).

— *Lamentations: Issues and Interpretation* (Minneapolis: Fortress Press, 1994).

— 'The Complaint against God', in Tod Linafelt and T.K. Beal (eds.), *God in the Fray: A Tribute to Walter Brueggemann* (Minneapolis: Fortress Press, 1998), pp. 233-41.

Wevers, John W., 'A Study in the Form Criticism of Individual Complaint Psalms', *VT* 6 (1956), pp. 80-96.

— *The Way of the Righteous* (Philadelphia: Westminster Press, 1961).

— *Ezekiel* (NCB; London: Nelson, 1969).

Whybray, R.N., *Isaiah 40–66* (NCB; Grand Rapids: Eerdmans, 1987; original edn, 1978).

Whitelam, Keith W., 'Elisha', *ABD*, II, pp. 472-73.

Widengren, Geo, *The Accadian and Hebrew Psalms of Lamentation as Religious Documents: A Comparative Study* (Uppsala: Almqvist & Wiksell, 1936).

Wilcox, J.T., *The Bitterness of Job: A Philosophical Reading* (Ann Arbor, MI: University of Michigan Press, 1989).

Wildberger, Hans, *Isaiah 28–39* (Continental Commentary; Minneapolis: Fortress Press, 2002).

Wilson, G.H., *The Editing of the Hebrew Psalter* (SBLDS, 76; Chico, CA: Scholars Press, 1985).

Wilson, Robert R., *Prophecy and Society in Ancient Israel* (Philadelphia: Fortress Press, 1984).

Wintermude, O.S., 'Jubilees', in Charlesworth, *Old Testament Pseudepigrapha*, II, pp. 35-142.

Wolde, Ellen van, 'Job 42,1-6: The Reversal of Job', in Beuken, *The Book of Job*, pp. 223-50.

Wolfers, David, *Deep Things out of Darkness: The Book of Job. Essays and a New English Translation* (Grand Rapids: William B. Eerdmans, 1995).

Wolff, Hans W., *Anthropology of the Old Testament* (Philadelphia: Fortress Press, 1974).

— *Joel and Amos* (Hermeneia; Philadelphia: Fortress Press, 1975).

Wolterstorff, Nicholas, 'If God is Good and Sovereign, Why Lament?', *Calvin Theological Journal* 36 (2001), pp. 42-52.

Wright, R.B., 'Psalms of Solomon', in Charlesworth, *Old Testament Pseudepigrapha*, II, pp. 639-70.

Zenger, Erich, *A God of Vengeance? Understanding the Psalms of Divine Wrath* (Louisville, KY: Westminster John Knox Press, 1996).

INDEXES

INDEX OF SCRIPTURE AND ANCIENT LITERATURE

HEBREW BIBLE

Genesis
4.9   189
4.13-14   30, 33, 35
6.1-6   182
15.2-3   30, 33, 35
18.17   20
18.23-32   20-21, 23, 27, 29, 155
18.23-25   20
18.27-32   21
18.25   20
19.18-20   32, 33
21.16   32-33, 35, 37, 61
24.12-14   18
25.22   14, 30, 32-35, 37-38, 61, 63
27.46   14, 30
28.1   30
30.24   18
32.10-13   29, 32-33, 35, 37, 61
36.24   28
42.36   17
43.14   18
47.15   16
47.18-19   16

Exodus
1.11-14   103
2.20   17
2.23   103
3–4   26
3.7   103
3.9   103
4.10   31, 33
4.13   18
4.24   195
5.15-15   16
5.22-23   19, 23
6.23   28
10.7   16
14.10   103
14.15   103
15.3   103
16   167
16.3   27, 167
17.2-3   27, 167
17.4   21, 23
21.12-17   118
32.11-13   21, 23
32.11   21
32.31-32   19
34.6   103

Leviticus
18   167
18.26-30   167

Numbers
6.24-26   192
10.35   97
11.11-15   31, 33, 35, 155
11.20   27, 167

14.2-3   27, 167
21.5   27, 167
22.28   17
22.31   141
26.30   28
27.3-4   16

Deuteronomy
1.27-28   27
3.24-25   18
5.21-24   16
5.24-27   16
7.1-3   167
12   71
14–16   71
21.18-21   118
23.3-7   167
32.30   94
32.39   139
34.9   26

Joshua
1.5   26
7   126
7.6   99
7.7-9   14, 19, 23, 26, 126
7.7   126
7.10-15   126
8   126
17.14   16, 44

Judges
2.1-5   125
2.1   141
3.15   28

6.13 19, 23, 26-27, 34
6.22 14, 29, 31, 33, 35
10.10 19, 164
10.15 19, 164
11.35 17
13.5 34
13.6 141
13.8 18
13.25 34
14.19 34
15.18 6, 14, 30, 33-35, 37, 38, 61
16.28 6, 32-33, 35, 37
17 157
20.1 125
20.3 125
20.18 125
20.19-28 157
20.23 100, 125
20.26-28 125, 169
20.26-27 100
21.1 125
21.2-4 99
21.3 14, 34
21.5 125
21.8 125

1 Samuel
1.11 31, 33, 35, 37, 61,62, 189
2.6-7 139
4.21-22 28, 62
4.21 9, 19, 23, 27-30, 34-35, 37, 39, 61
7.5-11 121
9.9 61
17.34-36 187
23.10-11 32, 33, 35
24.10-16 17
26.18-20 17
26.19 53
28.15 16, 17

2 Samuel
3.7 28
3.39 18
7 95
7.18-29 18
12.13 29
13.24-25 69
14 48
14.32 17
15.31 19
20.18-19 16
22 98
24.1 195
24.12-14 55
24.14 55
24.16 141
24.17 22-23, 98

1 Kings
1.24-27 16
3.6-9 32-33, 180
8 27
8.22-53 43, 98
8.23-53 18
8.31-53 126
14.1-5 40, 66
16.29–19.18 38
17.1 39
17.17-24 39
17.18 17, 39
17.20-21 31, 33-34, 39, 66
18.36-37 19
18.41-46 39
19.4 32-34, 64
19.10 31, 33, 35, 145
19.14 31
19.15-17 39
22 67

2 Kings
2.14 30, 33-34
2.16 17
2.19 16
4.1 17
4.14-17 39
4.17-37 39
4.28 17, 39
4.38-41 39
4.40 16
5 40
5.1-27 39
5.1-14 66
5.8 16, 17
6.5 17
6.15 16
6.24–7.20 39
8.7-15 39
9.1-10 39
13.14-19 39
13.20-21 39
19.15-19 22-23, 27, 43, 98, 100
20.3 29
20.7-11 66
22.18 61
25 120

Isaiah
1.7-9 90
1.21-26 90
1.21-23 92, 174
3.25–4.1 90
6 26
6.1-3 137
6.8-9 19
6.11 19, 23, 145
10.8-11 97
10.13-14 97
13.1-22 90
14.4-21 92, 174
14.13-14 97
14.24-27 139
14.28-32 90

Isaiah (cont.)		44.24-26	122	55.8-13	121
15–16	87, 90	44.24	132	58.3-7	100, 126
15.2-5	99	45.1-3	122	58.3	88
15.5	86	45.1-6	125	59	165
16.9-11	86	45.5-8	125	59.9-15	164, 165
22.1-14	90	45.7	139	59.9-13	96
23.1-14	90, 92,	45.9-13	121	59.15-20	165
	174	45.14-25	136	59.16	198
26.7-18	88	45.15	138	63.7–64.11	76-78,
26.13	88	45.18-25	121		80-81,
26.16-18	88	45.20	122		96, 99,
26.19	88, 100	46.5-11	121, 122		101, 118,
26.20-21	88, 100	47.1-15	90, 125		203
32.9-14	99	48.1-11	121	63.7-14	93, 164
33.2-6	89	48.3-8	122	63.7	91, 98
33.7-13	89	48.12-15	121-22	63.11-12	30, 79-80
33.7-9	89, 90	48.12-14	122	63.15	9, 30, 79-
33.10-13	100	49.1-6	123		80
37.16-20	22	49.7-13	121	63.16	118
38.3	29	49.14-26	121-22	63.17	79
40–55	100, 107,	49.14	87, 90-	64.4	79, 96
	120, 123,		91, 98,	64.6	79
	136		101, 122	64.7	118
40.1-2	124, 125	49.20	122	64.8	79
40.2	123, 124	49.21	87, 98	64.10	96
40.12-31	121	49.24	90	64.11	79
40.12-18	136	50.1-3	121		
40.22-24	122	50.1	94, 122	*Jeremiah*	
40.27	87, 90-	50.4-11	128	1	26
	91, 98,	50.4-9	123	1.6	31, 33-34
	101, 122	51.9-16	121	2.20-37	118
41.1-5	121	51.9-11	94	2.8	101
41.8-13	121, 125	51.17-23	107, 121	3.4-5	87, 91,
41.14-16	121	52.1-12	125		98, 101
41.17-20	121	52.1-2	90	3.21	99
41.21-29	121	52.13–53.12	123	3.22-25	164
42.1-4	123, 125	52.14	121	4–6	90
42.10-16	122	53	123-24,	4	165
42.12-20	125		128, 173	4.8	99
42.14-17	121	53.4	121	4.10	19, 23,
42.18-25	121, 123	53.5	124		126
43.1-7	121, 125	53.9	125	4.19-21	87, 91,
43.8-13	121	53.10-11	125		94, 98
43.16-21	121	53.10	124	4.21	87
43.22-28	121, 123	54.4-6	121	4.22	87
44.1-5	121	54.7-10	121	4.31	87, 91,
44.6-8	121	54.11-17	121		94, 98
44.24-28	121	55.1-5	121, 122	6.4	97

6.5	97		164	1–3	26
6.13-14	67	15.5-9	86	1.22-28	137
6.13	101	15.10-20	63	9.8-10	126
6.26	99	15.10-14	62	9.8	19, 23,
7	117	15.10	63-64		106, 126,
7.16	22	15.11-14	63		145
8–10	90	15.15-21	62	9.9-10	19
8.10	101	15.15-18	29, 63	11.13	19, 23,
8.18-23	20, 23,	16.19	97		106, 126,
	88	17.14-18	29, 62-63		145
8.18	20	18.13-17	86	11.14-21	19
8.18-19	20	18.19-23	29, 63	16	117
8.19-20	20, 88,	20.1	63	18.2	123
	91	20.7-18	131	19.1-9	92
8.21-23	20	20.7-13	29, 63	19.10-14	92
8.22	20	20.7-9	65	20.1	61
9.9	92	20.8	18	21.1-4	31
9.16-21	92, 174	20.14-18	29, 63-64	21.5	31, 33,
9.16-17	92	20.18	10, 64,		126
9.18	88, 91-92		190	21.6-10	31
9.19-23	100	23.11	101	23	117
10.17-25	122	23.16-17	67	26.15-18	90
10.17-18	87	28.1-10	67	26.17-18	92
10.19-20	87, 91,	30.17	97	27.1-11	90
	94, 98	31.18-20	118	27.3-26	92
10.21	87	31.29-30	123	27.26-36	90
11.14	22	32.17-25	30, 33-34	28.11-19	92
11.18-23	62	32.17	126	32.1-16	90
11.18-20	29, 63	41.4-6	125	32.12-16	92
12.1-6	62	45.3-5	34	40–48	138
12.1-4	29, 63	45.3	30, 33-		
12.7-12	86		34, 39,	*Hosea*	
14	76, 77		66	2.4-15	118
14.1–15.4	21-23,	46.3-12	90	6.1	99
	91, 106	46.14-24	90	8.2	14
14.2-9	122	47.1-7	90	11.1-9	118
14.2-6	89	48.1-47	90	14.3	99
14.7-12	126	49.1-6	90		
14.7-9	88-90,	49.23-27	90	*Joel*	
	101, 106,	50.1–51.58	90	1.5-15	89
	164	51.34-35	87, 91,	1.13-14	99
14.11-12	22		98	1.16-18	9, 21, 89,
14.13-16	111	51.34	87, 91		91
14.13	22-23, 67	51.36-37	87, 100	1.19-20	19, 21,
14.17	90	51.51	89		23, 89,
14.18	101	52	120		101
14.19-22	88-90,			2.17	90, 100-
	101, 106,	*Ezekiel*			101

Amos		*Zephaniah*		7	44-45, 47, 51-53, 73, 78

Amos
5.1-3 — 90
5.16-17 — 90, 99, 101
5.18-21 — 90
5.2 — 94
5.16-17 — 102-103
7.1-3 — 22
7.2 — 22-23, 145
7.4-6 — 22
7.5 — 22-23, 145
7.7-9 — 22
8.1-3 — 22

Jonah
3.5-9 — 99
4.2-3 — 31, 33-34, 64

Micah
1.2-16 — 90
1.8-16 — 99
3.5 — 67
3.11 — 67
4.9-10 — 90
7 — 87-88
7.1-4 — 87-88
7.11-13 — 100

Nahum
2.4-14 — 90
3.1-7 — 90
3.8-11 — 90

Habakkuk
1 — 76-77
1.2-2.4 — 19
1.2-4 — 19, 21, 23, 155, 175
1.5-11 — 19
1.2 — 18
1.12-17 — 19, 20, 23
2.2-4 — 19

Zephaniah
1.15 — 198
2.13-15 — 90
3.14-20 — 90

Zechariah
1.12 — 19, 23, 175
7.2-7 — 125
7.3 — 99, 101
7.5 — 101
8.19 — 101

Psalms
3-41 — 199
3 — 45, 47, 51-53, 78, 191
3.2 — 53
3.4 — 69
3.5 — 71
3.7 — 53
3.8 — 54
3.9 — 74
4 — 43-45, 51, 53, 73
4.2 — 44
4.3 — 53
4.6 — 71
5 — 45, 51-53, 67
5.3 — 70
5.4 — 48
5.8 — 71
5.9 — 53, 54
5.11 — 54
6 — 45-46, 49, 51, 55, 57, 59, 61, 195, 207
6.2 — 54, 60
6.3 — 60
6.4 — 49, 60
6.6 — 60
6.8 — 60
6.11 — 60

7 — 44-45, 47, 51-53, 73, 78
7.2 — 53
7.3 — 53, 145
7.4-6 — 134
7.12 — 70
7.17 — 54
7.18 — 71
9–10 — 43-44, 49, 80-81, 102, 104, 162, 204
9.6 — 102
9.10 — 104
9.16 — 102
9.18 — 102
9.20 — 102
10.1 — 79, 103
10.2 — 102
10.7-10 — 102
10.12 — 79, 102
10.13 — 79, 103
10.16-18 — 103
10.16 — 102
10.17-18 — 102
11 — 44-45
12 — 80-81
12.6 — 47
13 — 45, 49, 51, 57
13.2-3 — 49, 57
13.2 — 9
13.4 — 58
13.6 — 71
17 — 44, 45, 51-53, 73
17.3-5 — 134
17.10-12 — 53-54
17.12 — 53, 145
17.13-14 — 54
17.13 — 54
17.14 — 64
17.15 — 71
18 — 98
20 — 78

22	45, 49, 51, 57-58, 78, 196-97	27.12	54	38.23	69
		28	45, 51, 54-57, 73	39	43, 45, 49, 51, 55, 59-60, 66, 103
22.2-3	58	28.1	54		
22.2	49, 196	28.2	71		
22.4-6	69, 74	28.3	51, 54, 57	39.8-10	10
22.10-11	69, 135	28.9	74	39.8	69
22.12	54, 58	30	71	39.9	54, 60
22.14	145	31	45, 51-53	39.10	60
22.16	58, 60	31.4	69	39.11-12	49
22.17	58	31.6	196	39.12	60
22.20	54, 58	31.10-11	53	39.13	45, 54
22.21-22	58	31.11	51	39.14	60
22.23	74	31.12-14	53	40	43, 45, 51, 54-56, 73
22.26	71	31.12	53		
22.31	69	31.15	69		71, 74
25	43, 45, 51, 54-56, 66, 78	31.16-17	54	40.10-11	40, 56-57
		31.17	69	40.12	56
		31.18-19	54	40.13	56
		31.24-25	74	40.14-16	56
25.2	55	32	71	40.14	56
25.3	55	34	71	40.18	54, 56, 69
25.7	54-55	35	45, 49, 51, 57-58		
25.11	55			41	43, 45-46, 51, 54-55
25.18	55	35.11-16	58		
25.19	55	35.17	49, 58, 69, 144	41.3	54
25.20	11			41.5	44, 56
25.22	74	35.18	71, 74	41.6-10	56
26	44-45, 51, 54-57, 73, 76	35.22	54, 69	41.11	56
		35.23	69	42–43	45, 47, 49, 51, 57-58, 67, 74, 78, 199
		35.27-28	71		
26.2-7	134	38	45-46, 51, 54-55, 60		
26.6	71				
26.7	71	38.2	54	42.5	71
26.8	71	38.3-11	56	42.8	58, 145
26.9	54, 57	38.3	56	42.10	49, 58
26.12	74	38.4-6	56	43.2	49, 58
27	43-45, 51, 54, 57, 73, 81	38.4-5	44	43.3-4	58
		38.10	69	43.4	71
		38.12-13	56	44	49, 76-78, 80-81, 92, 94, 96, 98-99, 203
27.1-5	69	38.14-15	56		
27.4	71	38.16	69		
27.6	71	38.18	56		
27.9	50, 54, 69	38.19	56		
		38.20-21	56		
		38.22	54, 57		

Psalms (cont.)

44.5 — 77
44.2-9 — 93-94, 98
44.2-8 — 69
44.2-4 — 164
44.7 — 77
44.10-15 — 9, 79
44.12 — 94
44.13 — 94
44.15-17 — 112
44.16 — 77, 91, 98
44.18 — 93
44.20 — 79
44.24-25 — 96
44.24 — 79, 94
44.25 — 79
51 — 43-45, 47, 51, 54-55, 187, 194
51.3 — 55
51.4 — 55
51.10 — 10, 55
51.11 — 55
51.13 — 54
51.16 — 55
51.17 — 69
51.20-21 — 45
51.20 — 74
52 — 44
54 — 45, 47, 51-53
54.5 — 53, 74
54.6 — 69
54.8-9 — 71
54.8 — 71
55 — 45, 51-52, 54
55.2 — 54
55.10 — 69
55.15 — 71
56 — 45, 47, 51-53, 78
56.2-3 — 53
56.6-7 — 53
56.8 — 74
56.13 — 71

57 — 45, 47, 51-53
57.4 — 53
57.5 — 53, 145
57.7 — 53
57.8-12 — 102
57.10 — 69, 71
59 — 45, 47, 51-52, 54, 78
59.6 — 54, 74
59.7 — 145
59.9 — 74
59.10-11 — 69
59.12 — 54, 69
59.14 — 74
59.17 — 104
60 — 49, 76-78, 80-81, 92, 95, 101-102, 203
60.3-6 — 79, 102
60.7-14 — 102
60.8-10 — 47, 77, 93, 95, 164
60.12 — 79
60.14 — 100
61 — 45, 51-53
61.3 — 44, 53
61.9 — 71
63 — 44
64 — 45, 51-53
64.3-6 — 53
69 — 45-46, 51, 54-56, 145
69.2-3 — 56
69.6 — 10
69.9-10 — 71
69.10 — 54, 57, 69
69.18 — 196
69.22 — 56, 64
69.23-29 — 10, 56
69.27 — 56
69.30 — 71
69.31 — 71

69.36 — 74
70-71 — 45, 49, 51, 54, 57
70.6 — 51, 54
71.1 — 49, 54
71.5 — 69
71.6 — 69
71.9 — 50, 54
71.12 — 50, 54
71.16 — 69
71.18 — 50, 54
74 — 49, 76-78, 80-81, 92, 94-96, 99, 101, 104, 203
74.1 — 79, 96, 97
74.2 — 94, 96, 164
74.3 — 97
74.8 — 94, 97
74.10 — 79
74.11 — 79
74.12-17 — 69
74.19 — 79
74.20 — 93
74.22 — 97
74.23 — 79
77 — 43-44, 49, 80-81, 102-103, 106, 162, 204
77.1 — 103
77.2-4 — 103
77.5 — 79, 103
77.8-10 — 79, 103, 155
77.8 — 103
77.9-10 — 103
77.12-21 — 103
77.13 — 103
79-83 — 101
79 — 49, 76-78, 80-

81, 92, 94-96, 101, 104, 203

79.1   95
79.2-3   169
79.3   95
79.5   79
79.8-9   77, 80, 93
79.8   79
79.10   79, 90, 97
79.13   100
80   49, 76-78, 80-81, 92-93, 96, 99, 101, 104, 203
80.2-3   93
80.5   79
80.6-7   79
80.9-12   69, 93, 164
80.12   93
80.13   79
80.18   93, 98
83   76-78, 80-81, 92, 95, 97, 101, 104, 203
83.2   77, 79
83.5   97
83.7-9   95
83.10-13   93, 164
85   49, 78, 80-81, 102, 104, 176
85.6-7   155
85.6   79
85.7   79
86   45, 51-53
86.1   53
86.2   69
86.3   69

86.4   69
86.5   69
86.8   69
86.9   69
86.12   69
86.14   53
86.15   69
86.16   69
88   44-45, 47, 49, 51, 57, 59, 62, 64-65, 74, 195
88.7-9   49
88.7-8   59
88.7   198
88.12   59
88.14-15   59
88.15   49
88.16-17   49, 59
88.17-18   59
88.18   145
88.19   49, 59
89   49, 76-78, 80-81, 95, 98
89.2-38   77
89.2-3   98
89.4   93
89.20-38   69, 93, 164
89.31   164
89.39-41   79
89.43-46   79
89.47   79
89.48-49   97
89.48   98
89.50   79, 80
90   49, 80-81, 102-104, 162, 176, 204
90.7-9   104
90.7-8   104
90.8   79
90.10   104

90.13   79, 104
90.14-17   103
90.15   79, 103-104
91   191-93
94   43, 78, 80-81, 102, 104, 162, 204
94.3   79, 104
94.5-7   104
94.20   104, 155
94.22-23   104
101-150   185
102   45-46, 49, 51, 57, 59-60, 62, 78, 103, 185
102.3   54
102.4   59
102.11   9, 49, 59
102.13-18   59
102.13-17   59, 74
102.18-22   59
102.24   9, 49, 59
102.25   54, 59
102.27-28   59
106   152
107.12   198
108   49, 78, 80-81, 102, 105
108.2-6   102
108.7-14   102
108.12   79
109   45, 51, 54, 185
109.1   54
109.6-19   64
109.21   69
109.25   196
109.28   64, 69
115   80-81, 102
115.2   79-80, 90
116   71

Psalms (cont.)	
119	50
119.8	50
119.10	50
119.19	50
119.31	50
119.43	50
119.116	50
119.133	50
120	45, 47, 51-53
120.5-6	53
120.7	53
123	78, 80-81
126	80-81
130	43-45, 47, 51, 53, 55, 57, 72, 76, 185
130.1	44, 53, 145
130.4	44
130.7-8	74
132	50
132.10	50
137	78, 80-81
138	50, 71
138.8	50
139	44
140	45, 51-52, 54, 74, 185
140.8	69
140.9	54
140.10-12	32
141	45, 51, 54-56, 74, 76, 185
141.2	71
141.3-4	57
141.4	54
141.6	32
141.8	54, 57, 69
142	45, 47, 51-53

142.4	53
142.7-8	54
142.7	53
143	45, 51, 54-55, 57, 66, 73
143.2	54, 57, 69
143.3	57
143.5	69
143.7	54, 57
143.12	69
144	44, 78, 80-81, 98
Proverbs	
10–29	138
Job	
1–27	130, 142, 146
1–2	130, 142
1.11	129, 142
2.5	129, 142
3	131
3.3-10	131
3.11-19	131
3.11	190
3.20-26	131
4–21	131
4–14	131
4.17-21	133
6–7	34
6.2-4	132
6.11-13	132
6.14-27	132
6.28-30	134
7	132
7.3-6	132
7.11-21	132
7.17-21	155
9–10	34
9	132
9.1-12	132
9.8	132
9.13-20	133
9.17-18	132

9.22-24	132-33
9.25-28	132
10	132-33
10.1	132
10.2-7	132, 155
10.8-17	133
10.8-12	135
10.13-17	132
10.18-19	133
12–14	34
12.2-6	132
13.17–14.22	132
15-21	131
15–26	131
16.2-5	132
16.7-14	132
16.16-17	132, 134
17.3-4	132
17.6-7	132
17.12	132
19.2-5	132
19.6-12	132
19.7	18
19.13-20	132
21.34	132
22–27	129, 131
23.10-12	134
27.2-6	134
28	130-31, 139-40, 146, 205
28.10	140
28.12	140
28.13	140
28.16-19	139
28.20-22	139
28.20	140
29–31	130-31, 134, 142, 146
31.5-40	132
31.5-22	134
32–37	129-31, 139-40, 205
32.6-9	140
33.12-22	140
33.23-26	141

33.23	198
34.21-30	141
35.1-8	141
35.9-15	141
36.5-16	141
37.19-24	141, 164
38-42	130-31, 139, 142, 146, 205
38–41	130, 140, 145
38.8-38	145
38.13	144
38.15	144
38.25-27	144
38.39–39.30	145
39.5-18	144
40.5	145
40.8-14	144
40–41	145
42.2-6	142-43
42.3	145
42.7-17	131, 142
42.7	130, 142-43
42.15	145

Ruth

1.20-21	34

Lamentations

1–5	111
1–4	109, 111, 115
1–3	114, 115
1–2	91, 110-14, 117-18, 160
1	109-10, 113-15, 117
1.1-15	119
1.1-11	111
1.1-6	113
1.5	113
1.8	113
1.9	113
1.10	113
1.11-22	108

1.11	113-14
1.12-17	113
1.12-16	111
1.18-22	111
1.18	111, 113
1.20-22	113
1.20	113
1.21	113
1.22	113
2	78, 109, 113-15
2.1-10	111
2.1-9	113
2.9-14	113
2.9-12	119
2.11	108, 111
2.13-19	107-108, 111
2.14	111, 113
2.15-16	113
2.17	113
2.20-22	108, 111
2.20	113-14
2.21	119
2.22	113-14
3	110-15
3.1-39	111
3.1-24	44
3.1-18	114
3.1	112, 114
3.21-39	112
3.25-34	114
3.26-41	112
3.40-42	114
3.42-53	111
3.42-45	110, 118
3.42	111
3.43-45	111, 114
3.43-44	9
3.47-48	112
3.52	114
3.55	198
3.59-60	114
3.64-66	114
4–5	115
4	91, 109-15, 117-19, 125
4.1-20	114

4.1-15	119
4.1-10	111
4.1	107
4.4	114
4.6	114
4.10	114
4.11-16	111
4.11	114
4.13	111, 114
4.16	114
4.17-22	111
4.18-20	114
4.21	160
4.22	114
5	76, 78, 80, 109, 111, 114-15, 119, 127, 203
5.2-18	111, 115, 119
5.2-4	114
5.7	114-15
5.8	114
5.12-13	114
5.16	114
5.18	115
5.19	110-11, 118
5.20	79, 110-11, 115, 118
5.21-22	79
5.22	79

Daniel

4.31-32	139
4.32	139
8.13	19, 24, 27, 170, 175
9	165
9.4-19	19, 30, 152
9.4	164
9.7-15	164
9.7	159, 164
9.10	164
9.14	159, 164

Daniel (cont.)
9.16   166
9.19   159
12.6   19, 23,
27, 170, 175

Ezra
8.21   99
9   165-67,
169
9.6-15   19, 152-
53
9.7-13   164
9.8   166
9.10-11   164
9.11   167
9.13   167

9.15   159, 164,
167

Nehemiah
1   165
1.5-11   19, 151-
52
1.5   164
1.7-9   164
1.7   164
3.36-37   22-23, 27
5   105
6.14   32-33,
35, 37
9   165
9.5-37   19, 149,
152, 163, 166
9.6-31   164
9.14   164, 166

9.32   159, 164
9.33   159, 163-
64
13.14   18
13.22   18
13.29   22-23, 27
13.31   18

1 Chronicles
29.10-19   18

2 Chronicles
14.10   19
20.3   99
20.6-12   10, 21,
23, 27, 100
20.19   75, 199
33.12-13   179

NORTHWEST SEMITIC INSCRIPTIONS

Arslan Tash   193
Khirbet el–Qôm   193

Kuntillat Ajrud   192

Zakir Stele   98, 100

MESOPOTAMIAN LITERATURE

*The Babylonian
Theodicy*   53

Balag-laments
according to the
edition of Cohen
(1988)
p. 58
  ll. 28-38   81
  ll. 38-41   99
p. 59
  l. 62   81
  l. 65   82
p.70   ll.1-14
               82
p. 85
  l. 46   82
p.109
  ll. 90-98   81
p. 110
  ll. 108-28   82
p. 112
  l. 195   81

p. 138
  ll. 67-68   82
  ll. 79-101   82
p. 166
  ll. 24-29   81
  l. 30   82
p. 167
  ll. 84-92   82
p. 171
  ll. 247-57   82
p. 193
  ll. 73-74   81
p. 261
  ll. 41-44   82
p. 292
  ll. 29-33   81
p. 333
  l. 127   99
p. 340
  ll. 9-13   82
p. 382
  ll. 33-36   81

p. 398
  l. 204   99
p. 410
  l. 36   81
p. 719
  ll. 21-22   99

Eridu Lament
  ll. 7-8   82

Eršemma-poems
according to the
edition of Cohen
(1981)
p. 120
  ll. 1-14   82
p. 129
  ll. 33-34   82
  l. 36   82
p. 138
  ll. 30-31   82

I Will Praise the		*Lament over Sumer*		*Nippur (Nibru) Lament*		
Lord of Wisdom	53	*and Ur*	82		82	
		ll. 229-33	99	ll. 1-14	81	
Lament over Ur		ll. 241-42	99			
	82, 85	ll. 341-42	81	UDAM KI AMUS		
l. 372	82	l. 398	81		85	
l. 374	81	ll. 400-402	99			
ll. 376-77	82	l. 451	81	*Uruk Lament*		
				l.19	81	
		Man before his God				
			53			

APOCRYPHA AND PSEUDEPIGRAPHA (in alphabetical order)

Additions to Esther		*2 Baruch*		5.28	160
13.9-17	150-51	3.1-9	156	6.38-59	156
13.16	159	3.9	160	6.59	160
13.17	158	5.1	156, 160	8.20-36	152
14.3-19	148, 151,	10.6–12.4	153-54,	8.26-30	158
	184		160		
14.6-7	159	11.4	160	*Joseph and Aseneth*	
14.11	159	32.9	154	12–13	179
		46.1-3	154	12	179, 183
Apocryphal Psalms		48.2-24	152		
151A	180	48.14	158	*Jubilees*	
151B	180	48.19	159	1.19-21	157
152	179, 187,			1.19-20	159
	198	*1 Enoch*		1.19	158
152.2-3	183, 187-	47.4	175	10.2-6	193, 195
	88	84.2-6	178, 184,	10.3-6	179, 184
152.4	184		187	10.3	181
154	180	84.4	182-83	10.4	183
155	180, 182,	84.5-6	181	10.5-6	181
	186, 193			12.19-20	193
		1 Esdras			
Baruch		8.74-90	153	*Judith*	
1.15–3.8	153	8.87	166	9.2-14	148, 152,
1.15	164				184
1.15-20	159	*2 Esdras*			
2.6-10	159	2.41	175	*1 Maccabees*	
3.5	158	3–14	171	1.16-40	170
3.9–5.9	153	3.4-36	156	2	155
4.9-16	153-54,	3.30-31	160	2.7-13	154-55,
	168	4.23-25	156		168-71
4.9-10	153	4.23-24	160	2.7	154, 160,
4.10	153	4.33	156, 160		169
4.12	153	4.35	175	2.13	154-55,
4.14-15	153	4.36	175		160
		5.23-30	156	3.45	154

1 Maccabees (cont.)
3.47   155
3.50-53   154-55, 168-71
3.50   155, 160
3.51   155
3.52   155
3.53   155
3.55   155, 169
4   169
4.30-33   152
4.30   169
7.17   169
8.2-4   170

2 Maccabees
1.23   169
1.24-29   152
15.22-24   152
15.22   169

3 Maccabees
2.1   169
2.2-20   150
2.17   158
6.1   169
6.2-15   150

Prayer of Azariah
3-22   149, 151, 153, 162
4-5   159, 161
8-9   159, 161
11-12   159, 161
12   166
19   159, 161

Prayer of Manasseh
             179, 183, 187
13   181

15   184

Psalms of Solomon
1   153
1.1   185
2   153, 168, 185
2.3   166
2.13   166
2.15-21   159
2.15-16   164
2.25   159
5   152
5.6   158
7   152
7.1   159
7.2-3   159
8   153, 168, 185
8.4-5   185
8.7-17   159
8.11-12   166
8.22   166
8.30   159
9   153, 185
9.1-2   159
9.2   164
9.6   166
9.8   159
12.1   185
16.6-15   185
18   152

Pseudo-Philo
12.8-9   157
12.9   158
15.7   157
18.4   180, 182, 189
18.10-12   188
19.8-9   157

46.4   157, 160, 169, 171
47.3-8   157
49.6   157, 160, 171
49.7-8   157
50.4   180, 189
50.7   189, 190
60   194

Sirach
22.27-36   198
36.1-22(17) 152, 198
38.9-15   198
39.5   198
51.1-12   198
51.5   198
51.7   198
51.10   198

Susanna
42-43   181

Tobit
3.2-6   180, 184
3.3   181
3.5   182
3.6   181, 183
3.11-15   180
3.13   183
3.15   182-83, 190

Wisdom of Solomon
4.7-9   140
9   183
9.1-18   180-81
9.10   188
9.13-18   188
9.4   181

DEAD SEA SCROLLS

Hodayot
1QH^a
8.26   182
10.10-28   186

12.8-11   186
12.33-35   186
13.22-32   186

16.14-15   186
16.24-34   186
Frag. 4   193

Manual of Discipline
1QS
1.16–2.18   152

4QApocryphal
Lamentations A
4Q179   153-54

4QAramaic Levi^b
4Q213a   193

4QFragments citing
Lamentations
4Q282 (=4Q241)   153

4QApocryphon of
Joseph^b
4Q372
Frag. 1.16-31 181
Frag. 1.16   181, 183
Frag. 1.19   183
Frag. 1.22-31 184
Frag. 1.24   184

4QNon-Canonical
Psalms B
4Q381
Frag. 33–35.8-11
                  179
Frag. 45   182
Frag. 79   182

4QCommunal
Confession
4Q393
                  153
Frg. 1-2, ii, 7 159
Frag. 3   160
Frag. 3.3-5   159
Frag. 3.3   159
Frag. 3.5   166

4QLament by a Leader
4Q439   154

4QIncantation
4Q444   193

4QLament A
4Q445   154

4QLament B
4Q453   154

4QPrayer for Mercy
4Q481c   153

4QApocryphal
Lamentations B
4Q501   154
4Q501.1   159

4QWords of the
Luminaries
4Q504–506   153
45Q504   166
4Q504 Frag. 4.5-6 158

4QFestival Prayers^c
4Q509 I, Frag. 1-2 152

4QSongs of the Sage
4Q510-511   193-94

4QExorcism ar
4Q560   192-93

6QHymn
6Q18   193

11QPsalms^a
11Q5 (11QPs^a)
                  185
col. 19   185, 193
(Plea for Deliverance)
col. 24.3-17   186
(Psalm 155)
col. 27.2-11   186
col. 27.9-10   192
col. 27.11   197

11QApocryphal Psalms
11Q11   192-93

NEW TESTAMENT

Matthew
6.9-13   174, 195
6.10   213
8.6   195
8.25   174
9.18   195
15.22   195
17.15   195
23.37-39   173
26.39   196
27.46   196

Mark
4.38   174

14.36   196
15.23   196
15.29   196
15.34   196
15.36   196

Luke
8.24   174
11.2-4   174, 195
13.34-35   173
22.42   196
23.46   196

Romans
9.19-21   175

Hebrews
12.1-3   175

James
5.14   197
5.17-18   197

Revelation
6.9-11   174-75
6.10   174-75,
                  213
6.11   175

RABBINIC LITERATURE

Babylonian Talmud
Ber.
31b   190

Ta'an.
24b   170
25a   170

Yom. 53b   170

Jerusalem Talmud

Erub.
10.11   191

Midrash
Genesis Rabbah
39.6   172

Exodus Rabbah
5.22   172

Leviticus Rabbah

10.1   172

Numbers Rabbah
20.6   189

Deuteronomy Rabbah
11.20   172

Lamentations Rabbah
Proem 24   172
5.19   172

CLASSICAL GREEK SOURCES

Apuleius
Metamorphoses
11.2   183

Josephus
Antiquities 8.45   194

LATER JEWISH SOURCES

Eleazer ben Kallir
    209

Isaac bar Shalom
'There is none like you
among the dumb'
    210

Samuel HaNagid
'Short Prayer in
Time of Battle'
    207

Sĕlîḥôt   209

INDEX OF AUTHORS

Aejmelaeus, A. 5-6, 11, 13, 50, 61-62, 68
Albertz, R. 5-6, 12, 32, 43, 46, 48, 54, 69-71, 73-74, 78, 80-81, 92-93, 95-96, 100, 102, 107, 109-111, 113, 115, 120, 125, 134-35, 162, 207
Albl, M.C. 197
Alexander, P.S. 192-94
Amir, J. 51
Anbar, M. 37
Andersen, F.I. 87-88
Anderson, A.A. 44-45, 55, 98
Anderson, B.W. 43, 126
Anderson, C.B. 36
Armstrong, K. 137
Attridge, H.W. 175
Avalos, H. 39, 66-67, 200

Balentine, S.E. 3, 5-6, 10, 14, 18, 19, 21-22, 28, 32, 64, 126, 128, 137, 152-53, 164, 166, 212, 214
Baltzer, K. 124
Batto, B. F. 24, 94
Baumgartner, W. 8-9, 11, 47
Bautch, R.J. 6, 152, 161-63, 167
Beale, G.K. 174-75
Ben Zvi, E. 165
Benjamin, D.C. 38
Begrich, J. 1, 4, 17, 43, 50, 66, 69, 71-72, 78, 86, 97, 99-100, 185
Berlin, A. 154
Beuken, W.A.M. 89, 106
Beyerlin, W. 94, 97-98
Biggs, R.D. 66
Billman, K.D. 196, 212, 214
Blenkinsopp, J. 88-89

Bloom, H. 24
Blumenthal, D.R. 1, 4, 209
Boda, M.J. 6, 21-22, 26, 126, 149, 152, 161-62, 166-67, 169
Bouzard, W.C. 76-77, 80-81, 83-84, 86, 94
Brenner, A. 145
Brettler, M.Z. 43
Brichto, H.C. 35
Bright, J. 20, 87
Brown, S.A. 3, 214
Broyles, C.C. 1, 9-10, 47-49, 51, 58-60, 62, 73, 80, 94, 101-103
Brueggemann, W. 2-3, 5, 7, 42, 45, 47, 50-51, 57, 59, 73, 139, 211-12, 214
Buber, M. 51
Burchard, C. 183
Burnett, J.S. 9, 28, 39
Bustenay, O. 120

Carney, S. 7
Carroll, R.P. 20, 29-30, 63, 87-89, 96
Carter, W. 174
Charlesworth, J.H. 179-80, 187
Chazon, E.G. 153, 181
Childs, B.S. 24, 199
Clark, F.C. 146
Clements, R.E. 90
Clifford, R.J. 123, 124
Clines, D.J.A. 130, 146
Coggan, D. 195
Cohen, M.E. 81-83, 86, 92, 99
Collins, A.Y. 196
Cooper, B.Z. 129
Cousins, E.H. 217
Crenshaw, J. L. 21, 134, 142

Crow, L.D. 94, 98
Culley, R.C. 67, 68
Cunningham, G. 53

Dahmen, U. 186, 199
Day, J. 1, 43-45, 47, 71, 74, 101, 199
De Pury, A. 24
Dever, W. 118
Dhanaraj, D. 51, 74
Dhorme, E. 132, 141
Di Lella, A.A. 198
Diamond, A.R. 63-64, 66
Dion, P.E. 120, 123-24
Dobbs-Allsopp, F.W. 81-87, 90-92, 94, 97, 108, 117
Donin, H.H. 207
Driver, S.R. 23

Eisenstadt, S.N. 135-36, 213
Elkana, Y. 166
Emmendörffer, M. 78, 80, 83-85, 95-98, 101, 108
Erickson, S.A. 215
Eshel, E. 192-94

Faber, W. 66
Falk, Z.W. 48
Ferris, P.W. 68, 81-85, 99, 101, 108-10
Fleming, D.E. 129
Fløysvik, I. 59-60
Flusser, D. 148, 158, 174, 194, 196
Fohrer, G. 43
Ford, J. M. 175
Freedman, D.N. 87-88
Frerichs, W.W. 214
Fuchs, O. 1, 5, 13, 47, 70, 72, 74, 184, 191
Fullerton, K. 129

Garsiel, M. 109
Gauchet, M. 137, 213, 215-16
Gerstenberger, E.S. 5-6, 8-9, 11, 15-17, 43-47, 49-51, 53-54, 57-58, 60, 62, 65-68, 70, 72-73, 76, 78, 95, 98, 101-105, 109, 111-12, 135, 141, 154, 170, 191, 199

Girard, R. 134
Goatley, D.E. 211
Goldstein, J.A. 175
Gottwald, N.K. 23-24, 100, 121, 138, 164
Gowan, D.E. 118, 123
Green, M.W. 81-82
Greenberg, M. 6, 17, 37, 46, 62, 89, 188
Gross, W. 9, 50
Guest, D. 117
Gunkel, H. 1, 4, 17, 43, 50, 66, 69, 71-72, 78, 86, 97, 99-100, 185
Gwaltney, W.C. 108

Haar, M.J. 77, 92
Habel, N.C. 26, 144
Hackett, J.A. 188
Harrrington, D.J. 157, 171, 189
Hartley, J.E. 132, 134
Hayes, J.H. 95, 120
Heinemann, J. 2, 170, 172, 189-90, 206
Herman, J. 116-17
Hieke, T. 94
Hillers, D.R. 84, 88, 107, 109, 115
Hoffman, Y. 129-31, 140, 142-43
Holladay, W.L. 20, 30, 34, 87-89

Ignatieff, M. 216
Isaac, E. 182
Jacobsen, W.T. 81-82
Jakobzen, L. 53, 55, 102
Jaspers, K. 135
Jonker, L.C. 199
Joyce, P. 119

Kaiser, O. 88-90
Kaufman, I.T. 214
Kaufmann, Y. 66, 123-24
Kim, E.K. 97
Kirchener, D. 126
Kiss, J. 21, 23, 63, 77, 86, 106
Klein, R.W. 25, 199
Klijn, A.F.J. 154, 159-60, 171
Knohl, I. 166
Koch, K. 29, 64, 66-67

Kraemer, D. 3, 172, 207-208
Kuemmerlin-McLean, J.K. 195
Kuschel, K.-J. 1, 212
Kutscher, R. 83

Lane, B.C. 212, 216
Laytner, A. 1-4, 7, 21, 134, 170, 172-
   73, 206, 208-10, 216-17
Lemche, N.P. 120
Levenson, J.D. 52
Levine, B.A. 137
Lichtenberger, H. 192
Limbeck, M. 1, 162
Limburg, J. 43
Linafelt, T. 79, 107-108, 117, 122,
   207, 209
Lindblom, J. 27
Lindström, F. 43-46, 52, 144
Loretz, O. 47-48

Machinist, P. 136
Magdalene, F.R. 117, 130
Martínez, F.G. 158-60, 192
Mayer, W. 47
Mays, J. L. 199
McCann, I.L. and Pearlman,
   L.A. 116
McDaniel, T.F. 108
McEvenue, S. 120
Meichenbaum, D. 116
Menn, E.M. 187, 196-97, 199
Michalowski, P. 81-83, 99
Migliore, D.L. 196, 212, 214
Miller, A. 117
Miller, J.M. 95, 120
Miller, P.D. 3, 5, 8-11, 14, 17, 19-20,
   22, 30-32, 37, 46-48, 50-51, 53,
   65, 122, 159, 161, 164, 213-14
Moore, C.A. 149, 153, 161, 188, 190,
   200
Morrow, W.S. 24, 71, 85, 116, 120,
   129, 142, 144, 146
Mounce, R.P. 174-75
Mowinckel, S. 67, 78, 97, 101
Mueller, U.B. 52
Mullen, E. T. 24

Müller, H.-P. 54, 191
Newman, J. H. 33, 187-88
Newsom, C.A. 129, 132, 141, 144,
   146
Nickelsburg, G.W.E. 187
Nimmo, P.W. 144
Nitzan, B. 148, 184, 186, 190-91,
   194
North, C.R. 123-24

O'Connor, K.M. 111-13, 115-16
O'Connor, M.P. 21

Pardee, D. 110
Pardes, I. 146
Patrick, D. 129
Penchansky, D. 73
Penney, D.L. 207
Perdue, L.G. 130-32, 134, 140, 142-
   43
Phillips, A. 124-25
Porter, S.E. 129
Provan, I. 107, 112, 114
Puech, E. 192-93
Purvis, J.D. 121
Pyper, H.S. 116

Radday, Y.T. 24
Reif, S.C. 149
Rendsburg, G. A. 74
Reumann, J.H. 196
Reventlow, H.G. 5-6, 18-19, 22, 29-
   30, 33, 66, 70, 89, 126
Ringgren, H. 65, 67
Robinson, W.H. 123
Rofé, A. 38
Roloff, J. 175
Rosenberg, D. 24
Ross, J.F. 141
Rousseau, J.J. 191, 197

Sanders, J.A. 180, 187
Sarason, R.S. 149
Schmitt, J.J. 27
Schoors, A. 87-90, 100, 103, 107,
   121-22, 165

Schrage, W. 46, 54, 67, 191
Schuller, E. 148, 169, 182, 186-87
Scullion, J.J. 136
Scult, A. 129
Seitz, C.R. 130, 140
Seybold, K. 52
Shore, H. 24
Skehan, P.W. 198
Smith, M.S. 63-64
Smith, W.C. 165
Snapp, K. 129
Soelle, D. 212
Soll, W. 50
Sommer, B.D. 107, 122, 169
Sorenson, E. 190-91, 211
Stegemann, H. 186
Steinmann, A.E. 129-30
Stevenson, G.M. 103
Steymans, H.U. 81, 96, 101
Stolz, F. 197
Stone, M.E. 164, 171, 200

Tigay, J.H. 84
Tigchelaar, E.J.C. 158-60, 192
Tilley, T.W. 129
Tsevat, M. 144-45

Uffenheimer, B. 136

Van der Kwaak, H. 174
Van der Lugt, P. 131
Van der Toorn, K. 28, 53, 195
Van Grol, H.W.M. 89, 106
Van Seters, J. 24-25, 32, 37, 167
Van Wolde, E. 143

Veijola, T. 25-26, 32, 125-27, 162,
 164
Vermeylen, J. 29

Waltke, B.K. 21
Weber, B. 94-95
Weems, R.J. 117
Weinfeld, M. 137
Wendel, A. 14
Werline, R.A. 6, 152-53, 158, 160-
 62, 165-66, 171, 187
Westermann, C. 2-11, 13-16, 18, 20,
 24, 30, 34, 36, 38, 46, 76-78, 81,
 88, 90-92, 96-97, 99, 102, 108-
 10, 112, 115, 118-19, 121, 126,
 142, 149-55, 159-61, 165, 168,
 171, 179-80, 214, 217
Wevers, J.W. 31, 40, 44, 47-48
Whybray, R.N. 88
Whitelam, K.W. 38
Widengren, G. 81
Wiesel, E. 208
Wilcox, J.T. 146
Wildberger, H. 89-90
Wilson, G.H. 72, 199
Wilson, R.R. 26
Wintermude, O.S. 158, 193
Wise, M.O. 207
Wolfers, D. 134
Wolff, H.W. 29, 89
Wolterstorff, N. 211
Wright, R.B. 158, 171, 185

Zenger, E. 212

LaVergne, TN USA
01 November 2009

162700LV00001B/28/A